RICKENBACKER

RICKENBACKER

EDWARD V. RICKENBACKER

Prentice-Hall, Inc., *Englewood Cliffs, New Jersey*

Prentice-Hall International, Inc., London
Prentice-Hall of Australia, Pty. Ltd., Sydney
Prentice-Hall of Canada, Ltd., Toronto
Prentice-Hall of India Private Ltd., New Delhi
Prentice-Hall of Japan, Inc., Tokyo

To my mother,
ELIZABETH BASLER RICKENBACKER,
with love and appreciation;
her inspiration through life
never failed me.
To my wife,
ADELAIDE FROST RICKENBACKER,
whose constant confidence,
love and dedication
have always supported me
through failure
and success.

Acknowledgments

To my sons, David E. and William F. Rickenbacker, I offer my grateful thanks for their support and cooperation.

To Booton Herndon, I offer my appreciation for his editorial assistance.

E.V.R.

CONTENTS

ONE

BOYHOOD

My life has been filled with adventures that have brought me face to face with death. I still remember an early escapade that involved a terrifying roller-coaster ride into a gravel pit. I was about 8 years old at the time.

The pit was in a deep quarry near my home in Columbus, Ohio. The rock was hauled from the bottom of the pit by a small steel cart on rails, which was drawn up the incline out of the pit, a distance of more than one hundred feet, by means of a cable. The pit was closed down for the weekend every Saturday at noon.

One Saturday afternoon my friends and I—we called ourselves the "Horsehead Gang"—arrived at the pit. The cart was down at the bottom, but, with seven boys pushing and straining all the way, we inched it up to the top, where I secured it in place with wooden chocks. Everybody climbed aboard. I was the leader. I looked down the incline. It was like a ski jump, except that there was no landing place down there.

"Here goes nothing," I hollered and knocked the chocks from

in front of the wheels. Gravity took it from there. We began rocketing crazily down the incline, jerking and careening, uncontrolled and unstoppable. Then the speed became too much, and the cart flipped over. The other boys were thrown clear, but I didn't stand a chance. The cart went right over on top of me, bounced on me once or twice and went crashing down to the bottom of the pit. I was a mess. I was bruised and bloody all over. One wheel had passed right over my leg and laid it open to the bone. I still have the scar. It was one of my first; there were many more to come.

My earliest memory is of a pleasant summer day in 1893 when our happy little family climbed down from the East Livingston Avenue horsecar at the end of the line and struck out into what was then almost open countryside in Columbus. Though our destination was half a mile away and though Mother carried my baby sister Emma in her arms, we hurried along the unpaved street.

I was only 3 years old, but such was the excitement of the moment that I remember it to this day.

For the Rickenbacher family was moving into our new home. And that new home was more to us than a mere house on a lot; it was the end of a dream, the beginning of a reality.

To us, it was America. On that plot of onetime farmland was combined the best of two worlds. From the Old World my parents had brought a sense of duty and a tireless willingness to work. The New World provided what was to them a lavish amount of fertile soil, opportunity, and promise. I was a fortunate boy indeed in that I was able to pass my formative years in that favorable atmosphere of industry, production, gratitude and appreciation.

My parents, William Rickenbacher and his wife, Elizabeth Basler Rickenbacher, were both natives of Switzerland. They met in Columbus, fell in love and were married. Mother was fair-skinned, with lovely red hair. She was of French descent, devoutly religious and a lover of art and poetry. Father, a tall, strong, black-haired man with a heavy moustache, was of German stock, stern and serious. He had served his apprenticeship in construction work in Switzerland, but in his first years in the United States he worked as a laborer for the railroad. With their savings my parents bought a lot, 150 by 200 feet, in east Columbus, and with a little cash, a lot of credit and his own two hands my father built our little house. It had two rooms on the ground floor and two smaller lightless, unheated rooms in the attic, where the children slept. There was no electricity, no running water and no heat other than from the kitchen stove. It was our home, and we were proud of it.

On the day we moved in, Papa quit his job and became his own boss, subcontracting small jobs like pavements and foundations. It was a brave move to make, but he was a man of great self-confidence. He and his pretty young wife had come to this country virtually penniless, and now they had four children and their own home. America was truly the land of opportunity. His own strength and knowledge and energy constituted all the security he needed.

Four children were born in that little house. Mother had eight in all. Mary, Mother's little helper, was the oldest. Then came William, steady and dependable, and then me, Edward. Emma, a quiet girl who emulated sister Mary, was next. Louise died in infancy. Louis, the one happy-go-lucky Rickenbacher, was next, followed by Dewey, conscientious and industrious, and Albert, the baby of the family.

What a wonderful childhood we had! Of far greater value than mere riches was the opportunity to work together, play together, learn together and produce together, all under the loving yet strict Old World guidance of our parents.

How many children in America today, I wonder, are blessed with the opportunity to see the food they eat develop from tiny seeds placed in the moist spring earth? We little Rickenbachers enjoyed that privilege to the fullest extent. We made our own sauerkraut, from cabbage that we grew ourselves.

We grew our own potatoes too. I remember that one day, when I was 4 or 5 years old, Mama and I were out planting the potato eyes together. She, standing, would make a little hole with the hoe, and I, on my hands and knees, would put the cone-shaped pieces of potato in, then push the dirt over them. I must have moved too quickly toward the new hole Mother was digging, for instead of the hoe hitting the ground, it hit me, right in the head. One of the prongs actually pierced my skull.

Mama picked me up and ran to the house. There she washed my scalp and treated it with healing oil, then rocked me in her arms. What could have been a serious injury is now only a pleasant memory of being nestled in Mother's arms.

We raised many other vegetables, kept chickens and, from time to time, fattened and slaughtered a pig. Papa had brought with him from Switzerland a custom rare in this country. He bought a huge hogshead—about 10 feet high and 8 feet across—and we worked for hours digging a hole for it. The top was several feet underground. We climbed down into this underground storage chest by means of a ladder. Papa built shelves around the sides.

Our milk was goat's milk; goats are cheaper to feed. There was vacant land all around us, and nobody cared if we tethered them out to graze. As our herd grew, we had more than enough milk even for our large and hungry family. I delivered milk daily to several customers throughout the neighborhood.

There were also plenty of trees, and we would go out periodically, chop one down, saw it and split it for stove wood.

America the bountiful was symbolized to us by the figure 7 cents, a sum I'll never forget. I heard my parents mention it many times. Seven cents was the price of both a dozen eggs and a pound of sugar. When our chickens were laying well and we had an extra dozen eggs, we could always trade them for a pound of sugar. Then, with a little flour and some windfall apples from a neighboring orchard, Mama could make the most delicious dessert in the world, apple pie.

Where else, my parents would say, could a man begin with nothing and feed his children apple pie for dessert?

My father not only talked about his gratitude to America; he was also ready to back up his words with action. He was a peace-loving man. He used to tell us of the horrors of the constant turmoil in Europe. Yet, when war was declared against Spain in 1898, Papa went to the recruiting station and volunteered. Mama cried, but she bravely encouraged him.

He soon came trudging back, however. The war situation was not so drastic that fathers of seven children were being taken from their homes.

Though the episode ended happily and with a touch of humor, it exemplified the sentiment of my parents toward their adopted land and of us children toward the land of our birth. True and unashamed patriotism has been a part of my family life for as long as I can remember.

Above all, our parents taught us to love America. I have always loved this land of ours, and I shall never stop loving it.

Though the little house on Livingston Avenue was filled with happiness, there were periods of financial difficulty. I remember some lean years, particularly the winters. There were days when the wind blew strong and cold, the snow piled high and we children simply didn't have enough warm clothes to go to school.

And that was all right with me. I was so blond as a youngster that the other kids called me "Towhead." During my early years, before my parents became comfortable in English, German was our household language. I spoke English with an atrocious accent, and I was also called "Dutchy" and "Kraut." Towheaded and speaking "mit ein accent," I had to fight my way into school in the morning, stand up for myself at recess and fight my way home again after school.

As a small boy, I must confess, I was mischievous and devilish at times. I wasn't mean, but I was rebellious. I was so full of energy that I had to be active all the time. I resented my older brother's seniority. From the time I drew my first breath, I suppose, I wanted to be the leader in anything that was going on. But naturally Bill had the privileges and responsibilities that I wanted. On top of the four years he had on me, Bill was a strapping, robust youngster, whereas I was skinny and wiry. He could beat the daylights out of me, and he did more times than I like to remember.

But I continued to compete with him. I practiced hard at shooting marbles and became so proficient that I could beat him. We played for keeps, and I would wind up with all the marbles. Bill would get mad and start swinging, but I had the faster feet —and the marbles.

Bill and some of the older boys of the neighborhood, on their way home from school, used to leave the path and disappear into a thicket. One day I arrived at their secret meeting place first and shinnied up a tree. The older boys came along. They gathered under the tree, looked furtively around to make sure they weren't being watched and then rolled corn-silk cigarettes and began puffing away.

I wanted to do everything brother Bill did. "Hey," I hollered down, "I can see what you're doing. If you don't give me a smoke I'll snitch on you."

Well, that threw the meeting of the club into an uproar. They threatened me and pleaded with me, but I stood firm. "Give me a cigarette, or I'll tell Papa," I repeated. I won and smoked my first cigarette at the age of five. We soon graduated from corn silk to Bull Durham tobacco, at a nickel a bag. One day Papa caught Bill and me smoking in the barn, and he took a switch to both of us.

As more families moved into the neighborhood, I found other kids my age who were also plagued by the big-brother problem. We organized the Horsehead Gang. The title was inspired by the sign over the entrance to a nearby racetrack.

Some of our mischief was, I hate to admit, malicious and reprehensible. One night we went out and broke the globes on the gas-burning streetlights all up and down Miller Avenue. It didn't take the police long to find out who had done it, and one evening a policeman visited Papa for a little chat about the Horsehead Gang. I can feel that whipping yet.

Even during those rebellious years, one thing hurt more than a switching. That was the sight of Mama crying. She never remonstrated with Papa, for she knew that I deserved every lick. That made me suffer for her all the more, and I would make inward resolutions to reform. But somehow those periods of remorse never lasted very long.

And then something happened. Suddenly, out of the blue, the strange realization came to me that one day I would die and that the world would go on without me.

These few short words, accurate though they may be, do not begin to describe the depth of the emotion and perception that accompanied this seemingly obvious thought. What I felt was not merely fear of death or dying; it was more sensitively metaphysical. It was a cry of despair for the entire universe, centralized in the susceptible mind of a 9-year-old child. I could see time stretching on endlessly. As it continued, more and more wondrous marvels would be developed and become realities. But at some point along this interminable path, my life would stop, and time would flow on without me. In my despair, I would go off alone to the barn and sob for hours at a time.

On one of those occasions my father found me, sprawled face down in the straw and crying my heart out.

"What's the matter, Eddie?" he asked.

As best I could, I choked out, between sobs, the reason for my tears. Papa's reaction was typical, fitting and effective. He grabbed a switch. "You're too young to think of things like that," he said. (Whack!) "Life and death are my worry, not yours. Don't ever let me catch you crying about such foolish things again!" (Whack!)

That whipping did not dispel a sense of loss over what I would never live to see, but it did impress me with the futility of despair over the inevitable. I resolved to enjoy life as long as the good Lord would let me, but I never cried again over the unseeable occurrences of the future.

And so, at the age of 9, came the first turning point in my life. I still managed to get into a fight every now and then, and, if the apples looked particularly juicy, I might just shinny up someone else's tree and snitch one. But the days of rebellion, of destruction and meaningless mischief, were gone and gone forever.

Never, even during my most mischievous escapades, had I lost faith in God. Mama had planted the seeds of religion too deeply in all of us for that. All through my childhood there was a warm, continuing family ritual. After supper, when we had all helped to clear the dishes from the big kitchen table, Mother would ask one of us to bring in the Bible that she had brought with her from Switzerland. What an honor that was! It was big and heavy and bound in rich black leather. On the front, printed in gold in block capitals, were the words *"Heilige Bibel"*—Holy Bible. Mama would open it and begin to read. Her favorite passages were the Sermon on the Mount and the 23rd Psalm, and they are the ones I remember best. She would often stop reading to discuss the meanings behind the Scriptures and how we could apply the principles of Christianity to everyday life.

It was my mother who taught us to pray. She saw to it that each little Rickenbacher, the girls in their room, the boys in ours, knelt by the side of the bed each night and said the Lord's Prayer. But formal prayer was only the beginning. Mama taught us that the Lord above was a friendly God, a great Presence who was interested in our problems and sympathetic to them. Thanks to her influence, I have always talked to God in my prayers, with respect and awe but also with full confidence that He listens and responds. My prayers have been answered too many times for me to have any doubt at all that He hears me.

On Sundays we all dressed up in our best to attend Sunday-school services and, when we were old enough, morning worship at St. John's Lutheran Church in the south end of Columbus. The pastor of the church was Reverend Jacob Pister, one of the most forthright and inspiring individuals I have ever known. He christened me, confirmed me and, years later, performed my wedding ceremony.

I had another good reason for going to Sunday school in the mornings, as well as for attending Sunday evening gatherings. Her name was Blanche Calhoun, my childhood sweetheart. She was a lovely little girl, and walking home with her after church was a sweet and thrilling experience. When I was with her, the little ruffian Rickenbacher did not exist. Instead I was tender and artistic.

I loved to draw, and with Blanche as my inspiration I turned out one watercolor after another. My favorite subjects were flowers, landscapes and animals. I was so proud of a still life of a flower arrangement, on which I had labored several hours, that I framed it and presented it to my number-one sweetheart, my mother. For my father I painted several Swiss landscapes, based on his nostalgic word pictures of them.

Seeking still another means of self-expression, I purchased a battered little violin for a few pennies from a second-hand shop. I sanded and varnished it and put it into excellent shape. I learned to play a few tunes on it, but that was the extent of my musical interest.

My interest was turning instead toward the general field of mechanics. The girls and my mother were the inside workers, making the beds, keeping house, cooking and washing. The boys worked outside under Papa's direction, gardening, gathering wood and maintaining and improving the property. We added a room and a half to the house and a cellar to take the place of the old buried hogshead.

Though all those tasks were hard work and Papa was a stern taskmaster, I still loved to work alongside him. He would constantly advise us on why something was done this way and not the other. Through his own personal example, he inspired us to do the job right to begin with. He taught us to respect and take care of our tools. He had a phobia against leaving things lying around, and I caught it from him. My father taught me never to procrastinate, *to do it now,* and I have followed that practical axiom all my life.

He appreciated my pride in accomplishment and nurtured it. When I was only 7 years old, he taught me how to sew leather and repair shoes. When I became proficient and proud of it, he brought home a last, leather and nails. Before long I was actually putting new soles and heels on all the other children's shoes. As I worked with my hands, I automatically coordinated the work with my head. And hands and head are the winning combination in any endeavor.

Under Papa's influence and encouragement, I began to accept more and more responsibility for the work to be done about our busy little place. The more I accomplished, the greater the feeling of satisfaction and pride; I was thus constantly seeking new duties to be responsible for. Working long hours before and after school, even at the age of eight or nine, was not punishment, but a privilege.

My business career began before I started school. The original motivation was not of the highest morality, I'm sorry to say. I wanted money to buy Bull Durham tobacco so that I could smoke as much as my older brother Bill did. About that time, while I was looking for a source of income, who should come into the new, growing neighborhood but a junkman looking for rags, bones and metal. He went on to prosper, driving his own horse and wagon, but the first time I saw him he was on foot with a sack on his back. I knew him only as "Sam."

The discovery that Sam would give me money for things like rags and bones and old pieces of metal was almost like finding the money itself. Imagine getting money for bones! (They were ground up and sold for fertilizer.) I soon observed that bones found in mud puddles brought more money than dry ones. From then on I swished every bone around in a mud puddle before selling it.

Before long I had all the other kids in the neighborhood out collecting junk. We even pulled the rusty nails out of old boards. All the junk was brought in to me and I turned it over to Sam, keeping a percentage of the take. But I was such a determined little scavenger that my pile was always bigger than anyone else's. My bones weighed more too; the soaking process was a secret I kept to myself.

As I became more experienced in judging weight, the suspicion gradually dawned on me that I was being cheated. Somehow a big water-soaked bone didn't weigh as much on Sam's scales as I thought it should. I found a set of scales in a second-hand store. The price, a quarter, was quite an investment for a 6-year-old junkman, but I made the purchase.

I saw to it that they were set accurately. Then I weighed the items I had collected. When Sam came around, his scales showed fewer pounds—and fewer cents. I produced my own scales and weighed the same items again.

"Aw, Eddie," Sam said and began to argue, but his heart wasn't in it. He knew I had him. I believe he respected me all the more. He ungrudgingly dropped a few more pennies into my hand, and from then on, at least in his transactions with me, his scales gave honest weight.

When I was 10 years old, I became a newsboy for the old Columbus *Dispatch*. The job meant a steady income, a dollar or so every week. Newsboys started early in those days. I'd get up at 2:00 in the morning, walk the two miles to the *Dispatch* office to pick up the papers, then go on to my route.

This first job was as important as any I ever had. It was my initiation into a man's world. Being a newsboy taught me the meaning of duty, and without a sense of duty a man is nothing. Like the other newsboys, in Columbus and all over the world, I delivered my papers in the dark, in the cold, in the rain, in the snow.

In the spring I heard of a job picking strawberries for a penny a pint. It seemed more profitable than carrying papers, and I took it. The berries were smaller than the huge ones we have today, and it took a lot more to fill the pint boxes. It was hard work crawling down the row on my knees, picking, picking, picking, but I was right. It did pay better.

Still somehow there was time for play and hobbies. I was about 9 years old when I saw my first horseless carriage, a Duryea, at the circus. That led to the pushmobile. It was simply a long board mounted on wooden wheels. We sawed out the wheels ourselves, shaping them with a wood file. For axles we used plain old water pipes smeared with generous quantities of lard, which we filched from our mothers' kitchens.

Each pushmobile had a 2-man team, the driver and the pusher. We had some exciting races. We would go around and around our rough little track, jockeying for position, bumping and shouting. Sometimes we would wind up in a free-for-all, but I don't recall that anyone was ever seriously hurt.

One day I saw a lady walk by pushing a baby carriage. It rolled smoothly on ball-bearing wheels, and I knew then and there that I had to have a set of ball-bearing rubber-tired baby-carriage wheels for my pushmobile.

But how in the world would I get them? They had just come out. I couldn't find any in the second-hand stores. Then I had an idea. When Sam the junkman came by, I asked him if he could, as a special favor, find me four baby-carriage wheels, complete with axles. He said he'd look around. He must have known how badly I wanted them, because in a day or two, while making his rounds, he stopped in front of my house and proudly held up two sets of wheels.

"Here you are, Eddie," he said. "No charge. They're a present from one businessman to another."

I knew better than to ask Sam where he had found them. Somewhere in Columbus there was a baby carriage minus four wheels.

Those pushmobiles were the first of their kind. Many years later I told the Chevrolet people about them and inspired the now-famous Soap Box Derby.

The nearby racetrack occasionally featured bicycle racing. I'd sneak under the fence and watch the great bike riders of the day compete in the 24-hour races. These races gave me my first appreciation of physical fitness. It was obvious that bicycle riders had to be healthy and strong. Their muscles were the most clearly defined of any group of men I had ever observed.

I saved and scraped and finally was able to buy a used bicycle and to put it in perfect running condition. About the same time Roy Knabenshue, who was barnstorming about the country in a dirigible, came to Columbus. Everybody in town turned out, heads tilted back, to watch him float overhead. I lay awake nights wishing that I too could fly like Roy Knabenshue. Finally I figured out a way.

I bought a big umbrella, the kind we used to see on farm wagons, at a second-hand store and attached it to the bicycle. I planned to take the contraption to a neighboring barn with a steep-slanting roof and come roaring down the roof to the edge. With this combination of speed and height, I would fly like a bird!

But I was a cagey youngster. For days prior to countdown, I hauled sand to a spot beside the barn to provide a soft place to land just in case.

When the sandpile was high enough, my buddy Sam Wareham and I pulled the bike and umbrella to the top. With Sam steadying the bicycle, I climbed aboard. The ground looked mighty far away. But the promise of flight was greater than the fear of falling.

"Okay, Sam," I said. "Let go!"

Down the steep tin roof of the barn we went, bicycle, umbrella and Rickenbacher, gathering momentum. We left the roof. The umbrella gave a loud pop and turned completely inside out. The next thing I knew I hit the sand. Thanks to it and the good Lord, I was only stunned. The bike wasn't so lucky; it was demolished. And so ended Eddie Rickenbacher's first flight.

Even by that time in my young life, I had had several brushes with death. All boys, particularly those as harum-scarum as I was, have their moments of danger, but I had already had more than my share. It was a pattern that was to run all through my life, for I know of no man who has had more brushes with death than I.

Though I was only 3 years old, I remember vividly the first time the Grim Reaper reached out for me. In those days vegetable wagons would come through the neighborhood. One morning the vegetable man stopped across the street from us, and Mother took me by the hand and went over to see what he had.

When she had completed her purchases, I impulsively turned and started running home, back across the street. A horse-drawn streetcar was in operation on Livingston Avenue by then, and at that very moment it came along. I ran right into it. The force of the collision hurled me against the curb.

Although it later developed that my skull had taken a hard rap, and a big lump and two black eyes resulted, at the time I was too scared to feel any injuries. I jumped up, scurried upstairs as fast as I could and dived under the bed. Mama dashed after me. But I was still so frightened that it took a lot of pleading to lure me out from under the bed and into her arms.

Not long after we moved, I was at a neighbor's house watching some men digging a cistern. I turned away from the hole, lost my footing and fell backward. I landed on my head and neck and lay there, as limp as a broken toy. I learned later that they were all afraid that I had broken my neck. They lifted me out of the hole and carried me home. I was out for a couple of hours and was woozy for several more, but that was all.

Brother Bill and I used to go to the railroad yards to pick up coal from beside the tracks. I was fascinated by the switch engines, and, one day when I was about six, I ran out and hopped on the rear end of the coal tender as it went slowly by. The engine picked up speed, then stopped with a jolt. I lost my grip and fell off, flat on my back between the tracks. Stunned, I lay there helpless. The engine went on a few feet, stopped, then began backing up, right over me.

Bill came running, grabbed me and dragged me off the roadbed just in time.

On another coal-hunting mission, hurrying across the tracks in front of the switch engine, I stepped in an open switch. My foot was caught—and the engine was coming. Bill hurried up, and we yanked together. My foot came out of the shoe, and we both went back head over heels as the engine thundered by.

In the autumn we used to gather black walnuts. As I was more agile and daring than Bill, I was the one who climbed the tree to shake them down. Naturally, being me, I went higher up the tree and farther out on the limb than was necessary before I started shaking down the nuts. I slipped and fell, plummeting straight down to hit with a thump. The next thing I knew, I was waking up at home. The fall had knocked me cold. Bill had loaded me in the cart and dragged me all the way home.

Most of these misadventures were over so quickly that I didn't have time to be scared. The schoolhouse fire was a different story. It was in the dead of winter in my first year of school, at the East Main Street public school on the corner of Miller Avenue and Main Street. Some time during the afternoon a fire started in the basement and quickly spread.

The fire bell rang, and the teachers calmly but swiftly organized the kids and marched us all out safely. Soon the horses came galloping up, pulling the red fire wagon. It was all terribly exciting.

And then, suddenly, an awful thought hit me. I had left my overcoat and cap in the burning building. Without further thought, I dashed into the blazing building to get them. It wasn't that I was brave—just the opposite. I was afraid to go home without my coat and cap.

A sheet of flame roared out of the first classroom door. I didn't stop to think. I simply ran into it. The fierce heat scorched my face. I felt my eyebrows and hair being singed in the flames. Then I was through the wall of fire. I dashed into the coatroom, plucked my coat and cap off the peg and ran back through that blast of flame.

After I had passed through it the second time, the enormity of what I had done, the danger I had been in, reached out like another flame and grabbed me. I came skedaddling out the door and headed for home without slowing down. It was a good mile and a half, and I don't think I stopped once on the way. I ran in the door hollering for Mama, and I didn't stop until I was safe in her arms—with my coat and cap.

One evening about dusk I heard old Nanny, our goat, let out a bleat of terror. I ran out to investigate. A big dog had gotten through the fence and had her by the leg. I ran in and tried to pull him off with one hand and beat him on the head with the other. As Papa told me later, a dog vicious enough to attack a goat would probably counterattack a human, but danger did not enter my mind. I was protecting old Nanny.

The dog dropped the goat and turned and snapped at me. By that time Papa had arrived with a stick. Papa hit him a couple of times, and the dog yelped and took off.

Every boy has a dog at some time or another, I guess, and I was no exception. Mine was a medium-sized, tannish bitch, a mixture of many breeds, that I had found wandering, half-starved and homeless. I brought her home, fed her and named her "Trixie."

She was *my* dog, and she let everybody know it. Once, when Papa started to punish me, Trixie barked and snarled and tore at his trouser leg. He was trying to kick her away and hit me at the same time, while Trixie was trying to bite him. She finally succeeded. He let out a roar, stopped switching me and turned on her. Then it was my turn to run to her aid.

Fortunately, Father had a sense of humor, and he appreciated Trixie's loyalty. Sometimes, to tease her, he would pick up a switch just to hear her growl. But, on the occasions when he thought that I really did deserve a switching, he was careful to put Trixie out of the house first.

The robins who lived on our place became almost as tame as pets. They nested in the peach tree in the backyard. One year I built a well-appointed house for them, but they preferred to build their own.

As I watched them busily building their homes from dribs and drabs and odds and ends, I came to appreciate their skill. I began feeding them leftover crumbs, bits of meat and fishing worms. Gradually, they came to trust me and would perch on my shoulder and eat out of my hand.

One day I was standing under the nest when—thud!—a baby robin landed at my feet. He started walking around in a daze. Mother Robin came down and fluttered around him, noisily exhorting him to fly. Finally he moved his wings feebly a few times, and she cheered him on. Eventually she got the little bird airborne. Some of the young ones were able to take a few strokes with their wings on the way down and, one might say, soloed on their first flight. Over the years I would occasionally see one of the nestlings land so hard that it broke its neck, which always saddened me. I established a little burial plot especially for little robins who never did fly.

As the years went by on Livingston Avenue and the robins and the chickens and the goats increased in number, so also did the Rickenbacher family. As I entered my thirteenth year, there were seven of us children. We had increased the size of our house by two rooms and a cellar. Mary and Bill worked weekends and added to the family income. We were still a family of moderately low income, but the days of bitter discomfort were over.

Papa was doing what he wanted to do. Dependable, industrious and well-schooled in simple construction techniques, he had become foreman and equipment operator for a company building small and medium-sized bridges throughout central Ohio. He was proud of his work. He realized that in his own small way he was helping to build America. He had come from a tiny country in which three languages were spoken. Now he was in one great country with one language, one common goal.

Often Papa would take me with him to the sites of his various jobs. I stood by his side and looked out over the work in progress on bridges over Alum Creek and Big Walnut River, as well as over the bigger Olentangy. I could see the work progress from an empty expanse of water to naked piers to the final bridge.

Papa pointed out the meaning of his work to me. He would stoop over and point out the mark of a steel-rimmed wagon wheel in the rock of the riverbed. It was the way the early pioneers had come, crossing this river to build a nation. Sometimes they would have to go many, many miles off the most direct route in order to find a stream. As the bridge neared completion, his eyes would take on a greater sparkle of anticipation, his voice a lilt of enthusiasm.

"Soon it will be finished," he would say in good English but with a German accent I cannot reproduce. Then he would talk of the horses and wagons that would cross the bridge and of how the bridge would shorten journeys and bring people closer together, making our great land smaller in terms of transportation. Maybe even one of those new horseless carriages would be crossing that bridge. "And, mark my words, Eddie," he said, "you're going to see more and more of them."

For a time there in 1904, when I was $13\frac{1}{2}$ years old, he was running a pile driver on the night shift. One evening, on his way to work, he stopped in the little workshop back of our house to see what I was doing. It so happened that I was building a perpetual-motion machine, which I knew would bring me fame and fortune. It was a finely tooled apparatus. Gravity was its secret. The weight of a ball would push one part of the apparatus down. That power would be transferred through springs and gears to another part of the machine, which would lift a second ball up. Then the weight of the second would lift the first. This process would go on indefinitely—a true perpetual-motion machine. It never occurred to me that the power generated by the machine and the power required to keep it running canceled each other out completely. The machine could not possibly accomplish any task whatever.

Papa saw this basic fault immediately. "What good is it?" he asked. "What good does it do? A machine has to have a purpose. You're building it backwards."

And, putting his arm around my shoulder, he talked about the machines he used. His pile driver, a simple mechanism, would lift a weight and drop it down on one end of a pole. It would drive that pole into the riverbed to make a piling, on top of which a bridge would be built. That bridge would foster transportation and trade.

Then Papa asked me to remember two things: He told me never to get mixed up with a machine I didn't know how to control and that there was no value in a machine that didn't serve a useful purpose.

This talk brought to his mind the fact that not far away, in Dayton, a couple of brothers in the bicycle business were tinkering around with a flying machine. Many people who had heard of the Wright boys were saying that they would come to no good. But Papa had that wonderful quality, imagination. He stopped talking about bridges and started talking about the new horseless carriages and the still-imaginary flying machine, which most people scoffed at.

"Eddie," Papa said, "you're a lucky boy to be born when you were. There are a lot of new things in the making, and you ought to be ready to have a hand in them."

Those were the last words Papa said to me. That very night, while operating the pile driver, he was struck by a swinging timber. The blow fractured his skull. He was in a coma for many days. One day, as we all sat by his bedside, he regained consciousness sufficiently to recognize us. But that night he passed away. It was August 26, 1904.

Papa's body was brought home. Friends and neighbors came in to pay their last respects. Mama and all of us children were there, dressed in the dark clothes she had gone into debt to buy. After Pastor Pister had conducted the funeral services, all the friends, neighbors and relatives passed by the casket and left. Mama then gathered us around Papa's casket and said that she wanted us to look at him once more because we would never see him again.

She spoke quietly but very seriously. In the years ahead, some of us might be more fortunate than others; she asked each of us to promise her definitely that those who were successful would share with those who were not and would see that they would never be in want or need of anything within reason.

We all gave our solemn promise. I know that I have never meant anything so seriously in all my life, before or since, than the promise I made that day to my mother before my father's casket.

Papa was laid to rest in the cemetery, and we came home to a quiet house. Mama and the girls made a simple supper, and the family was in bed early. Thinking back, I can see how the older children would have suffered the most during that trying period and how, relieved to have the terrible ordeal finally ended, they would probably have dropped off to sleep. The younger ones probably did not realize the full import of Papa's death, that his widow and his seven children must take care of themselves. Whatever the others thought, I know that on that day I turned from a harum-scarum youngster into a young man serious beyond my age.

Unable to sleep, I heard a noise downstairs. I crept down and found Mama sitting at the kitchen table with her head in her hands. God knows she had cause to despair, left alone with seven children and considerable debts. Trying to comfort her, I made the very best promise I could make.

I said, "Mama, I'll never make you cry again."

Many years went by before I could appreciate what she did at that moment of her deepest grief. She reached out and patted me on the head, as if I were the one who needed comforting. Not knowing what else to do, I drew a chair up to the kitchen table and simply sat and said nothing. We sat together in silence.

Some time passed before I realized that I was sitting at the head of the table, where Papa had always sat. Mama knew where I was sitting, but she made no comment. Many years were to pass before I fully understood.

TWO

UP THE LADDER

I may have seemed the head of the house there in my father's chair, but to the world outside I was simply an undersized 13-year-old boy, still in the seventh grade. The acceptance of family responsibility brought with it the built-in attachments of financial concern and constructive thought. Where would the money come from? How could I get a full-time job? Would Mother let me take it if I could find it? The only answer to that was to get a job first, *then* to ask permission.

That procedure eliminated my older brother Bill as employment counselor. I knew that if I asked him to help me get a job he would tell Mother. But thinking of Bill gave me an idea. He had previously worked for the Federal Glass Factory on South Parsons Avenue. If the factory had employed one Rickenbacher, then maybe it would hire another one. In the morning I got up with the rest of the kids and started out with them as though I were going to school. Once clear of the house, however, I headed for the glass factory. It was a good two miles away. I went into the employment office, identified myself as Eddie Rickenbacher,

Bill's brother, and asked for a job. Bill had made a good impression; that was one foot in the door.

But a lot of me was still outside. Under the terms of the child-labor laws, the factory could not put me to work unless I was 14 years old and had finished the eighth grade. When I was asked how old I was, I stretched the truth a little.

"I'm fourteen," I said and quickly added, "I finished the eighth grade in school."

I am sure nobody believed me. Perhaps my determination shone through. Perhaps the company at that time had no scruples about exploiting children. Whatever the reason, I was told to come back at 6:00 that night.

"You'll work from six o'clock tonight till six o'clock in the morning," I was told. "That's twelve hours. If you don't think you can take it, don't show up."

"I'll be here," I said grimly.

I almost ran the two miles home. I had a job! My poor mother wasn't so pleased. "Oh, Eddie," she said. "You've got to finish your schooling!"

Her eyes grew moist. Quickly I began to plead with her. Not 24 hours had gone by since I had promised her that I would never make her cry again, and that was a promise I had to keep. But I had to have a job too. In the long history of boys talking their mothers into acquiescence, none was ever more persuasive than I. Finally she gave in.

There wasn't much else she could do. We had to have the money.

That afternoon I did my chores early. About 4:30, lunch pail in hand, I started out for the glass factory. I thought of taking the streetcar, but the fare was a nickel, and I well knew the value of a nickel: a quart of goat's milk, delivered. I walked.

I walked all night long too, on the job. The factory made glass tumblers. Skilled glassblowers fashioned them from molten glass by lung power, one at a time. Then I carried them on a heavy, awkward steel platter with a long handle to the tempering ovens. When we stopped at midnight for lunch, my legs were

Mother—
Elizabeth
Basler
Rickenbacher

Father—
William
Rickenbacher

As a boy

Rickenbacher home—Columbus, Ohio

As a boy at Zenker Monument Works, Columbus, Ohio

With group of fellow workers—Columbus Buggy Co., 1905

Mother—1919

Driving William Jennings Bryan on his lecture tour—Abilene, Texas, 1909

Courting days—author and his future wife

Wedding Day
With Pastor Jacob Pister

tired, and I thought my arms were going to drop off. I had hardly finished my sandwich when it was time to go back to work again. Somehow I finished the night and walked the two miles home. I went to sleep eating breakfast.

Payday eased the aches of tired muscles and made up for lost sleep. I had never thought to ask how much money I would receive. At the end of the first week, after six twelve-hour nights, I was given a small brown envelope. I peeped inside. In it were three dollar bills and a silver half-dollar. I'd never seen so much money at one time in my life before, and I had earned every penny of it. I handed it to my mother and watched her eyes light up as she took out the small fortune.

It was the proudest day of my life.

I had never formally quit school; rather, I had simply stopped going. One morning a school official came by to investigate my continued absence. Mother quietly led him upstairs to the bed where I lay sleeping and pointed to me. I was dead to the world.

"He's been working all night," my mother said softly. The truant officer looked at me for a moment, shook his head and tiptoed out of the room. We never heard from him again. That was the end of my public schooling, in the seventh grade. I never finished the seventh grade.

At first the night foreman in the glass factory, a rough-talking man named John Crawford, scared me to death. Gradually I realized that, under his harsh manner, he was actually considerate and helpful. As I showed interest in and enthusiasm for glass manufacture, he gave me the opportunities to learn more meaningful tasks than walking back and forth with a paddle.

First, he taught me how to line the insides of molds for the tumblers with a mixture of flour and molasses. After I had finished, I would sneak behind the ovens where it was warm and quiet and take a nap. Mr. Crawford would come and wake me up with a kick in the pants and threaten to fire me. But he always let me sleep a while first.

During the midnight lunch hour, one of the men showed me how to make flowers out of colored glass. It took a tremendous amount of lung power, but the way Mother's face lighted up when I took my colorful glass creations home and gave them to her made the huffing and puffing worthwhile.

With the nightly drudgery on top of my daytime chores and the long walk to and from work, I was continuously tired. Nor was there any future in glassblowing. It led to the grave. Toward the end of one long night I suddenly realized how dog-tired I was. I did not want to walk one more step in the Federal Glass Factory. I went up to Mr. Crawford and told him I was quitting.

"What's the matter, Eddie?" he asked. "Don't you like it here?"

"No, sir," I said, "I don't. I'm tired of working at night."

He looked at me and saw that I meant it. "Okay, Eddie," he said, "I won't try to hold you. But if you don't get another job, come back. This one will be waiting for you."

I walked out of there at 3:00 in the morning, unemployed at the age of 13. It never occurred to me that I might not find another job. I was tough and wiry and willing to work. About half a mile farther south on Parsons Avenue was the Buckeye Steel Casting Company. When the employment office opened at 6:00 in the morning, I was the first in line. I told the man who interviewed me that I was 14 years old, had finished the eighth grade and had great experience in making molds and castings.

"When can you begin?" he asked.

"Today!" I said.

"Then report back here at seven o'clock," he said. "You'll be making cores for steel castings."

I hung around until 7:00, then went to work. It had never occurred to me that it was going to be a long, hard day on top of a long, hard night. I had the confidence of youth and the adrenalin of enthusiasm for a new job. I quickly learned that about the only difference between making molds for glass tumblers and cores for castings was that my present job was even messier than the one I had left.

But there were compensations. I was now working not only in the daytime, but also an hour less each day, from 7:00 A.M. to 6:00 P.M. I had not asked what the pay would be, and my first paycheck was a welcome surprise. I was earning $1 a day—six whole dollars a week! With money like that pouring in, the Rickenbacher financial difficulties would soon be over.

I stayed at the foundry for about three months. When I heard of a job capping bottles in a brewery, which was closer to home and cleaner, I quit without hesitation. No worries, no fretting, no indecision. If I didn't like what I was doing or if another pursuit offered greater challenge or more advantages, I acted immediately, without fear of the future. I have never been afraid to quit.

Though my schedule might not be the envy of 14-year-old boys today, I considered myself fortunate indeed. Shorter hours at the brewery added time to my day, and the younger kids were now doing the chores at home under my supervision. A bowling alley had opened near home, and I would go over there after supper and set up pins for a nickel a game. On Saturday and Sunday nights I could bring home 50 cents or more.

I was beginning to look about me at the other houses and yards in Columbus, and I observed that many were nicer than ours. We had never been able even to consider beautifying our property. For a long time every square inch had been used to grow food. But now I thought that we too could have a front lawn. The nicest yards in the neighborhood were raised above the level of the sidewalk, and I set out to do the same with ours.

A vacant lot adjoined us, and, with the owner's permission, I moved dirt from it to our front yard, a wheelbarrowful at a time. It took hundreds and hundreds of loads. I worked on my project during the long summer evenings after coming home from work. When I had the yard two feet higher than the sidewalk, I put a layer of topsoil on it, then some good sod from an unused field. A white picket fence finished the job. It all meant a lot of work, but it did beautify our property so much that the accomplishment would have been its own reward, even without Mother's happiness and pride.

Working all day, I had lost contact with my friends in the neighborhood. The simple pleasures of the old Horsehead Gang no longer appealed to me; I worked as a man, and I thought as a man. Sunday became my day of relaxation and enjoyment, as it was for other men.

Every Sunday during the summer, after we had all returned from Sunday school, Mother would give me a quarter. It was wealth with a capital "W." The first nickel would go for the long streetcar ride to Olentangy Park, a pleasure in itself. At the park all kinds of marvelous adventures beckoned. I would usually go swimming, for that cost nothing. Then there were all the rides—the figure eight, the merry-go-round, the ferris wheel, the roller coaster. Each cost a nickel. I could ride on three; or I could ride on only two and spend another nickel for a box of Cracker Jack. And when my long happy holiday was at an end, I could spend my last nickel for the long, luxurious streetcar ride home over the quiet Sunday-evening streets, to end a perfect day.

In the meantime the smell of hops in the brewery was making me sick. Again, with no sense of impending insecurity, I quit. I had been replacing the worn soles and heels on all our children's shoes for some years now, and I found a job making heels at a shoe factory.

"With all the heels in the world," I told Mother after my first day, "it should fall to my lot to make more."

When winter put an end to my Sundays in the park, I thought of another use for my weekly allowance. For years I had been yearning toward art. I felt that, if only I had the time and the teaching, I could express myself with paint and brush. The only course I could take for a quarter a session was in woodburning, or pyrography, but it wasn't satisfying. It was not Art.

Mother was thinking of a headstone for my father's grave. A man named Zenker, who made cemetery monuments, came to the house with pictures and different designs for headstones. The idea struck me that, if I could not become a great artist, then perhaps I could become a great sculptor. I was persistent, and Mr. Zenker gave me a job polishing the stones with water and sandstone. It was a wet, sloppy, cold job, but I liked it. Within a few months I had participated in every phase of stone carving.

After I had become fairly proficient, Mr. Zenker offered me the opportunity to make my first monument—Father's. One of the accomplishments of my life, in which I have taken the most pride, was in fashioning my father's tombstone. It was a large marble stone of graceful design with the word "Father" carved in block letters across the top and the inscription set below. I cut every letter.

I loved working with stone. On my own time I fashioned a Bible out of white marble. I cut in the words "Holy Bible" myself. Then I sculpted a small angel out of stone. It was far more intricate and delicate, and I gave it to my mother. She liked it, but she did not like my working with stone. One day I overheard her talking with Mr. Zenker.

"Eddie is such a skinny boy," she said. "There was tuberculosis in my family, and I've often been afraid that he has a tendency toward it. Working in this kind of place isn't doing his health any good. Sometimes I don't think Eddie will live to be a man."

I thought about that remark during the rest of the day and most of that night. Dust masks had not come into use at that time, and it was generally accepted that the dust stonecutters constantly inhaled damaged their lungs and curtailed their life spans. I already had a slight cough and a constant tickle in my throat, and as I lay awake that night the cough became worse and worse. By the time the morning sun came up, the stonecutting profession had lost Eddie Rickenbacher.

Mr. Zenker tried to hold me. "Do you want more money, Eddie?" he asked. "You stay on, and I'll raise you to two and a half dollars a day."

That was the wrong thing to say. I had started at $1 a day, less than I had been making in my two previous jobs, and had then been raised to $1.50. I worked ten hours a day, from 7:00 to 6:00 with an hour for lunch, and it was hard work. I had never brought up the subject of wages, overtime or days off on any job I had held. I had always assumed that my employers had paid me what I was worth. Now I learned that this employer

considered my worth to be $1 a day more than he had been pay-
ing me. It was another reason to leave.

The next day I was downtown, strolling around and thinking
over my unemployed state, when I saw a small crowd gathering at High and Broad Streets. I hurried up to see what was going
on, and there was one of the most beautiful things I had ever
seen in my life. It was the brand-new two-passenger Ford runabout, the first one in Columbus. I had seen horseless carriages
on the streets, but nothing like this new little Ford turtleback
roadster, sleek, shiny, built for speed and all for $500.

Then the man who had brought this twentieth-century wonder
to Columbus began a kind of educational lecture, telling us of
the automobile's performance and how one of these days practically everybody would own one. When he finished, there was a
moment's silence. I swallowed, cleared my throat and got up my
nerve. "Mister," I said, "do you ever take anybody for a ride?"

He studied me for a long moment before he answered. "Why?"
he asked.

"Well," I said, scared to death but trying not to show it, "I'd
like to take a ride."

Again he looked at me and then at the crowd around us. The
wheels were going around in his head. Would any of the adults
in the crowd get into the car? Probably not. But here was this
boy who actually wanted to take a ride. He saw a desire and an
eagerness in me that struck a responsive chord. The automotive
industry was meeting sales resistance among adults, and winning
over the young people, customers of the future, was good long-
range public relations. And, finally, it would be good hard
salesmanship to let the people of Columbus see this boy riding
in the new Ford runabout.

"Sure, kid," he said. "Hop in, and we'll go around the block."

I climbed into the passenger seat, which was on the left. This
car, like all others then, had a right-hand drive. The salesman
set the levers on the steering wheel in proper starting position,
turned on the ignition and spun the crank. The motor caught
right away, with a series of explosions.

As we cruised along the streets of Columbus at a speed that must have been well over 10 miles an hour, I held on tight. What a lucky boy I was! Not one kid in a million had such an opportunity during those early days of the automobile.

That thrill would remain vivid all the rest of my life. And it had a direct influence on the course I would follow for many years.

But in the meantime, after the ride was over, I needed a job. The machine shops of the Pennsylvania Railroad were located in my general neighborhood, and I applied for a job as an apprentice. Back I went to $1 a day. My first job was cleaning out the passenger cars. It turned out to be surprisingly lucrative. Some days I'd find $2 or $3 behind the seat cushions.

Yet when I was transferred into the machine shop and lost my found money I had no regrets, for I found beauty to take its place.

As I discovered it at such an early age, I have always accepted without question the affinity between art and mechanics. People who have not been exposed to both do not see the similarity. To take a piece of rough steel and transform it on the lathe into a polished object that is not only shining and beautiful but also a functional part of an apparatus serving a useful purpose became, in my mind, even more fulfilling than the creation of a painting or sculpture. I loved particularly to work on the lathe.

The machinists saw my enthusiasm and encouraged me. They kidded me unmercifully too. "Hey, Eddie," one of the older men would say. "I need a half-round square. Go borrow me one."

"I don't have one," the first man I'd ask would say. "Ask that fellow over there." I would be passed from man to man, department to department, for that half-round square before it would dawn on me that there could be no such thing as a half-round square. The next day the whole procedure would repeat itself as I sought a double-ended punch or a left-handed monkey wrench.

But the same men who kidded me would help me to set up the lathe for my own projects at lunch hour. I turned out walking sticks and baseball bats for fun, in addition to machine parts for the shops. As my knowledge grew, so did my appreciation of machinery and what it could do for mankind.

I was at the lathe one day when a man came by pushing a load of heavy timbers on a hand car. A wheel dropped off the cart, and it capsized in my direction. The entire load slipped off and pinned me against the machine. It could have crushed both my legs, but again the good Lord was looking after me, for I came out of it with only bruises and a badly lacerated leg. But I couldn't work for weeks, and that was long before the days of workmen's compensation. I didn't work, and I wasn't paid.

Yet that accident turned out to be one of the most fortunate experiences of my life. Many factors that had bearing on my later years all came together in my mind during that period of enforced idleness. I had the time to think, to combine an analysis of my experience and knowledge with my intellectual leanings and desires. The result was a crystallized idea of just what it was that I wanted to do with this life of mine.

The beauty of machinery gave depth and meaning to the memory of that thrilling occasion when I had become one boy in a million to ride in the new Ford runabout. After my exposure to the creativity of machine design and production, I had a much better idea of what beautiful, functional, precision-made parts went under that shiny black hood to produce such perfection and performance. My 15-year-old mind was sufficiently able to project current knowledge into the future for me to realize that even that powerful engine could be improved upon. Someday, I knew, there would be more automobiles on American streets and even in the countryside. My new understanding of the creativity and functionalism of mechanics thus combined with the exciting promise and potential of the internal-combustion engine to produce an irresistible pull.

That's what I wanted to do, I decided. I wanted to become a part of the automotive industry.

Fortunately for me, a man named Evans, who owned a little bicycle-repair shop, had had the same idea not long before. Under the ambitious title of "Evans Garage," he had gone into automotive repairs and storage. From the sidewalk on Chestnut Street, I could look inside and see two or three automobiles. A Waverly electric was nearly always there, along with a single-cylinder Packard. Their owners kept them in the garage.

When my injuries had healed well enough for me to go back to work, I walked into the Evans Garage one morning and told Mr. Evans that I wanted a job. He could use a boy all right, if only to clean up around the place and mind the shop when he was out on calls, but paying a salary to that boy was another matter. We finally agreed on 75 cents a day. I didn't think of the reduced wage as a step backward. Even with my responsibilities as head of a household, the money was inconsequential. It was the future that counted, that and the meaning of my labor.

"You have yourself a boy, mister," I said. "Where do you want me to begin?"

My job in the Evans Garage was a rich and rewarding experience. Mr. Evans recognized and appreciated my willingness to work and my eagerness to learn, and he discussed the projects with me as we worked. At the time, horseless carriages were powered by three types of engines: steam, gasoline and electric. Steam engines were clumsy and cumbersome, and, besides, they blew up. The internal-combustion engine was complicated and still in its infancy. Electric power, on the other hand, was safe, gave smooth performance and started and accelerated simply by means of moving a lever. Its drawback was that the batteries had to be constantly charged. That was an important function of the Evans Garage: we not only charged batteries; we also built them.

With me in the shop, Evans could leave it to go out and solicit business. He would hardly be around the corner before I would be in one of the automobiles, first pretending to drive it and, eventually, actually starting it up and moving it back and forth a few feet at a time. That is where I learned to drive, in the small, gloomy interior of that little garage on Chestnut Street.

One afternoon I was driving away, back and forth, in such a

seventh heaven of happiness that I forgot to check the oil. The car I was using was the little one-cylinder Packard, and the engine simply stopped. It did not take long to figure out what must be wrong: the piston had stuck. I had never fixed one before, but sheer panic was a strong incentive to try. If Mr. Evans came back to find that I had ruined a customer's car, he would throw me out on my ear.

I took the top off the crankcase and looked inside. Sure enough, the piston was stuck tight inside the cylinder wall. It was completely dry; there was not a drop of oil. Desperate situations require desperate measures, and I stuck a crowbar behind the connecting rod and put all my weight on it. The piston broke loose. I poured a can of oil into the crankcase, replaced the cover, turned the engine over with the crank to work the oil in, then turned on the ignition and cranked it again. The engine started and ran very well. When Mr. Evans came in he found everything in good shape, with me busily working away patching a bicycle tire.

In the meantime, around home, I was bragging to my brothers and sisters and the kids in the neighborhood about how I was driving these automobiles all over the place. They did not believe me. The more I bragged, the more they scoffed. So when Mr. Evans told me that he was going to Toledo the next day, leaving me alone in the shop, I really did not have much choice but to announce that evening that the following day I would drive home in the Waverly electric.

The first thing I did when I opened the shop the next morning was to start putting a good charge on the batteries. I closed up a little early that night, and off I went toward home, sitting high and proud in the Waverly. Though I had never taken it out on the street before, it was not too difficult to drive. I made the trip home, a couple of miles, without mishap. I pulled the shiny horseless carriage smoothly to the curb in front of my house and pushed the button on the warning bell to announce my arrival. I swung down from my perch and walked with dignity to the house.

"I brought the car home, Mother," I called, as soon as I was inside. "Let's go for a little drive."

"Oh, Eddie," Mother protested, "you shouldn't have!"

But I insisted, and eventually she put on her newest hat, anchored it firmly with hatpins and we went down the walk together. I helped her into the seat, and then I swung on board. Off we went, spinning about the neighborhood, as all the neighbors came running into their front yards to see Rickenbacher taking his mother for a drive. We skimmed along at 10 miles an hour, Mother holding onto her hat and protesting prettily at the daredevil speed but flushed with pleasure and pride. It was the kind of experience that happens often in daydreams, but so rarely in real life.

After driving through the neighborhood, I took Mother home. All the kids from blocks around had gathered, and I gave them a lengthy demonstration.

After supper, I started back to the garage. Mr. Evans would be in early next morning, and I wanted him to find everything exactly the way he had left it. But I hadn't gone one-quarter of the way when the little car began to give signs that I had driven it too much. It slowed down and gradually came to a stop. It was out of juice. The batteries were dead.

Darkness was coming on, and I still had a mile and a half to go. There was no wrecker service to come and rescue me. There was only the Evans Garage, which was going to be minus its one employee should its irate owner return to find said employee out with a customer's car.

In discussing electric energy with me, Evans had observed that frequently a battery would regain some current if allowed to sit idle for a while. I sure hoped that he was right, because that was my only possible course of action. I decided to wait an hour. Never had time dragged so slowly. My Ingersoll dollar watch was in and out of my pocket a dozen times before the hour was up.

I gingerly pushed the control lever, fully expecting nothing at all to happen, but instead the little car lurched forward. We rolled along together for several blocks until again, gently, it died. Again I sat for an hour before touching the controls. The refreshed batteries took me a few more blocks. As the night wore on, the hope became shorter and the waits longer, but finally around 3:00 in the morning I reached the garage. I hooked up the battery charger and took the streetcar home. Mother, who had been worried because I hadn't come home earlier, heard me come in about 4:00. She got up and fixed me a good breakfast while I washed up. I ate, then went back to the garage. When I saw Mr. Evans coming, I pulled out the charging plug. The little Waverly was as good as ever.

Those were happy days at the Evans Garage. I learned about automobiles and drove automobiles at an age when most boys still had many more years of dreaming to do. After six months or so, however, I began to realize that repairing cars, charging batteries and patching bicycle tires did not satisfy my expanding ambitions. I dreamed of building automobiles, even of designing them. But first I needed to know more about automotive mechanics. I sat down and wrote, in a fairly good hand but in seventh-grade English, to a score or more well-known universities asking if such a course or courses existed. Some did not even reply, and those that did answered in the negative.

Then I heard of the International Correspondence School in Scranton, Pennsylvania. I wrote, and the answer came back promptly. Even then, in 1905, the ICS had exactly what I wanted, a course in mechanical engineering, complete with a special section on the automobile and internal-combustion engines.

The first lesson, I do not mind admitting, nearly finished my correspondence-school education before it began. It was tough, and I was a little rusty when it came to formal education. I had to teach myself to study all over again, and, furthermore, I had to teach myself to think. I did not realize then, as I laboriously worked away at the lessons all alone, that I was receiving a greater benefit from them than I would have received from the same courses in a classroom. As there was no teacher of whom I could ask an explanation, I had to work out the answers myself.

Once I reached the answer through my own individual reasoning, my understanding was permanent and unforgettable.

Being in the automotive business, as it were, I knew that only two blocks away from the Evans Garage the Frayer-Miller Company was actually making automobiles right there in Columbus. It turned out about one car a month. There was only one model, a touring car with a gasoline engine, and every component except the tires was made right there under one roof.

I was itching to see what was going on there, but, as I put in long hours at the Evans Garage, looking in on the Frayer-Miller plant was impossible during the week. However, I learned that Lee Frayer, who was the designer and chief engineer of both the engine and the car, was there every day, Sundays and holidays included. A great deal of activity took place there on Sunday mornings. Until then I had been attending Sunday school regularly, but I transferred that regularity to the Frayer-Miller plant. I went down there every Sunday morning and simply hung around watching.

In addition to the stock model, they were building three racing cars to enter in the Vanderbilt Cup Race. That set me on fire. Racing automobiles! What I would give to be a part of that exciting enterprise!

I came to know Lee Frayer by sight. He was a hardworking, ambition-driven man, and I would never have dared to bother him. But he noticed me hanging around, and one Sunday he called me over.

"What's your name, Sonny?" he asked.

I told him.

"You're around here every Sunday," he said. "What do you want, anyway?"

"Mr. Frayer," I said, "I want to help you build automobiles. Can I have a job?"

He shook his head. "I'm sorry, kid, but we're pretty busy here. There just isn't anything you can do."

It so happened that that very morning I had come to the conclusion that there *was* something I could do around that place. I had never seen a dirtier shop. I could clean it up.

"Mr. Frayer," I said, "I've got a job to do here. I hope you will like it. I'll be here first thing in the morning."

And I was, at 7:00 sharp. I didn't even take the time to go by and tell Mr. Evans that I was leaving him for a job I did not have. I found a broom and a heavy floor brush stuck away in a corner. I took them over to one wall of the machine shop and started working in toward the middle of the room. I took the brush and swept off the machines and the benches. With broom and brush I attacked the floor, pushing the dirt and shavings ahead of me. I left behind me a floor surface as clean as our floors at home.

Mr. Frayer came in about 8:30. I had finished about a third of the floor area by that time, including the machines and benches. On one side the place looked like a pigpen. On the other it was spotless. The contrast must have jumped at him. He stood there for a moment, looking over the room, and then he looked at me.

"You sure as hell meant it, didn't you?" he said.

"Yes, sir, I did," I said. "Have you any objections?"

He grinned. "No, you keep right on going. You've got your job."

I finished cleaning up the place, all three floors. When that was done, Mr. Frayer told me to report to an old German toolmaker named Schwartz, a genius at his trade, and help to make carburetors. This job was in itself a course in mechanics.

I continued my correspondence course, for working at Frayer-Miller whetted my interest in automotive engineering. In my enthusiasm for the course and my eagerness to complete it, I carried my lessons around with me all the time. If I had five minutes, I spent them on my lesson. Solid blocks of time, in which I could spend a full hour or more of uninterrupted concentration on my lessons, came in the early morning. I was too tired at night to concentrate, so I would get up at 4:00 A.M. to study before going to work.

Lunch hour provided another excellent study period. One day I was munching on a sandwich and reading my lesson when Mr. Frayer came up behind me and looked over my shoulder.

"What is that, anyway?" he asked.

I explained that it was a course in automotive engineering and handed him the lesson so that he could see for himself. He read part of it, then handed it back and walked away without saying anything.

The next day I was taken off my carburetors and put in engine assembly, spotting bearings. No sooner had I become fairly adept at that than I was moved on to another operation, another and another. Every phase of automobile manufacture, complete with sight and sound and smell, was impressed into my mind. Then, finally, I was assigned to assembly of the chassis, filing each handmade part to make it fit.

One morning, after I had worked in every phase of the mechanical department, Mr. Frayer came up to me and said, abruptly, "Eddie, I want you to go into the engineering department now."

With those few words, he opened up a new world. There were only three or four engineers in that department. They were designing and setting specifications for each part of the Frayer-Miller automobile. As the design for each particular item was finished, I would take it and make a one-dimensional drawing so that a machinist could reproduce the object in metal. My early interest in art paid off handsomely.

During those months Lee Frayer was also building the three Frayer-Miller entries for the Vanderbilt Cup Race to be run in the fall of 1906. Those three beauties were the pride of the factory. Every detail, every line, every part was dedicated to speed and endurance. Each car was little more than an engine and a pair of bucket seats set on a frame on wheels. Racing cars in those days did not even have seat belts.

As the race grew nearer, it was practically all we talked about in the factory. We discussed the history of the Vanderbilt Cup. Two years before, William K. Vanderbilt, Jr., an amateur racing enthusiast and a member of the famous New York family, who was known to the sports world as "Willie K.," had sponsored the first race as an incentive to the American automotive industry. First prize was the famous Vanderbilt Cup, a huge goblet of sterling silver that weighed 30 pounds, and prize money totaling $10,000. Though as a patriotic American youth I found it hard to believe, it was nevertheless true that the European automotive industry and its swift and sturdy products were years ahead of ours. One reason was the European emphasis on racing. As has always been true in automotive research and development, the race is the testing laboratory for the automobile. Driving an automobile all out for three hundred miles, which was the distance of the Vanderbilt race, over a period of some five hours, provided a test equal to one hundred thousand miles of routine driving.

The 1904 and 1905 races had been won by French cars. Every American manufacturer hoped that 1906 would be our year. Patriotism was not the only motivation, however, for winning the Vanderbilt Cup could mean a fortune. If Lee Frayer's car were to come in first, he would be able to sell every Frayer-Miller he could manufacture. His name would go down in automotive history.

Mr. Frayer planned to take the three cars to Long Island a month before the race, in order to test them on the course. He would drive one car himself. Frank Lawell and a man named Belden would drive the other two. Ike Howard headed the crew of mechanics.

The cars were to be shipped from Columbus to Long Island by railroad. I went down to the railroad yards to help load them onto the freight car. The last one was being put aboard when suddenly Mr. Frayer, who was supervising the operation, turned to me.

"How long would it take you to run home and get your bag?" he asked. "I want to take you with me."

"An hour at the most!" I said and took off running. I ran all the way home. Mother pulled what clothes I had out of drawers, and we stuffed them into an old cloth traveling bag of my father's. Then I ran all the way back.

Though I'd never been more than a few miles from Columbus in my whole life, the trip itself, even including my first sight of New York City, was only a minor attraction compared to the automobile race. We proceeded directly to a small inn near the course. It was all so exciting that I slept very little that first night. The next morning we unloaded the cars. When we finished Mr. Frayer handed me a leather helmet and a pair of Zeiss goggles.

"Here, Eddie," he said. "I want you to ride with me."

I wanted to let out the old Horsehead yodel, but I tried to be as calm as Mr. Frayer. "You mean I'm going to be your riding mechanic?" I asked.

"That's right," Frayer said. "I know you're young, and this is new to you, but you've got a good head on your shoulders, and I think you're going to make a good one. Now let me tell you what I want you to do."

Standing by this powerful little car, he began by pointing out to me the instruments on the dashboard. I knew them all, but I listened carefully. My major concern would be the dials showing oil pressure and gasoline pressure. As the gasoline tank was mounted on the tail end of the car, it was necessary to keep pressure in the tank in order to force the gasoline forward into the carburetor. When the pressure of either gasoline or oil fell below the minimum, I would have to pump it back up.

"The next thing you've got to watch for," Frayer said, "is the tires. Keep your eye on them, especially the rear tires, and let me know when the rubber begins to wear off. You can tell it easy, the fabric's a different color."

I nodded. "Watch the oil gauge, watch the gasoline gauge, pump the oil, pump the gasoline, watch four tires, especially the rear ones." "Yes, sir," I said.

"Oh, and there's one other thing," Frayer said. "I'll be looking straight ahead, of course, so if another car is coming up to pass me, I won't see it. According to the rules they can only pass on the left, and I've got to let them. So you keep a lookout to the rear, and let me know if anybody wants to pass. We won't be able to talk over the sound of the engine, so tap my knee once if somebody is coming up to pass me. Two taps mean a tire is going bad."

Our first trial run was scheduled for daybreak the next morning. The race itself would also start at daybreak to minimize the effect of the heat of the day on the tires. The tires were the weakest part of the automobile and therefore the most dangerous. At that time the average motorist was lucky indeed if he could get two thousand miles out of a tire. In a race, with accelerating, braking and screeching around curves, one hundred miles to a tire was the maximum.

On our first practice run, everything went smoothly. Frayer was feeling his way around the course. I sat in the bucket seat with the wind hitting my face, leaning with Frayer as we careened around curves; watching gas, oil and tires, and exulting in the joy of motion.

The engine, like all others of the period, turned over at a maximum of 800 to 1,000 revolutions a minute, even at its top performance of 70 miles an hour. The ride was not smooth but a series of lunges.

The second day Mr. Frayer opened it up a little more. We were rocketing along a stretch on the Jericho Turnpike, coming up to a sharp curve, when even I, with my limited experience, sensed that we were going into the turn too fast. We were not slowing down at all. I looked over at Mr. Frayer. His right foot held the brake pedal flat on the floor board. We had no brakes.

"Hold on!" Mr. Frayer shouted. He did not have to tell me. The road curved, but we kept right on straight. We went down into a ditch and up out of it. A sand dune loomed ahead of us. Frayer tried to steer around it, but we were still going too fast. The wheels dug into the sand, and we turned over. I flew out, soared through the air and skidded to a stop in the sand.

Mr. Frayer was also thrown clear. Neither of us was badly injured, only scratched and bruised. Though the car was scratched and dented, it too had come through without serious damage. It was towed in, and Ike Howard and his crew went to work on it. It was ready for the next day's run.

That time the brakes held. We spun around that sharp curve on the Jericho Turnpike at 50 miles an hour. Frayer jammed the accelerator down to the floor for the straight stretch ahead, and we must have exceeded the speed of 65 or 70 miles an hour. The sensation of speed brought intense exhilaration.

Suddenly, in front of us, a guinea fowl with an unfortunate sense of timing led his flock of hens across the road. We plowed right through them. Guineas, bits of guineas and guinea feathers flew into the air. One bird was sucked up into the big blower in the front. Our air-cooled Frayer-Miller picked him up, killed him, feathered him, broiled him and carved him all in a split second.

What a mess! What a stench! The blower was torn to pieces. We limped back to the shop, stinking to high heaven all the way. Ike Howard said that he smelled us coming. The combination of guinea grease, meat and feathers covered the entire engine. Every square inch of surface had to be scraped and cleaned.

Despite these mishaps, the cars were shaping up splendidly, and Belden and Lawell were also becoming familiar with the course. Each curve had a definite point of compromise between maximum speed and tire wear, and it was that optimum that our drivers had to attain to win the Vanderbilt Cup, the winner's share of the prize money and fame and fortune.

As Frayer became more secure, everyone became more excited. It was a colorful event. There were other racing cars from the United States, as well as from France, Germany, England and Italy. I remember the chain-driven Locomobile, the huge Pope-Toledo and a modified stock model of the Oldsmobile. Foreign cars included the French Panhard and Darracq, as well as a De Dietrich that was monstrous, and the already well-known Italian Fiat and German Mercedes.

Not all the twelve American cars would be in the actual Vanderbilt Cup event, however; each nation was limited to five entries. The American five would be determined in the elimination race held September 22. On the morning of this race, we waited our turn as Fred Wagner, the well-known starter, waved the cars ahead of us onto the course at 30-second intervals.

Our turn came. The flag went down, and Frayer let out the clutch and jammed the accelerator down. I sat beside him as tight as a spoke in a wire wheel. My eyes flicked over the instruments: oil okay, gas okay. I looked ahead as we came out on the course. We were going to win the race!

Frayer got everything out of the car that it could give. Perhaps he asked for a little too much on one curve, for the right rear tire blew out. Our rear end swung to the right, then fishtailed down the road at 60 miles an hour as Frayer fought the wheel to keep from piling into the trees. When he had the car under control, he pulled to the side. In a road race, one changed a tire wherever it blew. We had rehearsed the procedure over and over and were soon rolling again.

We hadn't continued much farther before I saw that the temperature gauge was in the red. I could sense Frayer's eyes flicking over it. I made certain that the oil pressure was up, but there was nothing further either of us could do. The pressure of the wind against my face decreased.

At first I heard only a faint knocking. It became louder and louder. Something was pounding in the engine. We were losing speed quickly. Behind us a car was coming up fast. I tapped Frayer on his knee. He nodded and gave way, and the big Loco thundered by, the engine at a steady roar.

Mr. Frayer continued on. He knew that his race was over, but it hurt too much to quit. The pounding grew worse. Any second now the piston would freeze tight to the cylinder wall. He sighed, let up on the accelerator, pushed in the clutch, turned off the ignition and coasted to a stop by the side of the road. We sat there for a long moment, and then he sighed and looked at me.

"We're through," he said.

That was all. A year of seven-day weeks, an outlay of $50,-000 or more, and he hadn't even finished the elimination run.

Yet his only remark was that quiet, "We're through." I never forgot it. Gradually, over the years, the significance of that remark sank in, and I drew inspiration from it. To spell it out: *Try like hell to win, but don't cry if you lose.*

One of the Frayer-Miller cars, the one driven by Frank Lawell, did survive the elimination race and competed for the Vanderbilt Cup. It was running well when, in the seventh lap, the crankshaft broke.

That was the last race for a car bearing the name of Lee Frayer. Many of the automotive features he pioneered were later accepted: left-hand drive, wire wheels and the low-slung chassis. His air-cooled engine was the forerunner of the power plant for the Franklin automobile, but that was long after he had left the Frayer-Miller Company.

About a year after the Vanderbilt Cup Race, he received an offer too challenging and too promising to resist. For many years one of the major industries in Columbus had been the Columbus Buggy Company. It turned out an excellent product and had distributors all over the country. Its president was Clinton D. Firestone, who made a continuous effort to keep his company abreast of the times. He had brought out an electric coupé and a motorized version of the famous Columbus high-wheeled buggy. Now he wanted his trademark on an honest-to-God automobile. Firestone offered Lee Frayer the position of chief engineer, with full authority to design and build the CBC entry in the automotive field. The first I knew of it was when Mr. Frayer came up to me in the engineering department of the Frayer-Miller Company and told me that he was leaving.

"I'd like to take you over there with me," he said. "We're going to build a brand-new automobile, and I'd like your help."

The day was bright again. "I'll go with you, Mr. Frayer," I said.

The opportunity offered by Mr. Frayer meant more to me than any I have ever received in my life. I had been fatherless for four years. Now someone whom I respected for his ability and knowledge was interested in me. It was an inspiration and an incentive to prove that his confidence in me was deserved. In fact, I would have gone with him as water boy but it turned out he had more ambitious plans for me.

There was a great deal of complicated engineering design to be laid out before we could begin building the new touring car. In the meantime, I was put in charge of the experimental department, which supervised the final tests on the high-wheeled motor buggy. It was a fairly large department, with twelve or fifteen men in it, and there I was, at the age of seventeen, with full authority. My salary was commensurate with the importance of my new job—a whopping $20 a week.

Testing those interesting little buggies and driving them over the streets of Columbus and out into the countryside, I came to know them inside and out. Some of my knowledge was gained the hard way too, such as the time I took a buggy out to test a new braking system that we had devised. I was going lickety-split down a steep hill when the new brakes failed completely. At the bottom of the hill, the road curved sharply to the left. There was absolutely nothing I could do but stick with it and try to make the curve. It was a graveled road and flat as a pancake—with no bank at all—and, when I eased the tiller bar gently to the right, the high, narrow, solid-rubber wheels simply could not hold it. Over the buggy went, catapulting me out. I hit the ground as the buggy jumped over me sideways. I could easily have been as badly battered as the buggy, but I found, somewhat to my surprise, that I could stand up and walk away.

These tests were invaluable, both for the quality of the product and for my own development. I would take one of the little buggies around a curve at a set rate of speed, then come back and take the same curve faster. I did it again and again until I finally reached a speed that would pull a wheel right off. Frequently, one of the connecting-rod bearings would burn out. I began carrying extra bearings, a can of motor oil and a bunch of waste with me at all times. I could put in a new bearing in less than thirty minutes.

Another weakness of the little engine lay in the intake valve.

The small locks that held the spring on the valve in place frequently shook loose. That would put the whole engine out of commission, because there would be no suction to draw in the fuel. I made it a point to carry a few spare locks in my pocket wherever I went.

One morning Mr. Frayer sought me out. "The old man is stuck up at the storage dam," he said. "Go up there, and see if you can help him."

He didn't have to tell me any more. By then I knew all about Mr. Firestone. He lived in the finest section of town, out on East Broad Street. On nice days he liked to take one of the buggies and drive over to the plant by way of the storage dam on the Scioto River. It was the long way around, and occasionally his buggy would break down. He would have to send to the plant for somebody to come out and help him. Sometimes it took a horse to haul him in.

Well, I was not taking any horse. By that time I had the little engine in the palm of my hand. I forgot that, although I was the superintendent of the experimental department, I was still a skinny 17-year-old kid who didn't look even that old. When I rattled up beside him, jumped out of the little mosquito and walked over to him, he looked at me dourly. I don't suppose he had ever seen me before.

"Good morning, Mr. Firestone," I said eagerly. "Mr. Frayer said you'd developed some kind of trouble and for me to fix you up."

He simply sat there and looked at me. He was a stout man, and when he finally spoke it was in a squeaky high-pitched voice.

"Hell," he said, "I asked for a man, not a boy."

"Well, maybe I can help you just the same," I said. The crank stuck out at the side, and I grabbed it and turned the engine over a couple of times. Sure enough, the thing went "swoosh." There was no compression. I knew without looking that the locks had bounced out of the spring. It took me less than five minutes to replace them. I spun the crank, and the little engine caught.

"It's okay now, Mr. Firestone," I said. He did not say a word; he simply slipped the little buggy into gear and took off. Later in the day, however, Mr. Frayer called me in.

"Say, what did you do for the old man?" he asked. "He thinks you're the seventh wonder of the world."

"Well, please don't tell him different," I said.

After that, Mr. Firestone seemed to make a point of coming around the experimental department, looking in on me and asking how things were going. He had found out my name from Frayer, and he ended every remark with it. "How are you doing, Eddie?" he would say. "What are you working on, Eddie? How are you getting along, Eddie?"

About that time a group of distributors of CBC products in New Jersey put on a demonstration of the motor buggies on the Million Dollar Pier in Atlantic City. They found that the buggies frequently got stuck in the sandy roads along the beach and called upon the home office for help. Mr. Firestone sent me. Though I had not aged appreciably since Mr. Firestone had referred to me, correctly, as a "boy," the distributors in Atlantic City accepted me as an emissary of the company. Mr. Firestone's praises had paved the way.

One of the local dealers took me out to the beach in a high-wheeled buggy to demonstrate the trouble. The narrow rubber tires worked right down into the loose sand, and the drag was so heavy that the clutch kept slipping. I fooled around with the clutch mechanism for a couple of days and nights, trying to work out a better method. It suddenly occurred to me that the brakes did not slip. I bought an old brake band in a junk shop and fitted it to the clutch mechanism. The little mosquito skedaddled along through the sand without trouble.

The dealers went wild. They insisted on taking the buggy to the sand dunes in back of the beach. No motor-driven vehicle had been able to climb those dunes, but our little mosquito, with its new clutch facing, skimmed right over them. The Atlantic City agent ran to the local newspaper to tell the wonders of the Columbus buggy, and a photographer came out to take a picture.

There I was, plain as day, right in the newspaper. I bought a dozen copies and took them back to Columbus with me.

I fashioned another clutch to show Mr. Frayer and the other bosses. They were so impressed with its efficiency that thousands were made and sent free as replacement parts to every buggy owner in the entire country. That was probably the first time that design service and parts service were handled properly by any factory.

And now our first touring car, the 5-passenger Firestone-Columbus was ready for final testing. It was a beauty. Into that car Lee Frayer had poured all his automotive genius. The early advertisement described the FC as "a mechanical masterpiece," and it was indeed just that. It sold for less than $2,000. At the car's peak the factory turned out from 1,500 to 2,000 models a year.

I tested the car to the point at which I could have taken it to pieces and put it back together blindfolded. The Northway engine that powered it, built to Frayer's demanding specifications, became as familiar to me as the little two-cylinder buggy motor. I learned, in a sense, to speak the language of the internal-combustion machine. Often when an engine was not performing properly and one of the engineers asked my advice, I would simply listen to it for several seconds and pinpoint the trouble. In nearly every case my diagnosis was correct. Put simply, engines have always talked to me.

The formal introduction of the new Firestone-Columbus was to be made at the Chicago automobile show in January 1909. My thorough familiarity with both car and engine was probably one reason that Mr. Frayer asked me to go with him. The trip itself would be the ultimate test of the automobile. The distance from Columbus to Chicago was at least 250 miles over the twisting dirt roads of that period. In winter, with the roads turned into ruts and mud puddles by melting snow, there was a good chance that we would never make it.

Mr. Frayer, however, insisted on taking his creation to Chicago under its own power. We made elaborate preparations for the trip, taking extra gasoline, oil, engine parts and tires. There were no road maps; we took with us only one Rand McNally map showing towns, railroads and rivers. We planned our route through Fort Wayne, Indiana, and allowed ourselves ten days for the trip. We hoped to spent the night at small hotels and inns in the towns through which we would pass.

Both Mr. Frayer and I knew the road to Marysville, Bellefontaine and Wapakoneta, Ohio. From there on it was necessary to stop at each town and ask the way to the next. We made good time to Fort Wayne, but from there on we had plenty of mud trouble. Through one stretch of so-called "road" across the level country of northern Indiana, we drove in low gear continuously and must have been stuck a dozen times. We came to know not only every farmer in the area but also his horse. We must have spent $50 having ourselves pulled out of mudholes. The car performed excellently when there was enough solid ground underfoot for leverage, and in spite of the mud we made the trip in five days.

In Chicago, we washed and polished the car, then took it down to the automobile show to exhibit it. People flocked around and made appointments for demonstrations. Mr. Frayer appointed me the official demonstrator-driver, and I took scores of potential customers for rides through the streets of Chicago, explaining the car's features truthfully as we drove. Largely as a result of this honest, factual approach, we took orders for no fewer than eleven automobiles during the few days we were in Chicago.

One of the best agencies for CBC products was the Fife and Miller Company in Dallas, Texas. Mr. Firestone sent the company three of the new automobiles—a carload. They arrived in June. A week or so later CBC received a furious telegram from Dallas. All three cars had been taken on test runs and each had broken down after only about ten miles.

Mr. Firestone came into my department, waving the telegram and shouting, "Where's Eddie?"

"Right here, Mr. Firestone," I said.

He showed me the telegram. "I want you to go to the treasurer and get some expense money and go down to Dallas and straighten this out," he said. "Get a move on now."

"Yes, sir, Mr. Firestone," I said, and that's how I found myself in Dallas. I had never been so hot in my life. The first thing I did when I reached Dallas was to find a hotel room and take off my long underwear. The next morning I went to the offices of Fife and Miller. Mr. Fife, a corpulent gentleman, was the one I saw first. When he saw that the factory representative was a skinny eighteen-year-old, his jaw dropped right down on his double chin.

"What the hell do you think you're going to do?" he asked.

"Well, I'm going to try to find out what the trouble is and fix it," I said.

He stared at me for several long seconds. "All right," he said. "I guess C. D. Firestone knows what he's doing. I'll give you a week."

I started one of the cars, and it told me in the language that we both understood that it was feeling fine. It was the middle of the afternoon and hot as blazes. After about five miles the engine began heating up. I kept going. I had driven that car or cars exactly like it thousands of miles, and not one had heated up.

But I had never driven one in Dallas in June. The radiator boiled over, the engine began to feel sluggish, the connecting rods began pounding and finally the engine stopped altogether. The pistons were stuck in the cylinders. I got nowhere, as it happened again and again, and for the time being I was stuck. There was no great mystery about what was causing the trouble. It was just too hot in Texas. The engine was equipped with a thermo-siphon cooling system instead of a water-pump system. It had worked perfectly in Detroit, in Columbus, in Chicago during the winter. It did not work in Texas in the summer. Nothing I tried would make it work, and my week was running out.

That Saturday I took the car into the country. It overheated again, and there I was, stuck ten miles from Dallas. There were no filling stations, no water. If there had been, pouring cold water into that sizzling engine would have cracked the cylinder jacket.

I was particularly anxious to make it back to town. I'd met a girl and had a dinner date with her that night. Looking around desperately, I happened to see a few cows bunched together around a water hole. I joined them, looking apprehensively at those longhorns, took off my straw sailor hat and filled it with water.

I knew better than to pour it into the hot engine, but I did not want to be late for my first date in Dallas either. I took a chance and poured a hatful of cold water into the radiator. It boiled out immediately, but I poured in another hatful and another, all the time listening for the cylinder water jacket to crack.

It creaked and groaned, but that was all. I filled the radiator—it took a dozen trips to the water hole—and drove back to Dallas in time for my date. We had a pleasant dinner and saw a good show.

The next day I took the same car out again. I waited for the engine to overheat, but nothing happened. Ten miles, twenty miles, thirty miles. Why didn't it overheat? Perhaps some chemical in the water had cured the trouble. I headed for the same water hole, shooed the cows away again and collected a sample in a bottle; then I paid a chemist in Dallas a small fortune to analyze it.

"Just plain old rain water," he said.

I reconstructed the whole operation from the beginning. What had happened when the engine got hot? The pistons had expanded and stuck in the cylinder walls. The engine manufacturer had fitted the pistons into the cylinders with the smallest possible tolerances. And then it came to me. Adding cold water had shrunk the pistons microscopically and had frozen them, in effect, in those dimensions. There was now sufficient clearance, even under extreme heat.

I took the second car out, drove it until it began pounding its head off and then, holding my breath, poured in cool water. The results were the same. I repeated the operation with the third car. All three ran perfectly for hour after hour.

"Your cars are okay now," I told Mr. Fife and Mr. Miller and proved it by taking them for a ride. I wouldn't tell them the details of the Rickenbacher cure; I was almost positive that I knew the metallurgical reason for my accidental discovery, but I was not ready to talk about it.

Satisfied by the performance, the two partners eagerly set out to sell the three cars. The cars went quickly, and Mr. Fife waddled off to the telegraph company to order more, provided that I would stay and help sell them. Back came a telegram to Mr. Fife, saying that the cars were on the way, and one to me from Lee Frayer, asking what in the world I had done. I wired him back that I would tell him when I returned to Columbus.

In the meantime, I stayed and helped to sell the high-wheeled buggies that were on hand. One of my first sales was to a doctor from the Waco area, who had a good understanding of mechanics. He quickly mastered the little two-cylinder engine in the motor buggy and got the most out of the odd little contraption. After that, whenever a prospect was wavering, I would ask him to wire the doctor, asking his opinion. The doctor would always shoot back a telegram—at my expense, of course—describing the excellent service that he received from the motor buggy.

I was not completely without guile. West of Dallas, near Fort Worth, lies a small range known as "Chalk Hill." A major criterion of automotive excellence was the ability of a car to take Chalk Hill in high. Prospects naturally demanded that the demonstration include this hill-climbing contest. We always made it, but one day, with a particularly heavy prospect aboard, I feared that we wouldn't.

In an effort to give the buggy every chance, I made a running start, and we approached Chalk Hill at 30 miles an hour. The little buggy bounced and skidded on the gravel road like a skittish colt just learning to gallop. We started up the grade, with my potential customer and me both leaning forward and pushing with body English.

Halfway up it became all too clear to me that we were not going to make it in high gear. Quickly I slammed on the brakes, and we came to a dead stop.

The customer turned to me, but before he could say a word I beamed at him with a proud smile. "How do you like those brakes?" I asked. "See how they hold us tight, right here on Chalk Hill."

He smiled back. "By Gad, they do hold, don't they?" he said. "Holy gee, that's great!"

He bought the car that afternoon, for cash.

As I traveled over Texas, helping dealers to sell both the motor buggy and the touring car, I began to recognize some of the factors upon which a successful operation was dependent. Our most effective dealers, I observed, were those who also believed in the product. They maintained efficient service departments with qualified mechanics. They were willing to invest capital in inventory, so that, when a customer was ready to buy a car, it was there waiting for him. Dealers who would order a car from the factory only when they had a customer sometimes found that by the time the car arrived the customer had purchased another make.

I bore these facts in mind when approached by local applicants for dealerships. I could tell them what it would take to be a successful dealer, and I could judge whether or not they were willing to pay the price. If a local businessman seemed a good prospect as a dealer, he and I could then go to the local banker. On the basis of my observations of the way that successful dealerships operated, I could set forth to the banker the profit potential in selling CBC products, and more often than not we walked out with the necessary capital to establish a new dealership.

My salary of $125 a month was more than adequate, even generous. With it I not only was able to support myself in Texas and contribute to my family in Columbus, but I also managed to pay off the mortgage on the house on East Livingston Avenue so that the Rickenbacher family owned it free and clear. But I was able to accomplish these ends only by keeping track of every penny I spent. One of the results of this care was full reimbursement of business expenses from the company. My expense account was honest but complete.

I had learned the importance of public relations as a business tool back in Atlantic City, and I kept my eyes open for opportunities to generate and use good publicity. I was in Abilene, Texas, when William Jennings Bryan, the famous orator and Presidential candidate, came to town to make a speech. I drove to his hotel in a shiny new Firestone-Columbus and went in to see him.

"Mr. Bryan," I said, "I've got a new Firestone-Columbus parked outside, and I'd be happy to drive you while you're here."

"Well, that's certainly very kind of you," Mr. Bryan said. "It would be a pleasure."

Naturally there was a parade in his honor, and thousands of people from miles around saw the great William Jennings Bryan in the back seat of my Firestone-Columbus, with me in the driver's seat. The picture was on the front page of the local paper.

One of the people who saw that picture was a local rancher named Hutchinson. He came into the showroom the next day, bringing with him two of his neighbors. I took them on a demonstration ride, and they all liked the car.

"I'll make you a proposition, young man," Mr. Hutchinson said. "If you can drive my family and me to my ranch and back safely and with no trouble, I'll buy this automobile. My friends here will each buy one, too."

Three sales! I agreed to pick him up at his house in town the next day. Only after he left did I learn that his 100,000-acre ranch was eighty miles away. Mr. Hutchinson, his wife and their seven children were waiting the next morning when I drove up. I packed them in, and off we went. A few miles out of Abilene the road became simply a wagon track cut through sagebrush and mesquite. By noon the sand was scorching hot. An inner tube blew out with a bang. I jacked up the car and changed it. Then another one blew.

As we neared the ranch, my attention must have wavered.

Suddenly there was a sickening thud, and we stopped dead in our tracks. I jumped out to see what we had hit. It was a big stump, at least six inches in diameter, sticking up right between the wagon tracks. It had bent the axle. I was sick. There went three sales flying right off with the angels.

"There's no point in trying to do anything with the automobile until the morning," Mr. Hutchinson said. "How would you like to take a ride around the ranch?"

"Why, I'd like to, Mr. Hutchinson," I said. We all went to the ranch house, freshened up, then strolled to the corral. The cowboys—there were a hundred of them—brought up a little cow pony all saddled and bridled.

"You may find this horse a little rough to start with," Mr. Hutchinson said, "but as soon as he gets acquainted with you he'll be perfectly all right."

"Sure," I said. As I was used to getting into automobiles on the right-hand side, I automatically went to the right-hand side of the horse. I put my right foot in the stirrup, gave a jump and tried to swing my left foot over the horse's back. He protested and kicked his hind feet almost straight up in the air. I went right over his head and hit the dirt about fifteen feet away. I could have broken my fool neck, but the cowboys thought it was the greatest show that they had ever seen and howled with laughter. I picked myself up and managed to get a sick grin on my face. It hurt too much to laugh.

The next morning we got down to work. The cowboys built a big bonfire, and, while it was building up heat, a couple of them helped me to take the front axle off the car. We heated it up, and I hammered it straight again, as good as new. We drove back to town the next day without a mishap. Mr. Hutchinson and his two friends each bought a car.

Meanwhile the Arizona distributor was having boiling-over problems. I went to Tucson and confidently proceeded to take a car out and give it the old Texas-tried Rickenbacher treatment. I was driving back to town, whistling away, when again the radiator boiled over, and again the car pounded to a halt. In Arizona

Deadman's Turn—1913 Vanderbilt Cup Race, Santa Monica, California

Elgin Road Race—1914

Author's first racing car accident—Red Oak, Iowa, 1910

A later accident

Driving Duesenberg at Indianapolis—1914

With famed movie maker Max Bennett, left, and Charlie Chaplin's brother, Sid, right—Hollywood, 1913

Driving 1914 Duesenberg at fiftieth anniversary of Indianapolis Speedway in 1961 with Colonel Roscoe Turner as riding mechanic

RICKEN

WINNER OF 300-MILE

Winner — Rickenbacher; time, 3:16:12.9. Secoond—Milton. Third—Lewis.

TACOMA SPEEDWAY, Aug. 5.—With but 15 of 150 laps in the 300-mile Montamarathan y
llowed, and Lewis was third, closely pressed by others. Drivers were tearing around the speed
e positions.

*Author and mechanic Fre
McCarthy looking like astre
nauts; this communication sy
tem was developed by the au
thor and is pictured at t
Corona, California, road race
1914*

SERVICE | PACIFIC NEWS LEASED WIRE

TRIBUNE

OVER
20,000
A DAY

AUGUST 5, 1916.   TWO COMPLETE LEASED WIRES

BACHER

PEEDWAY CONTEST

Palma.

nd ten cars o nthe track, an exciting finish was at hand. Rickenbacher was leading, Milton than 95 miles per hour. So close were the leaders that a stop would materrially change

Driving French Peugeot

Dario Resta,   *Ralph De Palma,*

Ralph Mulford,   *Spencer Wishart*

Louis Chevrolet,

First trophy won in racing career

Barney Oldfield,

At the 300-mile road race, Tucson, Arizona—1915

Towing record-breaking Blitzen Benz—1912

my remedy didn't work. I finally figured out why: the altitude at Tucson is 2,390 feet, and water boils at a lower temperature. This problem required a different approach. I bought a small water pump, bolted it to the side of the crankcase, connected it to the fan-belt pulley and forced the water through the cylinder jacket. That fixed it.

The owner of the car, a Doctor Fletcher, was most pleased. "Say, Eddie," he asked me, "would you like to go out in the desert and hunt jackrabbits?"

I had never shot a gun in my life, but Dr. Fletcher lent me a double-barreled shotgun, and out we went into the sagebrush. A jackrabbit took off in front of me. I jerked the gun to my shoulder, shot and missed him by a mile. The recoil was like a kick from a mule.

I figured out a way to do better the next time. I put my forefinger on the front trigger and my middle finger on the back one. That way I could get off the second shot immediately. Just as I had it all worked out, a big rabbit broke from practically under my feet. I jerked the gun up and fired before I had it to my shoulder. In the haste and excitement, I pulled both triggers and went flat on my back. But there was not much left of the jackrabbit.

I had been away from Columbus about a year and a half when I received a letter from Lee Frayer. The distributor for the north central states—Nebraska, Iowa, Wisconsin and the two Dakotas—was having difficulty with the high-wheeled buggy.

"How would you like to go up to Omaha, Nebraska, and straighten things out?" the letter concluded. There was nothing I would like better. Christmas was coming, however, and I received permission to go home for the holidays before going to Nebraska.

When I arrived home Mother hugged and kissed me, then took a step back and looked up at my face. "My, they grow them big down in Texas, don't they?" she said. When I left Columbus I had stood 5 feet 9 inches; now, just after my nineteenth birthday, the tape measure showed 6 feet 2 inches. I weighed 165 pounds.

But I was still pretty naïve about some things. I had bought presents in Texas for all the family, and while I was at it I bought a present for my childhood sweetheart, Blanche Calhoun, as well. It was, of all things, a diamond ring. She seemed a little puzzled when I gave it to her with the offhand remark, "here's something I brought you from Texas," but she accepted it graciously.

Within 48 hours it was all over the neighborhood that we were engaged.

I was scared to death. I was fond of Blanche, but I wasn't ready to get married. I was going to be traveling constantly for the next several months.

I did not know what to do. I simply went out to Omaha without saying anything more about it. Blanche later married a fine young fellow from Columbus, and whenever I saw her she was as friendly and gracious as though nothing had ever happened. But the next time I gave a girl a diamond ring I knew full well what it meant.

For the next several months I traveled through the north central states, tightening up the slipshod operation I found there. Both the motor buggy and the Firestone-Columbus were being oversold and underserviced. I staged a continuing educational program for our dealers. The work paid off in increased sales, and I was promoted to branch manager, complete with six salesmen and a salary of $150 a month.

Not a bad job for a 19-year-old—in March 1910—but I quickly found that selling cars was not enough. Dirt-track racing was just beginning to be popular throughout the Midwest at that time, and I naturally took an interest in this new sport. Driving my own Firestone-Columbus in those town races—and winning, of course—would be an excellent way to call my product to the attention of prospective buyers. I was seriously considering this move when one of the first of Lee Frayer's new models arrived.

Its most noticeable, and controversial, feature was its left-hand drive, the first in America. At that time all other American cars had right-hand drive, even though we drove on the right-hand side of the road. Lee Frayer argued that it was safer to have the driver sit on the left so that he could gauge the lateral distance between his car and oncoming cars. This innovation met the reaction to which all revolutionary principles are subjected, but Frayer made it stick.

The left-hand drive was only one of the several striking features. It was a small sport car, with only a 50-inch track, six inches less than the standard. It was powered by a four-cylinder high-speed engine, the first built in America, which provided smooth, even power and a quick getaway.

Working at night, I stripped the little car down, removing its body and fenders, reinforced the frame at critical points, put in a bucket seat and mounted an extra gas tank on the tail end. I painted it white and had a pair of white coveralls made for me. I wanted it to be spotless as well as speedy.

The first race after the little car was ready was a 25-mile event at Red Oak, Iowa. I drove over the day before the race and inspected the half-mile track. I remembered how Frayer had practically memorized every pebble on the road before the Vanderbilt Cup Race and how I had taken curves at ever-increasing speeds in the motor buggy to determine the safety point. Around and around the oval track I drove that evening, taking the curves at each end faster and faster, braking here, accelerating there, until I knew exactly the maximum speed I could attain at each point on the track. Strangely, this precaution did not occur to the other drivers.

Those county-fair contests of the Teens were interesting and colorful. At race time, usually on Saturday afternoon, the fair shut down, and the drivers took over with their roaring racers. Most of the cars entered in those events were stripped-down stock cars, driven primarily by agents like myself. We were in it, not only for the immediate prize money, but also for future sales. Winning a local race was the best possible advertisement for an automobile.

At Red Oak that day, thanks to my swift little car, I jumped off to an early start. Just behind me was a fellow named Walter Smith, the local Chalmers agent, driving a 30-horsepower Chalmers Detroit.

As the race wore on through lap after lap, little cars and big cars swung around the curves, gouging ruts and piling up ridges in the dirt track. But I kept piling into the curves with the same velocity as at the beginning of the race. Something had to give. It is the right rear wheel that takes the beating in a track race. Mine collapsed just as I went into a curve. The little car turned broadside, kept going right through the fence, leaped the ditch and landed on the other side, still going sideways. Then it rolled over, throwing me clear.

I got up and stood motionless for a moment in amazement that I was unharmed. Then I shrugged it off and went to check my car. I wanted to see what repairs it needed for the next race. For I knew there was going to be a next one.

Aksarben—"Nebraska" spelled backwards—Week is one of the biggest festivals in Omaha and the Midwest. Two days of auto racing were always the feature of the celebration. I entered every event, ten races of different lengths in two days. I tuned up the little racer until it purred. In the weeks before the races were scheduled, I drove the track over and over. It was a mile-long oval, and I got so that I could pull my car around each curve blindfolded. On the first day I won every race, five out of five. On the second day I won the first four.

I stayed out of the fifth race at the request of two of my competitors, the Chalmers dealer and the Cadillac dealer. They had a private bet, but neither could collect while I kept winning. They gave me first-prize money, the only time I ever won sitting in the grandstand.

In those two days I made close to $1,500 clear. I had hired a mechanic to help change tires and do other rough work, and I gave him $200 over his regular wages. It was an unheard-of amount and probably the first time he had seen that much money, but I thought he deserved it.

That summer I raced all over Nebraska and Iowa, winning more often than not. The prize money was my own, but the company benefited too. A restaurateur in Atlantic, Iowa, for example, was having difficulty making up his mind whether or not to buy a Firestone-Columbus from me. We had one in stock that was painted heliotrope, and he used to come to Omaha just to look at it. But he could not make up his mind to buy. At the fair in Atlantic, I won four of the five races. Then I cleaned up and went to his restaurant for dinner. He came running up to me.

"I want that car!" he cried. "When can you deliver it?"

"Do you want it right now or in the morning?" I asked.

"Tomorrow will be all right," he said. I ate, drove back to Omaha, washed and polished the heliotrope car and drove it to Atlantic in the morning. He had the cash waiting for me.

It was not always easy. Some of the tracks amounted to invitations to commit suicide. The one in Nebraska City was only a half-mile long around an artificial lake. One end of the track went over the dam.

The local Chalmers dealer was determined to beat me in that race; only the two of us entered it. He spent weeks preparing a little roadster for the big event, and he drove it like a madman. I stayed right on his heels.

Going into the curve over the dam, he blew a tire. The car started skidding sideways, directly in my path. The only way that I could miss him was to swing out. I hit the fence and went skittering along, knocking planks and posts every which way. It slowed me down, but I still went down the face of the dam at good speed and hit a tree with a good solid thud. I climbed out and crawled up the dam to the track. Neither the Chalmers nor its driver was anywhere to be seen. Both had completely disappeared. Then I looked out into the lake and there was the Chalmers driver, splashing around and swimming toward shore. His car was on the bottom of the lake.

Another accident occurred while my mechanic and I were driving home from a race one night. Though I had no lights on the stripped-down car, there was a full moon, and we kept going. We went around a curve, and there, right in the middle of the road, was a horse-drawn buggy. It had no lights either, of course. We went right into it. The people in it, a young man and his girl, went sailing out and landed in a field. I held onto the wheel, but my mechanic went right over the hood and skidded to a stop on the gravel. I ran to him. He was bruised and cut but not seriously injured. Moans and groans were coming from the field, and I hurried to help the young couple. Luckily a doctor making a night call came along just then. He determined that they were more scared than hurt and took them into town.

I paid the boy for his buggy. He later sued me for $5,000 but settled for $600. My car was banged up pretty badly. It was an expensive accident, but it could have been worse—we could all have been killed.

Back in Columbus, Lee Frayer was keeping up with my racing successes. One morning I received a long night letter from him. "How would you like to swap dust with Barney Oldfield?" he began. Frayer went on to say that the famous racing driver had entered a 100-mile race to be held at the Columbus Driving Park a half-mile from home. Frayer wanted me to bring my little racing car back to Columbus and help him beat the great Oldfield. I wired back that I was practically on the way.

In Columbus, Frayer proudly showed me the racing car he had built, his Red Wing Special. It had a 50-horsepower engine and was much faster on the straightaway than mine. But Oldfield's Knox was even more powerful. I did not see how Frayer could expect to beat him.

"I've got it all worked out," Frayer said. "He can outrun us on the straight stretches, but your lighter car can make better time on the curves. If you set the pace, he'll try to stay with you. But with that big monster he'll be driving, his tires won't stand up. He'll have to make several changes. I'll keep up a steady pace, and with less time wasted on tire changes I ought to stay pretty close. Then I'll give it all I've got at the end. Okay?"

"You bet!" I said. "We'll show him our dust!"

Oldfield even then had a magic name, and the whole town turned out for the race. It went just the way Frayer had predicted. Well before the midpoint of the race, Oldfield blew a tire. He was a lap ahead, but, by the time he had changed the tire and gotten back on the track, I was even with him. Again he pushed past me, and again he blew a tire.

At 75 miles I was leading, Oldfield was catching up fast and Frayer was holding a steady third. Oldfield blew another tire. Now I had him. Our plan was working fine, except that I was going to be first and Frayer second. But, with only a few laps to go, one of my connecting rods broke and, clattering and banging, I had to pull over to the side. Frayer came on strong, and Oldfield could not catch him. Our combination had won the race.

The Columbus 100-mile race was my first big event. I hoped it would not be my last. But, for the time being, racing was out. I had a long winter ahead of me selling cars in Nebraska. Then came another letter from Frayer. There was talk that the big new Indianapolis Speedway, which had opened in 1909 with a mishmash of 42 events in a 3-day schedule, was going to feature one big, 500-mile race in 1911. He wanted to enter it. We both knew that my little 30-horsepower Firestone-Columbus would not stand up against Speedway competition. For that matter, there was little reason to hope that his own Red Wing Special would finish anywhere near the money. But he still wanted to try, and he wanted me to be his relief driver. It did not require much coaxing.

The story of the Indianapolis Speedway is an exciting one, and I shall try to do it justice in a later chapter devoted exclusively to it. In 1911 I knew only that it was the greatest automotive event in the world. As the day, May 30, came closer I thrilled at the realization that soon I would be rubbing elbows with the great racing drivers of the period. There would be, among others, Wild Bob Burman; Spencer Wishart; David Bruce Brown, the wealthy sportsman; wily Ralph De Palma; the devout Ralph Mulford, and Louis Chevrolet. Ray Harroun, one of the drivers, was also chief engineer of the big Marmon Motor Company, with tens of thousands of dollars to spend on the development of his entry. Neither Frayer nor I knew it, but all that winter Harroun was not only building his automobile but also planning a campaign similar to the one Frayer and I had used at Columbus.

The talk of the race was Harroun's innovation: he would be driving without a riding mechanic. In order to see cars approaching him from the rear, he had rigged up a peculiar contraption, a rearview mirror. It was the first one ever seen.

Lee Frayer was at the wheel when the race began at 10:00. Carl Fisher, the Indianapolis magnate who had built the speedway, paced the group once around the 2½-mile oval. Then the race was on. I took over from Frayer later. I was driving when suddenly, right in front of me, the rim of an Amplex driven by Art Greiner tore loose. The car lurched. Greiner's mechanic went hurtling through the air to his death. It was the first time I had seen a man killed in a race. Greiner escaped with a broken arm.

Lee Frayer took over at the 400-mile point and drove the rest of the race. The Red Wing placed eleventh. The winner was Ray Harroun. He had held to his prerace plan, and it had paid off. His average speed was 74.59 miles an hour.

With the excitement of big-time racing in my blood, it was difficult to go back to selling cars and competing with local agents on dirt tracks. I stuck it out for another year; after all, it was profitable. For the 1912 Indianapolis Speedway race, Lee Frayer, who had decided to call it quits, turned his Red Wing over to me. I was running fourth when a crankshaft bearing burned out, and that was the end of the race for both the Red Wing and me.

It marked the beginning of the end of my career with the Columbus Buggy Company. For one thing, I could foresee the eventual demise of CBC. The top executives of the company, all men in their sixties, still considered the horse-drawn buggy its mainstay. Neither they nor their dealers had really entered the automotive age. Eventually the company went out of business, and the Firestone-Columbus became just another of the 1,600 discontinued American automobile brands.

For another, I was tired of the constant entertaining that was a part of automobile selling in those pre-Prohibition days. But more than anything else, I liked to race. I wanted to drive good cars fast, to pit my automobile knowledge and driving skill and plain old guts against the world's best. I liked the racing fraternity, and I wanted to be a part of it.

But how would I break into it? Over the previous year or so I had become increasingly interested in the Mason Automobile Company. It had started in Waterloo, Iowa, and had then moved to Des Moines. The chief engineer was Fred Duesenberg, a brilliant young man in his twenties. The two-cylinder, chain-drive Mason that he was building reflected his automotive genius.

One day I sent a telegram to Columbus, resigning my job, and bought a one-way railroad ticket to Des Moines. I walked into the Mason Company and asked Duesenberg for a job. The racing cars that he was building were nowhere near finished, so he did not need a driver. But, on the basis of my previous mechanical experience, he hired me as a mechanic.

In short, in the summer of 1912, I walked out of an excellent sales position at a salary of $150 a month and became a mechanic at $3 a day.

But I was on the way to becoming an automobile racing driver.

THREE

RACING DAYS

Automotive fans today remember the name of Duesenberg, the self-trained engineering genius whose car still lives as a symbol of beauty and excellence. Yet on the eve of the 300-mile race in Sioux City, Iowa, in 1913, the entire Duesenberg operation was perilously close to bankruptcy. With the exception of three sleek racing cars, which at that time bore the name "Mason" in honor of one of Fred's original backers, and a collection of parts, the 7-man racing team was reduced to the total assets of seven silver dollars, one cat and one bat. Under those circumstances the bat took on an abnormal importance.

My savings had long since been poured into the operation. First had come long months of 16-hour days, building racing cars virtually by hand. Day in and day out, lunch had consisted only of a chocolate malted milk shake, with two raw eggs, drunk on the job.

Duesenberg and his backers were in such desperate straits that he rushed the three Masons to the big race at Indianapolis. We painted them on the train heading east, and, even after we had arrived at the Speedway, we were still getting them ready for the race. The only time we took from working and sleeping was a few minutes here and there to attend to our mascot, Lady Luck. She had joined us in Des Moines as a kitten. I rigged up a little box for her and even took her with me on test runs. Lady Luck was practically a member of the team until she deserted us to raise a family.

Indianapolis proved to be a waste of time and money. The cars had not undergone sufficient testing. After that fiasco, we took them on the circuit, working on them and racing them at the same time. On the basis of my previous business experience, I had been put in charge of the team, and I drove us all unmercifully. The cars won a little money here and there, but it all went back into maintenance.

Though poor, our team had a great sense of dedication. In one race the rubber tread of my right rear tire broke in two and came off the casing. It became, in effect, a long, heavy lash. The rear wheels were right on top of the seat, and that heavy piece of rubber hit my arm with every revolution. The pain was excruciating. Suddenly the blows stopped. My riding mechanic, Eddie O'Donnell, had put his own arm out behind me and was taking the blows himself.

Racing and working, we finally put the cars in good condition, which was more than we could say for our bankroll. We had a few days off before the Sioux City race, and I squandered what money I had on a visit home. Mother listened to my troubles and came up with a solution. She had a book of Swiss folklore, which contained a recipe for success. All you had to do was find a bat, cut out its heart and tie it to your middle finger with a red silk thread, and you had it made.

It was a silly superstition, of course, but, well, we had certainly tried everything else.

At Sioux City we were so broke that I could not garage the cars but kept them under the grandstand. The crew slept on cots in a little adjoining room and ate on credit at a nearby greasy spoon. I talked a local farmer into giving me room and board for $2.50 a week, also on credit. After we won the $10,000 first prize, I told him, we'd have plenty of money. I told his children that I would give a silver dollar for a live bat. At 10:00 the night before the race, one of the boys brought in a mean-looking little mouse-colored creature.

Then I had to drive downtown to look for a spool of red silk thread. I finally found it in a little shop on a back street.

The next day, in secret, I performed the grisly operation. I hated to kill the little creature, but I had convinced myself that it was our only hope. Not being up on bat anatomy, I may have removed its gizzard rather than its heart, but, whatever it was, I tied it to my middle finger. I was invincible. Let the race begin!

The surface of the track was horrible. We called it "gumbo." When it was dry it broke up into chunks as hard as rocks. I fashioned a screen of wire mesh to shield us. Another problem was Spencer Wishart's powerful Mercer, the fastest car entered. Our only hope was for me to set such a pace, particularly on the curves, that Spence would wear out his tires. Our other drivers, Ralph Mulford and Tom Alley, would drive more conservatively and, with fewer tire changes, would, we hoped, place in the money.

The Sioux City race was a major national event. The press, there in full force, predicted that anyone who survived the race would win it. I was under no delusions about the danger. But I was the only one who had a bat's heart tied to his middle finger with red silk thread.

Race day was bright and sunny. The stands were full of spectators. If they had come looking for blood, they were going to get it.

We all got off to a good start. Just as I had figured, Spence outran the Mason on the straightaway, but I had done my homework on the turns, and I went into them at the top maximum speed for safety and perhaps a little bit more. It was the do-or-die race for both Duesenberg and Rickenbacher.

Roaring around the 2-mile oval, we soon gouged ruts in the surface. Never had I felt such vibration. My arms grew numb from trying to hold the wheel steady. But I still kept the accelerator on the floor. T. C. Cox, driving an Ogden Special, had to let me pass. But another car was coming up fast, and Cox cut back across in front of me. I wrenched the wheel hard to the right. My little Mason skidded sideways, and my left front wheel hit his left rear.

It was just enough to send his car out of control. He smashed through the fence, turned over, bounced high into the air and came down with a thundering crash. Both Cox and his mechanic were crushed beneath the car and killed instantly.

Spence and I were in a man-to-man duel. He'd pull out in front on the straightaway, but I would even up on the curves. We maintained that pattern for lap after lap. On the straightaway, as he pulled ahead, that gumbo came back from his rear wheels in a steady stream. It beat my screen down, pounded against my arm and poured in on my face.

With five laps to go, I was holding a slight edge. I glanced at the instrument panel. The oil pressure was low. I hit Eddie O'Donnell, my riding mechanic, with my elbow and made a quick gesture at the oil-pressure gauge. On the next straightaway, I checked it again. It was even lower.

"What in the hell is the matter with Eddie?" I thought. I shot him a quick look, and my heart went right down to the floorboard. He was slumped in his seat with a big bruise on his forehead. Obviously a chunk of gumbo had hit him. I did not know whether he was alive or dead.

The last thing I could do was stop. On the next straightaway, I grabbed the handle of the oil pump and gave it a few good licks. On the next straightaway, I pumped a little more. That was the way we finished the race. I beat Spence by exactly forty seconds. Tom Alley of our team came in third for $2,500. Eddie regained consciousness in the pit to find that we had won a total of $12,500.

We were rich. Whether it was strategy and hell-for-leather driving, those wonderful Duesenberg engines or the bat's heart on my finger I did not care. I took the team to the best hotel in Sioux City. We soaked the gumbo off in brimming tubs of hot water and went out to buy the finest food in town. We were able to continue racing. The great Duesenbergs of the early 1920s were incubated on the racing tracks of the Teens.

After two years on the circuit, I thought I was ready to strike out on my own with an established automobile. I wanted to drive the French Peugeot. At that time, before World War I had taken its tragic toll of the young men of France, the French were building superior cars, and the Peugeot was the best of them all. It had speed, endurance and maneuverability. I put my bid in and was accepted as a Peugeot driver, with all expenses paid and half the earnings, just in time to enter the Corona road race in California. I always preferred the challenge and the variety of road racing to going around and around like a ball on a string.

Before the race, I overhauled the car and painted it white. In an effort to provide an efficient verbal means of communication between driver and mechanic, I designed a simple system of speaking tubes. One tube ran from my mouth to the mechanic's ear, the other from his mouth to my ear. We wore face masks made of chamois skin and looked like men from outer space. The acoustics were fine, but in the race the face masks became unbearably hot and itchy. There went that idea. And, though the speedy Peugeot jumped off to an immediate lead in the race, the engine weakened, and we had to quit. When the same thing happened in the Point Loma race, I gave up the car and unloaded it on a famous automotive engineer named Harry Miller. That was the major mistake of my racing career because he made a tremendous car out of it. It had needed a more complete overhaul than I had thought necessary or could afford.

Once again I had quit one job without having another. The Maxwell Automobile Company had entered the racing field with a 3-car team and one extra car. Two well-known drivers, Barney

Oldfield and Bill Carlson, had already signed on, and I was the third. My role was to burn up the track and wear down the opposition while Oldfield and Carlson, less aggressive drivers, would hopefully come on strong in the last laps and win the race. Though we knew that the Maxwells were not superior racing cars, we hoped to hold our own in them through determination and driving skill, and it did work out that way.

That was a golden period of my life. Racing was fun, its rewards were great in both recognition and money and we all felt that we were making a contribution to the automotive industry. We had the satisfaction of participating in a clean, honest sport. There was never any suspicion of a fix.

We drivers all knew and respected one another. I have known drivers to sacrifice their own skins for one another. In a crash at Indianapolis, a riding mechanic was thrown into the center of the track and lay there dazed and battered, right in the path of Joe Dawson's oncoming car. Joe cut his wheels sharply, missed the injured man but piled into the retaining wall. He was badly injured in the crash, much more seriously than the mechanic whose life he had saved.

And Ralph Mulford, leading the grand-prize event at Savannah, Georgia, by eleven minutes, pulled off the road at top speed to avoid hitting a spectator who had no business being there in the first place. Ralph plowed through a cornfield, and, though he escaped serious injury, he lost the race as a consequence.

Just before the Elgin Road Race began in Illinois, a local farm boy, cranking Ralph De Palma's car, broke his arm. Ralph drove the boy to the hospital himself and returned to the race just as it was starting. He still won it.

But we were never averse to taking advantage of a rival's weakness. Oldfield didn't like it when the going got tough, and I could force him to give way. Louis Disbrow hated dust. Once on a dirt track at Libertyville, Illinois, he was coming up on the outside as we hit the first turn, and I skidded enough to kick up a cloud of dust into his face. On the next curve I let fly with a steady stream. I won the race by only ten seconds.

Small, light tires increased speed, but they had to be changed
more often. Heavy tires were durable but slower. Tires were a
major factor in one of my most exciting races, at Providence,
Rhode Island. It was a 100-mile race on a one-mile asphalt
track. All the great drivers were there—Burman, Oldfield, Mulford, De Palma. Practicing on it during the day with other
drivers around, I used—and wore out—small tires. Early in the
mornings I tested the big ones and concluded that they would
last out the race if I held the speed under 80 miles an hour.
On the day of the race, with all the other drivers, I ran the first
few practice laps on small tires. Three minutes before race time,
the members of my team all pitched in and changed to heavy
ones.

The other drivers, seeing them, held back. The pace was so
slow that my spark plugs fouled. Changing them cost me a lap
and a half. I built my speed up to 80 miles an hour and held it
there. It finally came down to a contest between Wild Bob
Burman and me. I caught up with him when he wore out one
set of tires and had to go to the pits. Back on the track again,
he gave it all he had, but I maintained that steady speed. His
second set of tires began to go, and he did not dare to barrel into
the curves. I passed him on the 98th lap and collected $10,000.
I have heard many racing fans say that it was the most exciting
race they ever saw.

Racing was a major sport, and drivers were lionized. We were
front-page news. At the beginning, I was advised to hire a press
agent. An older and wiser friend snorted.

"All you have to do is win," he said. "They'll print your name."

He was correct. Many a newspaper in those days carried a full
eight-column streamer: "Rickenbacher Wins."

Sportswriters called me the "Speedy Swiss," the "Baron," the
"Big Teuton," the "Dutch Demon" and a dozen other titles.
Another well-known racing driver of the day was the great Christian Lautenschlager, a real German. Just before World War I
broke out, Lautenschlager won the Grand Prix of France at the

same time that I won the big race at Sioux City. *Motor Age* published the following poem as a double tribute:

> *All Germany is on a spree*
> *And other lands is scorning;*
> *The Teuton clan now leads the van*
> *While France is wearing mourning:*
> *One, two and three in the Grand Prix*
> *First also at Sioux City—*
> *Just quaff your beer, don't shed a tear;*
> *The Dutch ask not for pity.*
>
> *Great Kaiser Bill has had his fill*
> *Of Pilsener and lager;*
> *He loudly boasts and drinks deep toasts*
> *In praise of Lautenschlager;*
> *Across the sea a victory*
> *Has led this peace-plan knocker*
> *To plan to knight in his delight*
> *That Deutscher, Rickenbacher.*

On one occasion I received far more publicity than I wanted. A young Los Angeles reporter cooked up a wildly imaginative story to the effect that I was really Baron Edward Von Rickenbacher, a Prussian nobleman. My stern father, a colonel of uhlans, had cut me off without a penny following an escapade, and there I was in the United States, proving to my Prussian papa that I could make good on my own.

By the time I saw the story, it was too late to do anything about it. I shrugged it off. How was I to know that that innocent story would, a few years later, help to bring about a serious and embarrassing situation?

Just as the real Rickenbacher differed from the fictional baron, so, to a lesser degree, did the hell-for-leather racing driver differ from the person I was away from the track. In my early days of racing I was much like the other drivers at first, and then one night I woke up with a start, terrified.

I had been dreaming that I was in a crash from which there was no possible escape. I woke up in the nick of time. I had had moments of fear before, but none as intense as that sudden terror in my dream. As I lay there shaking, it dawned on me how fortunate I had been to have lived through so many actual brushes with death. I recalled them back through the years, even to the time that I had been struck by the horsecar outside our house in Columbus, and counted fourteen separate episodes.

That night I re-evaluated my entire life. It seemed to me that surely the Lord above had shown a special interest in protecting me through so many hazardous experiences. It was about time, I realized, that I began to show some appreciation for this Divine consideration. The least I could do, in addition to keeping my faith steadfast, was to improve the condition of the body and mind that the Lord was obviously saving for some purpose.

I worked out a series of exercises, which I did—and do to this day—for fifteen minutes each morning and night to keep my body flexible.

I had always gone down on my knees and prayed before going to bed each night, and I continued the practice with even greater sincerity and gratitude. I did not then, I am sorry to say, talk of my religion and attempt to inspire others. I doubt if any of the millions of spectators who saw me blasting around curves with controlled madness ever dreamed that I would be on my knees that night, praying.

Though much of my association was with mechanics and other drivers, I also had the opportunity to converse with men in higher positions, automotive engineers and company officials. Maxwell's financial backer, for example, was Eugene Meyer, later treasurer of the Republican Party and publisher of the Washington *Post*. I saw him often. I listened carefully and marked well the way such men constructed and phrased their thoughts. I carried a dictionary with me always and used it. I have never slackened in the pursuit of learning and self-improvement.

I accepted racing as a great teacher of sportsmanship. Once I had been capable of throwing a monkey wrench over the grandstand when things were not going well; now I figured that I could not win them all, so I might as well accept with good grace those that I lost. I tried to get in the habit of wearing a smile. Who does not prefer to meet a person who is smiling?

I even gave myself a middle name. I was born "Edward Rickenbacher," but I thought that looked a little plain. I signed my name over and over, inserting a different middle initial each time. "Edward V. Rickenbacher" pleased my eye the most. For a name to go with the initial, I finally chose "Vernon."

During that period, I came to the conclusion that no important decision should be made before noon. At night, when the body is horizontal, more blood flows to the brain. It is the time for imaginative and creative thinking. But the ideas that come in the night should be examined and considered in the day before they are put into effect.

My new capability of smiling at adversity came in handy the night I was informed that Maxwell had decided to get out of racing and that I was out of a job. I hurried to Detroit. What about the cars? The company officials shrugged. Anyone who made a reasonable offer could have them.

I had saved $25,000, the price of the four cars, but it was only a drop in the bucket. I knew that it was only a portion of the capital required to operate a racing team. Money was necessary for spare parts and tires, salaries and travel expenses. I needed outside help.

I hurried from Detroit to Indianapolis and went to see Carl G. Fisher and James A. Allison, whom we shall meet again in chapter 8. They were two of the "Four Horsemen" who had created the Indianapolis Speedway. The other two were Frank Wheeler of the Wheeler-Schebler Carburetor Company and Arthur Newby of the American Chain Company. All four had created the Prest-O-Lite Company of Indianapolis, which built the gas tanks carried on the running boards for the gas headlights of all automobiles.

I outlined to them a proposition for buying and operating the four Maxwells. I would put up my $25,000; they would put up the rest. I would manage the team and drive one of the cars.

Out of what prize money we won I would pay all the expenses and share the profits with my backers. I pointed out that the war in Europe was curtailing the number of foreign cars racing in the United States. There would be less competition for prize money. Without financial backing, four more cars would be out of the Speedway the next year.

They agreed to the plan. Now at last I had my own racing team. Bill Carlson had been killed at Tacoma. Eddie O'Donnell, my former riding mechanic, took his place as one driver, and Pete Henderson replaced Barney Oldfield.

Instead of taking four cars to every race, I planned to use two two-car teams and leapfrog them. That way, while we were racing in one event, the other two cars would be en route to the next. On the completion of the first event, the drivers and mechanics would go by Pullman to the next while the cars went on to a third race. This system would enable us to make every major race in the country.

We rebuilt our four cars from the ground up. The engines were completely overhauled. We were receptive to every new idea, product and process, and we redesigned our cars completely to eliminate some of the weaknesses. I had new streamlined bodies built; streamlining alone added 10 to 12 miles an hour. The rebuilt cars were called "Maxwell Specials."

I worked out an incentive program by which every man on the team would receive a share of the winnings—and we all worked from 7:00 A.M. until late at night. I had always liked and been stimulated by music, and one day I brought a phonograph to the shop with some records of stirring marches. When the work began to drag, I put on a jolly, fast-rhythm song called "I Love You, California." We all perked up. From then on music was an important part of our operation—long before Muzak.

I solicited equipment manufacturers and oil companies. They furnished us with their products gratis and paid us for our sponsorship.

During that winter too, I wrote a little booklet of rules and regulations. Behind much of that advice, written by an unlettered racing driver over half a century ago, I stand today. It began: "Always conduct yourself as a gentleman. If you do not, you not only reflect discredit upon yourself, but also upon automobile racing, the means by which you earn a livelihood."

And it concluded:

If you don't like the way we do business, if you don't like your teammates, don't grouse and don't go around with a long face. Quit this job and get another one somewhere else. The trouble with a lot of people is that they are not willing to begin anywhere in order to get a fighting chance. My advice is: Throw away that false pride. No honest work is beneath you. Jump in and demonstrate your superiority. Once you get on the pay roll, make up your mind to master everything about your own job, and get ready for the job at the top. Your particular task is merely one end of a trail that leads to the driver's seat. That is my philosophy of success. It works, I have tried it and proved it.

I tried to spell out in advance every phase of every man's assigned activity, driver and mechanic, beginning with going to the rest room before the race began.

For the long races, we bound ourselves like mummies for protection against the incessant vibration. I would take a 20-foot length of burlap and, with another man holding it out from me, wrap it so tightly from hips to armpits that I could hardly breathe. At the end of a long race it would be loose.

Complete pit instructions were spelled out and practiced. A wheel was removed, for example, with one blow on the wing nut. We practiced it until we could do it.

Pit-stop procedure was rehearsed and carried out under the direction of a man with a megaphone. Every man had a specific job in the pit. Mine, for example, was to stop the car in the exact spot, then check the right rear tire, which is the most important tire on the car. To change it, I pushed the jack under the car and the handle down in one motion. I hit the wing nut once, removed it, removed wheel, replaced it, replaced nut, hit it once—and jumped in car, confident that all tires were changed if necessary and gas and oil added. Our 4-man crew could perform the entire operation in 39 seconds.

In that time a race could be won or lost. At Tacoma, Washington, we participated in a 300-mile race on a 2-mile dirt track. I knew that the surface on the curves would get badly cut up and cause excessive wear on the tires. Ralph De Palma and his Mercedes, a faster car than any Maxwell, would be our chief competition in that race, and on speed alone we did not stand a chance. That was where the pit procedure came in.

I pushed the Maxwell Special to the maximum, but still Ralph pulled ahead. At about the 225-mile mark, we both went into the pit. All four of my tires were replaced; apparently he replaced only his right rear. He spent 62 seconds in the pit; my crew had me out of there in only 33. I was leading, but that big Mercedes went by on the straightaway. He went into the curve too fast, and his left tire blew—he spent ninety seconds in the pit. With only fifty miles to go he could not catch up. I won by thirty seconds. If my crew had taken as long in the pit as his did, he would have won that $10,000.

One of our first races with the Maxwell Special was in my own hometown of Columbus. I determined to set a new world record for one hundred miles in this event. I picked the lightest man on the team, Eric Schraeder, to ride with me. The whole town turned out to see the local boy break a record. My mother came with my sister Mary and waved good luck to me before the race began.

I drove harder than I ever had before. At the 25-mile mark, I was a full lap ahead of my nearest competitor, Barney Oldfield. But that was one time when I was going too fast. The track was dry and dusty. Going into one of the curves at that terrific speed, I skidded out. Another car, right behind me, came by on the inside and kicked up a dust cloud. I tried to miss it, swung too far to the outside and hit the fence. We skidded along it, scattering planks and posts. I hit one post, dislodged it and kept going into the horizontal boards. One of them came through the radiator, knocked the magneto off the side of the engine and went through the dashboard on Schraeder's side. It kept coming, right into his stomach. Just as it touched him, the car stopped. Another four inches, and it would have cut him right in two.

As soon as we had the car back in the pit, I hurried up to the grandstand, where Mother was sitting. She was not there; she had left for home right after the accident. I cannot say that I blamed her. I had to leave immediately after the race for the next event, in Cleveland, but I still sent her my customary telegram, "Don't pay any attention to newspaper reports."

There were other times when the angel's wings were hovering. In Galveston, Texas, I was following Louis Disbrow at about 100 miles an hour when I saw a rock the size of a baseball coming right at my head. I ducked, and it struck me a glancing blow. I blacked out for a second but continued the race. If I had been going a hundredth of a second faster, it would have caught me right between the eyes.

In St. Paul, Minnesota, my car went off the track and did a complete flip. When we came down, I bounced out of the seat— we did not use safety belts—and landed on the track. I have no idea what part of my anatomy I fell on; for days I felt as though I had hit on every part.

In San Antonio, Texas, in my early days of racing, I think I saved my life by staying in the car. I had strengthened the cowl by fastening a strip of steel from a wheel under it. In the time trials, my time was faster than that of Louis Disbrow. He protested that the timers had made a mistake.

"OK, Louis," I said. "I'll do it again. This time you hold the watch."

I came by the starting line with the accelerator on the floor. It had rained, and the track was spongy. I went into the curve hugging the rail. My left front wheel hooked into a soft spot. I knew what was coming, and I let go of the wheel and dived forward under the cowl. I had no mechanic with me.

At that moment the car started to roll. It went over three times, then slid to a stop. I was tossed around like a man in a barrel over Niagara Falls, but my only injury was a dislocated collarbone. After that, everybody had some kind of reinforced cowl.

The car I was driving in the Elgin, Illinois, Road Race was so equipped, and my mechanic made full use of it. That was an eventful day. Spencer Wishart was driving the big Mercer. I was coming up behind him on the straightaway when his car started wobbling, left the road and crashed into a tree. The rear end rose up and smacked into the tree so hard that it wrapped around it. Spence was killed instantly. His head left a mark on the tree ten feet from the ground.

Regardless of my emotions, I had to keep going. After a couple more laps, I was coming up fast on Bill Endicott. He moved over to let me by, then his car hit a bump in the road and bounced back in front of me. I hit the ditch, just as poor Spence had done minutes before. I went up the other side of the ditch, hit the fence and bounced back down and up the other side. A telephone pole loomed. My mechanic dived under the cowl. I cut to the left, swung down through the ditch, bounced off the fence again and came back heading for another telephone pole. Back under the cowl went the mechanic. Down into the ditch I went again, careened off the fence and here came the third telephone pole. I finally wrestled the car back onto the road between poles, but I had bent an axle, and it twisted off. That was the end of that race.

With a dozen cars hurtling along at racing speeds, where the driver is is not as important as where he will be in five seconds and what the situation will be when he arrives there. Anticipation served me well in one of the richest of all speedway races, the Metropolitan on Long Island. First prize was $15,000, and additional awards would run the winnings up to perhaps $25,000. The best drivers in the country entered—Dario Resta and Johnny Aitken in their Peugeots; Ralph De Palma in his Mercedes; Carl Limberg in a French Delage; Barney Oldfield in a new creation, the Golden Egg, and, of course, my team of Maxwell Specials.

For the first three or four laps all of us stuck together closely, each waiting for someone else to set the pace. My car was the last in the pack, just behind Limberg. Going into a left-hand curve, Limberg blew his right front tire. The big Delage skidded into the wall. The wheel hooked into the wall, and the rear end hurtled into the air. Limberg and his mechanic were both thrown fifty feet and were killed instantly. The car came down with a crash and broke in two. The front end came down in front of me, just to my left. The other half bounced over me. A complete picture was stamped in my brain. The other drivers up ahead had seen nothing.

When we came to the scene of the accident again, orange flames and a huge cloud of dense black smoke were billowing upward, obscuring the track. The officials were standing there waving their flags and slowing cars down. According to racing regulations, in such situations, officials must give warning; drivers heed it at their own discretion. The other drivers had no idea what that cloud of smoke obscured and braked to a crawl.

But I knew the exact location of the two parts of the broken car. I knew that Limberg and his mechanic had been thrown off the track. So I ignored the officials completely and, with accelerator down, kept right on going into the cloud of smoke with full confidence that the track was clear. It was. By the time the other drivers had poked their way through I had built up such a lead that no one could overtake me. That glimpse of the accident meant $25,000 to my team.

Though we generally preferred the road races, with their challenges and variety, the exception was the Indianapolis Speedway, always the greatest event of all. And I can say it without prejudice, for I never won the "Big 500." The most exciting race I ever drove at Indianapolis was a special 100-mile event on Labor Day, 1916. The man I had to beat was Johnny Aitken, driving the same Peugeot that I had given up. It was 10 miles an hour faster than my car on the straightaway and would squat down on the curves and stick like glue. The only way I could win was to take the curves even faster.

Thanks to that driving plan and an Aitken pit stop, I was leading by a half-mile at 70 miles. We were both running well ahead of the track record.

Suddenly over my right shoulder I heard a sound like a rifle shot. A spoke in my right wheel had broken. The loss of one spoke would spread the strain over all the others. I kept going. I wanted that race. Another spoke popped, and they began going off like firecrackers. The wheel started to wobble. The boys in the pit tried to wave me down. So did the track officials. Even Johnny Aitken got into the act, pointing at my wobbling wheel. I kept going.

I went into the last turn, still holding onto my lead. After this turn, then the homestretch, the race, the record and the money would be mine. I was coming out of it at 100 miles an hour when the right rear tire blew out. I skidded to the right. The wheel collapsed, and the car began to spin. The left rear wheel collapsed. Tires and wheels were spinning off in every direction. I was going around, metal screeching and sparks flying, like a big pinwheel. I came out of the spin pointing toward the finish line, and I kept going on the brake drums.

All that time I had felt no fear. I believed that I could hold the car together with sheer mental power. As I limped along, I was practically doing just that. But where was Aitken? Finally he came by at about 25 miles an hour. His steering arm was dragging on the track. He was guiding the car entirely by the caster of the front wheels. If I had only known, I could have slowed down, and my car would have remained in one piece.

As I crawled across the finish line, I heard a tremendous roar. The crowd was standing and cheering. Everybody swarmed around the car, congratulating me on my escape from what seemed sure death.

"That was the most spectacular show I have ever seen on this course," one of the officials said.

I grinned at him. "I hope you never see one like it again," I said, and, brother, I meant it.

A big problem on the Speedway was the surface of the track. It ground the treads off tires as if it were an emery wheel. If we could only devise some method of saving my tires during the first one hundred miles, after which the worn-off rubber gave the track a coating, I would be able to build up a lead and joy-ride to the finish. We came up with a rather simple solution. We placed a tank filled with oil under the mechanic's seat and led tubes from it to the two outside tires, those that took the heaviest grinding, so that a stream of oil would flow over them for a few seconds when pressure was turned on. We tested the contraption in secret, and it worked. The problem was to get it into the race without the officials' knowledge.

On the morning of the race, I did not bring my car out until the very last second. I drove around the track, then stopped at the proper place. Two of my mechanics appeared and casually draped themselves over the outside wheels, hiding the tubes. The official starter peered at them curiously but went ahead and started the race.

The Rickenbacher tire-oiling system worked perfectly. I simply pulled out in front of everybody. It was as easy as that. At one hundred miles, I was a lap and a half ahead, and the treads on the tires looked as good as new. The rest of the race would be like a family drive on Sunday afternoon. And then the engine went bang and practically stopped in its tracks. A connecting-rod bearing had burned out. For me the race was over.

But the discussion was not. Regulations require that any car leaving the race be immediately inspected by the technical committee. Its members were at the pit waiting for me when I pulled in. There were those tubes sticking out over the tires, and the committeemen guessed their purpose immediately. Right there all such devices were ruled illegal on the Indianapolis Speedway. There went my greatest opportunity to win the "500."

That year, 1916, the Maxwell Special teams won seven of the thirteen major races we entered. Exhibitions and sponsors' fees brought in several thousand dollars more. At the end of the season we had a kitty of $78,000 to split among the personnel of the team, over what we had already drawn. I personally made $60,000 that year, in 100-cent dollars.

Late in the season I met a handsome, poised Englishman named Louis Coatalen, managing director of the Sunbeam Motor Works in England. I had raced against the Sunbeam, had great respect for it and told him so.

"There is no more racing in England now because of the war," he said. "However, we would like to continue racing in this country. May I ask if you have made plans for the 1917 season?"

"No," I said, "I haven't."

"Then would you be interested in joining our organization?" he asked. "I'm sure we could work out a mutually agreeable arrangement. We should like you to come to England at our expense and work with us in preparing the cars."

I had never crossed a body of water wider than the Mississippi River before, and a trip abroad, even in wartime, appealed to me immediately. He made me a fair proposition with an excellent potential, and I took him up on it. I ended my association with the Maxwell team and made arrangements to go to England right after Thanksgiving Day, 1916.

That was in October. I joined a team of Duesenbergs for the Vanderbilt Cup and Grand Prize road races to be held in Santa Monica in November. Several days before the first race, I happened to be driving near Riverside, California, when I saw an airplane parked near a small hangar on a grass field. I knew that aviation would someday be a major form of transportation, but I had never had the opportunity really to examine an airplane. On the spur of the moment, I pulled into the field and drove up to the hangar.

A young man about my age came out. He apparently recognized me from my pictures in the papers, for he stuck out his hand and said: "Hi, Eddie, I'm glad to meet you. My name is Glenn Martin."

Martin had been one of the early students of the Wright brothers. He had set up his own little operation and had secured a contract from the U.S. Navy to build a so-called "bomber." It was a two-place biplane. The pilot sat in the front seat, the gunner in the back.

As we were looking it over, he casually asked, "Would you like to take a ride?"

"Sure," I said. I didn't even think about my fear of height. I have always had a galloping case of acrophobia; looking down from a skyscraper window has always made me dizzy.

I climbed into the rear seat. Glenn spun the propeller to start the engine and jumped into the front seat. It was a smooth take-off. Finally I worked up my nerve and looked over the side. I was pleasantly amazed to find that I had no feeling of dizziness. We stayed up for about thirty minutes as Glenn pointed out the sights at the top of his voice. The whole flight was fascinating. He did not put the plane through any maneuvers; just staying up was enough in those pioneering days.

Finally he brought the plane down for a landing. The way the ground came swiftly up to meet us gave me a terrifying moment. If I had been at the controls, I would have tried to level off while we were still one hundred feet in the air. We taxied back to the hangar and climbed out. I told him how much I had enjoyed flying.

"But I wish you would tell me something," I said a little sheepishly. After all, I was known as a death-defying racing driver. "Why is it I didn't have a fear of height up there?"

"Because there's nothing to judge height by," he said. "There's no edge to look over."

I thanked him again and hurried back to the track in order to do a little bragging to the other drivers. I had flown in an airplane!

On another occasion, I happened to be driving through the countryside and saw a lone, single-seater military airplane sitting in a cow pasture. A man, who was obviously the pilot, was standing by it, forlornly poking at the engine. I stopped my car and went over to see if I could help. The pilot introduced himself as Major T. F. Dodd of the Army Air Service, then a part of the Signal Corps. "The engine runs, but it doesn't deliver enough power to remain aloft," he said. "Do you know anything about engines?"

"A little bit," I said. "Let's start it up and listen to it."

I could tell immediately that the trouble was in the ignition system. Further investigation revealed that the coupling had slipped off the magneto. I fixed it in a couple of minutes.

"Try it now," I said. He spun the prop again, climbed in and revved up the engine. It sounded fine. "Thanks a lot," he shouted.

"Glad to help you," I hollered back. He took off, and I went back to my car. I did not know how valuable that chance meeting with Major Dodd was going to prove before too long.

The Duesenberg I drove in both the Vanderbilt and Grand Prize races in 1916, the last ever held, broke down on me, and I did not finish either race. But at Ascot Park, Los Angeles, the car held together beautifully, and I won. I had no idea at the time that the Ascot victory would enable me to close my racing career as a winner.

It was the last race I ever drove.

FOUR

GERMAN SPY

I have often been asked how I managed to maintain my sanity, much less resist a feeling of bitterness and vengefulness during the ridiculous and frustrating experience that befell me in the winter of 1916–1917. All I can say is that the good Lord gave me a sense of humor, and somehow I held onto it.

The trip began most pleasantly. That in itself, it developed later, was part of the situation. At the time of my crossing in 1916, German U-boats prowled the North Atlantic, but American ships were supposed to have the freedom of the seas. My ship, the *St. Louis,* was small but comfortable. I met two congenial gentlemen who extended themselves to be friendly and pleasant.

After such a nice crossing, I was totally unprepared for my reception in Liverpool. As we disembarked, an English sergeant, a disagreeable-looking fellow with a long nose, called my name. I stepped up politely.

"What's your name?" he demanded harshly. I was a little surprised, inasmuch as he had just called it, and it was also written plainly on my passport, which he held in his hand. I repeated it for him, however.

"What is your purpose in England?"

I started to tell him, but he interrupted me. "Don't you know there's a war on?"

That one got under my skin. How could any intelligent person *not* know there was a war on? And it so happened that, although Americans were divided in their sympathies for the warring factions at that stage of the war and although I bore a German name, I believed fully in the cause of the Allies.

"Yes," I said a little sharply this time, "I know there's a war on."

"Then you ought to be aware of the fact that there is a government embargo on all steel or products containing steel being shipped out of the British Isles," he said. "Or don't you know that racing cars would come under that category?"

I said, quite honestly, that I did not know of any such embargo. It was my firm impression that racing the Sunbeam in the United States would mean money and goodwill for Britain. My answer was obviously not satisfactory. "Come with me," he said grimly.

I was beginning not to like my one-man welcoming committee. He conducted me to one of the cabins. There were my two shipboard companions, now cold as ice. They were both British agents. All that charm had been turned on to encourage me to talk freely.

What a dossier they had on me! They had traced my ancestry back to Germany and were obviously familiar with that ridiculous sports-page fiction about my being a German baron. Finally it dawned on me that I was suspected of being a German spy. Thank God for my sense of humor. The whole thing was so ludicrous that, instead of getting mad, I treated it as a joke. I answered every question truthfully and good-humoredly. Sometimes I couldn't help laughing. They probably figured me for the coolest enemy agent ever to seek to undermine the British Empire.

They made me strip down to the skin, went through every seam of my clothing and even pried the heels off my shoes. My baggage had obviously been given the same treatment.

They found nothing, for there was nothing to find. But still I was curtly informed that I could not enter England. I would have to stay on board the ship until its return. I was not permitted to communicate with Louis Coatalen. So there I was, stuck on that little bucket.

Several long, lonely and frustrating days went by. The captain was a fine old fellow, and he finally, on Christmas Eve, persuaded the British authorities at least to let me spend Christmas Day on shore.

"But you will have to be accompanied by two British agents," he said.

"That's okay with me," I told him. I was a lonesome Yankee far from home, and I would rather have the company of two gumshoes on Christmas Day than no company at all. With one agent on either side, I left the ship late in the afternoon of Christmas Eve and went to the Adelphia Hotel in Liverpool. We took three rooms, with me in the middle. I had a lonely dinner in my room.

I was so restless that I had to go out. The moment I opened my door, my two escorts opened theirs. They followed me downstairs and onto the street. It was a cold, foggy, nasty night. England had suffered several bombing raids by giant German dirigibles, and the only illumination was a tiny blue light on each corner. Suddenly, purely on impulse, I ducked into a side street and started running. A half-block down the street was an alley, and I turned into it and stopped. They pounded on by. Enjoying the game immensely, I called after them, "Hey, here I am."

It was a wonder they did not shoot me. But I was laughing my head off at the joke I had played on them, and, probably in relief that I had not escaped, they started laughing too.

"I'll buy an ale," I said, and they took me up on it. We had a high old time. I think I convinced them that I was not a spy. The next morning, Christmas Day, they let me call Louis Coatalen at his home in Wolverhampton. He promised to take immediate action and told me to meet him at the Savoy Hotel in London the next day. That very afternoon I was informed that I could proceed to London alone.

I arrived in London about 9:00 that night, in the midst of a double blackout; an intense fog cut off all visibility. There were no cabs in service. I asked the general direction of the Savoy Hotel and started walking. Every time I bumped into somebody, I would ask him where the Savoy Hotel was. A disembodied voice would tell me to go this way or that way, and I stumbled through the twisting streets for hours. In desperation I grabbed someone and told him that I was a lost American and would pay him any sum he thought fair to guide me to the Savoy Hotel.

"That won't be necessary," said a precise voice on the level of my chest. "If you hold onto my coattail I will be pleased to guide you to the hotel."

I grabbed hold, and off we went. After about a dozen twisting blocks, at 1:00 A.M., we reached the hotel. My volunteer guide would not take a tuppence. At the hotel the room clerk refused to give me a room until I had registered at the police station. Registration was apparently required of everyone, not only German spies. After I threatened to lie down right there on the floor, a porter guided me to the police station, where I was fingerprinted and registered. I went to bed at 3:00 A.M. and did not pick up my bags until the next day.

Coatalen arrived a few hours later with permission for me to return with him to Wolverhampton, provided that I checked in at the local police station morning and night. The next morning I set to work once again designing and building a team of racing cars.

As always, the work was hard, the hours were long but the job was interesting. The Sunbeam was an excellent model to begin with. The mechanics were efficient and helpful. I liked them and all the English people I met. I admired the quiet courage and determination that I encountered on every hand. I read up on current history and the war. More than ever I was convinced that Americans should join the Allies, then the underdogs.

Saturdays and Sundays I would spend in London at the Savoy, dutifully checking in at the police station on arrival.

From my room overlooking the Thames River, I could watch training planes flying along over the river. There was obviously a field nearby on the river. I found it when I visited the famous Brooklands Speedway.

The track was being used as a training field for the Royal Flying Corps, which later became the Royal Air Force. There were no security measures, and I strolled around and looked with admiration and envy at the airplanes and the young men—actually youths just out of school—who were learning to fly them.

My major activity in London became watching from my hotel window as the planes flew in formation down the Thames. At the airfield I talked with some of the older pilots, men in their early twenties who had flown in combat and were now serving a tour of duty as instructors, and thrilled to their stories of combat in the air. I told Coatalen that I wanted to join those brave Englishmen and fight the Germans in the air over France.

"You can serve us better behind the wheel of a Sunbeam Six," he said.

So I did not fly for England, but I determined that, if the United States came to the support of the Allies, aviation was where I was going to serve.

On February 3, after Germany declared unrestricted submarine warfare on the high seas, the United States broke off relations. The German government announced that Americans abroad would have five days to leave. That was the end of the Sunbeam racing team; I joined the rush of Americans trying to book passage home. I managed to get an upper berth in my old friend the *St. Louis*. My old nemesis, the grouchy, long-nosed sergeant, was standing at the gangplank. He appropriated my papers and books. On board my two pals from the trip over were waiting for me. I was still under suspicion. After a 2-hour interrogation, they somewhat reluctantly told me that I was free to sail.

I came into the salon and saw an old friend, Gene Buck, the songwriter. "Say, Eddie, have you heard the news?" he asked. "We've got a big German spy on board. That's why the boat is delayed."

"Yes, Gene, I know," I said. "That big German spy—that's me!"

I still felt that the Allied cause was just and that the United States should join in the fight. On the boat going home I worked out a plan for an air squadron composed of racing drivers; I knew that most of them would volunteer right along with me. I began advocating American entry into the war even before I set foot on American soil again, for the ship was met by New York reporters in the harbor.

Getting in touch with friends all over the country, I arranged to visit several cities where I was well known to make public pleas for all-out participation in the war. There was widespread sentiment that the United States should contribute munitions and money but not troops. My slogan was "The Three M's—Men, Money, Munitions." I spoke in New York, Columbus, Detroit and Chicago and then went on to Los Angeles. I still carried the glamor of racing, and people crowded in to hear what I had to say. Newspapers carried lengthy stories and interviews. Some people and papers attacked me as a warmonger, but I kept right on talking. I was paying my own expenses on that trip across the country, living on my savings—I had not earned a nickel since the Ascot race on Thanksgiving Day—and a little criticism did not bother me. Besides, I thought that if people would come out to hear what I had to say I could win them over.

In Los Angeles, a city that was a second home to me, I had my greatest success along this line. To the people on the West Coast the war in Europe was remote, almost meaningless. They wanted no part of it. But they did turn out to hear the true situation from the lips of someone they knew and trusted. I believe that in some small way I hastened their acceptance of their country's duty.

When I started the tour, I had the strange intuition that I was being followed. I gradually began to pick out one familiar face in each city I visited, that of a tall, sandy-haired man. I had never seen him before. After I had been in Los Angeles about ten days and had talked to several different groups with, I thought, some effect, the mysterious stranger came up to me in the lobby of the Alexandria Hotel. He introduced himself frankly and openly as a British agent and admitted that he had been on my tail all the way.

"I just want to tell you," he said, "that my government and I are now fully satisfied as to your status as a loyal and patriotic American. But I do want to thank you for the wonderful trip I've had, following you about this interesting country."

Before I could say a word, he turned and walked away. I never saw him again. That, I was sure, marked the end of my imagined career as a German spy.

But I was to find that the legend was still not dead.

FIVE

LEARNING TO FLY

On my return from England in 1917, while I was preaching money, munitions and men, I was making arrangements to be one of those men. My former racing companions, competitors and teammates, were enthusiastic about the flying squadron. Mature men of proven and swift reflexes developed at high speeds in competitive racing—what flyers they would make!

Even if the squadron did not work out, I was positive that somehow I would become a military aviator and fight for my country in the skies over France. I thought it would be wise first to attend to the tonsillitis from which I had been suffering on and off over the years. A throat specialist I knew in New York, Doctor Harold Foster, advised a tonsillectomy. It has always seemed ironic that, sandwiched between a period of racing cars in competition and flying airplanes in combat, one of my closest encounters with death resulted from a minor operation.

I wakened from the anesthetic to find myself bleeding from the throat. I spat out a lot of blood and doubtless swallowed more. At first I was too groggy to be alarmed, but gradually I began to realize that it was not a normal postoperative reaction. Blood was actually running out of my mouth.

I flagged down a nurse, who made some efforts to stop the bleeding, but it continued. Doctor Foster, after completing the operation, had left the hospital to see another patient. After wasting some time with me, the nurse went to look for an intern. He finally arrived, and, though he was concerned, he did not seem to know what to do to stop the flow.

I began to feel my life flowing away with my blood. Even though I was vaguely aware that I was in a critical stage, I felt no sense of discomfort, no panic. Rather, everything seemed serene and lovely. Still I continued to bleed, and still I remained in a quiet, almost pleasurable state accepting death.

Hallucinations began to enter my blood-drained brain. I lived again the happy scenes of my childhood. I saw strange shapes and beautiful colors. It was truly a sensuous experience. How easy it was to lie there and, with a heavenly sensation of contentment, die.

Then I realized that never, never in my life had I taken the easy way out. I had always fought, fought to win, to achieve, to accomplish. Now I had to face up to the greatest fight of all, the fight to live. I thought again of simply drifting off, but it was the determination to live, to fight, that was dominant. I simply refused to die. Somehow I called forth the will and the energy to tell the intern and nurse, who were still fumbling around ineffectually, to call my doctor. The nurse went off. I lay there, fighting off death until he came.

But I did not fight alone. I prayed for God's help. Together we held off the soft and insidious appeals of death.

I was still semiconscious when Doctor Foster came running. He forced open my mouth, shoved in a sponge, wiped away the blood and saw what had happened. He had inadvertently nicked a hole in an artery. He clamped it. That stopped the bleeding immediately.

And then he turned on the nurse and intern. No racing driver discovering a loose nut on his steering apparatus could have dressed down his mechanic in the way that he blistered that pair.

It was several weeks before I regained my full strength. Long before that, however, I was hard at work trying to sell my squadron of racing drivers to the U.S. Army. At that time, flying came under the jurisdiction of the Signal Corps. At the beginning of the war in Europe, aviation had been used almost entirely for observation. But swift changes had been taking place in this new military science. The airplane was developing into a weapon in its own right. The great value of aerial observation called forth the development of armed pursuit planes to destroy observation balloons and to drive off or shoot down observation planes. Each innovation incorporated into the equipment of one side was soon copied and improved upon by the other. Pilots were developing new techniques of combat flying. Military geniuses like Sir Hugh Trenchard of the Royal Air Force were developing the concept of the airplane as an offensive weapon. But, in our own military establishment, aviation was still no more than a means of observation.

By now several drivers—Ralph De Palma, Ray Harroun, Ralph Mulford, Earl Cooper and Eddie Pullen, to name only a few—had agreed to join me in the Aero Reserves of America. I took the proposal to the head of the Signal Corps, Brigadier General George D. Squier, who listened and passed me on to his assistants. They were not pilots either. They told me bluntly that the Signal Corps was not interested in racing drivers as pilots.

"We don't believe," one officer said, "that it would be wise for a pilot to have any knowledge of engines and mechanics. Airplane engines are always breaking down, and a man who knew a great deal about engines would know if his engine wasn't functioning correctly and be hesitant about going into combat."

It was difficult to argue with anyone foolish enough to make such a statement, but I tried. "But that's the key to the whole thing," I said. "These men can get the very most out of those engines. We can maintain them in the finest possible condition, utilize them to their fullest extent!"

I might as well have been talking to a stone wall. Furthermore, the fact that none of us had a college education was a mark against us. Applicants for flight training had to be under 25 (I was too old!) and have college education or the equivalent. I pointed out that the correspondence courses I had completed were the equivalent of a college education. The officers obviously thought that claim a joke.

"My correspondence-school courses taught me to think for myself," I said. "You're not under the impression that, when a pilot is flying his plane alone up there in the sky, he can raise his hand and ask a question of the teacher are you?"

I could have saved my breath. The Aero Reserves of America was never organized. I do not know of any other racing driver who became a pilot.

Disillusioned, I decided to wait and see what would develop. In the meantime, I had to earn a living. I agreed to drive a German Mercedes, an excellent vehicle, in the Memorial Day 500, which was to be run that year at Cincinnati, Ohio. During that period, incidentally, a racing driver named Jack LeCain and his daughter Mary Alice visited me one day. The little girl gave me an identification card and a crucifix in a little leather folder.

"As long as you carry it with you, you won't be shot or anything like that," she explained seriously. I thanked her and put it in my upper left-hand coat pocket, right over my heart. Since then I have never, not one day in more than fifty years, gone out without making sure that her little talisman is in that pocket.

One night I came into my hotel room from the track, where I'd been practicing, just as the telephone started ringing. It was Major Burgess Lewis calling from New York. Lewis was a racing enthusiast and an old friend.

"Eddie," he said, "we're organizing a secret sailing to France. We need staff drivers. Would you like to go?"

"It sounds wonderful, Burgess," I said, "but I'd like to think about it overnight. Could you call me again at 8:00 in the morning?"

"Sure, Eddie," he said. "You'll be hearing from me then. I hope the answer is yes."

I weighed the pros and cons for most of the night. No troops had yet been sent to France—it was May 1917—and I liked the idea of being the first. I figured that, if I could get overseas where the fighting was, I might circumvent the ridiculous regulations that were keeping me from flying. Finally, I realized for the first time that I had already been in hot water once because of my German name and there I was driving a German-built automobile in a race held in wartime. There might be unfavorable publicity, and the offer might not be repeated. I had better grab it while I could.

When Burgess called the next morning, promptly at 8:00, I told him that I would join him right after the race. There was a slight pause, then Burgess chuckled.

"If you aren't in New York tomorrow morning, Eddie, there's no use of your coming at all. That's how tight the schedule is."

"I'll be there," I said.

I worked like a beaver until noon turning the operation over to the crew chief. Finding a driver would be easy now that we had the car in good shape. I stopped over at Columbus for a couple of hours to see Mother, but I did not tell her that I was on the way to France. By noon the next day I was a sergeant in the U.S. Army, and the day after that I sailed with the American Expeditionary Force under General John J. "Black Jack" Pershing. The headquarters commander was a tall captain named George S. Patton, Jr., and also on board was Pershing's aviation officer, Colonel T. F. Dodd. He was the man whose airplane motor I had fixed in California not too long before.

Along with the other sergeant drivers, many of them well-known businessmen whom Burgess Lewis had rounded up, I was billeted in steerage. My bunk was a hammock. The ship was filthy, and the mess hall was filthier. Under the oilcloth the tables crawled with bugs. I could hardly wait to go up on deck. There

I ran into a doctor I knew, who had a comfortable second-class cabin.

"You're a sergeant just like me," I said. "How do you rate this when I'm down in the hold with the bugs?"

"I'm a sergeant first class," he said.

That was when I learned that there were different types of sergeants. The highest-ranking officer on ship, next to Pershing himself, was my old friend Colonel Dodd. I went to see him and told him that I wanted to be promoted. After all, I had been in the Army for 48 hours.

"Promotions come through meritorious service, Eddie," Dodd said. "Now how do you intend to go about that?"

"I don't know, Colonel," I told him, "that's why I brought you along."

He burst out laughing and promoted me to sergeant first class on the spot. I was assigned to a second-class cabin, which by contrast with the steerage was delightful, and to a far superior mess. I sweetened the chef's palm a little bit and came away with a basket of food and fresh fruit for my erstwhile companions in steerage. They were unaccustomed to such living, and my daily food deliveries helped to make the trip a little easier for them.

We disembarked at Liverpool. The first person I saw on coming down the gangplank was my old friend, the long-nosed sergeant. Now he was a captain, but he still had the same surly disposition. "Ah, you're back again," he growled.

"That's right," I shot back. He couldn't cause me any trouble now. I was in the U.S. Army. But it turned out later that I was wrong again.

The American Expeditionary Force proceeded overland across England and over the Channel; it landed in France on June 26. "Lafayette, we are here," said General Pershing. The war correspondents were out in full force and filed complete accounts of everything we did. In the world press I immediately became General Pershing's staff driver. Books on aviation and World War I persist to this day in identifying me as Black Jack's chauffeur. The truth is that I never did drive for the General.

But I did drive someone else who, I believe, made an equally great and lasting contribution to our national defense. One day I was on a mission with Colonel Dodd, when we came across a stalled automobile. I stopped. From the driver's description of the trouble, I concluded that the strainer in the carburetor was not letting the gas through. I took it out, and, sure enough, it was clogged with dirt. After I had cleaned it, the engine ran perfectly. The officer to whom the car was assigned was impressed. That was the first time I ever saw William "Billy" Mitchell, America's great air pioneer.

After that, Mitchell, then a colonel, requested me as a driver frequently. He had a big flashy Packard, and he wanted a well-known racing driver to go with it. I drove him all over the French countryside. On one occasion, we went to the village of Issoudun, where he selected the wheatfields that later became the Issoudun Flying and Training School.

On another trip we took a Hudson, which was always burning out its connecting-rod bearings. As usual, Mitchell wanted to pass everything on the road. Bang! went the bearing. I nursed the car to the nearest village and found a little garage. I heated some babbitt metal in a pot with a blowtorch, made a mold from sand and water and poured the babbitt into it. Then I filed it down and made it fit. We had a bearing. By 6:00 that night we were on the road again. Mitchell could hardly believe it.

Although I was a hero to Mitchell, to the counterintelligence corps I was still a suspected German spy. My long-nosed English friend had put in another report on me, and it had gone all the way to Washington. The head of the Secret Service, William S. Nye, was a racing fan and a good friend. He sent word to me that I was under surveillance by counterintelligence. After a while, I figured out that the agent checking on me was my tent-mate; once I had come in to find him rifling my belongings. From then on I enjoyed myself thoroughly with him. I would lead him on, letting drop mildly suspicious remarks, then, when his ears perked up, dropping the subject entirely. He was only doing his job, but I must admit that I did not make it easier for him.

I have always said that I would rather have a million friends than a million dollars, and it may be noticeable by now that the friends I have made in my lifetime frequently bob up at opportune times. One of them was New York banker James Miller. I bumped into him one afternoon on the Champs Élysées, and he told me that he was slated for command of the advanced flying school at Issoudun.

"You're just the man I'm looking for," he said. "I need an engineering officer."

"I'd be glad to do the best I could to help you, Jim," I told him. "But I think an engineering officer for a flying school ought to know how to fly himself."

Jim took the hint. "I'll see what I can do," he said.

Miller made a formal request for my services to Colonel Mitchell, and I approached him myself at an opportune moment. I think he honestly wanted to help me get ahead.

"Eddie," he said, "do you really want to fly?"

"Yes, sir," I said. "Anybody can drive this car. I'd appreciate the opportunity to learn to fly."

"I'll see what I can do," he said.

Mitchell must have snipped some red tape somewhere. A few days later I received orders to report for a physical examination for pilot training.

The doctor who gave me the physical turned out to be another old friend, a racing enthusiast from Chicago. He not only pronounced me fit but also wrote my age down, firmly, as 25, with my birth date as October 8, 1892. My true age, 27, would have disqualified me.

The primary flying school at Tours, France, southwest of Paris was operated by the French, with French instructors and French planes. There were only about a dozen of us in that class. Most were Red Cross drivers who, like me, had seized an opportunity to get to France before the troops arrived. Our first practice sessions were in a Morane-Saulnier, a funny little monoplane with a 3-cylinder engine. Its wings were clipped so that it would not fly. All I could do was run it back and forth;

it reminded me of a grasshopper. After a brief lecture, not even a demonstration, I climbed into it alone and started out. As an automobile driver, I was used to steering with a wheel held in my hands. But the little grasshopper, like all airplanes, had rudders, which meant that I had to steer it with my feet.

After the sputtering little engine had built up enough speed, I would push forward on the control stick, to lift the tail skid off the ground, and skitter along in that fashion. Steering with the feet and holding the tail up with the hands was like the old trick of patting your head and rubbing your stomach simultaneously. On my first practice run I went down the field wobbling from side to side, with the tail bobbing up and down, like a frightened roadrunner. After a day or two of practice, however, I had the hang of it.

The plane we used for flying was a Caudron. It had a tremendous wingspread and was powered by a 9-cylinder Le Rhône engine. It had a pusher-type propeller, mounted behind the pilot, which moved the plane along at a top speed of 80 miles an hour. I had two short flights with an instructor, and then it was time to solo.

I was scared to death. Everything started off wrong. I had trouble getting my six-foot-two frame into a cockpit built for smaller Frenchmen. A crosswind was blowing. Steering with my feet and trying to anticipate the right moment to lift the tail, I started across the grassy field. I felt the pressure of the crosswind, pushed down on the left rudder to compensate and overdid it. The plane, lumbering and bumping along, turned and headed straight for the hangar. The other students and the instructors were out watching, of course, and they scattered every which way. In desperation, I pushed down on the right rudder, and the tail began to swing around. I missed the hangar by a few feet and kept on across the grassy field, bumping and bouncing. One thing you could say for that tremendous wingspread: if the pilot built up enough speed he would fly almost automatically. I eased back on the stick. The plane lifted into the air. I was flying!

As the propeller spun in a clockwise direction, I had been advised by the instructor to make my first turn to the right, contrary to torque. I did what I had been told to do: I put the right wing down and pushed on the left rudder. It worked. I curved around gracefully to the right.

With all that wingspread, remaining aloft was easy. Coming down was something else again. I remembered how I had thought Glenn Martin was going to plow the plane right into the ground. Now, coming down slowly, I was scared stiff. The ground was coming up too fast. I eased back on the stick to let the tail drop and stiffened, waiting for the bump.

But there was no bump. I peered over the side, and there was the ground, still fifty feet below me. Fortunately, the training field was a broad expanse, for just that reason, and I was able to work the plane down step by step.

Our course of primary flying lasted exactly seventeen days, and some of those days were so cloudy or windy that flying was impossible. I put in a total of 25 hours of flying time and went forth a pilot and a first lieutenant in the Signal Corps.

Once I had learned to fly, it was time to fulfill my share of the bargain and report to Jim Miller at Issoudun as engineering officer. I arrived in the latter part of September. My new station was a mudhole. My duty was to organize the mechanical end of the school—repair shops, spare parts and other matériel, buildings and transportation. After a few days of indoctrination, I hurried off to Paris to requisition what we would need. I bought millions of dollars' worth of all types of equipment, including automobiles for transportation. I found a transportation officer in the same way that Jim Miller had found me, by bumping into an old friend named Spiegel on the street.

Miller had an adjutant named Wiedenbach. Wiedenbach's assistant was named Tittel. One day General Pershing came to inspect the field, and Captain Miller, who was a better banker than a soldier, forgot to salute him. That was the end of Jim Miller, and a regular Army officer, Major Carl "Tooey" Spaatz, came in to take command. When our first contingent of would-be aviators came in for further training, they found the field run by five officers named Spaatz, Wiedenbach, Tittel, Rickenbacher and Spiegel. They called us the "five German spies" behind our backs.

The new group had good reason to object to me personally. Its members were all young men of good family, recruited from Ivy League universities. Faultlessly attired in shiny Sam Browne belts, handmade boots and tailor-made uniforms, they came in expecting to find a flying school in full operation. Instead they found a mudhole and a tough Swiss-German engineer with a grammar-school education and the grubbiest of chores for them to perform. They made sarcastic remarks both behind my back and to my face, and I admit that I had some desire to get even.

The muddy field was strewn with rocks, which would fly up and break the wooden propellers. I was running out of props. One day I requisitioned a hundred buckets, put them in the hands of a hundred Ivy Leaguers and sent them out in the mud to pick up rocks. The groaning and moaning that day were music to my ears. But, though there was some antagonism between us, I must say that they were a fine bunch of kids, and many of them became excellent flyers.

The fact that they were perfecting their flying while I was working around the clock making their training possible did not decrease my resentment. The only way I could improve my own flying was to take a few minutes here and a half-hour there. I would duck into the lecture sessions between chores and pick up information when I could. To apply what I learned, I would have to sneak an airplane out and take it up without benefit of an instructor watching. Supervised instruction was dangerous enough; we had a graveyard right there on the field for those who did not apply what they learned in class. Without the benefit of classroom instruction, my surreptitious flying was doubly precarious.

We started out with the 23-meter Nieuport, so called because it had a wing surface of 23 square meters. It was old, slow and practically foolproof. As the flying art developed, Nieuport had brought out an 18-meter plane, which was a little faster. Then came the 15-meter plane, the smallest and fastest of all. I learned to handle them all fairly well.

I overheard the instructors and young pilots talking about one particularly difficult maneuver, the tailspin. It was a good stunt to know, as in combat a plane in a tailspin is hard to hit. To go into a tailspin, the pilot stalls the plane, then kicks the rudder hard. The nose drops, and the tail starts swinging around, building up centrifugal force. Knowing no more about the maneuver than what I had overheard, I took a small Nieuport out one day to try it. I flew about twenty miles from the field, so that no one would see me, and began trying to put the plane into a tailspin. I simply could not do it. My muscles simply would not obey my command. I came back to the field without making one effort, thoroughly ashamed of myself.

The next day I went out again. That time I steeled myself. I pulled the plane up into a stall, then put the nose down. It began falling, nose down and tail revolving above, like a leaf spiraling to earth. It was indeed a dangerous and frightening maneuver. I pulled the plane out after only one revolution and skedaddled home. One good turn did not deserve another.

By constant practice far from the field all by myself, I finally mastered the tailspin. I could flutter down almost to the ground. The other students were bragging about how many revolutions they could make before pulling out, but I kept my mouth shut.

Every Sunday afternoon at Issoudun, the college boys put on a football game. The big brass in Paris would make special trips to see the game. One Sunday I had to fly over to Tours, and I returned while the football game was in progress. Players were running up and down the field, and spectators were crowding in on the sidelines. It was an excellent opportunity to demonstrate a real tailspin. I came down low over the field at about five hundred feet, stalled and threw the little plane into a spin. Down it went, closer and closer and closer, right over the players. Frankly, it scared the pants off me too. Everybody beneath me, players and spectators alike, scattered for cover. Only then did

I pull out of the spin—and just in time too. I sure broke up that ball game.

Major Spaatz called me on the carpet as soon as I landed, gave me a blistering lecture and grounded me for thirty days. But it was worth it.

I had, in a sense, been obeying my mother's orders. I had written her that I was flying, adding that it was much safer than racing, as there was plenty of room in the sky. She wrote back saying that she was certain I knew what I was doing, but to be sure to fly slow and close to the ground.

In January 1918, the first group of pilots who had completed the course at Issoudun was ordered to the school of aerial gunnery at Cazeau in southern France. It was the final step before combat. I looked at the list of names, and mine was not on it. I hurried in to see Major Spaatz and asked him why.

"You're too important to me here," he told me bluntly.

"But I want to get into combat!" I said.

"I've given you my orders, Lieutenant," Spaatz said and turned away.

I had a miserable cold and was exhausted from doing a dozen jobs and sneaking off to fly. I went to the school surgeon, Major Goldthwaite.

"I've got a bad cold, Major," I said, "but the main reason I want to be hospitalized is to give Lieutenant Spiegel an opportunity to prove that he can do my job just as well as I can. Then maybe Major Spaatz will turn me loose."

The Doc chuckled. "Sure, Lieutenant," he said. "I'll be glad to put you in the hospital."

I had a pleasant two weeks. I really had been sick, as well as exhausted. Spiegel carried on perfectly well. I went in to see Major Spaatz again. Without saying a word, he handed me my orders to report to Cazeau. "Thank you, sir," I said. "But why the change of heart?"

"I'm onto your little game, Rickenbacher," he said. "But if your heart's set on going to Cazeau, you're no damn good to me around here." Then he grinned and stuck out his hand. "So good luck."

I never thought that at Cazeau I would find myself in a boat in the middle of a lake with a 30-caliber rifle in my hand. That was the way they started teaching us to shoot. I would stand up in this little boat, bobbing up and down, while another boat towed a target. I had only shot a gun twice before in my life, and at first I did not come close to the target. I blasted away at it day after day, until my shoulder was black and blue from the recoil. But finally I could hit it.

The next step was a little Nieuport with a machine gun. The target was a sock, about ten feet long and three feet in diameter, towed by two Frenchmen in a sputtering old Caudron. The first time I fired I shot the tow rope in two. The pilot put the old Caudron in a dive and landed. I followed, and they came running up to me, furious.

"Tirez là," they shouted, pointing at the sock lying on the ground, *"pas là, pas là,"* pointing to the plane. I got the message and, after burning up a few tons of ammunition, I got so that I could hit that target too.

And now I was a combat pilot, able to fly and to shoot. I was given a 10-day leave in Paris and then dispatched to a new unit that was just being formed. It was the 94th Aero Pursuit Squadron, one of the first all-American squadrons and the first to go into action on the western front. It was March 1918. It had taken me almost a year to reach the front as a combat pilot, but I was there.

SIX

UNCLE SAM'S HAT-IN-THE-RING SQUADRON

During the winter of 1917–1918, we had been hearing enthusiastic predictions of the thousands of airplanes that the United States was going to ship over to us. Editorial-page cartoons showed the skies black with American planes. Thousands of pilots were being trained to man this vast armada.

It was both a thrill and an honor for me to report for duty as an original member of the Air Service squadron that would undoubtedly be the first unit of the American air fleet to see action. The 94th Aero Pursuit Squadron was the first to be composed entirely of Americans. Its commander was Major John Huffer, an American who had lived most of his life in France. He had served with the famous Lafayette Escadrille, a unit composed of American volunteer fliers, which had been in action since the early days of the war.

Even more impressive was the presence of the greatest pilot of them all, Major Raoul Lufbery, the American Ace of Aces. He had shot down seventeen enemy aircraft. Lufbery, a native of France, had emigrated to the United States as a young man but had returned to fight for his native land. He was the idol of two countries.

The two new American squadrons, the 94th and the 95th, were assigned to the aerodrome near Villeneuve, about fifteen miles back of the front lines. Our quarters were comfortable and the field in reasonably good shape. Yet we were one disappointed group of fighter pilots. The planes we found waiting for us were old Nieuports cast off by the French. Even that was not the worst of it. The planes had no guns. And the pilots in the 95th Squadron had never been through gunnery training.

In preparation for the great day when our guns would arrive, I gathered up my courage and sought out Major Lufbery. Simply to be in his company was an honor, but of more practical value was his knowledge of air combat. He was a quiet individual with a dry sense of humor, and he recognized my eagerness to learn. We discussed every maneuver in which our Nieuports could be flown and every type of attack, all illustrated by his own personal experiences in combat. Many of his victories, he told me, had been gained while he was on lone patrol.

"There's a hell of a lot of difference," he told me, "in going out alone, no matter what the odds are against you, and in going out as a member or a leader of a group of pilots who may or may not be as good as you are. It's a great responsibility to shepherd these pilots out and get back home safe. I prefer to fight alone, on my own."

The weather was bad the first two days I was with the squadron, but March 6 dawned clear. Lufbery announced that he would lead a flight—three unarmed planes—on a patrol over the German lines. Of the twenty pilots in the squadron, which two would he choose to accompany him? There was a long moment of silence as he looked us over. Then his eyes met mine.

"Rick," he said casually, "you and Campbell be ready to leave at 8:15."

"Yes, sir," I said, trying to be nonchalant. Lieutenant Douglas Campbell, the third member of the flight, also made a brave attempt to conceal his emotions, but I knew the elation he felt.

Doug, a Harvard graduate, had had ground-school training in the United States but had not flown before his arrival in France. Assigned to the flying school at Issoudon, he had been called upon for staff work. He actually taught himself to fly, soloing in a 23-meter Nieuport used for advanced training. It was perhaps fitting that he and I, who had both learned to fly in spite of severe handicaps, should be chosen for the first flight with Raoul Lufbery.

The other pilots gathered around us as we went in for breakfast. A lot of jokes were made and well-meaning advice given. As we planned to fly only a patrol in our unarmed planes, there would be little chance of combat. But antiaircraft fire was something else again. Subsequently known as "ack-ack" or "flak," it was universally known as "Archie" in World War I, from a popular English song that ended with the words: "Archibald! Certainly not!" During breakfast that morning, Doug and I must have been reminded a dozen times of Archie. We were not likely to forget it in the first place.

At about 8:00 I strolled, as casually as possible, out to the hangar. Three mechanics were assigned to each of the twenty planes of the squadron. As I knew a bit about both engines and mechanics, my ship was in excellent condition. The crew walked it out of the hangar onto the field, put blocks under the wheels and proceeded to warm it up. One of the mechanics turned the propeller over a few times with the ignition off to bring the oil and gasoline up into the cylinders. Then, with a warning cry of "Contact!" another turned on the switch. The man at the prop pulled the blade down with one sharp motion and stepped back quickly. When the engine caught, the spinning blade would take your hands off if you left them there.

The engine started quickly and settled down to a smooth, even roar. It was ready, and so was I. Doug Campbell followed suit with his plane. At about 8:10 Major Lufbery walked briskly out. The three of us climbed into our fur-lined, fur-collared flying suits and put on our fur-lined leather helmets. It was cold enough on the ground in northern France in March; it would be a lot colder in an open cockpit at fifteen thousand feet. I squeezed into the cockpit and waited for Lufbery and Campbell to take off. Lufbery had instructed us to stay close to him, and it was not the kind of thing I had to be told twice.

In my conversations with Lufbery, he had described a kind of corkscrew maneuver that he used when flying near the lines. Flying in this manner, turning the head rhythmically from side to side, the pilot could sweep the skies with his eyes, checking everything above and below, to the right and to the left. I tried to follow his corkscrew path through the skies, but it did not come easily.

We were over the front lines between Rheims and Verdun. Below us was a scene that was appalling. Armies had been fighting over that once-beautiful farmland for more than three years, and what was left was wasteland. Not a house, not a barn, not a tree was left standing.

Tragic as was the sight beneath, I was becoming aware of something of even greater personal importance. I was getting airsick. At first I simply refused to believe it. Flying over the front lines in formation with the greatest American ace of them all was no time to get sick. But I felt the cold sweat break out all over me and the acute misery of nausea well up from my stomach.

I was on the verge of disgracing myself, when suddenly the plane rocked violently and a burst of light and sound hit my eyes and ears. Another blast rocked me and another and another. I looked behind me. Large puffs of black smoke marked my path through the sky. It was Archie. Down below men were shooting at me with 18-pound shells. Although I did not know it at the time, we were flying over Suippe, where one of the most accurate German antiaircraft batteries was located.

After my first moment of terror had passed, I realized that, in spite of all the turbulence and noise, neither my plane nor I had suffered a scratch. A delicate touch on the joy stick would compensate for the sudden buffeting of the shell bursts and smooth my little Nieuport out on its path again.

And, most wonderful of all, the Archie had scared the nausea out of me. I was no longer going to be sick. A feeling of elation surged through me. I had been fired at, and I had kept my wits about me. The flight home was one of my most exquisite flying experiences. I had passed my first test.

We landed and taxied up to the hangars. The other pilots and all the mechanics were waiting for us. Lufbery let Doug and me do the talking. Archie? Why the Germans must have wasted a million shells firing on us, but they had not come close. Enemy planes? We had had the air completely to ourselves; neither friend nor enemy had dared to join us in the sky.

Lufbery gave a dry little chuckle. "Sure there weren't any other planes around, Rick?" he asked.

"Not a one!" I said firmly.

Lufbery shook his head. "Listen," he said. "One formation of five Spads crossed under us before we passed the lines. Another flight of five Spads went by about fifteen minutes later, five hundred yards away. Damn good thing they weren't Boches. And there were four German Albatroses ahead of us when we turned back and another enemy two-seater closer to us than that. You must learn to look around."

Lufbery paused and looked at us as though we were inattentive children. Then he grinned and walked over to my plane. He poked his finger through a hole in the tail and another through the wing; then he pointed to where another piece of shrapnel had gone through both wings not a foot from the cockpit. Just a few inches and I would have been a hero all right—a dead hero.

I continued my sessions with Lufbery, trying to absorb all I could of his experience, and kept after him to take me with him again. In the meantime, I went up myself as often as the weather would permit. My flight with Luf had convinced me that a major factor in remaining alive in the air was the development of visual perception. I practiced focusing my eyes, not only on the ground or on a distant point, but also at intervals in the space between.

I practiced flying the corkscrew maneuver over and over until the misery and nausea of airsickness hit me. I would try to get sick over the side, but I didn't always make it. Too many times when I landed, the cockpit was a mess. While the mechanics were refueling the plane and cleaning the cockpit, I would stagger off in embarrassment to the mess hall to refuel myself. I'd force down a stack of wheat cakes, then come back and take the plane up again, corkscrewing through the sky until the nausea came on again. Then one wonderful day there was no airsickness, no nausea. It was all over; I was never airsick again.

All the time we were seething over our lack of guns and our resulting inability to start shooting down Germans, we were actually luckier than we realized. We were accumulating experience that would enable us to save our own skins and to shoot down our foes.

My old friend Captain James Miller of Issoudun days, now commanding officer of the 95th, became the tragic personal proof of this fact. One day he was invited to go on patrol with a French squadron in an armed Spad. Jim was ecstatic; the rest of us were envious. He went out with Major Davenport Johnson, an American flying with the French, and flew over the same sector that Lufbery and I had visited a few days before. They spotted two squadrons of German two-seater planes, each carrying an aerial gunner as well as a pilot, and attacked. Johnson's guns jammed, and he turned and came back to his field. Miller went on in. He did not stand a chance. His first combat flight was his last.

French fliers from neighboring fields would occasionally drop in and take us along on a patrol. It was a splendid opportunity to gain experience, and we took turns going. We came close to German planes on several occasions, but we always outnumbered them, and a fight never developed. The French never realized that our planes were not armed, and it never occurred to us to tell them. One day, however, a visiting pilot examined one of our planes closely and saw that it had no guns. That was the end of our French escorts over the line. We had all thought it was a big joke; the French thought we had lost our minds.

We never had the opportunity to fly with the English. They would probably have enjoyed the joke as much as we. Where the French were cautious, according to their considered military policy of getting the best possible results with the least expenditure of men and planes, the British were daring, almost foolhardy, also as a matter of military principle. They started flying combat at the age of 18, and a dashing style came naturally to them. American pilots were more daring than the French, more wary than the English. As for the Germans, they liked to fly in close formations, hunting in packs. Americans preferred an every-man-for-himself style of aerial combat.

When the big German spring offensive of 1918 began, we were moved back to a safer location at Épiez. It was a gloomy period, but the arrival of two experienced pilots from the Lafayette Escadrille, Captains David Peterson and James Norman Hall, revived us again. Both were aces, with more than five victories each, and their very presence inspired us.

Even more wonderful was the sudden arrival of our equipment, guns, ammunition, instruments, flying clothing, spare parts and spare planes. We were moved up to Toul. Once again we were only eighteen miles from the lines, but this time we were armed. Surely we would now be the first American squadron to go into action against the enemy.

The honor deserved a distinctive insignia. One of the pilots, Lieutenant Johnny Wentworth, was an architect, and he was asked to design it. We all threw out ideas. Major Huffer, the CO, suggested Uncle Sam's stovepipe hat with the stars and stripes for a hatband. Our flight surgeon, Lieutenant Walters from Pittsburgh, mentioned the old American custom of throwing a hat into the ring as an invitation to battle. And thus one of the world's most famous military insignia, the Hat-in-the-Ring, which became a part of my entire life from then on, was born.

The Hat-in-the-Ring was proudly emblazoned on my Nieuport on the morning of April 14, 1918, when Captain Peterson, Lieutenant Reed Chambers and I took off for a patrol of the lines in our sector. It was the first combat mission ever ordered by an American commander of an American squadron of American pilots.

It nearly turned into the first fiasco. The fog was so heavy that Peterson returned to the field. I thought he had turned back because of engine trouble, and Reed and I continued on. We became separated in the fog and were nearly lost. Two German planes pursued us, and they really became lost. Hearing them over the field, Doug Campbell and Allan Winslow took off to attack them. Winslow shot down his plane, and Campbell forced the other one to crash. On our first day of operations, the 94th had brought down two German planes. The people of Toul, who had been bombed nightly by the Germans, feted us in a great celebration. News of the 94th's double victory was flashed to the States, and cablegrams and letters poured in on our two heroes. There was even a happy ending for the two German pilots, for neither was seriously injured.

During the next few days I learned many lessons. On my second flight I trusted my judgment instead of my compass and wound up flying in the wrong direction. Then I jumped a French Spad and had to put my little ship through some tricky maneuvers, in order to show its pilot my United States markings before he could shoot me down. In the air one shot first and identified later.

On my next flight, just over Saint-Mihiel, I sighted an enemy plane and came in on him apparently unnoticed, even though shell bursts followed my path across the sky. At the last moment I remembered what Raoul Lufbery had told me a dozen times—*look out for a trap*. Coming in on top of me was an Albatros fighter. My little Nieuport could outclimb the heavier German ship, and I maneuvered away from him and came back down on his tail.

That time I had him, but again I thought of Lufbery's admonition. I looked around, and two more planes were coming at me. I banked and headed for home. The two planes stuck on my tail. I put my ship through every maneuver; they came on relentlessly, which was somewhat discouraging, as our planes were supposed to be faster than the German planes. The whole idea of aerial combat was to get on the other fellow's tail so that you could pour bullets into plane and pilot. I hunched over in dread expectation of the heavy slugs ripping into my back. Ahead was the most beautiful cloud in the world. I held my breath. Closer, closer—then I entered it. I was safe. I stayed in the cloud protection for several minutes, then poked my nose out for a look around. The planes had gone, and I proceeded on to the field.

There Doug Campbell and Charley Chapman, who had just landed, wanted to know why I had run away from them. I had been fleeing from two of my own buddies. Not only had they scared me to death, but because of my failure to identify them, I had lost what might well have been my first victory in the air.

But I was learning. I was lucky that I lived long enough to learn. Many a pilot went to his death before he gained the experience that would have kept him alive. All aces made their greatest numbers of kills against inexperienced pilots. The few pilots who had lucky victories at the very beginning found that, with instant fame, came carelessness and lack of appreciation for the true difficulties of aerial combat. Sooner or later what they had not learned caught up with them. My first flights were disappointing, but the experience I gained paid off later.

For several days it rained, and then came a double blessing. The sun came out, and I was ordered to go on a mission with Captain Hall, one of the greatest fliers and finest men I have ever known. Word had come that an enemy two-seater plane was flying south over the lines. We took off and went up to look for him. Once aloft, I saw a plane far off on the horizon and sped in its direction. Jimmy Hall ignored the whole thing and with good reason, for the plane turned out to be a French two-seater.

Looking around the sky for Hall, I saw a lot of German anti-aircraft activity in the direction of Saint-Mihiel. I knew it was German because the shell bursts emitted black smoke; allied Archie was white. I hurried to the area, and, sure enough, there was Jimmy amusing himself with the gunners on the ground.

He was baiting them with his entire repertory of stunts, having a wonderful time while the Germans below expended ammunition. When he saw me, he wiggled his wings and headed toward Pont-à-Mousson. I followed him.

From the German lines came a single plane, a new Pfalz. Hall was climbing into the sun, with me close behind, and the German was totally unaware of us as we kept between him and the sun. We had a thousand feet of altitude on him, and we were two to one. If he saw us coming, his only hope was to put his plane into a dive. The Pfalz, a sturdy ship, could outdive a Nieuport any day, for the main weakness of the Nieuport was a tendency to shed the fabric of its upper wing in a dive. If I had been that German pilot, I would have put my nose down and headed for Germany. I decided to get in position to cut off that form of retreat. I knew that Hall would attack when he was ready.

In a second I would go into my first combat. My heart started pounding. The image of a Liberty Bond poster popped into my mind. It was of a beautiful girl with outstretched arms. In big black letters were the words "Fight or Buy Bonds." Well, I did not have much choice.

As I came out of the sun to get in position to cut him off, the German pilot saw me. He stuck up his nose and started climbing. Jimmy came into range and let go a burst of bullets. The German instantly banked his Pfalz to the right and put it into a dive, heading homeward as fast as he could go. That was what I was ready for, and I was on his tail in an instant. The Boche ran like a scared rabbit, but I was gaining. I had my sights trained on the back of his seat. I pressed both triggers.

Every fourth shell was a tracer, and I could see two streaks of fire pouring into the Pfalz's tail assembly. I held the triggers down and pulled back on the stick slightly, lifting the nose of the plane. It was like raising a garden hose. I could see the stream of fire climbing up the fuselage and into the pilot's seat. The plane swerved. It was no longer being flown. I pulled out of the dive and watched the Pfalz curve down and crash. I had brought down my first enemy airplane.

We were over the German lines, and the angry antiaircraft gunners beneath filled the skies with shell bursts. I was ready to go home, but Jimmy Hall wanted to celebrate. He flew right into the barrage and stunted until the Huns exhausted their ammunition. I had withdrawn to a safe distance to watch the show, and Jimmy joined me for the trip home.

We came down together, jumped out of our planes and ran together with hands outstretched. It was one of the great moments of a lifetime. We were victorious. As we pounded each other on the shoulders, both talking at once, pilots and mechanics came running from the hangar. Some observer at the front had seen the fight and had telephoned the news back to squadron headquarters. Now the whole gang came to congratulate us.

Though pilots were lionized during the Great War, though news of my first victory went out all over the world and communications of congratulation came in by the hundred, the true gratification of an aerial victory comes from your fellow pilots. They know how easily it could have gone the other way, and their acclaim means more than all the applause from the outside world. There has never been a closer fraternity than the one that existed among the pilots of a squadron fighting together high in the sky, and no group of fighters had a greater spirit than those of the 94th Squadron. There on the muddy French airfield, surrounded by my fellow pilots of the Hat-in-the-Ring Squadron, I experienced the greatest elation of my life.

I had no regrets over killing a fellow human being. I do not believe that at that moment I even considered the matter. Like nearly all air fighters, I was an automaton behind the gun barrels of my plane. I never thought of killing an individual but of shooting down an enemy plane.

As for the method, that was how we fought. All pilots, German and Allied alike, strove to gain an advantage over the adversary. The advantage could have been in superior flying ability and marksmanship, in equipment, in numbers. When the sides were even and neither could gain the advantage, then there was no battle. Frequently two pilots of equal skill would spend an hour or more fencing in the sky, each seeking to obtain the superior position over the other. When one or both ran low on gas, they would simply give each other a wave and fly back to their respective aerodromes. Though we were out to shoot down planes and the best way to shoot down a plane was to put a burst of bullets in the pilot's back, there was never, at least in my case, any personal animosity. I would have been delighted to learn that the pilot of the Pfalz or any other pilot I shot down had escaped with his life.

The 94th ran up five straight victories before the inevitable happened. Good-natured Charley Chapman was one of our most popular pilots. He went out on patrol with Captain Peterson and two other pilots one afternoon. The four Americans attacked five Pfalz fighter planes and brought one down. During the fight Chapman spotted a German two-seater at a lower altitude and dived on it. A Pfalz got on his tail. Charley pulled out of his dive in order to meet his pursuer and flew right into a burst of bullets from the two-seater. Within seconds the entire Nieuport was in flames. Either Charley was mercifully killed by one of the bullets, or he was burned to death.

Death by burning was the death we dreaded more than any other. Our planes were constructed of wooden frameworks covered with fabric. The fabric was treated with "dope," a highly combustible fluid that drew up the cloth and stretched it tight. We Americans had no parachutes. Some German pilots and all their balloon observers were equipped with parachutes, and often I was pleased to see an enemy bail out of his burning plane or balloon and escape being burned alive.

We often discussed the question of whether we would jump to certain death or stay with the ship. Raoul Lufbery, whose every word I respected, was positive in his advice.

"I'd stay with the machine," he said. "If you jump you haven't got a chance. If you stay, you may be able to side-slip your plane down so that you fan the flames away from yourself. Perhaps you can even put the fire out before you reach the ground."

Years of flying in open-cockpit planes and living in cold damp barracks had brought chronic rheumatism to Lufbery. His assignment with the 94th was to advise and teach us, but it was impossible to keep him out of combat. One day I returned from a mission flown with Jimmy Hall with the tragic news that Hall had been shot down behind the German lines. At the time there was no way of knowing that Jimmy had suffered only a broken ankle in the crash and was being well taken care of in a German hospital. He lived to write *Mutiny on the Bounty* with Charles Nordhoff.

Lufbery naturally thought that his pal had been killed. He headed grimly for the aerodrome and pulled on his flying suit. His mechanics had seen him coming and had not waited for orders to run his plane out and warm it up. Luf spoke to nobody, and no one spoke to him. He climbed into the plane and took off.

For an hour and a half, he saw no German pilot on whom he could wreak his vengeance. He went deep into Germany and, with only half an hour's supply of gasoline left, spotted three German planes. He attacked. One Boche went down, and the other two fled. Luf barely made it back to the field. Jimmy Hall was avenged.

Four days later, on a lovely morning in May, puffs of white smoke in the air announced that an Allied battery was firing at an enemy plane. It was an observation plane, and the German flew it right over our field. Lufbery was in the barracks at the time. He ran out, jumped on a motorcycle and raced to the hangar. His own plane was being worked on, and he grabbed another. It was doubtful that either plane or guns were up to Lufbery's demanding specifications. In any event, he was unfamiliar with the machine.

At two thousand feet above the field, in plain sight of everyone below, Lufbery attacked the Albatros. He fired several bursts, then zoomed up and came in again for another attack. His guns

With French Nieuport

With the officers of the 94th Squadron in France—1917

Business end of the Spad fighter plane

With Spad 13

Mechanical crew members of 94th Squadron standing by author's Spad

French Caudron training plane at Tours, France

Manfred von Richthofen, leading German ace

Major Raoul Lufbery

Canada's leading ace—William A. Bishop

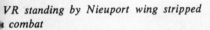

st landed from the Front after
sing leading edge and linen of
per wing

VR standing by Nieuport wing stripped
combat

author rides in parade of
welcome in Los Angeles

Author with Congressional Medal

jammed. Somehow he put them back in working order, then came around again. By that time he must have realized that this particular Albatros was heavily armored. His bullets bounced off the plane. Still he came on. He flew so close that the gunner in the Albatros could not possibly have missed him. Lufbery's plane burst into flames.

He held the plane on a straight course for about five seconds. Then, from the ground, eyewitnesses saw him squirm out of the blazing cockpit and climb onto the fuselage. Straddling it, he pushed himself back toward the tail. He rode in this position for several seconds as the flames fanned back over him. Then he jumped.

I returned from patrol to hear this shocking story. A phone call came in with the exact location of the spot where he had landed. A group of us jumped into a car and drove to the spot. He had fallen in a lovely little garden in a small town near Nancy. Nearby was a small stream; he may have been trying to land in the water. Instead his body had been impaled on a picket fence. Death must have been instantaneous.

After Jimmy Hall's crash, I had taken his place as commander of Number One flight in our squadron. I was honored, but I must admit it occurred to me that another pilot might soon be taking my place. For with leadership came responsibility.

In addition to leading my flight on routine patrols, I emulated Lufbery's example and flew my own lone-wolf missions over the lines. He always said that it was impossible to shoot down German planes sitting in the billet with your feet before the fire. I heeded his advice so well that I had more hours in the air than any other American flier.

Reed Chambers was a close second. At night and on rainy days Reed and I would discuss combat flying by the hour. In this completely new arena of warfare, we were convinced that if we thought long enough and hard enough we could devise some new strategy, some new technique, that would mean the difference between victory and defeat, life and death. One night we had an idea that was so simple that we both wondered why no one had thought of it before. Our plan was simply to take off well before dawn, climb as high as our Nieuports would take us and hover high over the lines waiting for the first German plane to come by.

My orderly pulled me out of bed at 4:00 on a chilly May morning. Reed and I met in the mess hall for some scalding coffee, then went out onto the lines where our shivering mechanics were warming up our planes, climbed into our fur-lined suits and took off. We pushed our little ships up to eighteen thousand feet. At that altitude, with our bare faces sticking out of the cockpits, the temperature was below zero.

Despite the numbing cold and the slight dizziness brought on by the altitude and our empty stomachs, we waited and waited, two specks in the sky three and a half miles over no-man's-land, patiently patrolling our sector. Dawn came on a beautiful cloudless day. Our scheme had worked perfectly; the only thing wrong was that the unpredictable Boches did not take advantage of these perfect conditions to photograph our lines.

I had about an hour's fuel left. At the aerodrome the other fellows were sitting down to a table loaded with hot food. Lufbery had said that you could not shoot down Germans at the breakfast table; well, those fellows were shooting down as many as I was, and they were warm besides.

Apparently Reed had given up and gone home. I was one lone speck in the sky. Why not try a better hunting ground? Twenty-five miles to the east was the famous old fortress city of Metz, with a German aerodrome nearby. I climbed to twenty thousand feet, seeing the first red arc of the rising sun, and headed into German territory. I felt invulnerable. Though the Germans manning the antiaircraft batteries below me could probably hear the sound of my engine, I was sure that they could not see me five miles up in the bright morning sky.

I flew over Metz several times, paying special attention to the aerodrome, but the Germans simply were not flying that day. Not much gas remained, but I decided to make one last check at a field near Thiaucourt. Still at twenty thousand feet,

I cut off my engine to save gas. As I silently circled the field, like a great bird of prey, I saw, far beneath me, three graceful German Albatroses taxi out onto the field and take off, one by one. They headed straight southward, climbing steadily, obviously unaware of my presence above them.

I continued circling, afraid even to breathe, until the last of the three was well on his way, with his back toward me. I put the little Nieuport into a shallow dive to start the propeller going and turned on the ignition. The engine caught, and I gunned my plane after the three Germans. I hoped to time it so that I would make my attack over the lines, rather than over German territory.

Closer, closer. My eyes were glued on the leather-jacketed shoulders of the German flying the rearmost Albatros. That is where my bullets were going to go. I was so intent on the pursuit that I completely forgot about a German stratagem. In front of the planes ahead, but higher, a black puff appeared in the sky, then another and another. The German batteries had seen me, and it was their way of warning the three planes in front of me. They were setting the fuse so that the shell would burst at approximately my altitude.

The pilot in front of me turned his head to look behind him. I saw the sun glint off his glasses. All three pilots immediately put their planes into a dive. I was now within two hundred yards of the last plane, and I had no intention of letting him get away. I knew the Nieuport's fatal weakness of shedding its wing covering in a dive, but in the excitement I did not think of it at all. I gunned the plane up to a speed of at least 150 miles an hour and closed in on the man in front of me.

At fifty yards I gave him a 10-second burst of machine gunfire. I saw the bullets hit the back of his seat. I felt no sympathy. He had made a stupid mistake in diving rather than trying to outmaneuver me.

By then the other two pilots had had an excellent opportunity to pull up and get on my tail. At that moment either of them could be sighting down my back. But I still wanted to make sure that I had killed my man. Not until I saw his plane go out of control did I try to pull my own out of the dive. I had to come out of it in a hurry, put the ship into a sharp climb and have it out with the other two. I pulled the stick back into my lap.

A ripping, tearing crash shook the plane. The entire spread of linen over the right upper wing was stripped off by the force of the wind. I manipulated the controls, but it did no good. The plane turned over on her right side. The tail was forced up. The left wing came around. The ship was in a tailspin. With the nose down, the tail began revolving to the right, faster and faster. It was death. I had not lost my willingness to fight to live, but in that situation there was not much that I could do. Even birds need two wings to fly.

The two remaining Albatroses began diving at me, one after the other, pumping bullets into my helpless Nieuport. I was not angry at the two men for trying to kill me; I simply thought that they were stupid. Why waste ammunition? Did they think I was playing possum, with the framework of one wing hanging in the breeze?

A crippled plane can take a long time to flutter to earth. I wondered exactly how I would die. Would the plane shake itself to pieces? In that case, I would go whistling down to hit the ground and splatter. If the plane stayed in one piece, it might crash in the trees beneath me, and I might only break a few bones. Which announcement would my mother prefer to read in the telegram from the War Department—that I was dead or that I was injured behind the lines?

I began remembering all the major episodes of my life, the good things I had done and the bad things. The bad seemed to outnumber the good. And then I remembered the Lord above.

"Oh, God," I prayed, "help me get out of this."

The earth was coming up fast. Without thinking, almost as though I were moved by something bigger than myself, I pulled open the throttle. The sudden extra speed lifted the nose of the plane. For a second there, I was horizontal. I pulled on the joy stick and reversed the rudder. I must have hit the one combination in a million that would work. The fuselage remained almost horizontal. The nose was heading for the American lines only a couple of miles away. If I could only hold her like that, I might make it.

I was at less than two thousand feet, and every antiaircraft battery, every machine gunner and practically every rifleman began sending a curtain of lead into the sky. I flew right on through it. I had no choice.

I talked to that little plane all the way home. Losing altitude, with the engine going full blast and the controls jammed in the only position that enabled it to stay aloft, my little plane and I crossed the lines. When I reached the field, I was flying at treetop height. I could not cut back the engine, for then I'd go straight down. I came in for my landing with the engine running wide open. Everybody dashed out to see what fool was coming in at full throttle. I grazed the top of the hangar, pancaked down on the ground and slid to a stop in a cloud of dust. I swung out of the bullet-riddled, battered little crate and tried to saunter nonchalantly toward the hangar as though I came in like that every day.

Reed came in for a landing a minute later. We walked in together. I felt perfectly calm. But, when I was alone in front of my bunk, suddenly my knees turned to water. The next thing I knew I was sitting down.

And then I uttered a little prayer of gratitude to the Lord above for my deliverance.

Every aerial victory had to be confirmed by another officer. There was no problem in validating that one, for the Albatros, with the dead pilot slumped over the stick, miraculously continued over the American lines and landed itself. It was my fifth victory. I was an ace. The French awarded me the Croix de Guerre. And again many messages of congratulations came in from the States.

During that experience, as in other close calls, I experienced fear only after it was all over. Other pilots were not so fortunate and permitted their fear to govern them.

It may seem strange that a man who had gone through flight training and had flown patrols in wartime would be leery of combat. Fighting, however, requires a different kind of bravery from that involved in flying. The combat pilot must be mentally prepared to shoot to kill and to be shot at in return. Some pilots had sufficient motivation and bravery to learn to fly, but going out to kill or be killed over the lines required a different type of courage. Some did not have it.

One of our pilots, a big, well-coordinated fellow, openly and goodnaturedly admitted that he was scared to fight. One day, when all the other pilots were out on patrol, the communications sergeant hurried to him.

"Two enemy planes have been spotted observing our lines in the vicinity of Saint-Mihiel, sir," the sergeant reported.

Standard order of procedure called for the officer on alert to start for his plane immediately. This fellow did not take his feet off the desk. "Well," he said, "let them observe! If you think I'm going to get shot down myself, you're mistaken."

Later, the lieutenant openly admitted the whole thing. He had a good excuse for not going, he said: He was scared. There was no further reason to keep him in the squadron, and he was transferred to a rear-echelon unit. None of us felt any rancor. It was obvious that he was not emotionally qualified to be a fighter pilot, and driving him into combat would be tantamount to killing him.

During June I suffered a recurrent fever and was grounded much of the time. Late in June the 94th was moved to Touquin, where we were quartered in a gorgeously furnished old chateau surrounded by well-tended shrubbery bursting into its full floral glory in the late French spring. Our sector of the front lay between Soissons and Rheims, including the German salient reaching as far south as Château-Thierry. It promised plenty of action. But my fever became worse, and the doctors put me in the hospital.

At first I fretted, but I later came to realize that those days in the hospital were the most important in my entire career as a fighter pilot. I had time to think. I had always, I realized, been striving for something. I had not yet decided exactly what it was I wanted or how to attain it. Aviation had been a mystery as well as a delight. With my background, it had seemed logical that I should learn to fly.

But after I became a pilot, events followed at such a whirlwind pace that it never occurred to me to review what had gone before. I looked back over the five aerial victories that had made me an ace. I recalled each maneuver that I had made in every combat and compared it with the one made by my adversary. I was already shaking with chills and fever, and I suffered another chill when I realized how many mistakes I had made. Other pilots had paid for such mistakes with their lives. I paused to utter a fervent prayer for my deliverance. It had happened too many times to be luck.

Many close calls were attributable to the antiquated and substandard equipment we were forced to use. Where were those twenty thousand American planes? There wasn't much that I could do about the airplanes assigned us other than to get the most out of what we had.

The continued jamming of our guns was something else again. Guns were mechanical contrivances, and I should be able to improve their performance. From then on, I vowed, I would have fewer gun jams than any other pilot in the service.

I was determined to begin a new career as a fighter pilot. I realized that I had repeated the same mistakes too many times and had been in danger of repeating them again. But now I had faced them and recognized them. As for my adversaries, I decided that all fliers were dominated by human qualities. My review of the Boche tactics enabled me to understand that there was nothing mysterious about them.

I must never let caution slip from my mind. Caution was important, yes, but never timidity. I recalled episodes in which boldness had been the most intelligent course of action and therefore the most cautious. It was said that I insisted upon getting close enough to my adversary to hit him with a baseball bat. I would continue to be bold but only at the right moment. Caution I must never forget.

I had looked deep within myself, and I was thankful that I had lived to enjoy that opportunity. I believe that any man who flies, any man who is in any way connected with keeping planes in the air, should know himself at least as well as he knows the machine that sustains him. This self-knowledge should apply to anyone in any activity. A man should periodically examine and test all the elements that keep him ticking. Any habit or technique, whether it is only blowing one's nose, should be reviewed and constantly revised and updated.

But procedures do not make the man. Only the man himself can make himself what he is, by taking full advantage of the excellent raw material supplied him by God.

While I was in the hospital someone suggested that I write a book about my experiences. From then on I kept a diary, making entries at the end of each day with religious regularity.

All along I had kept up my correspondence. We seldom flew at night, and on many days in France the weather was impossible. At such times I would write, in addition to letters to Mother and to members of the family, to old friends, acquaintances, even groups. I belonged to Elks Lodge No. 99 in Los Angeles, for example, and, when my fellow Elks sent me a ring as a token of their esteem, I wrote thanking them, enclosing a picture, telling of some combat experiences and calling for a helping hand for the war effort on the part of every man, woman and child. The story and picture were printed on page one of all the Los Angeles newspapers.

One letter I wrote had repercussions permanently affecting every member of my family. Winding up a letter to a friend in Detroit, I happened to sign my name "Eddie Rickenbacker" and to put a little bracket around the second "k" to call attention to it. My friend, eager to use any gimmick to help the war effort, promptly called in the wire services and showed them the letter.

Papers all over the country printed stories headed "Eddie Rickenbacker has taken the Hun out of his name!" From then on most Rickenbachers were practically forced to spell their name in the way I had written it on impulse that night on the western front.

I left the hospital on July 4 and went to Paris to celebrate. Paris was in a state of exhilaration. A month earlier the Germans had been thirty miles from the French capital. I had seen the terror and despair in the faces of both refugees and townspeople. American forces had played a major role in holding back the Hun on the Marne, and the people were grateful. They helped make July 4 a great day for us.

Next morning, on impulse, I went to the American experimental and supply aerodrome at Orly, just outside Paris. They gave me the good news that our squadron was to be equipped with new Spads. Three of our new ships were on hand.

I hurried to the field. There they were, three beauties. They were more impressive by far than any other airplane, any other automobile, any other piece of equipment I had ever seen. This new Spad would mean the difference between life and death. With it, a little luck and continuing aid from above, perhaps I could attain fame in the skies and join the great aces of the war—Lufbery, René Fonck; Billy Bishop, the Canadian, even the great Red Baron himself, Manfred von Richthofen. Well, at least I could dream.

The Spad was the ultimate aircraft of the war in which aviation was developed. In 1914, in the military mind, its only value lay in the simple fact that you could see more terrain from the air than from the ground. The war was only three weeks old when an English pilot in a fluttering crate saw the French Army proceeding the wrong way. On this information alone, British troops were pulled back in time to prevent their being encircled and captured.

Aerial observation became a vital factor in warfare. Observation balloons were used effectively, but a balloon observer's range was limited. An airplane could range far back over the enemy's lines, reporting not only on the disposition of troops but also on

the location of ammunition and food dumps and troop movements far to the rear. At first planes were unarmed, but it was
not long before airmen began trying to knock one another out of
the skies.

Planes on both sides developed rapidly. No matter what innovation one side might develop, the other was quick to find out
about it, copy it and incorporate it in a new design. In most cases
these secrets were learned from planes that had been shot or
forced down behind the lines.

A Frenchman named Roland Garros introduced aerial combat
as we knew it. He mounted a machine gun directly in front of
him, so that aiming the plane aimed the gun. To prevent the
bullets from shooting away the wooden propeller, he screwed
metal plates on the blades. He was a terror on his first forays
over the lines. It must have been like shooting fish in a barrel. He
became the world's first ace. But his engine conked out over
German territory, and the secret was out. The great Dutch plane
designer, Anthony Fokker, improved on Garros's principle by
synchronizing the gun with the propeller, so that the bullets
would fire through it. The Germans made several easy kills until
the Allies caught up. The first equalizer was the 15-meter Nieuport, which had a machine gun mounted on the top wing so that
it would fire over the propeller.

The Germans countered with the Albatros, in which Von
Richthofen scored the majority of his victories. Fokker's DR-1,
a triplane, was next. Hermann Goering flew a triplane, and Von
Richthofen was shot down in one while trying for his 81st victim. The D-7, maneuverable, speedy and tough, came out
in mid-1918.

The British produced several excellent planes, among them
the SE-5 and the Sopwith Camel, but I had no personal experience with them. The best ship I flew was the Spad, built by the
Société pour Aviation et ses Dérivés, whence it took its name.
The final Spad could do 130 miles an hour, climb to 22,000 feet
and stay together no matter what maneuvers you put it through.

It was the plane I saw July 5. It had the numeral "1" on its side. I wanted that plane.

"This is one of the planes for the 94th Squadron, isn't it?" I asked a mechanic.

"Yes, sir," he said. "She's ready to go."

"Well, I'm with the 94th Squadron," I said.

That was all it took. I had it gassed up, strapped myself in and took off. I could have been court-martialed, but I knew I had done right; that wonderful little machine told me so. I headed straight for Touquin, leaving my bag in Paris. I had a Spad.

Captain Kenneth Marr, who had been transferred from the Lafayette Escadrille to replace Major Huffer as CO, congratulated me and assigned the plane to me. I wasn't able to use it much at first. My right ear suddenly developed an excruciating pain. An abscess had formed, and I went back to Paris to have it lanced. But the pain came back more agonizingly than before. I could not afford to take any more time out of the air. To alleviate the pain at night, I had the cook heat a salt bag for me, and I slept with it over my ear. An ice bag would have been more effective, I learned later. During the day I do not believe anything could have dulled the pain. My new Spad had an altitude of 22,000 feet; try that sometime with an earache.

I had had far less opportunity than many other Americans to prove myself in combat. In March and most of April, we had had no guns; my first victory came on April 29. I had four in May, and then the fever came on. I had little flying time in June and no victories. July was no better.

I had a particularly miserable patrol during that period. I was leading a flight of six Spads over the enemy lines when I saw an aerial free-for-all in the distance. One group of planes skedaddled away from the fight, and seven planes continued on toward us. They were Fokkers.

I was long overdue for a fight. Seven eager pilots from the 94th in seven new Spads were surely more than a match for seven Fokkers. They saw us. Four turned off, and the other three kept coming. Three hundred yards from us, the three turned and, noses down, throttles wide open, headed for their lines.

It was obvious that the three planes were the bait. My flight was supposed to follow them down, whereupon the four Fokkers would come in on our tails. We did follow them but maintained our altitude. They outran us into Germany. Then I turned in the direction of the other four planes, climbing to about eighteen thousand feet. Sure enough, there came the four German planes back along the lines, unquestionably looking for us far below. They were either so busy looking below that they did not see us, or they thought we were friendly planes. At any rate, they stupidly flew right at us.

I picked the flight leader. I had him right in my sights. We were only fifty yards apart when he put his ship into a dive. I was waiting for just that maneuver, and I nosed over. It was a target I could not possibly miss. I pushed the trigger on both guns. They both jammed. The flight leader escaped without a scratch.

It was what Lufbery had warned me against, why he had preferred to play the lone wolf. I could not shoot down a German if he was ten feet in front of me. But I was the leader, and if I pulled out of the fight it would confuse my fellow pilots. I made my choice, and I stayed in the fight.

It was a twisting, turning melee. Frequently I could have shot a Heinie down if I had had guns. A couple of times the Germans nearly got me. Two of our pilots dropped out with gun or engine trouble and headed for home. We had all dropped to three thousand feet and were well inside the German lines. I saw two more flights of German planes racing up, and I called off my fighters and led them home.

I was furious. I had nearly been killed. Even worse, I had not killed any Germans, although they had been right there in front of me. And the whole right side of my head was one blinding mass of pain.

When I landed, my little gunner sergeant, a likable kid from Brooklyn named Abe Karp, came running up and asked his usual question:

"How did the guns work, Lieutenant?"

"They're no damn good and you know it," I snapped. "I . . ."

Abe interrupted me. "But, Lieutenant, I had them in perfect shape . . ." he began. I stopped him cold. It was the only time I ever pulled rank on an enlisted man over a personal matter.

"Abe, you're talking to an officer, so shut up and let me finish."

But still he wouldn't keep quiet. "Sometimes good comes out of an argument," he chirped. He was so serious, so positive, that the whole episode struck my funny bone. I started laughing and slapped him on the back.

"Abe, you win!" I said.

I had been thinking about those guns, and Abe and I sat down and began discussing my ideas for improving them. He was only about eighteen or nineteen years old, but he was sharp and alert, and he quickly caught on to some of my antidotes for the jamming of the guns.

One of the faults lay in the ammunition. Shell cases were not uniform in size and would stick in the chamber. Abe made a template calibrated to the exact size of the shell, and from then on each shell was tested and, if faulty, discarded.

In the low temperatures at high altitudes, the lubricating oil in the guns became heavy. It would stick in any rough spot on any sliding part of the gun mechanism. I obtained a little sharpening stone, and from then on you would usually find me with a gun part in one hand and a stone in the other, honing it smooth.

Suppose the guns still jammed? I remembered the copper-headed hammer of my racing days. Abe worked a leather thong through the handle of one so that it could be fastened to my right wrist and be always available. A sharp blow with it cleared many a jam.

The guns were easier to fix than my ear. Mastoiditis developed and practically knocked me out. One Sunday morning in August, I was only semiconscious and could not lead my flight. Eddie

Green took my place, with Walter Smyth and a new man, Alexander Bruce, flying number one and number two. I regretted not making that mission because I liked to fly with Walter Smyth. He was about twenty years old, honest, wholesome, with a grand sense of humor. He was brave, but he carried with him an atmosphere of melancholy; he seemed to sense that he was not going to live out the war. I was closer to Walter than to any other man in the squadron, and I tried to jolly him out of his black moods. We used to walk down to a little bridge over a canal and, leaning on the guard rail and looking down into the clear, still water, just talk.

On that Sunday morning, as I lay in a semicoma, I suddenly saw, as in a dream, Walter's plane collide with Bruce's. It seemed to happen in a cloud, yet I saw it clearly. Their wings touched and fell off, and I saw both planes plummeting to earth.

When I next opened my eyes, I saw Kenneth Marr standing by the bed. "I have terrible news for you," he said.

"I know," I said. "Smyth and Bruce were killed."

Marr's eyes opened wide. "How did you know?" he asked. "We just got the telephone message a minute ago."

"I saw it," I said. Later I learned that it had happened just the way I saw it in my mind.

With parachutes, both of those fine young men would have lived. It was absolutely criminal for our higher command to withhold parachutes from us. Men who could have lived on to serve America both in war and in peace perished in agony because of the lack of a parachute. What reward did Raoul Lufbery gain for his role in helping to develop American air mastery? Death on a picket fence when a parachute would have saved his life. Now Smyth and Bruce.

The Air Service had developed parachutes but only for balloon observers. They were too big and heavy for our small fighter planes. But we knew that it was possible to make a smaller parachute because the Germans were doing it. I experienced a sensation of actual pleasure when I saw my enemy bail out of his plane and float to earth safely. I never wanted to kill men, only to destroy machines. It seemed that the enemy cared more about its men than our higher headquarters cared about ours.

A major in the Paris headquarters of the Air Service told me that the service did not believe in parachutes. "If all of you pilots had parachutes," he told me coldly, "then you'd be inclined to use them on the slightest pretext, and the Air Service would lose planes that might otherwise have been brought down safely."

I got so mad that I started hollering at him. Other officers came in and broke it up. It was a good thing that I had a few ribbons on my chest by that time, for otherwise I would probably have been court-martialed.

Though it was of far less significance than the lack of parachutes, still the American uniform in World War I was a ridiculous sight. We wore funny-looking baggy pants stuffed into puttees and short ugly jackets that we called "see-more tunics." American troops abroad should make as fine an impression as possible. It was difficult for anyone to look his best in that ridiculous uniform.

And so I designed my own and had it made up for me by a Parisian tailor. The tunic was well cut, along French lines, with patch pockets. The trousers were trim, and instead of those awful puttees I had a pair of high laced boots, patterned after the French design. I wore an English Royal Flying Corps cap. One day I was walking down the Rue de la Paix when a hard-boiled infantry colonel, wearing his baggy pants and see-more tunic, took one look at me and stopped me right there on the sidewalk.

"Just a minute, Lieutenant," he said. "Tell me, just who in hell's army do you belong to?"

"Don't you like it, Colonel?" I asked.

That took him aback for a moment. Then he grinned. "Well, yes, I do," he admitted. "Where did you get it?"

I wrote down the name of my tailor on a piece of paper and gave it to him.

The last week of August I underwent my second ear operation. That time the trouble cleared up completely.

While I was convalescing, impatient to get back to the 94th and my Spad after almost three months of inactivity, a few of the pilots from the 94th dropped in for a visit. The news they brought from the squadron was bad. The 94th was not chalking up any victories.

"We wish you were back, Rick," one of them said. "Morale is low. We need a boost."

"We not only want you back; we want you back as commanding officer," another one said. "We've discussed this, and we're all in agreement. We want to go straight to Colonel Billy Mitchell and ask him to make you commanding officer of the 94th."

I was honored by their confidence. Though I knew from experience how the responsibilities of leadership could lead to uncomfortable moments in the air and could cut down on the number of personal victories, I would welcome the opportunity to lead the greatest fighting squadron in aviation history.

"If I am ordered to command the 94th squadron," I said, "I'll be proud to do so. But don't think that you'd have any gravy train with me as CO. I'd see to it that we all work, and work hard, at our primary job of fighting the Germans."

"That's okay with us," they all said. "That's all we have ever wanted, all along."

As events later revealed, it was not the period to discuss a personnel change with Billy Mitchell. He was, those first days of September 1918, planning the first great combined air-and-ground assault in the history of warfare. Air-power theorists had postulated such a campaign; now the flamboyant, volatile Mitchell put it into effect.

He was assigned the largest air force ever assembled—seven hundred fighters, four hundred observation planes and four hundred bombers—in support of five hundred thousand Allied troops in the attack on the German salient at Saint-Mihiel. The air mission was twofold. First, we were to contain all German planes within their own lines, preventing them from disrupting our own supply lines. Second, we were to cut off the Germans' rear by air as our ground forces pushed in on their front.

The weather, as usual, was lousy. It rained all morning of the first day of the offensive. All morning we heard the thunder of guns, but we were grounded. I fussed and fretted. About noon, when the other pilots were going into lunch, I grabbed Reed Chambers and suggested that we sneak upstairs for a look. Reed was always game, and we took off. Clouds were hanging at six hundred feet. We flew beneath them and had a good view of the show.

Our American doughboys were pushing in on both sides of the salient. We could see them moving forward. Their bayonets were fixed, and they were using them. They stormed the trenches, fighting with cold steel and rifle butts. From my comparatively safe place in the sky, I watched them with admiration. I have always maintained that American infantrymen were the heroes of the war and that Sergeant Alvin T. York, winner of the Congressional Medal of Honor, was the greatest hero of them all.

We could see the Germans beginning to pull out. They were hauling out all the supplies they could carry and burning the rest. One battery of horse-drawn artillery took up a half-mile of road. I nosed down, with Reed close behind, and sprayed the column with bullets. They ripped into men and horses; men fled, and horses stampeded.

"Now let's see you straighten up *that* mess," I thought as I turned away.

We hastened back to the field and phoned in information of the retreat to general headquarters. It was the news they had been waiting to hear. A colonel came on the line, and I gave him the exact coordinates of the column. A barrage of long-range artillery was laid down on the train of supplies behind the bottleneck we had created. Subsequent flights showed the success of the barrage; abandoned wagons, guns and supplies choked the artery completely.

The next day dawned bright and clear. I could hear the drone of bombers to the north, proceeding in the direction of Metz to seal off the German rear with bombs. I took off alone about 8:00. Over Pont-à-Mousson, south of Metz on the Moselle, I saw a group of American DH-4s returning from their mission. They came on majestically through the sky at twelve thousand feet. As I approached the group I saw, streaking after them, four Fokker D-7s. I climbed into the sun, let them pass under me, then dived on them. At fifty yards I fired a burst into the last one. The pilot never knew what hit him.

The other three turned to the right in a climbing banked turn. The sun glinted off their scarlet noses. I felt a little chill. Those red noses identified the most famous squadron in the war, the dread "Flying Circus" of Manfred von Richthofen, the Red Baron. Von Richthofen was no more, but the Flying Circus maintained its pride, excellence and discipline.

And they outnumbered me three to one. Within two minutes, I recognized them as the finest fliers I had ever faced. I did some fancy flying too, from sheer fright. The four of us whipped our ships around through the air for several minutes. They wanted to shoot me down; I wanted to get away. Suddenly an opportunity appeared beneath me. I turned my nose straight down and pulled the throttle wide open. It was for just such a moment that my mechanics and I had babied this engine, and now it delivered. We quickly pulled away. I hurried home to announce my first victory over this elite squadron—and my escape.

The next day I brought down another Fokker in the same area. It was my seventh victory. It would give me the most envied title of the war—"American Ace of Aces." It was an honor for which I had risked my life many times, but I had a strange feeling of dread. Four other fliers had held that title. All were dead. The honor carried the curse of death.

The two victories were confirmed immediately.

I was American Ace of Aces.

In my enthusiasm at succeeding to the title, I did not overlook the more significant victory of the Allies at Saint-Mihiel. The entire salient was wiped out. The Air Service had, for the first time, played a major role in a major campaign. Air power had wrought damage on and behind the lines, but, equally important, it had destroyed the morale of the enemy as well. American planes had ranged far behind the German rear, strafing, causing panic and bringing about the surrender of sixteen thousand German troops. Billy Mitchell was promoted to brigadier general and put in command of all Allied air operations.

My reign as American Ace of Aces was only temporary. The incredible Frank Luke, the most daring aviator of the entire war, went on a rampage at that time and shot down fourteen enemy aircraft, including ten balloons, in eight days. No other ace— Britain's Bishop, from Canada; France's Fonck, or even the dread Von Richthofen—had ever come close to that.

Then Luke succumbed to the curse of the title of "American Ace of Aces" and to his own incredible daring. On his last flight, he burned up three German balloons and was strafing a gun emplacement when a bullet hit him in the chest. He bounced his plane down in a clearing behind the lines. We learned later that he had crawled out of the plane, .45 automatic in hand, and waited for the Germans to come. A platoon of infantry arrived, surrounded him and called on him to surrender. Luke could have spent the rest of the war in comparative comfort. Instead he emptied his .45 at the enemy. They cut him to pieces. For his exploit that day he was awarded the Congressional Medal of Honor posthumously, the first flier to win the nation's highest award. After his death I again became the American with the most victories—and the title "American Ace of Aces."

Any envy I might have felt for the balloon buster was swept away on September 24. I was named commanding officer of the Hat-in-the-Ring Squadron.

I was simultaneously proud and humble. I thought of the great pilots who had made their contribution to this fighting squadron —Raoul Lufbery, Jimmy Hall, Dave Peterson, Doug Campbell, Walter Smyth. Now only three of those who had served in the 94th since the early days were left on active duty—Reed Chambers, Thorne Taylor and I.

The 94th had led all other squadrons in victories. On the day I assumed command, however, the 27th, thanks to Frank Luke's magnificent string, was six victories ahead of us. That situation was not going to continue. I do not like to come in second.

I called my nineteen pilots together and told them what I expected of them. The first thing was to help me put the 94th back in number-one position.

How would we do that? I passed along some of the techniques that I had worked out. From then on all pilots and their crews would follow my procedures to prevent gun jamming. I was getting one hundred hours out of my engine between major overhauls, whereas the rest of the squadron was averaging only about fourteen. When I needed maximum power in combat, my engine gave it to me. It could mean the difference between victory and defeat. "Baby your engines," I told them. "Do not run all out when it is not necessary. Save that reserve for when you need it. Take care of your engine, and your engine will take care of you."

We had no time to waste on military folderol. "I want no saluting, no unnecessary deference to rank. We're all in this together, pilots and mechanics. We need each other, and we're going to work together as equals, each man doing his job."

I assured my pilots that I would be a flying leader, a fighting leader. I would never ask anyone to fly a mission that I would not fly. When the request came down from headquarters for volunteers to fly a hazardous mission, I would be the first to volunteer, and only then would I ask others to join me. I gave them my assurance, proved on many missions as a flight leader, that I would never turn back from a mission but would lead them into combat and stick with them.

I warned each man to keep himself in perfect physical condition. There would be no drinking 24 hours before a mission, not even a glass of wine. Even a thimbleful of alcohol might tend to reduce the amount of built-in caution that each pilot should take with him on a combat mission.

Then I called on the other pilots for suggestions. Every man spoke up, some with excellent suggestions, all with pledges of support. I wound up the meeting with an old-fashioned exhortation to each man to give his best for America, for the Allied cause and for the best squadron ever to fly the skies, our 94th!

I held a similar meeting for the mechanics and ground crews. They too backed me to a man. Before turning in that night, I made a brief entry in my personal diary. I wrote: "Just been promoted to command of 94th squadron. I shall never ask a pilot to go on any mission I won't go on. I must work now harder than I did before."

I underlined that last sentence.

The best time to begin a new course of action is immediately. On the morning of my first full day as commander of the 94th, I set out early in the morning on a one-man mission over the lines. It was a wonderful day to celebrate a promotion. The sun was bright and the sky a brilliant blue. All I needed was a few German planes.

Over Verdun, I spotted them coming. Two LVG two-seater photographic planes were heading toward our lines. Above and behind them were five Fokkers, flying protection. I was east of them, in the glare of the sun. All seven went by underneath me. I cut back the engine and dived silently on the last Fokker. He glanced behind him at the same moment that I pressed my triggers. He tried to pull away, and that was his last living act.

The other four seemed to go to pieces. Instead of taking advantage of their superior numbers and attacking me, they fell off to the left and right, breaking up their own formation. I saw a narrow aperture leading to the photographic planes below. I slipped through and plunged after them. They had put their noses down and were trying to get away. The rear gunners were firing back at me. I dived under the tail of the nearest plane so that it blocked the gunner's fire. Then I zoomed up at his underbelly.

The pilot had obviously been in combat before. He kicked his tail around and gave his gunner a good shot at me. I had to stop pressing the attack in order to dodge. The other two-seater had circled behind me. A string of bullets went by my face so close that I could have reached out and caught them. I turned off and headed for the first plane, but before I could get him in my sights the second was on my tail again.

We went through this same maneuver over and over. It was working to my disadvantage, for the two LVGs were steadily retreating deeper and deeper behind their own lines. I should have quit when I was ahead. I had gotten a Fokker and foiled their photographic mission, but I still wanted one more plane: a doubleheader before breakfast.

The two-seaters were only fifty feet apart, and I was directly above them. I sideslipped my Spad to the right. One plane shielded me from the other. I leveled out, kicked my nose around to the left and began firing. The nearest LVG sailed right on through my bullets. It burst into flames and tumbled like a great glazing torch to earth, leaving a streamer of black smoke against the blue sky.

The four Fokkers finally awakened to their responsibility and came screaming down. I put my little Spad in a steep bank, gave it all she had and headed for home.

I landed at 9:30, stripped off my suit and hollered for Reed Chambers; the two of us jumped into the nearest automobile and headed for the front to get confirmation. Two hundred yards from the front we were halted by a French sentry, who said that the road was under artillery fire. Asked if he had seen the combat overhead that morning, he nodded his head enthusiastically, said "Oui, Capitaine" a half dozen times and added that the officers in the fort up ahead had also seen it. Reed and I dodged through the shell holes on foot. The French commandant wrote out the details of the two air victories and gave me a congratulatory handshake. We started back to the car.

I heard a strange whining noise. The next second an explosion knocked both of us down and kicked up a shower of dirt and rocks. Each time we started to make a run for it, the sound of another coming shell flattened us out again. Finally, we sprinted across the pockmarked terrain for our car and reached it safely.

Reed and I returned before noon. It had been a good morning's work. Two more confirmed victories were posted on our bulletin board. I had proved to the men that I meant my pledge of leadership. In 1930 this double victory brought me the nation's highest military award, the Congressional Medal of Honor.

My pilots had a chance to prove themselves the next day. September 26 was the beginning of the Allied offensive in the Argonne Forest. Our duty was to render ineffective the German observation balloons all along the front. I led a flight of five planes out before dawn. As we neared the front, we flew over the most fantastic fireworks display I have ever seen. The Allies were laying down an artillery barrage before the infantry attack. As far as I could see in either direction extended a solid belt of flashes, lighting up the world.

As I watched, I saw bigger bursts from high behind the German lines. German balloons were being shot down. The balloon that I had chosen for myself exploded in a great burst of light before I could fire. I glanced to my right and saw another airplane silhouetted against the artillery-illuminated sky. It was a Fokker. It was also a shock. The Germans rarely came out that early, and I had not been on the alert.

This one was looking for a fight. He gunned his plane, went out ahead, banked around and came at me head on. We both started firing at the same time. My ammunition was all incendiary, for I had come out to get a balloon. The German's ammunition was mixed. The four streams of bullets seemed to tie us together with ropes of fire.

We were coming together at a combined speed of four miles a minute. I thought that he had better get the hell out of my way. I certainly was not going to get out of his. Just as we were about to crash head on, he dived under my plane. I immediately put my Spad into a *renversement*—pulled the stick straight back to start a loop and simultaneously rolled it over in a half turn. I came over on his tail right side up and ready to shoot. I gave him a long burst of bullets. He began the long fall down.

My engine began vibrating so badly that it almost tore itself out of the frame. I throttled down. The plane continued to shake, but I could not cut the engine off all the way because I was still over German-held territory. I prayed that the thing would hold together long enough for me to make it back over the lines. I knew that there was a field only three miles within Allied territory, and, nursing the shot-up little ship along, I reached it and fluttered down. I climbed out and walked around to the front of the plane. There was just enough light in the early dawn to reveal that half my propeller blade was gone. That German had shot it off.

There were bullet holes all over the Spad. I counted a dozen or more holes within a four-foot radius of the center of the airplane. One hole was through the little quarter-moon isinglass windshield right in front of my face. I squinted through it. The line of sight led just exactly to where my forehead would be. Why hadn't it hit me?

Alone at dawn, I tried to figure it out. Then it came to me. Years before a hot cinder from a railroad locomotive had stuck in my right eye. A doctor had gouged it out, leaving a little black spot. My vision had not been affected, but I always favored my right eye.

The gun sights on a Spad were on the right side of the cockpit. If I had sighted with my right eye, as most pilots did, my head would be more or less in the center. But, because of that cinder, I had gotten in the habit of putting my left eye on the sights. That moved my head three inches to the right. I took off my helmet and looked at it. A scorched streak ran along the left side. That is how close it had been.

The mechanics at the field installed a new propeller for me, and by 8:30 my bullet-riddled little Spad was home again. A wild, shouting bunch of pilots ran out to greet me. Our First-Pursuit group had shot down ten balloons that morning. The 94th's total haul was two balloons and two Fokkers, including mine. What a day!

People unfamiliar with air combat in World War I may understandably tend to minimize the hazards involved in shooting down observation balloons. Hit one with an incendiary, and poof! It's all over. But give me an airplane as an adversary any day.

Balloons were important in World War I. From an altitude of two thousand feet on a clear day an observer with a telescope, comfortable in his wicker basket slung from the balloon, could see many miles into the enemy's rear. He was connected with the ground by telephone, and within seconds after he had made an observation the news was on the way to headquarters. The airplane observer, on the other hand, had to fly back to his field and land in order to report.

Balloons came complete with crews and trucks. They were anchored by steel cables played out on winches. They were usually let up in the morning and hauled down at night. The observers rode with them.

Balloons were ringed with antiaircraft batteries. It is true that pilots played down the effectiveness of antiaircraft. I knew of only one man brought down by Archie, and that was a freak and tragic accident. The victim was Lieutenant Hamilton Coolidge, a fine pilot and a highly respected individual. The shell that hit him was timed to burst at a much higher altitude than that at which Ham was flying. It did not explode but struck the plane like a projectile and knocked it to pieces. Ham fell to his death in the wreck. No, we had little respect for antiaircraft—unless it was protecting a balloon.

For in that case, there was no guesswork about the proper altitude for which to time the fuses. If the balloon was two thousand feet up, then any airplane attacking it must also be at or near the same altitude. When we came in to attack a balloon, therefore, we flew through a curtain of shells exploding at our precise altitude. We had to fly at that altitude for several seconds, for it took a long burst to ignite the gas—often it would not ignite at all. After the attack it was necessary to fly out through the wall of Archie on the other side.

Finally, balloons were of such military importance that, frequently, flights of Fokkers would be hovering above them, hiding up there in the sun. Again the fixed altitude of the attack added to the hazard. They always had the advantage over us.

Before I assumed command of the 94th, Reed Chambers and I had made an exhaustive study of the balloon situation. We obtained photographs of the German balloons in our sector and studied them, then flew over the balloons to make further investigations. We worked out what we thought was a foolproof attack plan and, with three other pilots, set out on a simultaneous dawn attack on five German Drachen.

We did not get one single balloon, even though three of us had actually pumped bullets into our targets. Comparing notes on the amount of Archie we had flown through, we all agreed that we were lucky to get back to the field alive.

The day after our tremendous success in destroying the balloons in our sector, I went on a lone patrol that took me behind the German lines. On the way home, flying low and looking for something to strafe, I suddenly came upon a new balloon being taken up to the lines. Its altitude was only five hundred feet. It was right in my path, and with no hesitation I attacked. I let off a burst of at least fifty incendiaries before pulling up.

But I was flying right in the path of the machine gun protecting it. As I pulled up, something exploded just behind my head. An explosive bullet had obviously hit something. I looked back. The balloon was still there, but the observer was in the act of diving out of his basket head first. I hoped his parachute would open in time. And just then that huge thing burst into a ball of flame.

At the field, I looked over my plane. Four inches behind my head rest was a bullet hole, and a neat row of holes extended on down the length of the plane. The explosive bullet had hit the longeron just behind me. I was beginning to get used to those near misses.

Those were hectic days. I put in six or seven hours of flying time each day. I would come down, gulp a couple of cups of coffee while the mechanics refueled the plane and patched the bullet holes and take off again. I caught an unguarded balloon while returning from a night mission, and Reed Chambers and I together brought down a Hanover. With the dead pilot at the controls, it glided to a perfect landing two miles within our own lines. We hurried to claim it and had it hauled back to our own field. Then Reed and I each dropped a Fokker in the same dog-fight. I shot down a German plane so far behind the lines that the victory was never confirmed. Our 94th squadron pulled out well ahead of the 27th, and after that our lead was never threatened.

In my 134 air battles, my narrowest escape came at a time when I was fretting over the lack of action. I was out alone one afternoon, looking for anything to shoot at. There was a thick haze over the valley of the Meuse, however, and the Germans had pulled down their balloons. To the south the weather seemed a little better; the American balloons were still up. German planes rarely came over late in the afternoon, and everyone had relaxed his vigilance. As I was flying toward the nearest Allied balloon, I saw it burst into flames. A German plane had obviously made a successful attack. Because of the bend in the lines of the front at that point, I saw that I could cut off the Boche on his return to his own territory. I had the altitude on him and, consequently, a superior position. I headed confidently to our rendezvous.

Guns began barking behind me, and sizzling tracers zipped by my head. I was taken completely by surprise. At least two planes were on my tail. They had me cold. They had probably been watching me for several minutes and planning this whole thing.

They would expect me to dive. Instead I twisted upward in a corkscrew path called a "chandelle." I guessed right. As I went up, my two attackers came down, near enough for me to see their faces. I also saw the red noses on those Fokkers. I was up against the Flying Circus again.

I had outwitted them. Two more red noses were sitting above me on the chance that I might just do the unexpected.

Any time one plane is up against four and the four are flown by pilots of such caliber, the smart thing to do is to get away from there. There is an old saying that it's no disgrace to run if you are scared.

I zigzagged and sideslipped, but the two planes on top of me hung on, and the two underneath remained there. They were daring me to attack, in which case the two above would be on my tail in seconds. They were blocking me from making a dash for home. I was easy meat sandwiched between two pairs of experts. Sooner or later one would spot an opening and close in.

For a split second one of the Fokkers beneath me became vulnerable. I instantly tipped over, pulled back the throttle and dived on him. As my nose came down I fired a burst ahead of him. Perhaps he did not see the string of bullets. At any rate, he flew right into them. Several must have passed through his body. An incendiary hit his gas tank, and in seconds a flaming Fokker was earthbound.

If I had been either of the two Fokkers above me in such a situation, I would have been on my tail at that very moment. I pulled the stick back in a loop and came over in a renversement, and there they were. Before I could come close enough to shoot, they turned and fled. I suppose that the sight of that blazing plane took some of the fight out of them.

It did not take any fight out of me. I started chasing all three of them back into Germany. We were already three miles behind the lines, but I was annoyed—with them and with myself.

My Spad was faster. One Fokker began to fall behind. He tried a shallow dive to gain speed, but I continued to close in. We were only about a thousand feet up. He began stunting, but I stuck with him and fired a burst of about two hundred shots. He nosed over and crashed. I watched him hit.

All around the crashed plane, I saw flashes of fire and smoke. I was only about five hundred feet above the deck, and the Germans on the ground were shooting at me with all the weapons they had. I could see their white faces above the flashes. The air around me must have been full of flying objects. I got out of there fast and went home to report that I had blundered into a trap and had come out of it with two victories. I now had nineteen.

During the month of October the fortunes of war shifted both on the ground and in the air. From the air we could see the German ground forces retreating, sometimes in complete disorganization. Our bombers were carrying the fight into Germany, and large numbers of German fighters were pulled back from the front in an effort to protect the civilian population.

All along the lines the feeling was growing that the war was coming to an end. I took a 3-day leave in Paris and, for the first time, found the streets illuminated at night and unrestrained gaiety.

During the month of October, I shot down fourteen enemy aircraft. On the 30th I got my twenty-fifth and twenty-sixth victories, my last of the war. My title "American Ace of Aces" was undisputed. The last victory for the 94th Squadron came on November 10. The Hat-in-the-Ring Squadron downed 69 Boche planes, more than any other American unit.

On the night of the 10th a group of us was discussing the next day's mission when the phone rang. An almost hysterical voice shouted the news in my ear: At 11:00 the following morning, the war would end. Our mission was called off. For us the war ended at that moment.

I dropped the phone and turned to face my pilots. Everyone sensed the importance of that phone call. There was total silence in the room.

"The war is over!" I shouted. At that moment the antiaircraft battalion that ringed our field fired off a salvo that rocked the building. We all went a little mad. Shouting and screaming like crazy men, we ran to get whatever firearms we had, including flare pistols, and began blasting up into the sky. It was already bright up there. As far as we could see the sky was filled with exploding shells and rockets, star shells, parachute flares, streams of Very lights and searchlights tracing crazy patterns. Machine guns hammered; big guns boomed. What a night!

A group of men came out of the hangar, rolling barrels of gasoline in front of them. Perhaps I should have made an effort to stop them, but instead I ran over and helped. We dumped them in an open place, and I struck the match myself. Up roared a bonfire that could be seen for miles. We danced around that blazing pyre screaming, shouting and beating one another on the back. One pilot kept shouting over and over and over, "I've lived through the war, I've lived through the war!"

Somebody emptied every bottle of liquor he could find into a huge kettle, and the orderlies served it in coffee cups, including themselves in. For months these twenty combat pilots had been living at the peak of nervous energy, the total meaning of their lives to kill or be killed. Now this tension exploded like the guns blasting around us.

We all ran over to the 95th Squadron. They had a piano, and somebody sat down and began banging the keys. We began dancing or simply jumping up and down. Somebody slipped and fell, and everyone else fell on him, piling up in a pyramid. A volunteer band started playing in the area outside. We ran outside again to continue our dancing and jumping and shrieking under the canopy of bursting rockets. Again somebody went down, and again we all piled on and made a human pyramid, this time bigger and better and muddier, a monument to the incredible fact that we had lived until now and were going to live again tomorrow.

In the morning orders came down that all pilots should stay on the ground. It was a muggy, foggy day. About 10:00 I sauntered out to the hangar and casually told my mechanics to take the plane out on the line and warm it up to test the engines. Without announcing my plans to anyone, I climbed into the plane and took off. Under the low ceiling I hedgehopped towards the front. I arrived over Verdun at 10:45 and proceeded on toward Conflans, flying over no-man's-land. I was at less than five hundred feet. I could see both Germans and Americans crouching in their trenches, peering over with every intention of killing any man who revealed himself on the other side. From time to time ahead of me on the German side I saw a burst of flame, and I knew that they were firing at me. Back at the field later I found bullet holes in my ship.

I glanced at my watch. One minute to 11:00, thirty seconds, fifteen. And then it was 11:00 A.M., the eleventh hour of the eleventh day of the eleventh month. I was the only audience for the greatest show ever presented. On both sides of no-man's-land, the trenches erupted. Brown-uniformed men poured out of the American trenches, gray-green uniforms out of the German. From my observer's seat overhead, I watched them throw their helmets in the air, discard their guns, wave their hands. Then all up and down the front, the two groups of men began edging toward each other across no-man's-land. Seconds before they had been willing to shoot each other; now they came forward. Hesitantly at first, then more quickly, each group approached the other.

Suddenly gray uniforms mixed with brown. I could see them hugging each other, dancing, jumping. Americans were passing out cigarettes and chocolate. I flew up to the French sector. There it was even more incredible. After four years of slaughter and hatred, they were not only hugging each other but kissing each other on both cheeks as well.

Star shells, rockets and flares began to go up, and I turned my ship toward the field. The war was over.

SEVEN

THE CAR WORTHY OF ITS NAME

Out on the desert the air is clear and pure. The loneliness is absolute. In the late summer of 1919, I wandered over its limitless expanse, aimless and unhurried. At night, snug in my sleeping bag, I would look up at the glorious mystery of the brilliant stars and dream and think and plan without pressure or tension.

Alone under the stars, I readjusted my mind to serving mankind constructively in peace, rather than through destruction in war, and stabilized my nerves and physical condition. I had been living under great pressure for the past few years. In my continuing competition with the Grim Reaper, I had endured 134 aerial encounters in which other humans tried to shoot me down. I made no effort even to guess at the number of times I had been shot at. So many close calls renewed my thankfulness to the Power above, which had seen fit to preserve me.

When the war was over I sometimes wondered which was worse, combat or the onslaught of well-wishers, hero-worshippers and fast-buck operators. I had never sought to become a hero, only to serve my country. I knew that with the title "American

Ace of Aces" would come an awesome responsibility. Because of it I now represented the spirit of American aviation, especially to the youth of the nation, and I must never permit that image to be cheapened. I knew that it would be easy to go from hero to zero.

While I was still in Europe after the Armistice, Edgar Wolfe, a member of the Wolfe publishing dynasty of Columbus, had crossed the Atlantic to present me with an unusual opportunity. The Wolfes wanted to head a public subscription drive to buy a home for my family and me in Columbus. I had to decline. Although I was proud of my birthplace, I did not plan to live there the balance of my life.

Against my personal wishes, I was separated from my beloved Hat-in-the-Ring Squadron in January 1919 and brought home to assist in the Liberty Bond drive. Reporters, photographers, agents, committees, friends and curiosity-seekers met the ship at the dock. Wherever I went, I was the center of a small mob scene. Promoters offered me huge sums of money to endorse various products—cigarettes, chewing gum, wearing apparel. Of course I refused. Publishers were after me to have my story "ghosted" by any one of a number of prominent writers. I refused them too, although later I did write my memoirs of World War I, *Fighting the Flying Circus*. It went through many printings and was brought out again in 1965.

Theatrical agents tried to book me for vaudeville tours, and scores of get-rich-quick schemes were presented. Finally, a group of friends actually locked me up in the Knickerbocker Hotel for my own protection.

The most persistent pursuer was Carl Laemmle, the head of Universal Studios, who wanted me to appear in a motion picture. He approached me himself several times, and his assistant Irving Thalberg actually followed me around the country, booking compartments next to mine on trains and rooms next to mine in hotels. On one occasion, he produced a certified check for $100,000 made out to me.

By that time I was pretty nearly broke, as my savings had

gone to support my family during the war, but I never considered accepting the offer. I could just see myself up there on the screen making movie love to some heroine. I was fully aware of my potential influence upon the youth of America, and I intended to continue to do my best to inspire them by both deeds and words. Depicting myself in the movies, I felt, would degrade both my own stature and the uniform I so proudly wore. The studio continued to pester me until I threatened suit to make Laemmle leave me alone.

There were many attractive offers, of course. I could have written my own ticket as a racing driver with nearly any automobile manufacturer. I had, however, determined not to return to racing. I had garnered enough glory; it presented no further challenge, and I could make no further contribution. As to the other propositions, I had plenty of time to consider them during the Liberty Bond tour.

It had not occurred to me that the tour might be a difficult job. I hadn't been shy speaking to my racing crew or to the 94th Squadron. But on February 3, 1919, I found out how little I really knew about public speaking. That was the night of the first banquet held in my honor after my return from World War I, given by a group of automobile associations at the old Waldorf-Astoria Hotel in New York.

Representative Clifford Ireland, Chairman of the House Ways and Means Committee, was toastmaster, and one of the many speakers was Secretary of War Newton D. Baker. I will never forget that part of his speech in which he said:

Captain Rickenbacker is one of the real crusaders of America—one of the truest knights our country has ever known. He will find his greatest delight, when the evening of his life comes, in looking back on his experiences. He will never forget the thrill of combat in the clouds where it was his life or his adversary's. He will always know this thrill even when he awakes from his deepest sleep. But his life will always be gladened as he looks about him and sees men and women and children walking about free and unafraid and when he thinks that he has given his best and ventured his own life to bring this about.

The featured speaker was Dr. Henry van Dyke of Princeton University, one of the great orators of the day. At the conclusion of his address, an oration filled with poetic phraseology and delivered in impassioned style, I was presented with a pair of jeweled wings and called upon to respond. I had never before known such a moment of helplessness. Standing before that august assemblage I became frightened and embarrassed.

Looking in confusion about the room, my eye fell on my mother, who was described in a newspaper article the following day as "a beaming little woman in black silk whose eyes shone proudly through gold-rimmed spectacles." On a sudden impulse, I held out the jeweled wings in her direction and said, "For you, Mother." Then I sat down.

Everyone present, ladies and gentlemen alike, rose to his feet and applauded. Some stood on chairs and tables. I saw tears on the cheeks of both men and women. We were living in an emotional period, and that was one of its great moments. My sincere love and appreciation for my mother, coupled with blind luck, had enabled me to make the perfect response.

But even then I realized that I could hardly repeat that performance on my forthcoming tour. I would have to prepare a moving speech and deliver it properly.

In the meantime, sitting next to Secretary Baker, I tentatively suggested a project that Reed Chambers and I had discussed and that General Billy Mitchell had informally approved: a transatlantic flight to prove the feasibility of air transportation. Mitchell had recommended a three- or four-engine plane and warned that a successful flight could be made only with governmental resources. Baker listened to me about thirty seconds, then politely indicated that the government couldn't care less. His speech that night was the first public exoneration of those industrial leaders entrusted with the aviation program during the war. Baker denied the charges of corruption and chicanery, and I agreed. The miserable failure of the American aviation effort was caused by lack of foresight and mismanagement but not by corruption.

Baker did invite me to come to Washington and discuss military aviation with interested parties. I spent a week with congressional and military leaders. I pulled no punches, pointing out that American equipment was inferior to that of England, France, Germany, even Italy. I believe that these discussions did help in some way, although it would be hard to prove in the light of ensuing developments or lack of developments in American aviation. The idea of a transatlantic flight received no encouragement.

The week of high-level discussions heightened my determination to take a greater interest in my country's affairs. It represented a postwar mood shared by hundreds of thousands of other American veterans. One of the results was the formation of the American Legion, through which those of us who had served our country could present a unified voice.

I was proud to be one of the charter members of the American Legion. Years later one of the greatest honors of my life came when I was chosen honorary national president of the Society of American Legion Founders at their annual dinner in Dallas, Texas, on September 19, 1964. General John J. Pershing was the first to hold that office, General Douglas MacArthur was the second and I was the third. Tenure is ended only by death.

In the meantime I was getting nowhere with the speech I would deliver on the Bond tour. At that time writing speeches was hardly my line. In desperation, I called on Damon Runyon, the great newspaper reporter and short-story writer. We had become good friends in France, where he had been a war correspondent. The speech that resulted was perfect.

Runyon also showed me how to remember it by writing each major subject on an individual card. As I finished each subject, I would put that card in my pocket and look at the next.

My delivery was flat and dull. Damon specified that I should describe some technical maneuvers extemporaneously, in my own words, and I could see him wince as I tried these passages out on him. At that time my vocabulary still contained the word "ain't," and I am afraid that I mispronounced a word here and there too.

To correct these defects, Damon sent me to an elocution teacher at the Metropolitan Opera House in New York. She was a stout woman. She stood me on the stage, while she perched in the topmost balcony—she called it the "chicken roost." I would then shout my speech up at her, and she would bellow instructions down at me.

"Louder!" she would shout. "Raise your right arm . . . Raise your left arm . . . Look up!" She corrected my English and recommended a book called *Modern Eloquence*. I memorized passages from it and practiced in front of a mirror. I also bought and studied a book on etiquette. I had much to learn, and I knew it.

The first major stop on the Bond tour was Symphony Hall in Boston. Six thousand people were there. I was scared to death—until the Governor of Massachusetts, Calvin Coolidge, started introducing me. He spoke in a high, whiny voice, and his delivery seemed to me to be worse than mine. If he could get to be governor, then I had no worries. Years later, when he was President, I visited him at the White House and told him that he was one of the great inspirations of my life and why. It was one of the few times I saw Silent Cal smile.

The next night was in Worcester, Massachusetts. The man chosen to introduce me had attended the Boston appearance. In his introduction, he talked for half an hour, practically repeating my speech word for word. I had to think out a new speech as he talked.

I didn't want it to happen again. In Omaha I learned that I would be introduced by a long-winded local gentleman. I called some of my friends there and asked them to bring their children and sit them in the front row. Sure enough, the introduction began turning into an oration. After a few minutes, I deliberately uncrossed my legs. That was the signal. The youngsters started shouting: "We want Rick! We want Rick!"

My long-winded friend wound up his introduction in a hurry.

Several cities in which I had raced—Indianapolis, Detroit, Sioux City, Dallas and Los Angeles, in particular—considered me a hometown boy and insisted that I make official homecoming visits. The delegation from Los Angeles had met me at the boat, and when I did not accept its invitation immediately the Mayor sent me a long telegram. It accused me, between the lines, of thinking I was too good to come to Los Angeles. I wired back the hour and the day that I would arrive.

That Los Angeles celebration outdid them all. The official program had full-page advertisements from all the movie stars. The day began with a barbecue given by the Elks Lodge and attended by thousands. In the parade I rode in a mock-up of an airplane covered completely with flowers. It was stunningly beautiful, but I felt like an idiot riding in it for three hours.

In practically every city there were old friends with marriageable daughters. I managed to avoid getting involved.

Little incidents for which I was totally unprepared kept happening all the time. On my first visit home to Columbus the Pullman conductor shoved a $20 bill at me and asked me to autograph it. I thought it a strange use for good money, but I complied. He showed the bill along the train, and people waving bills of all denominations descended on my compartment. I signed my name on money half the way to Columbus.

A song entitled "I'm Glad To Be Back in the USA," with my picture on the cover, sold ten thousand copies in Columbus alone. Years later, incidentally, not one single copy could be found.

The frenzy, the adulation, the pressure were all taking their toll. One night, sound asleep in an upper berth, I got in a terrific dogfight in the skies over France. I pulled my ship up into a loop, and the next thing I knew I was in the aisle of the Pullman car. It was a good 5-foot drop. I continued sleepwalking for years, until I fell off a 25-foot balcony. After that I called upon mental discipline to control the problem and was no longer bothered.

When the Bond tour ended, I was released from active duty with the rank of major. I never used the title. I felt that my rank of captain was earned and deserved, and that is what I have been called ever since.

I realized that before entering civilian life I had better take time to clarify my thoughts and determine what I was going to do. A friend in New Mexico had asked me to visit him. After a few days there, I bought a secondhand flivver, a sleeping bag and a complete grubstake and took off alone into the desert. For a period of six weeks I would repeatedly spend a day or two, sometimes a full week, in the desert, relaxing and thinking about what I was going to do.

I did not want to return to racing or to take any position offered on the basis of my publicity value. I was interested in both military and commercial aviation, but it had been pretty well demonstrated to me in Washington that, although I was ready for aviation, it was not yet ready for me.

For years, one of my most steadfast aspirations had been to build an automobile of my own design. In it I would incorporate all the new features and developments that automotive designers, engineers and factories were then capable of producing. One of my reasons for changing racing cars so frequently had been to study the different designs and performances. In quiet days on the front I had thought about building an automobile—and building it under my name. In the quiet of the desert, I decided that what I wanted to do was to build the Rickenbacker automobile.

First, the car should have a high-speed motor. There was none on the market at that time. I believed that I could overcome the objections—excessive vibration and gasoline consumption —through engineering improvements that I had in mind. Second, it should have a lower center of gravity for both safety and comfort. I was positive that a double-drop frame could be designed to make it possible.

The most dramatic Rickenbacker innovation would be the introduction of a four-wheel brake system. I was convinced, through my experience with racing cars, that four-wheel brakes would be an absolute must on the automobile of the future.

I came away from New Mexico with my future charted. I would build an automobile, an automobile named "Rickenbacker," an automobile worthy of its name.

Detroit was the automotive capital then as now. One of my

first contacts was with an old friend named Harry Cunningham, a former racing driver, a creative engineer and entrepreneur and a great salesman. Cunningham had had a successful agency for the EMF automobile. The EMF's name came from the initials of three well-known automotive executives, Barney Everitt, William Metzger and Walter E. Flanders, who built it. The EMF company had been purchased by the Studebaker Corporation when the famous old wagon company decided to bring out a horseless carriage, and the EMF had become the Studebaker.

Everitt's primary interest was in automotive bodies. Flanders was a production genius. It was he who was actually responsible for the famous Ford assembly line. Metzger was practically retired. It was thus Cunningham, Flanders and Everitt who became my partners in building the Rickenbacker.

It would be a six-cylinder car in the middle price bracket, between $1,500 and $2,000. There was no point in competing with Henry Ford's Model T for the low-cost customer, and Cadillac and Packard shared the limited high-priced field. Our car would appeal to the white-collar worker, the junior executive, the fairly prosperous farmer and the woman of taste. Finally, it would earn the appreciation of anyone who recognized fine engineering and workmanship.

After weeks of planning, in which I am sure we used up a ton of paper drawing designs, work started on the prototype early in 1920. The first two cars were built practically by hand. Although I kept in close touch, it was Cunningham, not I, who looked after the details. I was not even in Detroit.

I realized that my greatest contribution would be in sales. I was therefore not the president of the Rickenbacker Motor Company, but the vice-president and director of sales. Everitt was president. It had been a long time since I had sold automobiles, and I needed a refresher course. General Motors had just introduced the four-cylinder Sheridan and had no California distributor. I applied for the agency and won it.

I arrived in San Francisco in December 1920. The postwar depression was beginning, and well-known makes of automobiles were meeting sales resistance. Under such conditions I was to introduce and sell an unknown product.

One way to publicize the new car was obvious: aviation. I would be the first sales supervisor to cover my area by plane. The only ship available was an Italian single-seat plane, a Bellanca, owned by a small San Francisco corporation. I had an American six-cylinder engine installed and arranged to lease the plane when I needed it. I would fly into a California community, land on the cow pasture nearest town and be met by the Sheridan dealer in a new automobile. Naturally there would be pictures taken for the newspapers, and people would start talking Sheridan.

In establishing a new dealership, we worked out a simple but effective method of advertising. For days in advance, we would take a full-page advertisement saying, in big black letters, "Sheridan is Coming." Just as we had everybody talking about who Sheridan might be, we would run a full-page ad saying, "Sheridan is here," with a photograph of the automobile. In my first year in California I built up an organization of 27 dealers and sold more than seven hundred cars.

We made plenty of mistakes. Some of my dealers were not aggressive; others made too many wild trades. Others gave poor service and maintenance. It was up to me to apply the remedy for each failure. That was why I was there. I wound up with more than fifty dealers in the state and sales figures in the thousands.

In the meantime, I was making regular trips back to Detroit. I test-drove the Rickenbacker for many thousands of miles myself, on the hot plains of Texas, on the gumbo roads of Nebraska and Iowa, through the snows of Minnesota, across the mountains of Montana. It stood up.

But I was still not satisfied. We were planning to sell our car not to expert test drivers but to average motorists. While my impatient partners fretted, I put the car in the hands of a group of people who had never driven before. Again it stood up.

The delay worked to our benefit. The depression continued

through 1921 and 1922. They were not years in which to bring out a new automobile. In the fall of 1921 we sold about $5 million worth of stock to some thirteen thousand stockholders. My three partners and I retained about 25 percent of the total. Factory space was going begging, and we picked up an excellent building at a reasonable cost. Then we went to work producing automobiles.

The first Rickenbacker cars were shown at the New York Automobile Show of 1922. The three displayed represented not only the entire Rickenbacker line but also the entire output of the factory at that date. They were a touring car, which sold for $1,485; a coupé, for $1,885, and a sedan, for $1,995. All three were the most handsome automobiles of that day. They had automotive sex appeal. The new features—high-speed engine and low-slung body, among others—made sense to the car-buying public. People obviously believed our slogan, "A Car Worthy of Its Name," for the orders began pouring in.

Just as I had flown about California in the little Bellanca, so for the first year I flew over the entire United States in a big German aluminum Junkers, piloted by Eddie Stinson, setting up dealerships. Flying about the country was national news. On my visit a local delegation headed by the mayor would meet the plane at the field nearest to the city, usually a cow pasture, and one of the service clubs would arrange a gathering.

The car began to sell immediately. Not many cars had been sold in the past two years, and a natural market existed. We had a phenomenal growth; at its peak the Rickenbacker Motor Company had some 1,200 distributors and dealers in the United States and about 300 throughout the world. In our first two years we built and sold fifty thousand cars. Profits were low, for we had to build a better car and sell it for less in order to compete. Our original capitalization of $5 million was small potatoes compared to that of the big manufacturers.

But we had no complaints. Later we brought out a higher-priced model powered with a straight-eight engine, and it did well. Almost forty years later, incidentally, in 1963, I heard from an owner who still had one. He had put over two hundred thousand miles on it and said he was still getting excellent service out of it.

The Rickenbacker Motor Company did so well from the very beginning that, for the first time in my 31 years, I could dare to think about taking on the responsibilities of a wife and family. Because I was constantly on the road and because of the obligation to my mother and younger brothers and sisters back home in Columbus, it had not been possible for me to consider matrimony. Over the years, whenever anyone started talking to me about a sweetheart, I would always answer, "I have always had one, the most wonderful sweetheart in the world, my little mother."

After the war, at a party given by a friend in New York, I happened to see a young lady named Adelaide Frost Durant, whom I had met in California before the war. We had dinner together, and she later permitted me to escort her to a New Year's Eve party in New York.

And there Dan Cupid shot me down in flames. The romance began and blossomed into lasting love, admiration and respect. We were married on September 16, 1922. Pastor Jacob Pister, who had christened and confirmed me, performed the ceremony. We left immediately afterward for a 6-week honeymoon tour through Europe.

Our marriage has been a happy one from its beginning to the present. We have been blessed with two boys, David Edward, born January 4, 1925, and William Frost, born March 16, 1928. Note that neither is a "Junior." I have never liked the name "Eddie"—in my mind it depicts a little fellow—and I saw to it that neither of my boys would be so called.

Before I went to Europe for the auto show of 1923, I asked the office manager of the Rickenbacker Motor Company to employ a good secretary for me. When I returned from Europe, I found that my new secretary was Miss Marguerite Shepherd, an attractive, well-educated and serious young woman from Hamilton, Ontario, Canada.

I remember telling the office manager that I wanted someone willing to work and who wasn't interested in getting married for several years. Well those "several years" have, at this writing, stretched into 44 years of dedicated and loyal service. Day and night, weekends and holidays, whenever an emergency arose, "Sheppy," as she is known to thousands throughout the country, ungrudgingly performed whatever was required.

After several years as secretary, she became my personal office manager, personal accountant for Adelaide and me and practically a member of the family. She has been of particular help to Adelaide during my lengthy absences from home and the office occasioned by both duty and misfortune. Throughout the years, she has accumulated and documented my activities, good and bad, fortunate and unfortunate, as reported both in print and in photographs. This meticulously kept and thorough collection of material covering an entire lifetime has been of great value to me in composing this autobiography, and I give Sheppy due and honorable credit.

In 1924, despite some reluctance on the part of my partners, I determined that the time had arrived to bring out the world's first production passenger car equipped with four-wheel brakes. It is difficult today, after more than forty years of four-wheel brakes, to explain the pandemonium that the introduction of this eminently sensible braking system caused in the automotive industry. I had driven racing cars with four-wheel brakes and had personal proof of their superiority. To me it was a simple, straightforward matter of arithmetic: four is greater than two.

We secretly devised and manufactured a four-wheel brake system, mechanical rather than hydraulic, and tested and improved it until it was as dependable a system as could be built at that time. When we had a stock of automobiles equipped with four-wheel brakes on hand, we broke the news in full-page ads all over the United States and in every foreign country where we had dealers. It was the automotive sensation of the year.

What I did not realize in my bullheaded determination to bring the superiority of four-wheel brakes to the nation was that the other automobile companies could not afford to be taken unaware. The industry had hundreds of millions of dollars' worth of automobiles with two-wheel brakes in inventory or in production. There were cars in showrooms, cars in warehouses, cars en route to the dealers, cars on the assembly line and cars in pieces en route to the assembly line. To sell those cars the entire automotive industry had to convince the public that four-wheel brakes were inferior, even unsafe.

The Studebaker Corporation, a major manufacturer, took full-page ads in newspapers all across the country attacking the four-wheel brake system as extremely dangerous. In every community, all the other dealers and salesmen ganged up on the Rickenbacker car and its four-wheel brakes. Some said that the car would turn over on a curve when the brakes were applied. Others claimed that all four wheels would skid, rather than grip. Some said that the four-wheel brakes would stop the car too quickly, throwing the occupants up against the dashboard and injuring them.

Although there were some customers who were mechanically inclined or sophisticated enough generally to realize that four are better than two, the adverse publicity could not help but affect our sales. We could not return to two-wheel brakes, not after our glowing announcement of the superiority of four-wheel brakes. The other companies were feverishly retooling to bring out their own four-wheel brake systems anyway. The only thing to do was to stick it out and try to sell the cars we had. On top of everything else, the country entered a recession in 1925, and sales in general went down.

No automobile manufacturer is stronger than his dealers. They sell the cars. When the dealers are solvent, the company is solvent; when the dealers go broke, the company goes broke. Our dealers could not sell the car, and they were going broke. It was up to us to shore them up. I put all the money I had into the Rickenbacker Motor Company, and when that was gone I went out and borrowed more. I borrowed from banks and from suppliers. One single bank loan was $50,000. My total personal indebtedness came to $250,000.

The company continued to flounder. Dealers went out of business; the value of the stock went down. Walter Flanders was killed in an accident, and his loss was felt immediately.

I forced myself to realize that my dream bubble had blown up in my face. There was no hope of regaining the position we had held during our first years. As is normal when a company begins to go on the rocks, the leaders began squabbling among themselves. The only hope I could see for the company to survive was for me to leave it. Perhaps then a miracle might happen. I wrote a brief note of resignation, effective immediately, and departed. The miracle did not happen; the company went into bankruptcy a year later in 1927.

I was 35 years old. I was also unemployed, flat broke and $250,000 in debt. Several friends suggested that I declare bankruptcy, but I did not consider it for even a moment. I owed the money, and I would pay it back if I had to work like a dog to do it.

I was not ashamed and not afraid. Failure was something I had faced before and might well face again. I have said it over and over: "Failure" is the greatest word in the English language. Here in America failure is not the end of the world. If you have the determination, you can come back from failure and succeed.

A few days after I resigned, Frank Blair, president of the Union Guardian Trust Company of Detroit, called me and asked me to come and see him. When I arrived, he went to the point immediately.

"You're a young man," he said, "and knowing you as I do, I'm sure that you will find a new line of endeavor. When you find it, and if you need financing, come in and see me. I'm pretty sure we'll be able to help you."

I walked out of his office as spry and chipper as a young man just beginning a new business. It is not every week that you can go broke to the tune of a quarter of a million dollars and have a banker tell you that your credit is good. I might have failed, but there was still someone who believed in me.

And that made two of us.

EIGHT

INDIANAPOLIS SPEEDWAY

The paradox of being unemployed, a quarter of a million dollars in debt and at the same time in search of a business to buy brought to mind Frank Blair's suggestion. In my frequent trips to Indianapolis over the years, I had been impressed with the Allison Engineering Company, a little gem of a plant. James A. Allison, one of the builders of the Indianapolis Speedway and a successful businessman, had originally started the company to build racing cars, but it had since gone into other activities. One of Allison's products was a special bearing used in most of the aircraft engines manufactured in the United States. It was building superchargers for General Electric and reduction gears for Navy dirigibles.

I knew that Jim Allison had partially retired, and I went to Indianapolis to ask him to sell me the company.

"Well, Eddie, I'll tell you," he said, "it's true I spend most of my time in Florida these days, but when I do come home for the summer I like to have a desk I can put my feet on. But I have a better idea, one tailor-made for you. Why don't you take over the Speedway?"

The Speedway had been built by four men—Allison, Carl G. Fisher, Frank H. Wheeler and Arthur C. Newby. "The way it stands now," Allison said, "Frank Wheeler is dead, Art Newby is no longer interested and Carl Fisher is spending all his time developing Miami Beach. I'd like to see it in younger, capable hands."

I told Jim quite truthfully that I had never thought about buying the Speedway, but I began to think about it at that moment. I went out and took a look at the property. When the Speedway had been built in 1909, it had been far out in the country, and its 320 acres had been acquired for $72,000. But now it was practically surrounded by the city, and its real-estate value alone had multiplied many times.

Allison gave me a price of $700,000 and a thirty-day option. I had a survey made, which verified my belief that the price was fair. The more I thought of it, the more enthusiastic I became. Owning and operating the Indianapolis Speedway, home of the world's greatest automotive event, would be a thrill in itself.

Allison had strongly hinted that, if I did not take it over, it would probably be sold to real-estate speculators. The Speedway would be razed and the land subdivided. To someone who had been as close to the Speedway as I had been for so many years, such an idea was unthinkable. Fleeting nostalgic scenes of color and excitement raced through my mind, beginning with the very first "500" in 1911. That was when, as a 20-year-old amateur from the dirt tracks of Iowa, I had relieved Lee Frayer in his Red Wing Special.

And the wonderful, dramatic race of 1912. Joe Dawson won it, driving a National, but it was Ralph De Palma, a great sportsman and a gentleman with a heavy foot, who won the cheers that day. He was the favorite in that second running of the Big 500. His Mercedes gleamed like a Tiffany showcase. The German craftsman who built it had fashioned it with the care of a watchmaker. It was long and low and powerful and could do 120 miles an hour on the straightaway.

Another popular favorite was Bob Burman in a car made to his measure: a Cutting, with a whopping piston displacement. The man I thought we would have to beat was Teddy Tetzlaff, in an old Fiat with cylinders the size of beer kegs.

As we lined up, 24 cars driven by some of the greatest names in racing, the band was playing "Everybody's Doing It Now." The morning air was fresh and cool, but we all knew how long that would continue. My car broke down on the 43rd lap. I climbed out of the cockpit, soaking wet with perspiration. By that time De Palma had been leading the pack for forty laps. A superb driver in a superb machine, he hurled that car around the turns with little slackening of speed. The crowd loves a winner, and he received a great cheer each time he passed the grandstand.

The heat was taking its toll in tires. You could smell the rubber burning as it shrieked over the hot bricks. De Palma came in for a change, but his pit crew worked so swiftly and efficiently that it cost him little time. Bob Burman put off making his change too long, and two of his tires went out on a turn. The big Cutting rolled over, but Bob came out of it alive. Tetzlaff moved into third place. Joe Dawson had been hanging onto second. But De Palma was seven laps in the lead and still gaining. That Mercedes charged around the track making a noise like a battalion of artillery. On the 197th lap, with only three to go, he was eleven minutes ahead of Joe. In seven and a half miles and five and a half minutes, he would rake in the biggest prize money of his career.

On the 198th lap, a piston broke and smashed through the crankcase. The engine was hitting on only two or three cylinders and leaking oil. Joe Dawson caught the frantic signal from his crew and jammed the accelerator down all the way. He had a chance.

Ralph De Palma came limping around the turn, sounding as though the engine were being pounded with sledgehammers, and continued on down the track, that sleek, proud Mercedes crawling like a hurt animal. Joe was pushing ahead at full throttle.

Less than a mile from the finishing line, the Mercedes gave up the ghost. Ralph simply sat there for several seconds. Then he and his riding mechanic climbed out and, keeping close to the inside edge, began pushing the crippled car home.

As they trudged along, Dawson crossed the finish line.

I was watching the Dawson crew's victory celebration, when I heard a roar go up from the grandstand. With everyone else, I looked around and saw Ralph pushing the car down the homestretch. He had lost the race, he had no chance yet he doggedly continued to push that car to the finish line. The cheers and the applause were even louder for this man who did not win than for the winner himself. Ralph De Palma had failed, but he had failed in a wonderful way, and we were all with him.

Though I had not raced after my return from World War I, I had kept in close touch with the Speedway. In the first race after the war, I had accepted Carl Fisher's invitation to serve as referee. And I remembered how, in 1925, I had proudly paced the race in a Rickenbacker Straight 8.

There was no doubt about it. If the Indianapolis Speedway passed out of existence, its loss would be felt with nostalgia and grief the country over.

But thrills and excitement are only by-products of the Speedway. I thought also of its more important function, to serve as a proving ground for the development and improvement of features that increase the performance, economy and safety of the American automobile. Practically every major development in the automobile had been tested on the Speedway. Continuation of the Speedway as the world's greatest testing laboratory was vital to both industry and motorist.

And all I needed was $700,000. I first tried to raise the money in Indianapolis. No one was interested, which was typical of the city's attitude in those days. Indianapolis had been the cradle of the American automotive industry. Some of the cars that had been manufactured there were the American, Pioneer, Marmon,

Stutz, Empire, Willys-Overland. But the more aggressive community of Detroit had taken over the automobile industry.

My option ran out, and Allison gave me a thirty-day extension. Several real-estate operators had heard about the opportunity by that time and had moved in with their bushel baskets, ready to pick up the option when it expired. Recalling Frank Blair's promise, I hurried back to Detroit and put the package before him at the Union Guardian Trust Company. He arranged to float a bond issue in the State of Michigan. We raised the $700,000 in 6½ percent bonds with only an hour to go before the option ran out. I kept 51 percent of the common stock as a bonus, and the bank took 49 percent for its effort in marketing the bond issue. On November 1, 1927, I assumed control of the Indianapolis Speedway and immediately set to work improving it. After the success of the bond issue, I had no difficulty in raising additional capital from the local banks.

The original surface of the Speedway was composed of gravel and tar. It had broken up in the bloody three days of racing with which the Speedway had opened in 1909. In one accident five people were killed. The track was then repaved with large bricks. I was dissatisfied with this surface, and I had the Speedway completely resurfaced with Kentucky rock asphalt. It gave a much smoother surface than the paving blocks and also provided a greater coefficient of friction. Tires gripped the surface.

One of the great dangers in a race was going over the walls. I rebuilt them, strengthening them with steel supports; no driver has gone over the wall since. I also rebuilt the curves, improving the angle of bank, which improved both safety and speed.

When I bought it, the Speedway was functional but hardly beautiful, and it was idle 364 days a year. I put in an 18-hole golf course, which brought in about $10,000 a year, enhanced the beauty of the Speedway and helped to provide for year-round maintenance.

From the beginning, the Speedway had enjoyed excellent coverage by the newspapers and had cooperated with them fully.

Steve Hannagan, who went on to become one of the world's best-known publicists, got his start with the Speedway.

But the new entry in the communications field, radio, was hard to sell. To enable the Speedway to take its rightful place in the parade of youth, I thought we ought to put the show on the air. I prevailed upon Merlin H. "Deac" Aylesworth, president of the National Broadcasting Company and an old friend, to be my guest at the first race run during my stewardship. I took him out to the track at midnight before the race. A police escort was necessary to get the car through. For miles, from the heart of town to the Speedway, two rows of cars were lined up, waiting patiently. In subsequent years I persuaded the city to build a 4-lane highway to the Speedway; then, on my midnight trips, I would see the cars lined up *four* abreast for miles.

We returned for the opening of the gates at 6:00 A.M. It took three hours to get all the cars in. In the meantime I was constantly receiving weather reports, as I had been doing for days and would continue to do right up to the last minute. A heavy rain would compel me to delay or postpone the event. You can imagine my consternation when, with 425 miles down and 75 to go, a few drops of rain began to fall. At the time, four cars were battling for the lead. Rain on the oily track makes it slick, and the caution flag was brought out. All drivers throttled down. But the shower ended, the track dried swiftly and the race continued.

The shower marked a complete change in the race. Louis Meyer, a veteran driver, and Lou Moore, a rookie, had been holding back, nursing their engines. Now they both made their bids. Meyer, driving a Miller Special, pulled out in front. Moore stayed on his tail but could not pass him. He finished a close second. It was an exciting race; the customers received their money's worth.

So did Deac Aylesworth, and from then on the race was covered by radio, as well as by the press. Today, of course, many more thousands of spectators can see the Big 500 in theaters all over the country on closed-circuit television.

I had barely put the Speedway on its feet when the 1929 Depression began. Our bond issue was the only one of its kind in the State of Michigan that weathered the crash; we even continued to pay interest. After 1928 I devoted only a few weeks a year to the Speedway, leaving the day-to-day operation to T. E. "Pop" Myers, the capable general manager, but the responsibility did not lessen.

Few racing fans realize how close the Memorial Day event once came to being terminated. All drivers are given a thorough medical examination several days before the race. In 1933 the medical staff reported that a driver named Howard Wilcox had a diabetic condition that made it unsafe for him to drive. I informed him that he could not participate.

Wilcox, known to all of us as "Howdy," was a likable fellow, and the other drivers jumped to his defense. I liked Howdy too, and that was one of the reasons I did not want him to kill himself or inadvertently cause injury or death to the other drivers. The owner of the car, Joe Marks, made arrangements with Mauri Rose to drive in Howdy's place. I gave official approval, with the proviso that the car move back to the rear of the field for the start of the race. That should have ended the matter.

But, as Memorial Day draws closer, tension increases. Nerves grow tauter. I could sense that the Wilcox matter was growing out of proportion. Finally the drivers got together and announced publicly that they would not participate in the race unless Howdy was permitted to drive.

That was the situation at 9:40 on the morning of the race. The cars were in position behind the starting line, the drivers grouping at the line for the customary picture-taking ceremony. I stepped forward as usual and called the drivers around me. Howdy Wilcox was there, ready to drive. So was Mauri Rose. I looked at the faces in front of me, faces of men I had known, liked and admired for years.

I said I knew how they felt about Howdy but that I could not permit him to endanger himself or the others.

"And now I advise you to get into your cars and get ready," I said. "If you don't, I'll get on the public-address system and tell everybody here in the Speedway grounds and people listening in on the radio all over America that it is you drivers who refuse to go on because of the medical disqualification of another driver. I will return every single dollar we've taken in, call off the race and close down the Speedway."

The fifteen-minute warning bomb went off. I gave the traditional order: "Get in your cars and start your engines."

Nobody moved.

"Now!" I snapped. "Otherwise I'll cancel the race and close down the Speedway forever."

That did it. The drivers started to their cars. The race started on time.

I exulted in the color and competition of the Speedway right along with all the other thousands of spectators. But there were many times during my years with the Speedway when I had to avert my gaze from the track. I simply could not look.

It always occurred during the first official lap. When the starter drops the green flag, it's like pulling a trigger. The drivers jam the accelerators to the floor. They barrel down the straightaway into the first turn. That was when I would nonchalantly turn and look toward the backstretch, away from the scene of action. If anything happened, I did not want to see it.

Many years later what I feared did happen. It was in 1964. Dave MacDonald's car hit the wall and burst into flames. MacDonald jumped out in flames.

Eddie Sachs, a witty, likable driver, had no chance. He piled into MacDonald's car. He was dead when they pulled him out of the cockpit.

Then Johnny Rutherford came through the fire on the track and jumped completely over two cars—MacDonald's and Bobby Unser's. Unser's car went on into the pile-up. Ronnie Duman, driving his first race, slammed into the first two cars. Norm Hall, not the author Norman Hall of the 94th Squadron, plowed right into the whole mess, and two more cars, driven by Johnny White and Chuck Stevenson, were also involved in the chain-reaction accident.

Sachs was dead. Dave MacDonald died on the way to the hospital. Duman was seriously injured. Rutherford suffered burns. The other four drivers involved in the eight-car crash, the most spectacular in Speedway history, escaped with minor injuries.

In 1966 another spectacular crash occurred on the first turn. Nobody was seriously injured, but 11 of the 33 entries were forced out.

When I first drove on the Speedway, the race was won by an average speed of 74 miles an hour. In 1966, thanks both to my reconstruction of the track and to the general improvement in every phase of the industry, a new record of 166.328 miles an hour for one lap was set during the qualifying trials. Winning the race today means $600,000. It would take more than that to lure me out there again.

The real gratification in operating the Speedway came from the realization that we were enabling the automotive and allied industries to make great strides in their art. Those grueling five hundred miles on Memorial Day are equal to one hundred thousand or more miles of ordinary driving on the highways and byways of America. It would require ten years, perhaps even fifteen, of routine testing to equal the job done on the Speedway in one day. Without the Speedway, in other words, your new automobile would be no better in many ways than a 10-to-15-year-old car.

Imagine driving an automobile over today's superhighways with two-wheel brakes. Well, four-wheel brakes were tested and proved on the speedways of the world. So was the expanding type of brake in use on most cars today and the newer disc brake. Hydraulic shock absorbers were developed on the Speedway. So was the low-slung frame.

Through racing, countless improvements have come about under the hood. I remember the 12-cylinder Packard and the 16-cylinder Cadillac; today automotive engineers receive more power from lighter, smaller 4-cylinder engines than both those heavy old motors could produce, thanks to design and materials tested in competition.

The tire industry has benefited greatly from racing. The Firestone Tire and Rubber Company has spent millions perfecting tires for Speedway use. In the early days we would wear out twenty, even thirty, tires in a single race, some of them from dangerous blowouts. Today racing cars can drive the entire five hundred miles without changing tires. Tires produced for the average motorist have kept pace. I remember reading, as a teenager, a tire advertisement guaranteeing three thousand miles. Today's motorist expects thirty thousand miles.

Fuels have been improved on the speedways. I sometimes think that what they are burning in those souped-up engines is closer to nitroglycerine than to gasoline. Oils and lubricants, subjected to the test of racing, have improved tremendously.

Every year the leading engineers of the automotive industry meet with the leading drivers to consider the conditions and formula for the next race. For years I was chairman of that group, the Contest Board of the American Automobile Association. In 1933, I recommended a drastic step: a limitation on the amount of gasoline and oil to be used by each entrant. The maximum amount of gasoline was set at 45 gallons. Furthermore, we prohibited adding any oil at all during the race.

Under the impetus of this regulation, petroleum engineers developed new oils and fuels that would give more mileage. The oil limitation forced engine designers to make sweeping improvements. My express intention in putting the new regulation into effect was to eliminate accidents caused by oil leaking onto the Speedway. It forced the engineers to provide better pistons, better cylinder walls and better valve operation. In short, they had to build engines that would run five hundred miles at tremendous speeds with only limited amounts of oil. By meeting this challenge, automotive engineers have improved the durability of engines to the point that today manufacturers guarantee their engines for as much as fifty thousand miles.

These benefits have not accrued solely to the automotive industry. The fuel-injection system, perfected on the Speedway, became standard on all aircraft piston engines. The low-pressure tires developed on the Speedway have also been adapted for use on airplanes. I could name a hundred improvements brought about in the automotive world alone by racing.

Important as the Speedway was, it became obvious as World War II got underway that all the fuel, oil, rubber materials and countless hours of time that would be consumed in the race and in preparing for it would serve a more vital purpose in national defense. Following the 1941 race, I closed down the Speedway.

When the war was over, instead of reopening the Speedway myself, I looked around for a buyer. By that time my other operations were too demanding for me to devote the time necessary to put it back into shape after five years of idleness.

All along I had felt that the ownership should be in Indianapolis, or at least in Indiana. I picked Wilbur Shaw, an Indianapolis boy who had won the event three times, as a natural leader to attract state capital. Wilbur interested an able young man named Anton Hulman, Jr., of a wealthy Terre Haute family, in the Speedway. I sold it to Tony for the exact price I had paid for it, writing off completely the hundreds of thousands of dollars I had put into it. Tony has done a marvelous job. He has put millions back into the Speedway, and it is in magnificent shape. The Speedway is the richest event in the world by far.

There is an interesting postscript to this story of the Indianapolis Speedway. Not long after I had bought it, Jim Allison, whose engineering company had been the property I had first wanted to acquire, dropped dead from a heart attack. His executors advised me that the Allison Engineering Company would go to the highest bidder. Just about everybody in the aircraft industry or who wanted to get into the aircraft industry was after the company. Through my associations, I was kept informed of the prices being offered and was able to raise my own bid as necessary. I finally bid $5,000 more than the highest bidder up to that time, and Allison was mine at a price of $90,000. I did not have $90,000, of course; I borrowed it from an Indianapolis bank. I also optioned the land around the company for future expansion.

After acquiring the property, I suddenly realized that I had neither the time to run it properly nor the money or credit that would be required for proper expansion over the next few years. During months of ownership, for example, I arranged with the Navy to build the prototype of a 12-cylinder, water-cooled aviation engine with 750 to 800 horsepower. To develop that engine and manufacture it in large quantities would require the investment of millions.

At the time, the Fisher Brothers Investment Trust was buying into the aviation industry and agreed to take it off my hands. A few months later, General Motors decided to go into the aviation industry, and the Fishers turned the Allison Company over to GM for the same price they had paid me for it, including a liberal commission. GM poured millions into the development of the company before selling the first Allison engine. It eventually sold eighty thousand of them; the Allison engine powered the P-38 and the P-51, among others, during World War II. In 1928, however, such an investment was far out of my reach.

As it was, we all came out ahead. I had the Speedway, GM had Allison and the nation had a superb, workhorse engine that powered thousands of planes for use in war and peace.

NINE

FLYING IN THE 1920S

When a man is determined to pay off a moral obligation of a quarter of a million dollars, one job is not enough. I drove myself hard in those years following the failure of the Rickenbacker Motor Company, and I was all the better for it. Not only did the last few years of the 1920s constitute one of the happiest and most productive periods of my life, they also served as excellent preparation for the bitter Depression of the 1930s.

For while others more fortunate than I were clipping coupons during the boom, I was working hard to pay my debts. When the crash came in November 1929, driving many men I knew well to ruin and suicide, I simply kept plugging along. I was used to eighteen-hour days, and no adjustment in my life was necessary. Thanks to my apprenticeship during the boom, I actually prospered during the Depression. And, through hard work and some fortunate business deals, like the one involving the Allison Engineering Company, I was able to pay back every penny of that $250,000.

One venture that provided a lot of fun as well as profit was an adventure cartoon strip, *Ace Drummond,* based roughly on my own wartime flying experiences. I wrote the continuity myself. At the peak of Ace's popularity, the strip ran in some 135 newspapers.

After getting the Speedway operation off to a good start, I looked about for other opportunities. In 1927 General Motors brought out a new automobile, the La Salle. It was manufactured by the Cadillac Division and featured a V-8 engine. I had had some experience introducing two new automobiles to the American public, and GM offered me $12,000 a year to help market the new La Salle. I joined them on January 1, 1928. It was understood that I would continue to give the Indianapolis Speedway my full attention during the month of May.

Before assuming duties with La Salle, I put in a few months on Cadillac. The automobile was, then as now, one of the finest cars manufactured in the United States. The first Cadillac had been built in Detroit in 1902 on the two hundredth anniversary of the first settlement on that site by the French explorer, Sieur Antoine de la Mothe Cadillac. The very first Cadillac produced was a model of superior workmanship, and the standard was maintained over the years. GM had bought the company for $4,500,000 cash in 1909. Cadillac had the first electric self-starter in 1912, the first synchromesh transmission and, with the La Salle, the first shatterproof glass all around.

But in 1927 the Cadillac met some sales resistance. I undertook to find out the reason and attempt to do something about it. The only way I could see to accomplish this twofold mission was to visit every single Cadillac distributor and dealer in America.

On my swing about the country, visiting some 75 cities in 81 days, I learned that the fault was not in the automobile but in the attitude of the dealers and distributors. Many had come to take their franchises for granted. Service departments were the key to the problem; they were in awful shape. Garages were dirty, with tools lying around everywhere. This slackness frequently had spread throughout the entire operation.

The remedy was obvious. I would simply call the entire gang together—boss, salesmen, mechanics, *everybody*. We would parade through the entire operation together, as I pointed out examples of slovenliness.

"Look at that," I would say, pointing to a messy showroom, dirty repair shop, poorly kept tools. "Is that Cadillac quality? Is that representative of America's finest automobile?"

Without exception, every dealer whose operation needed attention saw his mistakes and began putting my recommendations into effect immediately. I then assumed my duties with the La Salle Division. Again I worked with distributors and dealers all over the United States. Incidentally, it soon became apparent to me that General Motors was competing against itself; La Salle cut into Cadillac sales. I recommended that it be discontinued, and eventually it was.

In my travels about the country for the Rickenbacker automobile, for Cadillac, for La Salle, I always made a practice of speaking to civic clubs, chambers of commerce, American Legion posts, high-school and college students and other groups. I could hardly give a blatant sales pitch for my own products, and increasingly I found myself talking about the future of America. Some of my comments caused bitter controversy, as when I predicted that in the future cities would be bypassed by highways four lanes, even six lanes, wide. Merchants and newspapers protested vigorously—they wanted all through traffic to come right down Main Street—but most of them lived to see this prediction borne out.

Many of my listeners laughed at me when I talked about television—remember, it was in the 1920s. I suggested that the day would come when a lady could watch a New York fashion show in full color on a television screen in her local store, pick out the dress she wanted, have it flown to her and wear it the next night. This remark frequently brought a polite but wistful laugh from the ladies in the audience.

When I said that by 1950 there would be 50 million motor cars in America, my listeners would look at one another, smile and shake their heads. I hit that figure right on the head; the number of motor vehicles registered in the United States did reach 50 million during 1950. As highways became more and more crowded, I prophesied, there would be no place to go but up. And this point led into the main message of all my talks: aviation.

The world is surrounded by an ocean of air, I stated, and every city in the world could, thanks to air transportation, become a port on that ocean. In my speeches in the 1920s, I predicted, based on the comparative speed of rail travel, that, from a transportation point of view, aviation would reduce the United States to the size of Texas. I underestimated; by the same standard of comparison, the country has been reduced to the size of Pennsylvania.

Many major cities in the United States had no airports whatever worthy of the name during the 1920s. When I was in such a town, I hit the lack of aviation facilities and hit it hard.

I would point out the analogy between a community without an airport and those communities in the Midwest and West that, in the period of railroad expansion, had refused to permit the railroad to come through. Those towns that resisted progress were still the same. Lack of foresight had stunted them forever. The same fate would be suffered by the modern community without an airport.

I remember well the headlines in the Washington papers when, speaking before the Washington Board of Trade on November 22, 1928, I said:

> The fact that Washington doesn't have an airport and is not participating in the progress of today is a source of shame to every Washington citizen, member of Congress, and to the country at large.
> Transportation is life itself. Wherever we find rapid means of transportation and communication we find happiness, peace and prosperity. But where we do not find modern methods of transportation and communication, we find poverty and misery.
> We are on the threshold of a new era. There has come into our lives a science which is going to be a blessing to every human

being, the science of aviation. It is for you to recognize its existence today. Already it has come and is going beyond you. There are 35,000 route miles being flown every day in this country by airmail, passenger and transport planes, a greater mileage than is being flown in all the rest of the world combined. See it, recognize it and grasp the opportunity it offers. This new science will someday be the biggest industry in the world. It is your duty and obligation to prepare for what is coming, what in fact already has come. Passengers, mail, parcel post, express and light freight are going from the steamships and the railroads into the air.

The District of Columbia today is on an aerial highway over which the planes are about to operate from New York to Buenos Aires, and yet you are totally unprepared. The cost of an airport of the kind that the capital of a nation should have is nothing compared with the cost of the penalty which you will pay for failure to provide it.

Not long after, work was begun to reclaim 450 acres of land from the Potomac River on which the National Airport was built.

In about 25 major cities, I was directly instrumental in convincing the city fathers to buy land for the development of airports; I picked the sites in many cities. In some communities the only areas close to the hearts of the cities were the speedways or fair grounds. The Sioux City Speedway, where I had won my first big race with the Duesenberg team, was turned into an airport—Rickenbacker Airport.

One of the cities in which I was particularly active was Cleveland. I visited there several times, talking aviation. One day City Manager William R. Hopkins got in touch with me in Detroit and asked me to come and help him select a site. We saw several sites of a few hundred acres each, then visited a large acreage farther out in the country. I immediately recommended that the city buy one thousand acres.

Hopkins proposed that a bond issue be put through to buy the site. The members of the city council, however, felt that too much acreage was involved. Hopkins again got in touch with me in Detroit and asked me to return to appear before the council. I did and spoke for several minutes on what aviation was going to mean to Cleveland in the future.

"Gentlemen," I concluded, "you'd better buy this land now because you'll never get it this cheap again."

The vote was taken immediately, and the bond issue passed. The land was purchased and the airport built.

Incidentally, I never had a pilot's certificate or, for that matter, an automobile driver's license. I was both pilot and driver before they started issuing certificates. On the two or three occasions that I have been asked by a policeman to show an operator's license, I have instead produced the solid gold life membership card given me by the Los Angeles B.P.O. Elks Lodge No. 99. It has always proved sufficient.

A group in Indianapolis once asked me to speak on the subject of home. "You've probably seen more homes than any man in America," their spokesman explained.

I immediately recalled how, when I had returned from World War I and was flying around the country, I used to look out over the side of the cockpit of my plane and marvel at the number of houses I saw below me. No one realizes how many houses there are in the world until he sees them from the air.

Flying has enhanced the meaning of home. "Home" is one of the most all-embracing words in our language. It is the landing place where comfort, joy, happiness and love find their greatest expression.

After some of my flights in the early days of commercial aviation, I was indeed fortunate ever to see home again. I frequently hopped rides on the mail planes and sometimes flew them. Those were hair-raising flights; most of the planes were the old flying coffins, DH-4s.

In 1920 a friend of mine named John M. Larsen tried to sell the Post Office Department on an airmail and passenger operation. The year before, the Junkers Company in Germany had brought out a four-passenger low-wing monoplane built of duralumin, a new aluminum-base alloy that was both light and strong.

In order to promote air transportation, I helped Larsen to arrange a cross-country tour. I believed that duralumin pro-

With President Herbert Hoover at presentation of Congressional Medal of Honor

At Indianapolis Speedway—1932—Eddie Rickenbacker, Henry Ford, Edsel Ford, Harvey S. Firestone, Jr., Henry Ford II, Benson Ford and Harvey S. Firestone

With Marshal Foch at first American Legion convention, Kansas City

With sons David and William

With Orville Wright, left, and Major R. W. Schroeder, World Altitude record holder at that time

C. M. Bunting

Flying with the mail to California—1922

Author made this nose landing at Elko, Nevada, in 1922

With General Billy Mitchell

*Rickenbacker "Super-Sport"
coupe (rear view)*

*Rickenbacker "Super-Sport"
coupe (front view)*

*Rickenbacker "Vertical-8
Superfine" coupe-roadster*

Rickenbacker "Vertical-8-Superfine" Brougham

Rickenbacker six-cylinder sport Phaeton

Rickenbacker "Vertical-8-Superfine" Phaeton

With President Calvin Coolidge

vided the answer to some of our major problems in aircraft construction, and I wanted to demonstrate it. I invited Edward E. Allyne, director of an aluminum company, to go with us.

We left New York in three planes, piloted by Harold Hartney, who had commanded the 1st Pursuit Group in World War I; Bert Acosta, a famous name in aviation, and Samuel C. Eaton. In Cleveland we arranged for Hartney, our best pilot, to take Ed Allyne's entire family, wife, son and daughter, on a flight over the city. On his takeoff the plane smashed into a telephone pole. There were some tense moments until we learned that no one had been hurt. I was afraid that Allyne might reconsider the trip, but he continued with us. The plane did not.

We went on to Chicago, Des Moines and Omaha. The day we left Omaha was a scorcher. The air was hot and thin. I was riding with Hartney. We started across the field, but we could not build up enough speed to get off the ground in the thin air. We hit the ditch at the end of the field, jumped completely over the road and smashed into a house. We hit so hard and so fast that we collapsed it completely and moved it right off its foundations.

The end of a two-by-four came through the side of the cabin, missed my head by inches and went on out the back. The plane was a total wreck, but again no one was injured. The people in the house were standing outside the house watching us try to take off and escaped injury. As I told the reporters later, the only injury involved was a severe fracture of a straw hat.

Another plane was flown out from New York, and we continued on to Oakland, California, then down the coast to Los Angeles. We left Los Angeles early in the morning, hoping to make El Paso, Texas, by nightfall, and stopped at Tucson for lunch. It was hotter than blazes. Our regular procedure was to use gasoline on the takeoff, then switch to benzol when aloft. Taking off at Tucson, however, the pilot forgot to cut back to gasoline. Burning benzol, the engine overheated, and loss of power resulted. We fluttered on over the sagebrush and finally came down on our nose. The landing gear was knocked off—more emergency repairs.

Flying low along the Mexican border to El Paso, I saw orange flashes and little puffs of smoke beneath us. Mexican border guards must have thought we were the forefront of a gringo air invasion. At any rate, somebody was shooting at us. I suggested to Sammy Eaton, our pilot on that leg, that we seek a little higher altitude.

Crossing the Sacramento mountain range between El Paso and Roswell, New Mexico, I made the suggestion again and not so mildly. The top altitude of our airplane and that of the mountains were just about the same. We finally managed to get about two hundred feet higher than the ridge ahead of us and started over. At that moment the gas pump broke. The engine sputtered, and we started to lose altitude. The top of that mountain began coming awfully close. But Eaton spotted the trouble immediately, and a few strokes of the manually operated wobble pump forced gasoline into the carburetor again. We scraped on over the mountain, holding our breaths.

I had a new shaft for the pump fashioned and installed at Roswell, and from there we went to Kansas City, St. Louis and Columbus. Fog forced us down near Bellefonte, Pennsylvania, a well-known airfield in those days. But Acosta stayed with the plane while the rest of us hitchhiked into Bellefonte. The next morning the fog lifted. We were waiting at the field when we heard an airplane coming. It was Bert, and he was headed for New York at an altitude of about ten thousand feet. He did not even slow down, let alone come down. As we learned later, he had a date in New York that night, and Bert Acosta was not the kind of man who would let a stranded group of people endanger his punctuality with a girl friend. The rest of us finished the trip by train.

A few days later, a similar plane crashed and burned at Morristown, New Jersey. I went to look at it but saw only a mass of melted aluminum. Not long after, another crashed and burned. It was finally determined that the cause of both crashes lay in the gasoline line between the tank and carburetor. The line, of half-inch copper tubing, had no hose connection or flexibility, and it would crystallize and break under pressure and vibration. The engine, starved of fuel, would backfire, which would in turn ignite the spilled gasoline. I will never understand how we completed our trip without burning up.

Early in May 1921, General Billy Mitchell called me in San Francisco to invite me to a dinner commemorating the sailing of General Pershing and his staff on the *Baltic*, back in 1917.

"That's fine, General; you can count on me," I said. "And say, here's an idea. If you authorize Captain Arnold down at the San Diego Air Force Station to fix up a DH-4 with extra gas tanks I'll try to break the transcontinental record."

"That *is* a good idea, Eddie," Mitchell said with his customary enthusiasm. "I'll get in touch with Arnold right away."

Captain Arnold was Henry H. "Hap" Arnold, who later became the first commanding general of the U.S. Air Force. A few days later he called me to say that the plane was ready.

"I'll be there the first thing in the morning," I said.

The plane was an Army DH-4. I planned to make my official start from San Francisco, which would require crossing the Sierra Nevada range with a full load of gasoline. Testing the rate of climb with full tanks, I ran into a layer of clouds over Los Angeles and a violent snowstorm over the Tehachapi range north of the city. The only thing I could do then was to fly out over the Pacific in hopes of finding a break in the cloud layer. I found it and came back to Los Angeles and Rogers Field under the clouds.

There was no way for the people at the field to tell me that the field was soft and muddy from the rain. I landed and taxied for about one hundred feet, and then the wheels dug in, and I somersaulted right over on my back. It broke the rudder, smashed the propeller and knocked the tips of the wings off.

I called Hap Arnold, and the next morning another DH-4 arrived. We cannibalized it to repair my plane, and the next morning I proceeded to Redwood City, south of San Francisco.

The dinner was to be held in Washington on Saturday, May 28. I took off at 4:00 A.M. Thursday, May 26, right into a heavy fog and almost took the top off Goat Island in San Francisco Bay. I hurried back to the field and waited until 8:00 A.M. for the fog to clear.

It took me an hour and a half to reach sufficient altitude to cross the Sierra Nevada. There went more precious time. I gave the old Liberty engine all it would take, but it began getting dark long before I reached my scheduled stop, Cheyenne, Wyoming. I came down over the Union Pacific tracks and followed the signal lights into the city.

I had sent on a request that the field be illuminated, and, as I came over the city, a hundred or more automobiles rimming the airport turned on their headlights. Then the flaming "T" was ignited. It was a standard procedure for emergencies in the early days of flying. It was composed of oil-soaked rags and was placed at the beginning of the field against the wind. I came in and put my wheels down one hundred feet before the "T," rolled into a 6-foot ditch and somersaulted. They had put the "T" at the wrong end of the field, with the wind.

The plane, or what was left of it, was upside down, straddling the ditch. Both the engine and the tail had been knocked off. I was hanging by my safety belt, head down. It was a discouraging situation. The bottom of the ditch was several feet below me. I have never been a very patient individual. I pushed the button on the safety belt buckle, and I landed on my head. I had to laugh at my own impatience.

I was still laughing when my rescuers came up. I heard one of them say: "We'd better rush him to the hospital. He's knocked cuckoo."

I called General Mitchell from the field and told him I would take the next mail plane out, riding on the mail bags, to Chicago via Omaha.

"Stay there," Mitchell said. "I'll call you in an hour."

He did, with the news that he had arranged for another DH-4 to meet me at the Chicago airfield. I would fly it to Dayton, where the commandant of the Dayton-Wright field would turn over his own long-range DH-4 to me for the last leg of the trip.

Everything worked well. At Dayton I found the long-range DH-4 warmed up and ready to go. I took off immediately for Washington.

Over Wheeling, West Virginia, I ran into a terrible storm. I came down low and made it to Pittsburgh. I knew that the Monongahela River ran through the mountains east of Pittsburgh, so I picked it up and followed it. About five minutes up the river, I saw something pass just over my head. It was a high-tension electric wire. I decided I had better get away from the river. I started winding through the valleys. After a few minutes of that, I reached the point where I had no idea which way I was going. A large pasture loomed up ahead of me, and I landed to find out where I was. The ground was soft, but the plane rolled to a stop without mishap.

People began arriving and told me I was near Hagerstown, Maryland. I decided to drain off some of the gasoline to lighten the plane, so that I could take off from the soft field.

A couple of the local farmers hurried off for milk cans into which to drain the gasoline. I didn't cut the engine off because I wasn't sure that anyone there could swing the heavy wooden propeller to start it again.

As the crowd grew larger, including small children, I became afraid that someone might run into it. When the gas cans arrived and I had to crawl under the plane to drain the gasoline, I posted guards. I filled the first milk can and turned it over to one of the farmers. At first he thought I was trying to sell it to him; he was amazed to find out that he was doing me a favor to take the stuff. I crawled under the airplane again and drained the second tank, and just then I noticed a pretty little girl about seven years old start to walk straight for the propeller. I shouted at her to stop, and while she hesitated somebody ran out and grabbed her. I crawled out from under the plane, chewed out everybody in sight and doubled the guard.

After draining about 75 gallons, I managed to take off without difficulty and flew straight to Washington and landed at Bolling Field about 6:00 P.M. Congressman Clifford Ireland of Illinois was there to meet me. I changed at his apartment and arrived at the Metropolitan Club at 7:00 sharp.

Sometime after that I was approached by Will Hays and Albert Lasker, the national chairman and treasurer respectively of the Republican Party, who asked my advice on building an image for their Presidential candidate, Warren G. Harding of Ohio. After several conferences with Harding, he mentioned that he planned to make a front-porch campaign from his home in Marion, Ohio. I hurried back to Chicago and called a meeting with Hays and Lasker.

"We can buy an airplane," I said enthusiastically, "and I'll fly him back and forth between your national headquarters in Chicago and his front porch."

They bought the idea immediately. A flying candidate! I made arrangements to buy a DH-4 and designed some modifications for it. One was the installation of a little canopy over the rear seat for my distinguished passenger. The total bill would run to about $500,000. But, before I could buy the plane, the Democrats accused the Republicans of having a $5 million slush fund, and in the face of this adverse publicity Hays and Lasker decided that the party had better not spend a half-million flying Harding around. As far as I know, Harding was never consulted, one way or the other.

After Harding became President, he asked me to deliver a personal letter to the Shriners convention in San Francisco. I flew with the airmail all the way. My old friend of the Junkers trip, Sammy Eaton, was the pilot on one leg. We stopped overnight at Elko, Nevada, and, when we awakened early in the morning, we found that it had snowed during the night. We all pitched in to clear the runway. In taking off down the narrow cleared strip, however, we skidded just enough to hook a wing in a snowbank. The impact swung us around and rolled the plane up in a knot, but neither Sammy nor I received a scratch.

Another DH-4 happened to be available, and we took off in it. We had to stop at Reno for refueling before proceeding to San Francisco. It was snowing heavily when we arrived. Sammy circled low over the field, and we could tell by the snow on the rooftops that about a foot had fallen. The field was one unbroken expanse of snow, but we were short on fuel and had to land.

Sammy mushed the plane down, and we rolled along in the deep snow for about one hundred feet. Then the plane flip-flopped over on its back. It was practically demolished, but again Sammy and I were unhurt. Another plane was sent from San Francisco. We cleared a runway for it, and it took me to San Francisco without mishap. I delivered the letter personally. We had cracked up two planes getting it there, but we had saved the price of an airmail stamp.

To visit distributors and dealers for the Rickenbacker automobile, I had chartered a Junkers monoplane owned by Eddie Stinson, one of aviation's pioneers. On one of our trips, Steve Hannagan, then a handsome young man, who could not have been more than 22 or 23 years old, went along. He had never been in an airplane before.

En route to Cleveland we ran out of gas and had to put down in a wheat field. From Cleveland we went to Detroit. There a couple of mechanics were working on the plane during a thunderstorm when lightning struck it. It knocked the two mechanics out cold, but they quickly recovered, and the plane was not damaged.

The following day, over Ypsilanti, Michigan, we broke an oil line. That time Eddie chose a corn field for his emergency landing, we repaired the line and proceeded to South Bend, Indiana. There we discovered that we had sprung a leak in the water system.

For a few days everything went smoothly. We visited Chicago, then started for Omaha. We were flying along nicely when suddenly, over Dexter, Iowa, the engine froze and Eddie put us down in a clover field. We were standing up to our knees in clover, trying to figure out what to do, when a tall, lanky farmer boy wearing a straw hat and blue overalls came up with a pitchfork over his shoulder.

"Is Eddie Rickenbacker on board?" he asked. There had been a great deal of publicity on the trip.

I took a chance. "Yes," I said, "that's me."

"Gee, Mr. Rickenbacker," he said, "my dad will sure be glad to see you. You sold him a Firestone-Columbus automobile thirteen years ago. You drove it here yourself from Omaha."

"Did the car perform all right?" I asked cautiously.

"Oh, yes," he said. "We've still got it."

The three of us went home with the boy, met his parents, had a wonderful farm meal and met all the neighbors for miles around who dropped in. I called the airmail boys in Omaha and arranged for them to wrap a new cylinder and piston in burlap and drop it on the clover field. We made the repairs and went on to Omaha for the night.

The next morning, fully loaded with gasoline, in hopes that we could reach Denver without refueling, we prepared to take off. Although it was only 5:00 in the morning, the day was already hot. The air was calm and dry. Eddie opened up the throttle, and we picked up speed, but we just rolled and rolled and rolled. That plane had no intention of taking off.

I saw what was going to happen, and I hollered, "Hold on!" The plane plowed into a road, bumped over it, went into a field, bounced high into the air, came down so hard that it knocked the landing gear off and then stood up on its nose and stayed there. Steve and I both slid down into the front of the cabin. He was first, and I landed right on his back with both feet.

The first thing I think about in a crash is fire, and it was an automatic action for me to open the door and start out. Steve picked himself up just in time to see me leaving the plane.

"My God, Rick, don't jump, don't jump!" he hollered. He thought we were still in the air.

That ended that tour. I gave Eddie enough money to have his plane fixed up, and Steve and I continued by train.

During the Rickenbacker automobile period, I had also designed a simple, compact star-shaped engine for a small plane. Its five cylinders produced eighty horsepower. It weighed less than two hundred pounds. When I finally finished building it, with the help of a young engineer named Glenn Angle and a mechanic named William Kimsey, we gave it exhaustive tests on the block, and it held up very well.

I wanted to test it in the air too, but there was no small airplane being manufactured into which I could put it; I would have to build one myself. I called in an aircraft designer named Ivan Driggs, told him some of my ideas for a small plane and set him to work designing one. The result was a small high-winged monoplane seating two passengers side by side. It was the first small plane ever built with landing flaps and with a tail wheel instead of a tail skid. I flew it from Dayton, Ohio, to Detroit, a distance of 220 miles, in two and a half hours, using twelve gallons of gas and one pint of oil. I had a small two-speed transmission built that would make it possible to use the plane as an automobile. You could land on a cow pasture or highway, fold the wings back against the body, disconnect the propeller and drive off.

Unfortunately for me, I was in the same situation with the plane as I had been with the four-wheel brakes. The public was not ready for a small plane. I sold the design of the little engine and plane separately to two different companies for satisfactory prices.

My most important aviation project during those years was Florida Airways. It had had its beginning in the minds of Major Reed M. Chambers, my old flying companion of the 94th Aero Squadron, and myself in 1925. By that year the practicality of airmail had been proved.

The toll had been great. Flying obsolete equipment and taking off and landing in fields little better than cow pastures, 31 of the first 40 pilots hired by the Post Office had sacrificed their lives trying to get the mail through. Sammy Eaton was one of them. But enough mail did get through for Congress, in the Air Mail Act of 1925, to authorize the Postmaster General to contract for airmail service with private operators.

Under the terms of the Air Mail Act, private operators could apply for a Civil Air Mail route from the U.S. Post Office. Hundreds of inquiries poured in from people interested in operating airlines. One of these inquiries came from Florida Airways, of which Reed Chambers was president. Associated with him was a fine group of maintenance men and pilots.

Reed had helped me with the financing of the Rickenbacker Motor Company, and we had always talked about the possibilities of commercial aviation. I looked toward Florida as the place to start. Someday, I knew, there would be extensive air travel between the two American continents, and Florida was the logical gateway. Florida Airways applied for and received Route No. 10, Miami to Jacksonville by way of Fort Myers and Tampa, at a rate of $3 a mile per pound of mail.

Along with others, I put up several thousand dollars to get the company under way. The rest was raised by public subscription. Selling stock in an airline was difficult in 1926, as there were few people then who wanted to try this promising new field. Reed and I, as World War I aces, had the confidence of the public, however, and we finally financed our airline. We worked closely together in setting up the company. He would come up to Detroit, or I would take a trip down to Florida, tying it in with promotion for the Rickenbacker automobile.

One of my activities was promoting the development of airports. I persuaded the city of Tampa to buy a cow pasture to use as an airfield. Today, it is one of the United States' finest airports.

On April 1, 1926, Florida Airways began one of the nation's first regularly scheduled airmail, passenger and express services with one Curtiss Lark.

The Ford Motor Company was producing a duralumin monoplane powered with a Liberty engine. Referred to as the "Tin Goose," it had eight wicker seats for passengers.

Ford made a straight deal with Florida Airways for the purchase of its stock.

There were plenty of good service-trained pilots available, and four fine pilots were hired and sent to Detroit to pick up the new planes. They proceeded south, stopping over in Nashville, Tennessee.

The arrival of four planes was cause for a celebration in those days, and the whole town of Nashville turned out to speed the Florida Airways fleet on its way. The planes were parked in formation for the farewell ceremonies. On their completion, the pilot of the first plane taxied out to the runway and started to take off. The tail skid began fish-tailing on the grass, and the pilot found himself headed directly for the mayor and his party of dignitaries. To avoid wiping out the entire governing body of Nashville, the pilot jammed the throttle wide open and whipped the plane around. He missed the mayor, but he managed to crash into all three of the other planes.

The way the company had procured the planes paid off in this instance. To protect the value of its stock, Ford had little choice but to send a crew of mechanics to Nashville. The four wrecked planes were transformed into three whole ones, and they proceeded to Florida.

The company started expanding the airline from the very beginning. I had dreams of a north-south airline. A natural extension was up the coast to Atlanta. With the help of an enthusiastic young assistant city attorney named William B. Hartsfield—later one of America's best-known mayors—we arranged to use the infield of the Atlanta speedway for an airport. On September 15, Florida Airways began flying from Atlanta to Miami with a dogleg through Tampa.

One of the agents came up with a brilliant idea for airmail. He found that by soaking a blotter he could double its weight. The agents did a rushing business sending one another wet blotters. We could afford to buy the stamps and make a 50 percent profit. Frequently this method was the only way Florida Airways could build up a pound of mail.

It worked fine for a while, but then the boys became greedy. They began shipping one another bricks, carefully wrapped and addressed. At $3 a pound per mile the company could afford to buy the stamps and make a 100 percent profit on the bricks.

The system was working well until one of the agents took a day off. His assistant, charged with the duty of mailing a brick but uninstructed on the complete details, simply tied a label with stamps onto a bare brick. A postal inspector spotted it and asked questions, and that was the end of Florida Airways' airmail-augmentation program.

As for passengers, the public was not ready. It was a rare day indeed when the company had one frightened customer in our wicker chairs. The hurricane of 1926 was the final blow. At that time, I was having enough trouble with the Rickenbacker Motor Company, and Florida Airways eventually went into bankruptcy. Harold F. Pitcairn, a young Philadelphia millionaire who had acquired the CAM route between New York and Atlanta, picked up what was left of the Florida Airways for a song. His line was known as Pitcairn Aviation, Inc. It later became Eastern Air Transport. And that, for the time being, ended my participation in airlines on the East Coast.

One other involvement with commercial aviation during that period is worth a mention. Donald Douglas, Glenn Martin's chief engineer, quit Martin and tried to start his own company. He too found money hard to raise and offered me a half-interest if I could raise $50,000 for him. I had all I could handle at the time and could not take advantage of his offer.

Not long after that, I dropped in to see my old friend Harry Chandler, publisher of the Los Angeles *Times*. Harry asked me about Don Douglas. I was so enthusiastic about the potential of both the aircraft industry and Don Douglas that after lunch Harry held up his hands and said, "All right, all right, that's enough."

He put up $10,000 of his own money, then called several friends and raised a total of $100,000. That put the Douglas Aircraft Company in business.

It was not until twenty years later that I told Don about my conversation with Harry Chandler. "That explains a lot of things I never understood until now," he said.

Throughout the 1920s, therefore, although I was involved in

other enterprises, my interest in all phases of aviation, rather than waning, became stronger and stronger. I talked aviation in my travels about the country, and I talked aviation in company and social gatherings back home in Detroit. I saw a lot of William S. Knudsen, president of Chevrolet in those days, and, like everyone else, Bill had to listen to me talk about aviation. He reported this interest to the late Alfred P. Sloan, Jr., then president of General Motors and one of America's great industrialists.

And that put me in aviation, this time to stay.

TEN

HOW TO BUY AN AIRLINE

Early in June 1929, Charles E. Wilson, vice-president of General Motors in charge of aviation activities, phoned me and asked me to stop by his office. When I arrived, he told me that GM had taken over the Fokker Aircraft Company and would like me to move to New York and be vice-president in charge of sales. Naturally I said that I would be delighted to accept.

Later it occurred to me that, if I had remained with Cadillac, the possibilities of my moving up to the higher echelons of General Motors would have been enhanced, but that June day in 1929 I never even thought of it. Aviation was where I wanted to be. I believed that in this great new industry I could best serve my country and civilization. I moved to New York and commenced my new duties on July 1, 1929.

I had helped to negotiate the purchase of the Fokker Company. I had been familiar with planes designed by Tony Fokker ever since World War I, when they had given me too many close calls, and I was convinced that he was building a superior product. His newest design was the famous trimotor, the F-10. Its fuselage was of steel tubing covered with linen and its wings of laminated wood. The price was $54,000, which some airline directors considered exorbitant, but I still sold several of them. My customers included the Army Air Service, Western Air Express and Pan American, which was then flying between Miami and Havana.

Tony, a colorful individual who liked loud sports jackets and golf knickers, also built an even larger airplane, the F-32. It was a four-engine, 32-passenger monoplane made of steel tubing and plywood. The engines were in tandem, one pair on each side of the fuselage. They had an unfortunate habit of blowing the cylinder heads off. When that happened in one of the forward engines, the cylinder head would usually fly back into the propeller of the rear engine, which would throw it in any direction. A friend of mine was riding on one of those big planes between San Francisco and Los Angeles, when he saw the cylinder head go hurtling past his nose, through the cabin and into the engine on the other side. There went three of the four engines right there.

While I was with Fokker, I also negotiated the purchase of Pioneer Instrument Company, which made precision instruments for aircraft. It became the Bendix Aviation Company.

The 1929 stock-market crash hit the budding new aviation industry hard. Partly for economy reasons, General Motors moved the Fokker operation to Baltimore, where it became General Aviation, Incorporated. A young aeronautical genius, E. H. "Dutch" Kindelberger, was employed to run it. It later moved again, this time to California and, as North American Aviation, manufactured some famous planes, including the World War II fighter plane, the P-51 Mustang.

But I was no longer with the company. I had moved my family from Detroit, and we lived in the pleasant New York suburb of Bronxville. Though I did not want to leave General Motors, I resigned on March 31, 1932, rather than move to Baltimore.

Once again I had left a good position with a good future. But I had no regrets. For it happened that my departure from Gen-

eral Motors resulted in my taking an active role in one of commercial aviation's most fascinating episodes.

When, in the late 1920s, it began to appear that aviation offered an exciting opportunity in the world of finance, two
personable young men on Wall Street, W. Averell Harriman and
Robert Lehman, organized a giant holding company called "Aviation Corporation," or "AVCO." It acquired many aviation properties, including several small airlines scattered roughly east
and west across the country. AVCO put this conglomeration
together and called it American Airways. It operated half a
dozen different types of airplanes on a generally haphazard basis.
It was losing money. I joined Aviation Corporation as vice-
president of American Airways on April 29, 1932.

One of my major duties was to visit Washington regularly in
an effort to develop and maintain governmental goodwill. Being
in the airline business, I naturally traveled, when possible, by
air. The only line between New York and Washington at that
time was Eastern Air Transport, owned by another large aviation
holding company, North American Aviation, Inc. Eastern was
flying an uneconomical plane made by the Curtiss Aircraft Company, called the "Kingbird." Curtiss was also controlled by North
American Aviation; they would build a plane in one subsidiary
and run the bugs out of it on another. Flying from the little Newark Airport, which served New York City at that time, down to
Washington and other southern cities was more or less a gypsy-
type operation. If the weather was good, one flew; if it was bad,
one did not.

But still I could see a great advantage in combining the east-
west operations of American Airways with the north-south operations of Eastern Air Transport. American Airways did its best
business in the eight months of the spring, summer and fall. The
winter months were the busiest for Eastern, which ran all the
way to Florida. There was not a great deal of passenger business
for Florida then, but someday, I was positive, Florida would
attract great numbers of vacationists. It was a 30-hour train ride
from New York to Miami, and many of those vacationists would

prefer to get there more quickly by plane. Merging the two lines would give them a year-round peak. It would cut costs tremendously through eliminating duplication in facilities, offices, overhaul and practically every phase of operation. Most important, it would permit the transfer of airplanes from American to Eastern during the winter months and from Eastern to American during the rest of the year.

The controlling interest of North American Aviation, Inc., and therefore of Eastern Air Transport, was owned by Clement M. Keys, who had almost single-handedly created the huge holding company. In 1933, after too many years of the Depression, he went into bankruptcy. On my strong recommendation, Harriman and Lehman began making arrangements for AVCO to buy the Keys company from its receivers in order to obtain Eastern Air Transport and the north-south route.

But dealings in high finance are never simple. Shortly before, Aviation Corporation had taken over the Century Airline from the man who had built it, Errett Lobban Cord, giving him AVCO stock and a directorship in the company. I had known E. L. for years, dating back to when he had run a car-washing operation in Los Angeles; he was a sharp and energetic entrepreneur who loved to manipulate stock. At one time, incidentally, he had manufactured the Auburn and Cord automobiles. Looking further into AVCO, he learned that it had $30 million cash on hand. He immediately began negotiating for the purchase of more properties, which he figured would increase the value of the stock. He also began buying all the stock he could lay his hands on. Harriman and Lehman controlled the corporation with only about a seven percent interest, and they looked upon Cord's activities with some concern.

My suggestion that AVCO purchase North American Aviation provided them with an excellent opportunity to resist Cord's inroads. Instead of using AVCO's cash reserves, they would issue an additional two million shares of stock, which would have the effect of reducing Cord's interest. When E. L. heard about this new plan, he exploded. He was so angry that he threatened to put not only this particular controversy but also the airline situation in general before the public.

I considered this move most unwise. I knew as well as Cord that some mistakes had been made and that some skulduggery had taken place in the early days of the aviation industry. But the industry was becoming mature and capable of clean and efficient operation. Washing our dirty linen in public might lead to a congressional investigation and government action. It would be American aviation that would suffer. Personally, I did not care who controlled the company. My interest was in building an air-transport system of major proportions to serve the American people.

I thus found myself attempting to serve as peacemaker between the two factions, Harriman and Lehman on one side, E. L. Cord on the other. Fortunately, they were geographically convenient. Cord lived in the Waldorf-Astoria Towers, and Harriman and Lehman maintained company suites there. I had breakfast, lunch or dinner with one, two or three of them every day for two months. At least E. L. took no drastic action. When he seemed to have simmered down a bit, I began a long-postponed business trip across the country. In Los Angeles I was told by long distance to hurry back, that Cord was going to blow the lid off. I left that night by plane, but bad weather grounded the flight in St. Louis. Before I could make it back Cord had begun a free-for-all proxy fight that made headlines.

My loyalty was to Harriman and Lehman, and I worked for them in the proxy battle, but it was obvious that Cord was going to win. He did. He fired the old board of directors and installed his own. I waited in my office, and, when the board meeting was over, about 6:00 P.M., he came in. Before he could open his mouth, I said, "Well, E. L., when do you want it?"

"Want what?" he asked.

"My resignation."

"I don't want it."

"You've got to take it if you hope to retain any esprit de corps in your personnel," I said. "You know and they know I was on the other side. If you keep me on, your people would lose confidence in you."

E. L. saw the logic in what I was saying. "Well, all right," he said, "but I'd appreciate it if you'd stay around for a couple of months to finish up what you've been doing."

I agreed. A few weeks later he moved the home office of American Airways to Chicago. That was my excuse to leave. My two boys were in school in the New York area at the time, and I did not want to uproot them. I parted with E. L. Cord and American Airways on the best of terms on February 28, 1933.

As a result, I was once again out of a job. The C. M. Keys empire, North American Aviation, Inc., a holding company, was still in receivership. Included in its holdings were large blocks of stock of Pan American, TWA, Western Air Express and China National Airways, and it owned outright the Sperry Gyroscope Company and Eastern Air Transport Company. Whom could I interest in buying and operating North American Aviation? General Motors, of course, first came to mind. One of my good friends at GM was Ernest R. Breech, the assistant treasurer, who was enthusiastic about the potential of aviation. I outlined to him my proposal that GM buy North American.

Ernie was interested. Encouraged, I then went to several of the top people in GM—John J. Raskob, a vice-president; Donaldson Brown, treasurer, and, of course, William S. Knudsen and Alfred P. Sloan, Jr. Ernie presented the plan to the board of directors, and it was approved. GM bought a 30 percent control of North American Aviation, effective February 28, 1933. Later Ernie Breech became president, and I became vice-president.

Our job was to resuscitate those operations that held some promise and to unload those that did not. One property on which the wrong guess was made was the Sperry Gyroscope Company. It was manufacturing and developing revolutionary new instruments, including the automatic pilot, which were enabling aircraft to fly in almost all types of weather. If I had had my way, this highly productive company would have remained in the

General Motors family. It was sold, however, at the ridiculously low price of $2 a share.

It was during that period that one of the great blots on the history of commercial aviation occurred. As I had feared, E. L. Cord's bitter attacks on the AVCO management had called attention to the Wall Street involvement in commercial aviation as a whole.

Attacks also came from other sides. Tom Braniff, then operating a small line in Oklahoma and Kansas, failed to win a mail contract and blamed it on Wall Street influence. Charges were made that there was collusion between certain airlines and the Postmaster General in the Hoover administration, Walter F. Brown. I believed that Brown and the Post Office Department were primarily interested in furthering a dependable airmail service over the entire nation.

Abuses had unquestionably taken place in commercial aviation during the 1920s and the early 1930s, but the hearings held on the matter by Senator Hugo Black, later a Supreme Court justice, and his committee went too far. So did the committee's recommendations, one of which was that President Roosevelt cancel all airmail contracts.

At that time, in January 1934, I had no great love for Franklin D. Roosevelt. I had supported him for the Presidency in 1932, believing that his platform, which to me seemed sound and conservative, was what the country needed. No sooner had he taken office, however, than he had made a complete 180-degree turn and taken off in the other direction toward liberalism and socialism. I no longer supported him, but I did not believe that he would go so far as to cancel the airmail contracts.

I should have known better. One night in February I was having dinner in the Central Park Casino in New York with a large group of people, including Mrs. James A. Farley, the wife of the Postmaster General. The main topic of conversation, naturally, was the airmail situation. Bess Farley looked at me deliberately and said, "Eddie, you haven't seen anything yet."

She was right. On February 9 Postmaster General Farley announced from the White House that all airmail contracts would be canceled, effective at midnight February 19. Three days later Roosevelt himself announced that the Army Air Service would fly the mail. Like most people familiar with the situation, I was shocked and astounded by both announcements. Colonel Charles A. Lindbergh sent Roosevelt a critical telegram, which was carried in full by the press. Newspaper reporters came to me in my office and asked my opinion. It was a dreary, foggy day in New York, and for an answer I waved to the window looking out on leaden skies.

"The thing that bothers me is what is going to happen to these young Army pilots on a day like this," I said. "Their ships are not equipped with blind-flying instruments, and their training, while excellent for military duty, is not adapted for flying the airmail. Either they are going to pile up ships all the way across the continent, or they are not going to be able to fly the mail on schedule."

Though the airlines of the United States were just beginning to realize their potential, they were flying two hundred thousand miles in every 24-hour period. Standards were already high. No chief pilot flying for a commercial airline in February 1934 had fewer than four thousand hours of flying time. A few had from six thousand to nine thousand hours accumulated in the previous five to fifteen years. Only men with at least one thousand hours were being hired as copilots. Copilots were required to sit alongside the chief pilots for at least one year, perhaps five years, before attaining the rank of chief pilot—and some did not make it then. Airline pilots had the experience of flying day in and day out on predetermined schedules, in rain or shine, day or night, spring or summer, fall or winter. Those men had come to know every building, every tree, every housetop on their routes, and they were prepared through experience for whatever weather they might encounter. Planes were equipped with the best instruments for blind flying available at that time, including 2-way radio communication, and the pilots knew how to use them.

And suddenly, in contrast to those mature and experienced men and their specialized equipment, young Army officers were going to attempt to fly the mail in military planes. At that time there were only three Army pilots who had five thousand hours of flying time. For the past several years, because of limited appropriations by Congress, military pilots had been restricted to flying only about 170 to 180 hours a year. To airline personnel that kind of flying meant absolutely nothing. We all knew that those few hours had been flown in sunshine.

Most of the planes assigned to the airmail were open-cockpit jobs. None had adequate instruments for night flying or flying through weather. The airlines employed seven thousand technicians; the Army assigned 200 officers and 334 men to the program. I considered the whole thing shocking, and I said so.

The cancellation had an additional direct effect on the three airlines owned by North American Aviation Corporation—Western Air Express, TWA and Eastern Air Transport. We had been helping the Douglas Aircraft Company to design and build a new air transport. It was the best plane in the world at that time, and we were all proud of it. Jack Frye, vice-president of TWA, and I were planning to fly the plane from California to New York in March, hoping to break the transcontinental transport record. The Army was scheduled to begin flying the mail on February 20. If Frye and I wanted to make our transcontinental flight carrying airmail, we would have to time our departure from Los Angeles in order to arrive in Newark before midnight on the 19th. Several journalists had requested permission to participate in this history-making flight, and I rounded them up and hurried to Los Angeles. We arrived on Saturday morning, the 17th.

At the airport a call came in from New York with the report that a tremendous storm was brewing over the Great Lakes region and was expected to be over Newark on the evening of the 19th. It would be impossible for us to land there. We checked more closely with meteorological experts, however, and received a precise forecast of when the storm would hit Newark. If we left at our previously announced time of 9:00 P.M. Sunday (midnight Newark time) and made the trip in fifteen hours, we would arrive at our destination just twenty minutes before the storm. I determined to follow our original schedule and announced this decision to the press. I wanted the American people to know that air transport had progressed to the point at which we could call our shots with this degree of accuracy. It was taking a great chance, but, in the light of what was happening to the entire air-transport industry, it was a chance that we should take.

This decision made, we all sat down to breakfast. Someone brought in the morning papers. Big black headlines jumped at us. Three Army pilots had been killed in two separate crashes. All three had been flying to their assigned stations in order to begin flying the mail on the 20th. Two of the boys, reserve second lieutenants on active duty, hit a mountaintop in Utah during a snowstorm. The other, also a reservist, crashed in a bomber in fog in Idaho.

"That's legalized murder!" I said.

The newspapermen grabbed their pencils. "Can we quote you, Eddie?" they asked.

"You're damned right you can," I said. I was furious. In New York, the National Broadcasting Company had asked me to speak on a fifteen-minute coast-to-coast program before taking off on what we hoped would be a history-making, record-breaking flight. Well, now I knew what I was going to say. I went to my old friend, Harry Chandler, publisher of the Los Angeles *Times*.

"I'm going to make a speech, and I want it to be the most vitriolic attack that ever blistered the airwaves," I said. "I want you to lend me your best editorial writer to help me write it."

Harry agreed.

"Now will you object if I go to the *Examiner* and get their best man to help too?" I asked. Harry also agreed to that, and so two editorial writers from rival newspapers sat down with me to help me write a speech. We worked on it the rest of Saturday and all day Sunday. The speech we turned out was vicious, as I wanted it to be.

About 6:00 Sunday evening, as I was getting ready to leave for the airport, William B. "Skeets" Miller, who was in charge of special events for NBC, called from New York with the incredible report that orders had come from Washington to cut me off the air if I said anything controversial.

It wouldn't do me any good to argue. "Thanks for the warning, Skeets," I said. "I'll keep it reasonable."

I must have been so disappointed that I actually tore the speech to shreds. At any rate, I cannot find it, and I have a copy of every other important speech I ever made. During the ride to the airport, I called upon my mental discipline both to bring my anger under control and to formulate at least a general outline of what would be a fifteen-minute extemporaneous speech to a national radio audience. It went off fairly well. I could not help but inject one or two controversial remarks, but they were temperate under the circumstances.

Only after the broadcast could I relax and take some time to admire the plane that, we hoped, was going to take us to New York in record time. It was a beauty, the culmination of seven years of developmental work by the foremost airplane manufacturer of the day, my old friend Don Douglas. It was the DC-1, the experimental daddy of the famous model known as "Douglas Commercial No. Two," or "DC-2." In only a few years it would be superseded by the great DC-3, but there in Los Angeles in 1934 this sleek, shiny plane was the queen of the skies.

We took off on schedule, at 9:00 P.M. California time and climbed to an altitude of fourteen thousand feet. Our supercharged engines pulled us through the rarefied atmosphere at a far greater speed than Douglas had promised us. We had been assured of an approximate speed of 180 miles an hour, but from Los Angeles to Albuquerque we averaged 230 miles an hour. We refueled in ten minutes at Kansas City and took off into the gray dawn. At ten thousand feet the top of the sun appeared, rising out of the Atlantic. Although we had three veteran pilots and an automatic pilot on board, Jack Frye sat at the controls most of the time, and I could not resist putting in a few minutes in the copilot's seat. It was the biggest and best plane I had ever flown, and it was a thrilling experience.

We had planned to make a second stop at Pittsburgh, but computations indicated that we would be catching up with the storm there. We refueled at Columbus instead. When we did catch up with the storm, we simply climbed to twenty thousand feet and into the sunshine. The automatic pilot took us smoothly along.

We outdistanced the storm over eastern Pennsylvania and came into Newark with overcast skies but good visibility. Total flying time was thirteen hours and two minutes, a new record for commercial aircraft. No transport had ever before crossed the continent with such a load and only two stops. Two hours after we landed, the storm closed in, and it was one of the worst I had seen in years.

During the last leg of the flight, I had been busy writing another speech, to be delivered, according to a previous arrangement, over NBC on our arrival at Newark. Skeets Miller, however, met the plane with the announcement that NBC had been ordered to cancel my speech entirely. My remarks the night before, mild as they had been in comparison to what I had really wanted to say, had proved to be too controversial for Washington.

And so President Roosevelt had the last word that day. He kept me from telling the truth to the American people over a national radio hookup. But he could not silence me beyond that point, and over the years I have repeated it a thousand times: Sending the Army pilots out to fly the airmail was legalized murder.

More men were killed flying the mail during the ensuing weeks. Finally the administration, through Postmaster General Farley, came up with a face-saving device: Airmail contracts would be relet but not to any airline accused of collusion with the former Postmaster General. The presidents of three airlines, all able men, were blacklisted. The airlines involved put through token reorganizations. Some changed their names slightly. Eastern Air Transport, for example, became Eastern Air Lines, and American Airways became American Airlines.

Though I disagreed vehemently with the means, some of the results of the airmail investigations and the subsequent legislation were good for the growing air transportation industry. One of these results was the provision divorcing aviation manufacturing companies from aviation transport companies. It set the airlines up apart from any other industrial association, the way they should be. Four years later the Civil Aeronautics Act of 1938 modified some of the provisions of the 1934 Air Mail Act. It set up the Civil Aeronautics Authority, with authority over practically all the technical details of commercial aviation—airports, air aids, radio and instrumentation, airmail. It has generally worked well.

Under the terms of the 1934 Air Mail Act, North American Aviation, an affiliate of General Motors, was required to divest itself of interest in several aviation holdings, including Western Air, TWA, Pan Am and the China National Airways. Purchasers were found for those properties. GM also tried to sell Eastern Air Lines, asking only $1 million for the entire operation, but no one except me was interested, and I could not raise a fraction of that $1 million. Under a legal technicality, however, GM was permitted to retain ownership of both the General Aviation Manufacturing Company (the old Fokker Company) and Eastern.

But Eastern was no great asset. It was in bad shape and getting worse. In December 1934, Ernie Breech asked me if I wanted to run the line. I thought for a long moment before I answered. I knew the situation looked bad. But the route did have potential. It served the entire East Coast. I still believed that someday there would be extensive travel between New York and Florida by air.

More important, healthy air transport was, is and always will be of vital importance to our country. Only through the normal demands of a growing air transport industry could a healthy aircraft-manufacturing industry grow and prosper. In the years to come, I firmly believed, the state of the entire aeronautics complex would directly affect both the economic well-being of the nation and its capability for national defense. I wanted to accept the challenge of building Eastern Air Lines. But if I had not wanted to, it would still have been my patriotic duty.

I agreed to take the job but with one proviso. As I told Ernie and the board of directors: "As it stands today Eastern Air Lines is held up by government subsidy. I believe it can become a free-enterprise industry, and I will pledge all my efforts and energies to making it self-sufficient. But if this airline cannot be made to stand on its own feet and must continue to live on the taxpayers' money through government subsidy, then I want to be relieved of that job."

I was accepted as general manager on that basis.

At that time Eastern Air Lines was a comparative peanut, flying only 3,358 route miles with fewer than five hundred employees. Its equipment consisted of a mismatched assortment of planes. Salaries were low, and so was morale. But, when the personnel saw that I was willing to travel all night and work all day to build an airline in which we all would prosper, they pitched in and helped. In 1934 the line lost a million and a half dollars; in 1935, my first full year, we actually made a little money—$38,000, with scrupulously honest bookkeeping. There was still much to be done, but at least we had proved that we could do it.

One day in the early part of January 1938, I received a call from Leslie Gould, the financial writer for the Hearst newspaper chain. "Eddie," he said, "I've just learned that John Hertz has taken an option on Eastern Air Lines for $3 million. What can you tell me about it?"

I had a sudden sensation in my stomach as though I were in a plane falling straight down and out of control. "I can't tell you anything about it, Leslie," I said. "This is the first I heard of it."

I was angry and hurt. Two years before, GM had not been able to sell Eastern for $1 million; now they were selling it right out from under me for $3 million. It was I who had increased the value of this property—to *more* than $3 million, in my opinion—

and my reward, in effect, would be to be kicked out on my ear. There was no love lost between John Hertz and me.

John had built the Yellow Cab and Coach Company, which included the Hertz Drive-Your-Self System, and had sold it to GM for $43 million in 1925. He had then become a partner in Lehman Brothers. When North American Aviation was forced to sell TWA, it was Hertz who bought it. One of the points on which we disagreed was the cost of air travel. He wanted to raise fares; if anything, I wanted to lower them.

One night some months before, the phone had rung in my home in Bronxville. I heard a voice I recognized as that of John Hertz say, "Eddie?"

"Yes," I said. When Hertz began talking, it dawned on me that he had called my number by mistake. I realized that he had said "Ernie," not "Eddie." He obviously thought that he was talking to Ernie Breech, who lived in nearby Scarsdale. Breech had been associated with Hertz in the Yellow Cab Company, and the two were close. Before I could break in and tell Hertz who I was, he began talking about me. From then on I listened. Hertz went into great detail about how he was going to get that Rickenbacker. He must have talked for half an hour.

When he was through, I said gently, "John, this is Eddie Rickenbacker you are talking to." There was a very loud silence, and then Hertz hung up.

And so I knew that if Hertz bought Eastern there would be no place for me in the line. That was not my major concern; I would not have stayed anyway. More important, I knew that Hertz was not dedicated to aviation. Eastern Air Lines would be simply another property to him and a small one at that. But to me Eastern Air Lines was everything. It was my life. Its employees were my personal friends and my personal concern. I wanted to keep Eastern and continue to make it grow. I did not want to lose it.

After Leslie Gould's call, I hurried over to see Henry M. Hogan, general counsel for General Motors and North American Aviation. Henry confirmed what Leslie had told me.

"Do you see any reason why I shouldn't go to see Mr. Sloan about this personally?" I asked.

"No I don't," he said. "Go ahead."

I called Mr. Sloan and asked if I could have a word with him. He recognized the urgency in my voice and told me to drop in right away. Mr. Sloan and I had talked many times before, and he had always listened to my suggestions and proposals. I told him the whole story of Eastern Air Lines.

"I think I'm entitled to as much of an opportunity as any outsider to bid for Eastern Air Lines," I said. "If I can't outbid John Hertz, then I'm the loser. But isn't it fair to give me a chance to try?"

"Let me look into this, Eddie," he said. "Come back and see me in a few days."

In the meantime, I went to my old friends Bill Knudsen, by then president of General Motors, Donaldson Brown, at that time the financial genius of GM, and several other top executives. I received no help from Ernie Breech. Though we had been friends before and would be friends again, in this instance he was on the other side of the table.

When I returned to Mr. Sloan, it was apparent that he had thoroughly investigated Eastern Air Lines and my participation in it. Neither he nor anyone else had intended any slight to me by giving Hertz an option. Eastern was such a comparatively small part of a giant corporation that the top management had simply not thought much about it one way or the other.

"I agree with your position, Eddie," he said. "GM will give you a 30-day option, equal to that of John Hertz, for an equal amount." He went on to explain the terms of Hertz's option—$1 million down and the rest in long-term notes.

"I think it should be a cash transaction," I said. "Mr. Sloan, if I can offer you three and a half million dollars cash for Eastern Air Lines before the option runs out, would you be inclined to sell it to me?"

Mr. Sloan was a forthright gentleman. "Yes, Eddie," he said. "I would."

Where in the world would I find that much money? I called everyone I knew in Wall Street. One was an old friend named William Barclay Harding of Smith, Barney and Company, the investment bankers. Harding was particularly interested in the aviation industry and believed that it was right for investment. His own firm did not have the money, but he took me to see John Schiff, Frederick M. Warburg and Hugh Knowlton of Kuhn, Loeb and Company. After a thorough investigation, they agreed to advance the money for me to buy the airline. They would organize a new corporation and raise the money through public subscription. I would be president of the company.

Then I had to win approval of my bid from the directors of North American Aviation. A meeting of the board was called in the General Motors building at 57th Street and Broadway in Manhattan. Accompanied by my financial backers and attorneys, I appeared before the board and made my offer. I received no concrete answer. We talked and talked but got nowhere. It was obvious that Ernie Breech was stifling my bid in favor of his friend John Hertz.

At 6:00 P.M. the board had still come to no decision. I suggested that we adjourn for dinner and meet at a later hour.

Before we ate I went to a phone and called Knudsen in Detroit. I was furious with Ernie Breech and his outright favoritism for Hertz, and I protested bitterly to Bill. He heard me out. "Go ahead with your meeting," he said in his soft Norwegian accent. "I will ask Mr. Breech to refrain from participating."

Both groups went over to the University Club for dinner, eating separately in two of the small private dining rooms.

After dinner we continued the discussion, but separately. My attorney, Alexander B. Royce, served as mediator. He would go over to the GM group and deliver our message, then come back with their response. Ernie Breech, he reported, was not participating in the discussion. At about 3:00 A.M. Alex came back with the news that the GM group would like to come over to our room and state its position. We extended the invitation, and the group arrived. Alex reiterated our original offer. Henry Hogan, speaking for GM, accepted, with no provisions whatever.

That was Friday morning. My 30-day option expired at 6:00 P.M. Sunday. I began worrying about where Schiff and Warburg would find $3.5 million on Sunday. By Saturday night I had fretted to the point of desperation. I called Mr. Sloan at his apartment at 11:00 P.M. and asked if I could see him for fifteen minutes. "It's of vital importance," I explained.

He told me to come on over and received me in a robe over his pajamas. He had obviously been in bed. I poured out my fears that my banker friends would not have the money on Sunday and asked for a 10-day extension. Mr. Sloan listened to me for an hour and a half. Finally he stood up and looked me in the eye with a whimsical little smile.

"If I were you, Eddie," he said, "I wouldn't worry."

I went home and went to bed, but I did not get much sleep. Sunday morning Freddy Warburg called. "Where do you want your three and a half million dollars, Eddie," he asked, "and when?" He sounded as though he made such calls every Sunday morning.

I replied just as calmly. "If it's convenient, Freddy," I said, "make it the Eastern hangar at Newark airport at 10:00 A.M. tomorrow."

"I'll be there," he said, "with a certified check."

I called Mr. Sloan to apologize again for keeping him up the night before and told him of the conversation with Freddy Warburg. "I am confident that he will be there with the money," Mr. Sloan said. "Now stop worrying. Everything is all right."

I was at the airport at 8:00 the next morning. It was a long two hours. At 10:00 sharp Freddy Warburg and one of his associates walked in. He handed me a certified check for $3.5 million.

"Thank you," I said calmly. I was standing up straight, but I really wanted to go down on my knees. That night at home, I did kneel. I thanked God first, and then I murmured thanks to everyone else who had helped me. That included Mr. Sloan, of course. I had presented the check to him personally, and I have never forgotten his words. He said:

"Congratulations, Eddie, and God bless you, and I wish you every success in the world."

By that time my group had all the organizational details worked out for the new corporation. Two important features were the provision for a half-million dollars in working capital—more money than I had thought there was in the world—and an arrangement by which I would have an option on 10 percent of the capital stock. There would be roughly 416,000 shares, to be sold to the public at the issue price of $10 a share. The issue was considered to be oversubscribed three to one, but on the day the stock went on sale Germany invaded Austria. The international reverberations caused the oversubscription to evaporate; only about one-half the issue was taken. I had to take to the road myself to help sell the stock. But eventually we raised the money, and I had the airline.

It was April 1938. I realized fully that on that day my life had changed. I sat down and wrote the following:

My Constitution
April 1938

(1) My goal will be to do a good job and sell, sell, sell Eastern Air Lines at all times.

(2) I will plan my work and work my plan each day arranging details in advance as far as possible.

(3) I will make a business of arriving on duty on time and then think of nothing but doing my best to help make Eastern Air Lines the best airline in the world.

(4) I will spend my time just the same as I would spend my money, as it is the only capital I have to invest, and I will keep a strict accounting of every hour.

(5) I will try to do nothing at any time which will undermine my health, as clear thinking and effective action depend on feeling fit.

(6) I will stress as well as I can and keep my mental attitude right never allowing myself to think of my work as a "GRIND" but rather as a pleasure and a privilege.

(7) I will endeavor to give careful thought as to the needs of our company and its customers.

(8) I will avoid misrepresentation as dishonest and poor policy.

(9) I will be fair competition but be firm, using diplomacy, remembering "a knocker never wins, a winner never knocks."

(10) I will always keep in mind that I am in the greatest business in the world, as well as working for the greatest company in the world, and I can serve humanity more completely in my line of endeavor than in any other.

(11) I will become an expert by continuing to study and learn.

(12) I realize that most of salesmanship is "MAN," and that success depends on the superiority of Eastern Air Lines' service.

"A winner never quits and a quitter never wins."

ELEVEN

HOW TO BUILD AN AIRLINE

And now that I was at last president and general manager of Eastern Air Lines, I could not help but observe that in thirteen years I had made a full 360-degree circle and, in a sense, wound up right where I had started. For an important section of Eastern was the same route that Reed Chambers and I unsuccessfully pioneered with Florida Airways so many years before. Its purchase by the Pitcairn Aviation Company had extended Pitcairn's New York-Atlanta route to Miami. It flew a tiny biplane called the "Pitcairn Mailwing."

On May 1, 1928, when the Pitcairn line began operations, there had been 44 people on the payroll. In that first month the little line flew eight thousand pounds of mail. It carried no passengers.

Once he had an opportunity to do both, Harold Pitcairn found that he preferred designing and building planes to operating an airline. C. M. Keys was then building his aviation empire, North American Aviation, and he bought Pitcairn for $2 million cash. The route included service between New

York, Philadelphia, Washington, Atlanta, Jacksonville and Miami.

Keys called his new line "Eastern Air Transport." On August 18, 1930, with eleven cash customers and five pounds of mail, Eastern flew the first passenger service between New York and Washington. Keys used planes made by his manufacturing subsidiary, the Curtiss Airplane Company. Curtiss made a 2-engine plane called the "Kingbird" and a bigger plane of newer design, also a bimotor, called the "Condor." It was made of fabric over steel tubing and was powered by two big water-cooled 12-cylinder engines. No other airline would buy it. It was up to Eastern to fly it, develop it and perfect it.

In addition to those planes, Keys somehow managed to pick up a couple of single-engine Stinsons. By the time I had prevailed upon General Motors to buy North American Aviation, Eastern Air Transport had a fleet of 23 planes ranging from the tiny Mailwing to the lumbering Condor.

We did the best we could with this hodgepodge. It was in 1933, I recall, that we put a couple of berths in the tail end of the Condor and called it a "sleeper." I flew from Atlanta to New York in it. At every stop all night long, I would climb out of bed and display myself in pajamas to the reporters and photographers waiting at the airport.

Air travel was by no means fully accepted in the early 1930s. The New York-Washington run was the only one that came near paying for itself. Planes flew empty or with only one or two passengers. Our employees were not selling their product.

In a way I could not blame them. When I became general manager of Eastern Air Lines in January 1934, morale was right on the ground. For years there had been no continuity of management. Every six months or so a new president or general manager would come in, add to the confusion and depart. Personnel on the managerial level, up and down the line, had learned to keep their mouths shut and their costs down if they wanted to hold their jobs. No one stuck his neck out with a new idea for fear that he would get his head hacked off. Salaries were ridiculously low. Salesmen, who were supposed to be walking into the offices of prominent local business-men and selling them on air travel, were receiving as little as $60 a month; only a few made $100. And they were men who were expected to exude confidence in air travel and to impress the public with its advantages.

Low morale among our nonflying personnel was bad enough; in the air it could mean life or death. Our chief pilots were reasonably well paid, but they had many other problems—domestic and physical. Copilots were underpaid to the extent that they could not possibly give the company their best efforts. Some had spent their life savings trying to support themselves in their chosen careers. Most were married, with children. Some actually had outside jobs. Yet we were asking them to devote full concentration to their development into chief pilots with all the responsibilities the title entailed.

No major effort had been made to expand the line. It ran from New York to Atlanta, from New York to Miami, from Chicago to Atlanta and from Atlanta to New Orleans. The leadership of any operation should want to make it grow.

On top of everything else, the Eastern route had probably the worst weather of any airline in the country. Storms came from over the Gulf of Mexico, the Great Lakes, the North Atlantic and the Caribbean. Fog would roll in from any of these directions, bank up against the Appalachian mountains and stay there. On one occasion the entire route was blanketed for seven full days. Not one mile was flown for one entire week.

Air travelers today, who are used to looking into the gray nothingness of clouds for long periods of time without think-ing anything of it, may wonder why planes could not fly on instruments. But when Eastern first started, instruments were in their infancy. Without instruments, the pilot of a plane can reach the point where he doesn't know whether he is right side up or upside down.

Here, then, were some of the problems that I faced when I first took over Eastern Air Lines. One thing was certain: I was not going to understand the problems, much less solve them, from a desk in New York. One doesn't make dollars by depositing his quarters in a swivel chair. I don't like second-hand information.

So I went out on the line to obtain my information first-hand. I traveled at night and worked in the various stations by day. I could always take time off to talk with the personnel, watch them in action, get my own firsthand impressions and facts. More often than not, I would work with my people as I talked with them. I changed tires and loaded luggage. I have changed spark plugs many a time. I also checked people in at the counter, called hotels for accommodations for passengers when weather forced us to cancel flights and made railroad reservations for them.

In this way, combining my own firsthand investigations with the inevitable paper work, I soon knew more about the airline, its condition and its problems than did any other man in the company—including the operations manager, the treasurer and the traffic manager. I never boarded a plane or visited a company operation without introducing myself to those I had not already met, visiting with my people, listening to their problems and suggestions and in general constantly keeping my eyes and ears open. Believe me, when I dropped in on one of the smaller stops at 3:00 A.M. and showed an earnest and sincere interest in the welfare of the people on duty, those people talked with me frankly. They also realized that they were no longer faceless figures on a payroll sheet, but men and women with distinct names and personalities, members of a team.

I was on the New York-Miami flight when bad weather forced us to land at Charleston, South Carolina, at midnight.

We had two full sections, and there on the ground was one employee, a long lean country boy. When he finally realized that he was responsible for the welfare of 24 passengers, his eyes lit up.

"You know, Cap'n," he said, "I've been dreaming that some-time something like this would happen, and by golly, here it is."

We worked from midnight until 3:00 in the morning find-ing accommodations and arranging transportation.

The next morning when the skies cleared and the flights were resumed, several passengers complained that the cab-drivers had been surly and had demanded exorbitant fares. A few days later I returned to Charleston on a late flight un-announced and took a taxi into town. The driver overcharged me several dollars. The next day I rode cabs all over town, making notes on the distances and fares. I then went to see the owner of the cab company. He cleaned up the situation immediately. After all, he never saw any of the extra money his drivers were collecting. The entire cab-riding population benefited and not only the airport passengers.

Straightening out this problem was just one of the little extra services that the general manager of an airline can perform.

Esprit de corps can not completely make up for a skimpy pay envelope. I fought for pay increases for those employees who most needed them. One of the first groups I worked with was the traffic, or sales, department. We went out on the streets and made calls on businessmen, industries and in-stitutions, aggressively selling air transportation. I have al-ways referred to this work as "hoof-and-mouth disease"— "hoof it" to get to your prospects and "mouth it" to tell them about your product. In order to be successful, it was neces-sary for me to reorganize the entire traffic department by raising salaries, attracting top-quality personnel, developing knowledge, inspiring dedication.

We had a service to sell. If we presented it enthusiastically and honestly to the public, then the public would buy it. Our business would then be built on a sound foundation.

As soon as increased revenues made it possible, we increased the salaries of our copilots. No prior announcement was made. One payday they found their paychecks substantially larger. Other steps were taken to advance them up the seniority ladder. A systematic, planned vacation schedule was worked out for the chief pilots, for example, which gave the copilots additional opportunities for responsibility and advancement.

I wanted to start expanding the route as soon as I could, but at the beginning we could only put on additional service along our existing route. In our first year, we added five round trips between New York and Washington, putting on fourteen more the next summer and twenty the third. This expansion increased the openings for chief pilots and gave copilots more flying time.

Within three years, every man who had been a copilot when I became general manager of Eastern Air Lines had become a chief pilot. Their individual contentment with their jobs added up to a positive asset for the company. For one of the greatest safety devices in the world is a free state of mind, a happy state of mind, on the part of those at the controls. I would rather have it than all the instruments on the dashboard.

The problems of the chief pilots were more complex. They could be solved only by individual understanding and guidance. I know of no finer group of men than airline pilots. They carry a terrific responsibility. They are the most self-disciplined body of men in the world today. They must constantly school themselves. They must watch their health and their physical condition to the degree that their freedom is voluntarily restricted.

Associating with the pilots was one of the greatest fringe benefits for me as an airline operator, for I enjoyed their company. The very environment of their occupation, high above the vibrations and noises and petty irritations on the earth's surface, is conducive to a broader, wiser, calmer outlook. I know that many a time, when I have been trying to work out some apparently unfathomable problem, I have looked for an excuse to go somewhere, just to take a ride in an airplane. Up in the sky, in the unpolluted air, thoughts come more clearly, and concentration is easier.

Yes, there is a poetry in the sky. There is poetry in the clouds, in the moon, in the sun, in every phase of the universe.

The men who live in the heavens above the world have a spiritual brotherhood. Whenever I boarded a plane, I would introduce myself to the crew and would usually be asked to come and visit in the cockpit during the flight. I soon came to know every pilot by his first name. Incidentally, I later came to learn that the crews were always prepared for me. Whenever I scheduled a flight, the ground personnel sent word to the crew by means of a simple code: "orange on board." That orange was Rickenbacker.

It was through visiting with our pilots on their home grounds that I gained their confidences on what, if anything, was bothering them. I was able to help several of them to reorganize their lives and their finances in order to enjoy the standards and additional pleasures to which their incomes entitled them.

One of our best known pilots was Henry T. "Dick" Merrill, a man whose name is prominent in the history of commercial aviation. Dick Merrill, with Jack Lambie as copilot, made the famous transatlantic flight of 1937 in which the pictures of the coronation of King George were brought to the United States. Two years before that he and Harry Richman, the entertainer, had made a transatlantic round trip.

Dick was a great pilot in the air, but he had a weakness on the ground: He liked to play the horses. I have flown with Dick right after he has won or lost large sums at the racetrack, and, though I have noticed no apparent difference in his flying skill, I have felt that he could not help but be affected by his gambling activities—particularly when he lost. One day I had an idea. Dick had just married a beautiful starlet, Toby Wing. At a party one night I drew her aside.

"Toby," I said, "you ought to have a better house. It would be a good investment, and if Dick had to meet a big payment every month I don't think he'd take a chance on gambling it away."

I didn't have to tell a woman as pretty as Toby how to talk her husband into a new home. Not long afterward, I was invited out to the Merrills' housewarming in Miami Beach. It was a beautiful place, with a mortgage in proportion. Dick had to forgo the ponies to pay for the house. I felt better flying with him, and he went on to become chief check pilot of Eastern Air Lines.

Other pilots were in more complex difficulties. I helped many of them straighten out. Simply enabling them to realize that they were destroying their careers and their lives was a major factor in steering them back to the right road.

Some of our pilots had physical problems. At that time medical examinations were far less rigorous. Any authorized physician could give a physical examination. Few doctors had any interest in, let alone knowledge of, aviation medicine.

It was a vital problem that affected the entire industry, but neither the industry nor the government was doing anything about it. Most of our senior pilots had, by that time, devoted some fifteen years to flying and were largely untrained for any other profession. Their continued employment depended upon the semiannual physical checkups given by a doctor who was, in effect, judge, jury and executioner and who usually had no continuing contact with the pilot. It would be natural for a pilot to withhold any symptoms that he might think would result in his being grounded. Some pilots actually bribed doctors to sign their health certificates.

As general manager of an airline, I was responsible for our passengers; I wanted to know positively that the man to whose hands they were entrusted was in the finest physical condition, regardless of what a medical examiner might write on his card. In short, I wanted our own aeromedical department. The board of directors was somewhat skeptical of my proposal to set up an expensive operation to provide what the government was supposedly providing free, but finally it did approve my proposal. Our medical department was set up on July 1, 1936. It was the first of its kind.

Back at Issoudun in World War I, I had known a fine young doctor named Ralph H. Greene, who had been the first medical officer ordered to fly. I found Doctor Greene in Jacksonville, Florida. He was a colonel in the Medical Corps Reserve, a pilot and a consultant in neurology and psychology, in addition to being an excellent practicing physician. We discussed the area of aviation medicine for hours.

Though I knew little about how to keep the human mechanism operating, I did know something about preventive maintenance for the airplane. This system calls for constant surveillance of the aircraft and an hour-by-hour and day-by-day record of the performance of engines, propellers and airframes. Why, I asked Doctor Greene, could we not apply the same principles to the men who would fly the machines?

He went right along with these ideas and became the world's first medical director for an airline. We set him up in his own aeromedical laboratory in Miami. There he could make his own thorough and exhaustive examinations of our pilots' physical conditions. More important, he became the family doctor for those men. He saw them frequently, he flew with them and he saw them socially as well as medically.

At first some of our pilots, particularly the older ones, were suspicious and distrustful of the program. They thought that I was trying to "get" something on them to railroad them out of their jobs. But Doctor Greene won them over. He could appraise them psychologically as well as physically. Frequently he saw symptoms of approaching ill health in time to take preventive measures. He was able to detect signs of hypertension before the pilots themselves were fully aware of what was happening to them. Through frank and deep discussions of their problems, he was able to relieve their anxieties.

The Eastern Air Lines aeromedical laboratory carried on a far more comprehensive technical program than I can discuss here. From the first year's findings alone, Doctor Greene published several technical reports. Our findings were made available to all other airlines, and within a short time practically all of them had their own medical departments. We helped several get started and even accepted assignments from other airlines. The special research that Doctor Greene did for Pan American World Airways, for example, led to a new system for the control and prevention of certain tropical ailments that flight personnel operating beyond our international borders were beginning to contract in serious proportions.

We also set up a meteorology department under the direction of a young scientist named Joseph J. George. Again and again, in the early days of commercial flying, the U.S. Weather Bureau, on the basis of reports covering an entire area, would ground our planes. Our own meteorology department in Atlanta, however, could pinpoint weather conditions at local stations and frequently would permit planes to go through. One shipload of passengers could pay the cost of a week's operation of the meteorology lab. It paid for itself over and over. And there were times when our department recommended that we not fly even though the U.S. Weather Bureau gave the go-ahead.

Though we could do nothing about the weather itself, we could certainly do something about flying through it. We were fortunate in the early years in having a pilot named Howard C. Stark, who was a student of blind flying.

"I got to thinking I was pretty good at blind flying," he told me once. "I used to go into clouds deliberately to practice it. One time I was flying through a cloud, practicing my blind-flying skill, patting myself on the back for keeping the plane straight and level. Suddenly I burst out of the bottom of the cloud. I was in a spin, heading straight down at 160 miles an hour. Lucky for me the ceiling was about seven hundred feet, and I had time to pull out of it. But after all the practicing I had done, there I was in a spin, and I didn't know it."

At that time instrumentation was still being perfected. There were two types of equipment on the market, the turn-and-bank indicator group and the Sperry group. Stark made a study of each method and wrote what I believe was the first manual on instrument flying. I exploited his interest and experience. Some of our pilots, even in the 1930s, resisted and were skeptical of this new science, but I encouraged Stark to persist. As a result, Eastern Air Lines had the first instrument-oriented group of pilots.

Weather was the initial cause of one of our most fortunate early changes. Primarily to ensure better living for our employees, I moved our operations headquarters from Atlanta to Miami. Atlanta has always been one of my favorite cities, but I chose Miami simply because of the climate. I believed that the Florida climate would be delightful to work in, living costs would be less and the employees would appreciate the opportunity for year-round outdoor recreation. The directors objected to the additional expense, but I finally convinced them, and they approved the move. As we added new routes and stations, the Miami move paid for itself in maintenance. By scheduling planes due for periodic checkups to terminate at Miami, the end of the line, we were able to effect great savings.

When I took over the line, I traveled its length and spoke at all the different stations. "It makes no difference to me what you think of my ability or my qualifications to run Eastern Air Lines or my knowledge of air transport," I said.

There is one thought I wish to register with you, though, and I hope you will never forget it. That is that my job is to see that you members of Eastern Air Lines are a happy, successful lot, that you get everything that can be given you. If I do that job properly, I need not worry about the rest of my duties. You men and women will take care of that automatically. We can't help but succeed.

Increasing the number of flights between New York and Washington was one of the early proofs that I meant what I said. The merry-go-round, as we called it, kept not only our pilots but also all our personnel busy the year round. We lost some money, but the benefits more than made up for it. The merry-go-round increased the training and the expertise of all employees and ended layoffs completely. From then on, all Eastern employees knew that, barring unforeseen events, they were assured of year-round work and regular paychecks.

But overcoming a disgruntled attitude on the part of all personnel takes time, particularly when that attitude has been justified by general lack of concern at the top levels. Our mechanics and maintenance men had been particularly neglected. Many of them wanted a union to come in and fight their battles for them. Others believed that I was doing my level best to improve their working conditions and increase their salaries and remained loyal. Conflict between the two groups developed to the point at which there were fistfights on the job.

In November 1937, I received word that the mechanics at Newark planned to strike. I was just beginning to develop some esprit de corps in the organization at that time and had singled out several loyal men down the line. On the day before the strike was to begin, I brought some of those men into Newark. When the strikers walked out at midnight, my men walked in. Cots were set up and food brought in.

I knew several of the boys who were out on strike and knew them to be intrinsically decent people who were simply being misled. I kept in contact with them. One was a particularly nice young fellow, a lead mechanic with a definite future in the organization, and I talked to him myself on several occasions. One of my main arguments was that a union was not going to do one thing more for the employees than I was, and I hammered this point home.

The union advocated lumping individual workers into different classifications. I do not believe in the classification of any American. My policy in hiring men and women to work for Eastern Air Lines was simply that I did not want anyone who did not want to be president of the company. Desire for leadership could be our measuring stick, not some stultifying classification.

At 4:00 one morning, I received a telephone call from Beverly Griffith, our public-relations director. Bev liked to go out and talk to people too. He had just been told by the young lead mechanic that he was walking off the picket line and going back to work.

"I couldn't wait to call and tell you," Bev said.

"I'm glad you did," I said. "That starts the ball rolling." Within a few days, the strike was over.

I have heard it said that I am against labor unions and the laboring man. Such statements are ridiculous. In the first place, I myself am fundamentally a workingman. I have worked hard all my life. Nor do I have anything against the legitimate labor union that provides an honest service to its members. It is those so-called "unions" dominated by racketeers and Communists that I abhor.

During the strike I realized that some men would honestly feel more secure with a union negotiating for them. I quietly began looking into this union business. After some research, I determined that the International Association of Machinists was the best union to serve my people. I set up an appointment with its president, George M. Brown. "I want to unionize my mechanics," I told him bluntly. "How do you want to go about it?"

He looked at me as though I had lost my mind. Only a few months before, I had successfully fought off a union; now I was inviting his union in. After several bargaining sessions that were no more difficult than I expected, the union and the company reached an agreement.

But a union could never take the place of consideration and concern for our Eastern family. I tried to stay ahead of it by providing our employees with the compensation and benefits they deserved.

Eastern was the first airline to put in the 40-hour week for maintenance employees. Eastern had the first pension plan. It took a great deal of research and negotiation, as I wanted it to cover the high-salaried pilots, as well as everyone else down the line. We also put in a group insurance plan, the first in the industry, which, over the years, held many a family together when the breadwinner died. It was followed by a comprehensive medical-insurance plan.

In the early days of Eastern, employees had learned to go about their work as inconspicuously as possible. I wanted to convince them that I needed their help, that it was *our* airline. Even a turtle has to stick its neck out to get anywhere. We set up an idea bank to stimulate new ideas. Anyone proposing an improvement that would save the company money or increase efficiency or revenue would receive 10 percent of the savings or earnings for the first year. Ideas poured in, and their creators received thousands of dollars over the years.

A great many improvements were inspired through my continued custom of simply visiting with members of the Eastern family. One day, for example, as I was having a cup of coffee in the employee lunchroom, I happened to notice a bandage on the hand of a young maintenance worker sitting next to me. I inquired about it.

"I hurt it on a jack," he said. "If you want to know the truth, our jacks are no damn good."

He turned out to be right. Under the pre-Rickenbacker policy of "say nothing and keep the cost down," no one had had the courage to bring up the matter of these defective jacks. I had them all thrown out and more reliable equipment purchased. They paid for themselves in greater efficiency and less time lost through accidents, with a boost in morale as a bonus.

During my first three years as general manager of the airline, some of the mechanical personnel were given several raises. Eastern had men in the maintenance department who were being paid at much higher rates than any union scale in existence. Every man received two weeks vacation with pay.

Thanks to their esprit de corps, coupled with efficient schedules and work programing, we built up a greater utilization rate per plane. By 1941 we were obtaining a daily average of 12 hours and 45 minutes of flying time from each of our planes. This utilization figure topped all others in the industry.

When the new company was organized in 1938 and I became president and general manager, I insisted that an option on 10 percent of the capital stock be held for me for five years at the issue price of $10 a share. This scheme provided an incentive and a reward, for, should the stock increase in value, I would still be able to buy it at the issue price.

As the line began to prosper, I realized how much I owed to our employees and also how the company would benefit if all the employees had similar incentives. I split my option with the employees. We worked out a formula by which employees were entitled to buy those shares in varying amounts, depending upon their jobs and the length of time they had been with Eastern. Pilots and executives were at the top of the list.

In making stock options available to the employees, I went out of my way to impress the members of the Eastern family with the opportunity they had. I wanted everyone to realize how his own efforts, directed toward making his company successful, would increase his nest egg for the future. Furthermore, this opportunity would tend to hold down administrative salaries. As the nation came out of the Depression, many companies were beginning to pay exorbitant sums to their top administrative personnel, a practice that has increased. Through the Eastern stock-option plan, we were able to compensate our people without inflated executive salaries. I set my own salary at $50,000 in 1938 and did not raise it a penny during the quarter of a century that I was to continue as head of Eastern.

While the stock was still selling for $10 a share, I warned everyone against getting too excited if it should go higher than that. I frankly though ruefully related my own experience with General Motors in the early 1920s. I had bought five hundred shares of GM in 1920 for $10 a share. When it reached $17 a share, I thought I had Wall Street licked and sold it for a profit of $3,500. Well, if only I had hung onto those five hundred shares, they would be worth several million dollars today.

"If it develops that selling these shares on which you have options will bring in a profit and you need that money to buy a home or pay medical bills or take care of some extreme emergency, then I won't object," I said. "But, if I find anybody selling his stock to buy a big red automobile or something equally frivolous, I warn you right here and now I'm going to get mad as hell."

Over the years I prevailed upon the board of directors to approve additional stock that could be taken up by the new employees on the same option basis. Some years later the Internal Revenue Service issued a directive nullifying the option plan. I arranged a conference with Senator Walter E. George of Georgia, a fine gentleman, and convinced him of the fairness and advantages of the stock-option plan. He introduced and served as floor manager of a bill to reinstate the benefits of the option agreement between company and employee. The bill became law. Not only the thousands of Eastern employees, but probably millions of other employees of American corporations as well, benefited. After that I obtained and portioned out two hundred thousand more shares.

In the meantime the stock had gone as high as $134 a share. Its activity became erratic because of the limited number of shares publicly owned. Purchase of a comparatively small amount of stock in one day would cause the total value to leap five or ten points. In order to stabilize the value, the board of directors approved a four-to-one split, creating a total of some 2 million shares.

Those employees who had purchased $100 worth of stock in 1938—and there were many who had—saw their holdings increase in value to $4,000 when the stock passed the $100 mark in 1966. Many a happy home has been paid for with the profits resulting from the sale of this option stock. Many small businesses have been started, many youths sent through college, many family emergencies or tragedies alleviated by this system of rewarding our people.

In all these years, I know of only one employee who abused the stock-option privilege. His problem was alcohol, and he did not remain with Eastern Air Lines.

Concern for our people included protecting them from the occasional crank or ugly customer who came along. One of our regular passengers seemed to take a psychotic delight in making life miserable for Eastern personnel. I heard about him from reservation clerks, stewardesses, even pilots. One day, coming north from Atlanta, I was sitting in the front seat when a passenger plopped down beside me and told me his name. It rang a bell. "You're the man I've been looking for," I told him. He looked at me in surprise. "You've been making life miserable for people on this line, and they don't deserve it. They're trying to do the best they can for the customers. When you browbeat them over something they can't control, like weather, it's you who's wrong, not they. Personally I don't care if you ever ride this airline again."

He gulped and said, "Oh, Captain, don't talk like that."

"That's just exactly what I'm trying to get you to do—not talk like that," I said. "If you want to talk hard to somebody, talk to me—or try to. I don't think you're worth listening to."

We rode all the way to Washington. He didn't say a word. The flight was terminated there because of bad weather in New York, and we were taken to Union Station for the midnight train to New York. The next morning when I got up, he was waiting in the aisle. "Won't you have breakfast with me, Captain?" he said.

"I've got to have it some place, and I might as well have it with you," I said. I was civil but not friendly.

When we parted, he said: "You know, you really have been a great help to me. I want to give you this. It's a good-luck piece."

It was a silver dollar. I still have it. That man became one of our most considerate passengers and gained the friendship and respect of those who served him.

On another flight, a passenger sitting behind me said in a loud, harsh voice, "What's wrong with Eastern is it's got lousy management."

I turned around. "Rickenbacker's my name, general manager of Eastern Air Lines," I said. "What's your name? What's your business?"

He turned bright red, but he told me. I recognized him for another chronic complainer.

"Do you tell your salesmen to go around telling everybody your competitors' management is no good?" I asked. He said no. "Well then, what right have you to criticize the management of Eastern Air Lines? I don't give a damn whether I ever see you on board one of our planes again or not."

When we got off he came running up behind me, put his arm over my shoulders and asked if he could call me "Eddie."

"You are a hundred percent right," he said. "I've been jumping on people along the line for things they weren't responsible for. You don't ever need to worry about me again."

I never heard another complaint about him. All the kids wanted to know what I had said to him to turn him from an ogre into a fairly nice individual. Episodes of that kind travel the length and breadth of an airline. I was asked about it everywhere.

One day I was up in the cockpit when the stewardess came in. Her face was contorted. "What in the world is the matter with you, Betty?" I asked.

She started crying. "That man back there keeps making insulting remarks to me," she said, sniffling and poking at her eyes with a handkerchief. "I can't stand it any longer."

I went back into the cabin, found the man who had made the insulting remarks and took him aside. "Are you a married man?" I asked. He said he was. "Do you have any children?" He said he had two girls. "How old are they?"

"One's ten, and one's eleven," he said proudly.

"Well when they grow up," I said, "are you going to tolerate a damn stupid ass like you making vulgar advances to them? Our hostesses are ladies and are entitled to your respect, not your insults."

He took it in silence, but when we deplaned he came up to me and said: "Captain, I apologized to that young lady. I had one drink too many. But I'm glad in a way, because you pictured something to me that I had never thought of before."

That story spread like wildfire over the line too. It increased the respect my employees had for me—Rickenbacker stood up for his people. I was happy and proud to have that reputation, but my action in such episodes was spontaneous. It was certainly not staged to make an impression on my employees.

One of the employees who might not have felt that I was supremely on his side was my own son David. When he was a teenager, I found him a job out at the airport during the summer vacation and told his boss not to show him any favors. He would leave every morning at 6:00, bright and chipper, and come back looking as though he had been dragged through a sewer pipe feet first. After about three weeks I casually inquired how things were going at the airport.

"Okay, Daddy, okay," he said.

"What have they got you doing?"

"Well, I'm in charge of the latrine division," he said. "I pull out the full ones and put in the empty ones."

They certainly had taken me at my word. I know of no worse job on an airline than cleaning the chemical toilets.

It goes without saying that full emphasis was placed on courtesy to the passengers from our employees. A typical exhortation is this one, taken from the minutes of one of our employee gatherings:

Our passengers are paying your salaries which amount to millions of dollars a month, plus ten million dollars we have to pay for parts, supplies and materials. Sure, I know you get irritable as you get the pressure put on you, but you shouldn't. The difference between leadership and the lack of it is to be able to control yourself under pressure. Anticipate your problems and then be courteous.

If some of you, when you get angry at someone, would stop to think how you would feel if you were treated as you treat our customers, you would soften up quickly and recognize your responsibilities and obligations to those customers.

When I took over the general management of Eastern, I told the board of directors that I was going to operate an airline as a free-enterprise company or that I would not operate it at all. One of my first duties, therefore, was to inform the United States government that we did not want any more of the taxpayers' money. Eastern was the first airline to operate without a subsidy from the Federal government, and for many years it was the only one to do so. The taxpayers did not support Eastern Air Lines. We did not fly the mail free; we charged the Post Office Department the agreed-upon service fee. But there was no subsidy.

There had been a time, at Eastern Air Lines as well as at all others, when a subsidy had been necessary to get the line going. It was reasonable; all modes of transportation have needed government assistance at the beginning. Many airlines, particularly the regional lines, have continued to need taxpayers' subsidies up to the present.

Through subsidizing the airlines, at the beginning of commercial air transport, the government actually saved hundreds of millions of dollars in the long run. With this government assurance, private enterprise could take over, raise and spend hundreds of millions of dollars for equipment and development of equipment and thus build an air-transportation system. But, once an airline can support itself honestly on its own efficient operation, it should do so. Eastern could and did.

I saw no reason to continue our Washington office. All we were doing there was lobbying, trying to get something for nothing.

We had more vital operations to spend money on, operations that would develop public confidence in our business and provide honest earned income. If we were honestly and fairly entitled to something that Washington could give us, then we would go down there and walk in the front door with our heads up, demand it and fight for it.

Building public confidence in air travel in the 1930s was a major job in itself. I had always maintained a policy of checking in with local organizations before I arrived in any town, and I continued. I had standing invitations from several different civic groups in every fair-sized city. I began welcoming invitations from women's organizations. I would try to convince the ladies that, when their husbands took business trips, they would come back not only safely but also more quickly if they flew.

"And by the way," I'd add, "have you thought about going with him on one of his trips? You'd find out for yourself how nice it is to fly in an airplane."

Frequently, at the end of a local meeting, women would come up to me and protest that they were simply too scared to permit their husbands to go off on trips by air.

"And as for flying myself, I'd be petrified!" they'd say.

During all those years, Eastern Air Lines—and that included Eastern Air Transport, Pitcairn Aviation and even Florida Airways—had never lost a passenger. Every safety measure available at that time was utilized to the fullest extent. The engines on those lumbering Condors were being overhauled every two hundred hours, and maintenance was constant. I would reiterate these facts, again and again, and I'm sure they made some impression on my listeners, but still the ladies were hesitant to fly.

When the idea of having women hostesses on airplanes was born, Eastern Air Transport embraced it immediately, partly to allay the fears of our potential lady customers.

Thus began a whole new career for women, that of airline stewardess. At the beginning, all Eastern stewardesses were registered nurses. Nurses are trained to face emergencies calmly, and from this group we sought exceptionally poised young ladies.

They were an instant success and had a tremendous impact on air travel.

Over the years, Eastern switched back and forth between stewardesses and male stewards on two separate occasions. It has been almost impossible to keep a stewardess on the job for much more than a year, on the average. The career is the greatest marriage market in the world. At first the stewardesses married the pilots and the copilots. When they ran out of flying personnel, they began marrying the customers. We would put $1000 into training each attractive girl, and the next thing we knew she would have a ring on her finger.

After the primary success of hostesses, we replaced them with flight stewards. These young men were fortunate indeed; they could learn more about human nature in a year's time in those cabins than in a lifetime in another job. Many of them went on to make their careers with Eastern as pilots or in other capacities. During World War II, however, military service captured stewards at a greater rate than marriage had relieved us of stewardesses, and the girls came back to stay.

When the new airmail contracts were let, following the cancellation of the old ones in 1934, I wanted to apply for new routes in addition to the old ones. Studying the map of the United States, I saw a definite figure-eight pattern. It took in Chicago and New York in the North and New Orleans and Miami in the South, with Atlanta in the center. To be precise, the routes included Chicago-New York, New York-New Orleans via Atlanta, New Orleans-Miami, and Miami-Chicago via Atlanta. By using this figure-eight pattern, we could keep our planes circulating constantly, with greatly reduced periods of idleness between flights. Airlines make no money when their planes are not flying.

In addition to the figure-eight pattern, I wanted the New York-to-Miami route straight down the coast. And in the back of my mind was a dream, a transcontinental route through the southern tier of states.

The figure-eight pattern did not come off. At that time, I was only the general manager of the line; Ernie Breech was president of the holding company. He would not consent to the application for the Chicago-New York route. He did not believe that we should try to take it away from American Airlines. (If I had been permitted to bid, Eastern would have won the route. The figure I had decided on was lower than the one that won.) He had already agreed to the Atlanta-Chicago route and the Atlanta-New Orleans route, however. We did not win the New Orleans-Miami route, and my dream of a figure-eight pattern was reduced to an "X," with an additional route down the coast from New York to Miami.

The next step westward was Houston. The New Orleans-Houston route was vital to our expansion for two important reasons. First, from Houston we could go south to Brownsville on the Mexican border, the gateway to Mexico and Central America. In the mid-1930s I had no immediate hopes for an international extension, but I could dream. Pan American Airways was already operating in Mexico, and by getting the Houston-Brownsville route we could stop them at the border.

The second reason was my dream of a southern transcontinental route. How many people realize today, I wonder, that the first route across America, long before the Pony Express, was the old Spanish Trail, beginning at St. Augustine, Florida, and proceeding almost directly west to San Diego, California. The first transcontinental flight of any consequence was across the southern tier of states.

In the 1930s the South was an unwanted stepchild. President Roosevelt called it the nation's "number-one economic problem," a statement with which I publicly disagreed when I called it "economic opportunity number one." I believed that it had enormous potential. History, I am happy to say, has borne out this belief, but at that time neither bureaucratic Washington nor even the communities along the way showed any interest in the southern transcontinental route. I knew better than to go all out for it. But I thought that I could sneak up on it by going first to Houston, then, hopefully, to San Antonio and westward.

One of my good friends in New Orleans was Harry P. Williams, who had bought one of my sporty Rickenbacker straight-eight roadsters a few years before. He operated a small airline called Wedell-Williams between New Orleans and Houston. I had told him about the Lockheed Vega, an excellent little 4-passenger airplane, and he had purchased three Vegas on my recommendation. Now I wanted to buy those Vegas—along with the rest of the airline.

It was not easy to persuade Harry Williams to part with it. I made fifteen separate trips to New Orleans, sitting up all night both ways, before he finally sold us the line for a basic consideration of $160,000.

In the meantime, I had, of course, been flying over to Houston on the Wedell-Williams line occasionally. On one of my visits, several civic clubs organized a luncheon meeting and asked me to speak. Some 1,200 people, the leaders of the community, were in attendance. My speech was not exactly tactful. For many years, I had been hearing Texans brag about what a great state they had and about how progressive and forward-looking they were. But, in spite of all that talk, they had yet to recognize the age of aviation.

"With all your braggadocio," I told the gathering bluntly, "with all your talk about Texas and Houston, you still haven't even thought of an airport. And, ladies and gentlemen, let me tell you, without an airport, your city is going to be as dead as a community which ignored the railroad a hundred years ago."

Not only were the newspaper reporters present, but also the publishers themselves, and I fully expected to receive a little of my own medicine back in the newspapers that night and the next morning. Instead, the Houston newspapers supported my stand on aviation completely and directed their criticism at their own community leaders. As a result of the speech and the ensuing publicity, a committee was set up to seek a suitable site for an airport.

The location recommended was a poor choice. Fog was frequent on that side of the city, and yellow dust from a nearby sulphur operation compounded the problem. It became a hot political issue; I stayed out of it, however, and the airport was built in the wrong place. Many a time I've had to overfly Houston and go on to San Antonio because of that combination of fog and sulphur at the airport—when other parts of the Houston area were perfectly clear.

Some years later Glenn McCarthy, the multimillionaire oil-man, offered the city one thousand acres of land on the opposite, fog-free side of the city at the price he had paid for it some years before. He asked me to come down and help persuade the city government to take advantage of his offer. I checked out the proposition, determined that it would be in the best interests of the community and went to Houston to recommend its accept-ance. McCarthy made an excellent presentation of his proposal to a large gathering of civic leaders, and I backed him up. But the city fathers turned it down, and at this writing the airport is still frequently fogbound.

In the meantime, we had purchased the New Orleans-Houston route, and we were flying a regular schedule. It was time to make the move south to Brownsville and west to San Antonio, which involved penetrating the priority route structure of Braniff Air-ways or, to put it another way, jumping feet first into both Texas and national politics.

The first stumbling block thrown in my path was pressure on the Post Office Department not to accept bids for the route but to postpone all action until the Civil Aeronautics Act went into effect on August 1, 1938. After some intensive politicking, I was able to convince Congressman Richard Kleberg, a part owner of the enormous King Ranch in southern Texas, of the soundness of our position. His bill, authorizing the Post Office to call for bids for the Houston-Brownsville-San Antonio route, was passed and became law. Then all we had to do was make the low bid. The entire airline industry was buzzing over the im-pending battle.

The Braniff brothers, Tom and Paul, had influential friends. One of them was Jesse Jones, later chairman of the Reconstruc-tion Finance Corporation and a power in both Texas and the nation. I had also known Jesse for years. When I had visited Houston on behalf of the Cadillac Motor Car Company back in 1928, I had learned that one of our major problems there was Jesse Jones. He owned the Packard agency, and the pressure he could bring to bear on local businessmen to talk them out of Cadillacs and into Packards was overwhelming. We later became good friends, and I would nearly always drop into his office when I was in Houston or Washington, to pay my respects. About two weeks before the deadline for the presentation of the bids, I dropped in to see him in his Washington office. Also waiting was A. P. Giannini, president of the Bank of America in California. Jesse asked us both to come in together. I demurred, but he insisted.

"I'll be through here in a moment, Eddie," he told me and then turned to his other visitor. In all my association with business and finance, I have never heard such a blistering, vitriolic lecture as Jones gave Giannini there in my presence. When it was over and Giannini had left like a culprit, Jesse called me over.

"Sit down, Eddie," he said. He was all smiles and charm. "I want to talk to you."

For several minutes, we discussed business affairs in general. Suddenly, out of the blue, he asked, in a casual tone of voice, "Eddie, what are you going to bid for the mailing contract between Houston, San Antonio and Brownsville?"

Totally disarmed by the abruptness of the question, I replied truthfully, "If we have to, we'll go as low as a cent a mile."

It was some time before the significance of that question sank in. I realized with a sudden sinking feeling that I had told Jesse Jones exactly what Tom Braniff wanted to know. All Braniff Airways had to do to get that route was to bid less than a cent.

How much less than a cent could either of us bid? The answer, of course, was zero. But would that be possible? Could we or any other enterprise offer to carry on the government's business with no compensation whatever? I had our lawyers check out the question carefully and discreetly. They informed me that there were several cases on record, none involving airlines, in which services had been offered for exactly zero and accepted by the government. The situation in each, of course, was similar to that of Eastern. By providing the basic service at no cost, a firm could gain affiliated advantages. In our case, unless we won the mail contract, we would not be able to win the passenger, express and freight business, which was what we also wanted.

I determined to put in a bid for exactly nothing.

The deadline for the presentation of bids was less than a week away. The issue had gone all the way to the White House. Roosevelt's son Elliott had visited with Maury Maverick, the New Deal Mayor of San Antonio and a friend of the Braniffs. As a result, Roosevelt was trying to prevent the bids from being opened at the appointed hour. My friend Joseph B. Keenan, the Assistant Attorney General, and other Cabinet officers made known their belief that proper procedure should prevail. On the day before the bids were to be opened, Keenan reported to me that the President had finally given in and said, "Oh, let the Postmaster handle it."

Postmaster General Farley was out of town on a political junket. His assistant, William H. Howe, was also out of the city. We started tracking him down and learned that he was in Louisville, Kentucky. I explained the situation to him on the telephone and finally importuned him to catch a plane out of Louisville that night. Paul Brattain, our vice-president in charge of sales, and I met his plane at 1:00 A.M. We drove to the Post Office building, took a secret elevator to Howe's office and sat there discussing every angle of the problem until 3:30 A.M. Then Paul and I drove Howe to his apartment and went back to our hotel.

I snoozed for a couple of hours, had a quick breakfast and called our lawyers together for a final discussion of the zero bid. In the meantime, fully aware of the lateness of the hour at which Howe had retired, I sent Paul Brattain to his apartment to drag him out of bed by the heels if necessary. Paul was to bring him to the Post Office building, along with a notary public from the local Eastern office to witness the bid.

At 11:00, in the office of Charles P. Graddick, Superintendent of Air Mail, with the notary public there to witness, I carefully wrote in three zeroes and the word "cents" on the proper line of the bid, then signed my name. My hand was shaking so that the writing was barely legible. I put the bid in an envelope, sealed it and took it up to Howe's office by way of the secret elevator. Paul Brattain had carried out his mission successfully, and Howe was present, though a little sleepy-eyed.

He signed the sealed envelope in the proper place, according to regulations. Leaving the envelope with him, Paul and I slipped out the side door into the corridor, walked around the corner and made our official entrance into the anteroom, as though we had only arrived in the building. Tom Braniff was already there, along with representatives of other airlines interested in the route. There was no question, of course, that the contest was between Braniff and Eastern. Just before 12:00 we were all asked to come into Howe's office for the formal opening of the bids.

The bids were opened in alphabetical order. Braniff's bid was first. It was opened and read—$0.00001907378. Eleven digits adding up to less than a cent. The sound of murmurs, whispers and subdued laughter filled the room.

Then it was Eastern's turn. Howe's assistant opened the envelope, looked at the figure, gulped, looked again, then blurted out: "Zero, zero, zero cents!"

Everyone sat in stunned silence. Then Braniff was on his feet with a roar. Everyone began talking at once. Several minutes elapsed before Howe could resume opening the bids. None, of course, was less than zero. Eastern had the route.

Or did we? Braniff and his lawyers and political friends continued to seek ways to defeat our zero bid. In the meantime, I took my family on one of our rare vacations. We had made reservations for an ocean tour to northern Europe and up the coast of Norway. It was a restful and fascinating experience. Every day, in each little port along the coast, a telegram would be waiting for me from Paul Brattain advising me of the day's developments at home. Then two days went by with no word. On the third day, I put in a call to him by transatlantic telephone.

"I didn't dare wire you the information I received," he told me, "but I knew that if I sent you no communication at all you'd be on the phone. Here it is. President Roosevelt passed through San Antonio a few days ago. Obviously somebody got to him there. He has advised the Postmaster General to hold up the certification of the Eastern zero bid until August first when the new Act goes into effect."

That would be the same as throwing it out completely. "I'll get there as soon as I can," I told him.

The ship was leaving for home the next day. Paul met me at the dock in New York, and we left for Washington on the first Eastern flight early the next morning.

President Roosevelt, in the meantime, had continued westward to California and was returning east by cruiser via the Panama Canal. In Washington we were able to see the legal division of the Post Office Department, which advised the Postmaster General that he did not have the authority to hold up our legal bid. With a few days still to go before August 1, the Eastern routes in southeast Texas were certified.

Still Braniff refused to give up. He persuaded some influential citizens of the cities involved to protest to the President and Postmaster General. To counter this opposition, we loaded one of our new DC-2s with community leaders from some of Eastern's cities—Atlanta, Washington, New Orleans—and flew to Texas. We visited Houston, San Antonio, Corpus Christi and Brownsville. In each city, I attempted to sell air transportation in general and Eastern Air Lines in particular. The community leaders who accompanied me spoke frankly and warmly of the service Eastern provided to their hometowns.

In Brownsville, Texas, I was in the middle of a speech to the Chamber of Commerce when someone handed me a folded piece of paper with the underlined words "Very Important" printed on it. The message advised that Tom Braniff was to meet with the board of directors of the Houston Chamber of Commerce at 4:00 that afternoon.

"Mr. Chairman, ladies and gentlemen," I told the assembled

group, "I must leave immediately. I am terribly sorry, but I have no choice."

We hurried to the airport, flew to Houston and landed there about 3:45. By the time I arrived at the Chamber of Commerce, Braniff was in the board room discussing the situation with the directors. I had to wait outside, but I could hear some of the conversation. Tom did not speak softly. His main point was that the competition furnished by Eastern would destroy Braniff Airways, which, he kept repeating, was a Texas operation. The line was actually based in Oklahoma City.

Finally, I was permitted to enter the board room. I took Tom's arguments apart, one by one, as best I could. I concluded by answering the charge that I would destroy his airline.

"Gentlemen, and that includes you, too, Tom," I said, "you simply do not realize the vast potential of your own state and community. There is enough business here for both Braniff and Eastern to prosper. If you really seriously feel that additional air service would destroy the existing service provided by Braniff, let me make this statement. I am willing to guarantee you and Tom Braniff here and now that, should the day ever come that he is carrying one passenger less on an average than he has been carrying all along, then I will take our own sales force off the job here in Houston and turn them over to Braniff Airways. I make that guarantee here and now, in good faith, before witnesses."

The board then went into executive session and voted by a substantial majority to support Eastern Air Lines in Houston. From then on, our problems diminished. The new routes were added. Within a year, owing in large measure to the enthusiastic selling of air transportation by our traffic personnel, the number of passengers carried by Braniff Airways had doubled. Eastern, of course, because of the number of cities we served to the northeast, carried more. But there was definitely enough business for both of us, and we both prospered.

By 1938, we had practically doubled Eastern's mileage. Both by adding new route mileage and by adding cities along existing routes, we had increased the number of cities served from 14 to

34. This expansion involved the creation of new airports in several of these communities.

I was walking through the lobby of the Mayflower Hotel in Washington one day when I bumped into Abe Shushan. Abe was one of Senator Huey Long's henchmen in New Orleans.

"You're just the man I wanted to see," he said. "I came to Washington hoping I could get money to develop a new big airport in New Orleans, but the people in the Reconstruction Finance Corporation won't listen to me."

"You ought to talk to Harvey Couch," I said. "He's the chairman, and I know him very well. He's from Mississippi, and he ought to be responsive. Let's sit down and see whether we can't work out some kind of a pro forma balance sheet."

We went up to his room and spent about three hours working up a balance sheet. I told Abe that I would not hesitate to put my name on it. I called Harvey about 8:15 the next morning, and he said that he would be eager to talk to Shushan about the airport. I called Abe, woke him up and told him to get on over to the RFC in a hurry.

"Oh, my God," he moaned, "I'm not dressed. I haven't had breakfast."

"To hell with breakfast," I said. "You get on over there."

When I returned to my room later that day, the phone was ringing. It was Abe. "You're fantastic," he said. "Mr. Couch told me that if Eddie Rickenbacker would put his name on that balance sheet he would too. So I'm going to get the money." He paused. "Now I've got to perform," he said.

"Well, that's your worry, not mine," I said.

Shushan did perform. The project cost about $25 million before he finished. It was necessary to fill in a portion of Lake Pontchartrain. Abe called it "Shushan Airport," and he put his name or initial all over the place, on every doorknob, even in the paving. After Huey Long was assassinated in 1935, the Long political machine fell apart. The name was changed to "New Orleans Airport," and a crew went around removing every vestige of his association with it.

With Mrs. Eleanor Roosevelt christening Eastern plane

Ford single-engine plane of Florida Airways

Mailwing

DC-3

Super Constellation

Douglas DC-8

With Anthony "Tony" Fokker, airplane manufacturer, and Sir Hubert Wilkins, explorer

With Ernst Udet—Richthofen's successor as leading German ace

A Margaret Bourke-White Photograph

With Amelia Earhart at Indianapolis Speedway

Wreckage of the Atlanta crash, February 27, 1941

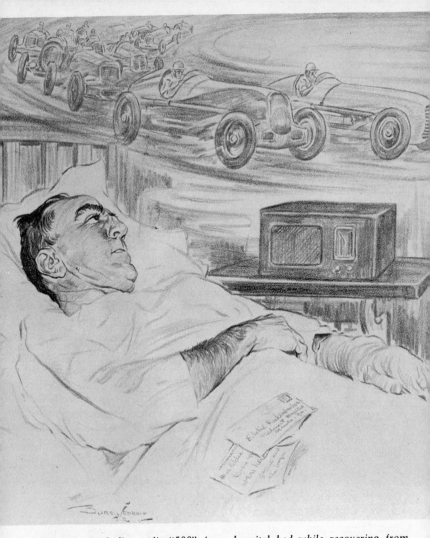

Listening to Indianapolis "500" from hospital bed while recovering from Atlanta crash

As Eastern extended westward, we found ourselves in the awkward situation of flying new routes with obsolete planes. For years I had been keeping up with Don Douglas' operations on the West Coast. He was developing a transport plane that many of us felt would revolutionize the industry. His first model was called the "DC-1," the plane in which Jack Frye and I had set a new transcontinental record on the eve of the airmail cancellation. Many of the airline operators were called in to inspect it and make recommendations. We made so many that Douglas just about started all over again with the DC-2.

The 12-passenger DC-2 was superior in every way to the planes Eastern was flying. It was made of duralumin and powered with modern 9-cylinder, air-cooled engines, tough and sturdy. The new Douglas would eliminate many of the problems of our fabric-covered, water-cooled fleet. It was much more reliable, more comfortable, and faster.

I prevailed upon Ernie Breech and our board of directors to buy ten of the new DC-2s. GM's credit rating did not hurt us any with Douglas. As soon as we received delivery of a new plane from Douglas, we would put a corresponding Condor on the ground and leave it there, depreciating it as if it had been a used car. When we finally did sell off all our old planes, we had depreciated their value to the point at which we actually made a nice little profit on the sales.

I was inordinately proud of our fleet of silver planes. "The Great Silver Fleet" popped into my head. That was truly what those ten new planes constituted. From then on, in all our advertising, Eastern Air Lines was "The Great Silver Fleet." I thought the duck hawk, a speedy bird of graceful lines, epitomized our operation, and a silhouette was painted on the rudder of each ship.

The individual components of our Great Silver Fleet were so handsome that I wanted the world to know whose they were. At every airport, when one of those sleek planes landed and taxied up to the gate, it would attract the attention of everyone present.

On each one we had painted in bold black letters the length of the fuselage: "FLY EASTERN AIR LINES."

Each plane became a flying billboard.

It had been some years since I had had an encounter with the Grim Reaper. Then came two brushes with death, each involving a new DC-2.

I was returning from California in one when, ten thousand feet above Richmond, Indiana, a loud noise pulled me right up in my seat. I knew exactly what it was. A piece of the propeller blade had broken off and hit the fuselage. Instantly the engine on the right side began vibrating furiously.

"Shut it off, shut it off!" I hollered to the pilot and copilot in the cockpit. They did not hear me, of course, but I kept yelling anyway. Several seconds passed before they woke up and cut off the engine.

The pilot began letting down on one engine, and we landed at Columbus. On the way down, I couldn't help wondering why it had taken two men so long to cut that engine. Such an action should have been an instantaneous reflex. Then the answer came to me. This plane was equipped with an automatic pilot. We had been experimenting with this new flying aid on Eastern, and I had come to the conclusion that it had not yet been developed to the stage of complete reliability.

More important, I wanted our pilots and copilots, particularly the copilots, to be developing their knowledge and improving their flying skill every second they were in the cockpit. The copilot was there to learn. With the automatic pilot in operation, all he could do was sit and watch it fly the plane.

When we landed at Columbus, the crew and I climbed out and inspected the right-hand engine. Sure enough, about eight inches had broken off one tip of the propeller. The resulting vibration of the engine had broken three of the four mounts that secured it to the wing. It was hanging by only one support.

The captain and I looked at it silently. "You were on the automatic pilot when that propeller let go, weren't you?" I asked.

"Yes, sir," he said. "How did you know?"

"Because it took you so long to realize what happened and take the proper action," I said.

He had to agree with me. There was not much else he could do. Later I learned that he had been reading a magazine when the propeller broke. He was not tuned into the vibrations of the airplane at all. As far as instant remedial action was concerned, he might as well have been on the ground.

It was many years before Eastern Air Lines used automatic pilots, and by that time there was a third man, an engineer, in every cockpit.

Not long after that experience over Indiana, I came even closer to cracking up in a new DC-2. I am convinced that once again I was saved only by direct intervention from above.

As was our custom, we planned a special inaugural flight for the opening of the Chicago-Miami route. We planned to fly a new DC-2 to Chicago from Newark on Sunday for the Monday flight. The captain was Robert Chew, a stocky red-headed veteran. Sumner Sewall, the governor of Maine, also went along. Sumner had been a combat pilot in World War I, and I had organized a group of fellow pilots to stump the state for him in an aerial caravan during his campaign. He was elected by a large majority. Now he was on his way to Chicago, and I offered him a ride.

It was in the middle of December, and the weather was miserable—snow, sleet and ice. We were held up in Pittsburgh for an hour before we were given clearance with the warning that there was ice at 1,500 feet and higher. There are no hills over seven hundred feet high between Pittsburgh and Chicago, and we figured that this ceiling would give us plenty of margin. We flew through the clouds toward Columbus, following the radio range. I was in the cockpit with Bob Chew, sitting in the copilot's seat.

Suddenly, we lost the radio beam. We began flying back and forth all over the state of Ohio, looking for that beam. We lost our bearings completely.

"Maybe we'd better go down and take a look," I told Bob.

He did, very slowly. The driving sleet covered the windows,

and I opened mine to look down. My face was freezing. Tree-tops appeared beneath us. We were barely fifty feet above them. My left hand went out automatically and yanked the wheel back. Bob shoved the throttle forward. We went up fast.

"Let's take it easy for a few minutes and think this through," I said when I felt that I had my voice under control.

Back at Pittsburgh the weather maps had shown unlimited visibility at St. Louis and Kansas City. I suggested that we head west. Then the radio went dead. Now we had no range, no radio, no communication whatever. At the time, we learned later, we were over Cleveland, Ohio. They heard us but did not know who we were. I had no intention of telling them. I did not want to notify the world that we were lost.

We kept flying. We had been up seven hours and were running low on gas. Suddenly our fog light showed the slightest break in the fog beneath us.

"Mush down," I said. "Go easy."

Again Bob let down slowly, slowly. Again we burst out of the fog. We were directly over a 4-lane highway.

"That road goes from one place to another, or it wouldn't be there," I said. "What does the compass say?"

"Northwest," Bob answered.

"Okay, follow it," I said. "That's where we want to go, to Chicago."

I happened to glance to my right. At that precise instant, a light flickered in that direction. If I had not been looking directly at it, I would never have seen it. I kept my eyes fixed in that direction.

"I see a light in the northeast," I said. "Let's go over there and see if we can recognize the code number."

Bob banked the big plane to the right. It was still daylight but murky. There was snow on the ground. Suddenly, in the distance ahead of us I saw a faint glow reflected from the snow. That could only be a city.

"That way!" I said, pointing.

A river appeared beneath us, leading toward the glow in the

distance. We followed it. Then we were approaching a city. A huge illuminated sign dominated the city landscape. Its warm glow was reflected on the surface of the river. I strained to read it. Soon it became legible: "Toledo-Edison." We were coming into Toledo, Ohio. Our altitude was lower than the sign.

He came in over the field and let down. When we filled the tanks, we found that we had had only seven or eight gallons left, ten more minutes of flying at most.

Both the beam antenna and the voice antenna had iced up and snapped. That was why we had no radio. Neither antenna had a tension reliever or spring. There was no give and take. I made a report on this problem to the manufacturers with a recommendation. Within thirty days the antennas on every airplane were equipped with some form of tension reliever. Today even automobile aerials come equipped with springs of some kind; take a look at the next police car you see.

That episode proved once again that, even though our antennas were broken, we were tuned into a Divine Providence. I like to think that it was the "Big Beam" that kept us going, the Holy Spirit that keeps us all flying safely through the fog and night to some mysterious and important goal. I did not forget that the Big Radio is a two-way job, and that night on my knees I gave thanks for the light in the fog.

I have never liked to use the word "safe" in connection with either Eastern Air Lines or the entire transportation field; I prefer the word "reliable." For whenever motion is involved, there can be no condition of absolute safety. The only time man is safe is when he is completely static, in a box underground. With motion comes the inexorable possibility of accidents; it is the price we pay for motion. A human being, because he is alive, because he moves, is subject to many dangers, diseases and breakages. A person can insulate himself from the world, but as long as he moves he is subject to injury, if only from tripping over the rug.

With our expanding situation and with the increasing swiftness of all forms of transportation, the price is even higher. With all the safety devices on the railroads of the world today, accidents still occur. Even on the high seas, ships equipped with every modern device, including radar, and proceeding at comparatively slow speeds and with vast spaces in which to maneuver, still manage to run into each other. There will always be accidents on the highways, just as there will always be accidents on the sidewalks.

Air travel, the swiftest of all, can hardly be expected ever to be immune to danger. Those of us in the transportation industry can inspire, develop and install the most intricate devices, but still there will be accidents. The human element is still involved. In nine of ten accidents, the basic cause is simply that somebody neglected to do the right thing at the right time.

For many years the safety record of Eastern Air Lines was the envy of the industry. In 1937 we received our first safety award "in recognition of outstanding record in safe air transportation" from the National Safety Council. We had not had a passenger fatality during our entire operating history, 1930–1936, with an accumulation of 141,794,894 passenger miles.

Only four months later, the inevitable happened. On August 10, I was a guest on board Alfred P. Sloan's yacht at Newport when word came to me over the ship-to-shore telephone—one of our planes had crashed at Daytona Beach, Florida. I made my apologies to Mr. Sloan and immediately headed back to New York by train. From New York I took the first plane for Florida. I was in Daytona Beach that evening.

The plane involved was a DC-2 on the Chicago-Miami route. It had come into Daytona at four in the morning, discharged passengers and mail and taken off on schedule. At the end of the runway, just as the plane became airborne, it had hit an obstruction. It had hurtled over a clump of pines and landed in the midst of a palmetto thicket. Four men were killed, including the captain, Stuart Dietz. Five passengers were injured.

What had caused the accident? A human error that seems unbelievable. The day before the accident a violent storm had struck Daytona Beach. An underground transmission line ran alongside the road at the end of the airfield. The storm had caused a short circuit in the underground conduit. The repair crew of the Florida Power and Light Company, which owned the line, had set up two poles and strung a line between them to bypass the shorted circuit.

One of those two poles was at the exact end of the runway, right in the path of any airplane landing or taking off. The poles had been put up during the night, but no lights had been placed on them. No one from the power company had bothered to inform anyone at the airport that they had been erected. The first Captain Dietz knew of their existence was when he flew into one of them.

What a tragedy of errors! I have never felt more frustrated in my life. Even though I was there on the scene, there was nothing that I could do. The people were dead; the plane was demolished. Although blame was later laid squarely on the electric company by the Department of Commerce, still the airline was responsible. It all came back into the lap of the local manager. He should have known everything that went on at his field.

The one action I could take was to see that such a tragedy would never happen again. We notified all municipalities served by Eastern and all the power companies in the Eastern area of what had happened and why. They in turn advised all other cities with airports around the world. From then on, at least, no more poles were casually stuck up around airports.

During the 1930s I studied two other types of aircraft, the autogiro and the lighter-than-air dirigible. In 1939 Eastern actually operated an autogiro airmail service between the airport at Camden, New Jersey, and the roof of the Philadelphia general post office, which continued for one year. The distance was six miles, and we flew five round trips a day. It was successful in that we delivered the mail without mishap. But it was a constant headache, for the autogiro contained plenty of bugs. The operation never paid for itself, and the Federal government took up the slack through subsidization.

That, in effect, ended the autogiro. The industry began looking instead to the helicopter, a more complex machine but one with a greater potential, and it was gradually perfected. In 1941, in an article in *Fortune,* I predicted that the helicopter, then in its infancy, would in the near future be basic to every urban transportation setup. It took 25 years, but helicopters have become an integral part of the New York transportation system. From my office in Rockefeller Center I can see them landing and taking off at the Pan Am Building in midtown Manhattan.

Twelve years after I made that prophecy I had the opportunity to prove it to myself. On September 8, 1953, I landed at the Dayton, Ohio, airport at 5:30 P.M. in the midst of a big air show. It was to end at 6:00 P.M., and fifty thousand spectators would head for home. To enable me to avoid that traffic jam, the airport personnel, who knew that I was to make a speech at the Biltmore Hotel that night, had arranged to fly me to the roof of the Biltmore by helicopter.

We took off a few minutes before the close of the races and were over the heart of Dayton in approximately six minutes. I kept looking around for the hotel. The pilot saw me peering down.

"It's down there next to that church steeple," he said. "It will get larger as we get closer."

Actually we landed on the roof of the elevator shaft, which was forty feet square. The hotel people had placed a ladder against it for me. I was in my room seven minutes after leaving the airport.

The dirigible, I had every reason to believe in the 1920s and 1930s, would someday provide a major form of long-distance air transportation. In 1928 the German dirigible *Graf Zeppelin,* with 20 passengers and a crew of 38, flew from Germany to Lakehurst, New Jersey, in two days. A year later it flew around the world, again with twenty passengers, in twenty days.

In 1936 I spent several hours on board the new German dirigible, *Hindenburg,* as a guest of its captain, Hugo Eckener. I was tremendously impressed. We flew quietly and comfortably all over New England and part of the Middle West. The ship had a salon, a dining room and roomettes for the passengers. Its danger lay in the highly explosive gas, hydrogen, with which the envelope was filled. We in the United States had plenty of helium, a noncombustible gas with a lift potential 92.6 percent that of hydrogen, but it was not available to the Germans.

On May 6, 1937, while flying home from Chicago on United Airlines, I happened to look out the window as we came in for a landing at Newark. Suddenly I saw a terrible blinding flash. When we landed, I found that it was the *Hindenburg.* No one ever proved what caused the explosion, but the investigating committee reported the possibility that there was a gas leakage that came in contact with static electricity.

It was the third major dirigible disaster in the United States in four years, and it marked the end of the dirigible's future as a passenger or cargo carrier, at least for several decades. I do not believe, incidentally, that the world has seen the last of the dirigible. We shall soon break through the problem of applying atomic power to dirigibles, and then they may well become great liners of the air. They will be capable of cruising at a speed of 150 miles an hour and will take people comfortably and with comparative reliability to Europe in more time than a jet—but in less time than a surface ship.

As the 1930s went by, Eastern Air Lines showed a steady, healthy growth. By 1940 we were serving 80 percent of the population east of the Mississippi. In 1934, when I became general manager of the line, we flew a total of 3,360,257 plane miles over a 3,358-mile route. By 1940 the total mileage had more than quadrupled to 16 million miles over a 5,381-mile route. The number of our employees had increased from 473, with an annual payroll of $876,000, to just under 2,000, with a payroll of nearly $4 million.

In 1934 Eastern carried 52,820 customers and had a gross revenue of $1,565,020. In 1940 we carried 368,436 passengers, with a gross revenue of $10,700,578. Our net profit had increased in the same period from minus $698,539 to plus $1,575,456.

In 1940 World War II had already begun in Europe, and in the United States we were belatedly beginning a rearmament program. Obviously Eastern was going to need many new airplanes. Don Douglas had by that time perfected the airplane that became the foundation of the air transport industry, the famous 21-passenger DC-3. It was the ship we needed in quantity. For funds with which to purchase the planes, we arranged with a group of investment bankers to underwrite a $3 million stock issue.

Some of the best financial brains in the country, men on my board of directors, disapproved of this method of raising money. They suggested that instead we go directly to our stockholders, giving them preferential rights. But I insisted on playing it safe. I was scared to death of the European situation. After a couple of sleepless nights, I called a special board meeting and fought my own ideas to a successful conclusion.

The stock was then selling for $40 a share. The bankers underwrote it at $32.50. Soon after the agreement was made, Belgium surrendered to the invading German army, leaving the British Expeditionary Force seemingly at Hitler's mercy. Our stock, like that of everyone else, dropped severely. I doubt that we could have sold $3 million worth to our stockholders for $15 a share—much less than $32.50. But by that time we had the money in the bank, and we did not owe anyone a single dime.

The new equipment we were able to buy with this money enabled Eastern Air Lines to provide at least a large portion of the service for which we were called upon during World

War II. We sold our ten DC-2s to Australian interests, thus enabling us to receive authorization from the priorities board to purchase ten more DC-3s. In that one transaction we more than doubled our passenger capacity.

As the line expanded, we began to be cramped in our small offices in the General Motors building. I learned that Lawrence A. Kirkland, who handled leases for Rockefeller Center, was negotiating with Pan American Airways to take space in one of the Center's new buildings. Kirkland was a stockholder in Eastern Air Lines; Laurance S. Rockefeller was a member of the board of directors.

"Why are you negotiating with somebody else?" I asked. "Why don't you negotiate with yourself? Come to Eastern first."

It was obvious that Rockefeller Center and midtown Manhattan were going to be the executive and administrative headquarters of commerce in America for many years to come. There should be an airplane building in that great complex. I sold the idea to both Rockefeller and Kirkland. Then I went one step further: "As long as we're going to have an airline building and Eastern will sign a 10-year lease for the top floor, why don't we just go ahead and call the building the 'Eastern Air Lines Building'?"

Again they agreed. We signed the lease in a fitting ceremony in a DC-3 over Rockefeller Center. We gradually expanded to the point at which today Eastern occupies five floors in the Eastern Air Lines Building.

World War II was by then raging in Europe. Soon, I knew, the United States would be in it. Eastern Air Lines would enter another period of change, but, before turning from that stage of growth, development and stability, I should like to repeat with pride some of the major firsts of Eastern Air Lines during those years.

Eastern was the first airline and the only line for many years to operate without government subsidy. We did not take the taxpayers' money to keep us in business.

It was the first line to show a profit. Our entire Eastern Air Lines family, stockholders, personnel and customers, benefited from our operations.

Eastern was, in sum, the first airline to operate as a free-enterprise company, just as I had insisted we would operate when I took it over back in 1934. Even greater days were in store for Eastern Air Lines, but that story will come in a later chapter.

TWELVE

THE ATLANTA CRASH

For weeks, during the months of January and February 1941, members of the Birmingham Aviation Committee had been writing, calling and wiring invitations for me to come down and speak to a combined civic-club luncheon sponsored by the committee. I was well aware of the importance of this meeting. Leaders of both city and state would be there. It would be an excellent opportunity to discuss ways of providing Birmingham with direct air service to the Miami gateway to the Southeast and the Chicago gateway to the Northwest.

The city needed and could support this route. Eastern Air Lines would benefit in two ways. We would be able to provide better service to a major city. We would also be able to increase still further the utilization of our equipment.

Important as this visit to Birmingham would be, however, I repeatedly, though reluctantly, turned down the invitations. I was also preparing a program to put before my board of directors' meeting in Miami on February 28. I hoped to persuade the board to approve the purchase of some $5 million worth of new equipment. The Birmingham meeting was set for February 27; I simply could not squeeze it in.

On the afternoon of the 26th, a bleak, rainy Wednesday in New York, the people in Birmingham really began putting the pressure on. From the tone of the conversations, I was beginning to realize that they all thought that I considered myself too big to visit Birmingham. When this fact finally dawned on me, I immediately decided to go, and I so advised them.

I put the papers I would need for the board meeting in my briefcase, went home and packed a little bag with a clean shirt and other travel necessities, then proceeded to the airport. My plane was Flight No. 21, departing at 7:10 P.M. for Washington, Atlanta, Birmingham, New Orleans, Houston and Brownsville. I planned to get off at Birmingham, catch a few hours' sleep, attend the luncheon and take the afternoon plane back to Atlanta; I would fly on to Miami that night.

The Mexico Flyer was a DC-3 sleeper equipped with berths. It had a little private room behind the cockpit called the "sky lounge," and I made myself comfortable there with my paper work. Over Spartanburg, South Carolina, the pilot came through the doorway from the cockpit.

"Captain Rickenbacker," he said, "the weather in Atlanta isn't too good. We may have some difficulty getting in."

The captain, James A. Perry, Jr., of Atlanta, was a fine young man with an excellent record. Having the boss on board was bound to have some psychological effect on him, and I immediately assured him that he was in command and should do whatever he thought best. That was my standard policy.

The plane continued on toward Atlanta. It was a smooth and even flight. I was sitting by the window. The flight steward, Clarence Moore, was next to me in the aisle seat. We passed through scattered showers, but occasionally the clouds thinned out. I recognized the lights of the Atlanta Federal penitentiary as we flew over it.

The field reported a low ceiling, and we were making an instrument approach. According to this procedure, we would follow the radio beam in over the airport, fly past it, make a 180-degree turn and come back on the beam.

I had come into Atlanta on many another cloudy night, and this time everything seemed routine. I felt the pilot put his left wing down to go into the 180-degree turn. There was no way for me to know, and obviously the captain didn't know either, that we were about one thousand feet too low. We shall never know why. Either the field had given him the wrong altitude when he was coming in, or the copilot had misunderstood.

Suddenly I felt the left wing scrape the treetops. The captain felt it simultaneously, for he instantly yanked the left wing up and put the right wing down. I jumped from my seat and began moving swiftly toward the tail of the plane.

Everything seemed to go. I was in the aisle when the right wing hooked into the trees. The wing was ripped off. The plane veered to the right and went up on its nose. I resolved that, if the plane started burning, I would open my mouth and suck in the flames. It's quicker that way.

The lights went off as the pilot cut the switch. I was bouncing around inside and came down on the arm of a seat so hard that my left hip was smashed completely. The plane kept turning over in a somersault. It landed on its tail and broke in two pieces in the middle. I was right where the break occurred. That's where I found myself when the tearing noises stopped—wedged tight in the wreckage. I was lying on the body of Clarence Moore. He was dead.

My head was held tight between the bulkhead and a gas tank. Something had dented my skull. Along the temple over my left eye was a groove you could lay your little finger in. I had a big egg on my forehead.

Wreckage had packed in around my left arm, shattering

the elbow and crushing the nerve. The arm was clamped tight. My left hand stuck out of the wreckage, but I couldn't move it at all; it was paralyzed and terribly painful. Later I found that several of my ribs were broken, some in two or three places. Two jagged ends had broken out through my sides. In addition to the crushed hip socket on the left side, my pelvis was broken on both sides. A nerve in my left hip was severed, and my left knee was broken. I couldn't move my body or my entire left leg at all. My right hip and leg were pinned too, but they were not broken. The only part of my body that actually had any movement was my right hand and forearm.

I was soaking wet with a combination of blood and high-octane gasoline. The tanks had ruptured, and gasoline was everywhere. I remembered how the lights had gone out just before the crash. The last action of the pilot and copilot, both of whom were killed instantly, must have been to cut off the ignition to prevent an explosion. At least those of us who were still alive were saved from burning to death.

I began to hear talking around me in the dark. Of the sixteen people on board, eleven were still alive at that time. Some were seriously injured, but others seemed only shaken and dazed. They were the people who had been in the tail. Some were in nightclothes. One man was wandering around in his underwear.

A woman was moaning. There were groans and cries of pain. The rain was falling, and it was cold and wet.

A man's voice said, "Hey, let's start a bonfire and get warm."

"*No!*" Fear wrenched the word out of me. With hundreds of gallons of 100-octane gasoline soaking everything, we'd all have gone up like a torch.

"Don't light a match," I shouted. The ends of my broken ribs grated painfully against one another as I cried out. "You'll set the gasoline on fire. For God's sake, *don't light a match!*"

There was silence for a moment. "Who is that?" somebody asked.

"Rickenbacker," I said. "Don't light a match. Just sit tight and wait. Somebody will come and get us."

In the meantime, I was in agony. Of all my injuries, my left hand was the most painful. I felt for it with my right hand, took hold of the ends of my fingers and yanked as hard as I could. I was desperate enough to try anything. It did relieve the pain slightly, but I didn't have the strength to continue.

In addition to the pain, being so completely immobilized was frustrating and exasperating. Lying on the steward's dead body added to my mental discomfort. In a frenzy, I tried with all my strength to wrench my head loose. It moved a few inches, just enough to make contact with a jagged piece of metal that was sticking out just above my left eye and that I did not see in the dark. It ripped my eyelid, right in the center, and my eyeball popped out of the socket and fell down on my cheek.

But I still wanted to get myself loose. I struggled again, this time with my shoulders and chest. Several ribs snapped. I heard them give. It sounded like popcorn popping.

There were two other passengers trapped in the wreckage near me. From their groans, they seemed to be in even worse shape than I was. I tried to comfort them as best I could. I kept reassuring them that help was coming. I told them that I was sorry, on behalf of the airline. Thinking of ways to comfort and control them kept my own mind active. But comfort alone could not keep them alive, and they both slipped off during the night. Now there were seven dead, nine living.

Three of the passengers, all men, had escaped major injury. If they could find a house or a road, it would definitely hasten our rescue. On the other hand, it would be easy for anyone to get lost stumbling around in the hilly pine country on that black and rainy night. I solved this dilemma by instructing one of the men to proceed out from the wreck as far as he could and still remain within the range of my voice. When he had reached that point, I sent a second man out past him along the same projected line to the point where he could barely hear the first man's voice. The third man repeated the procedure.

Though this line extended several hundred feet from the wrecked plane, it was not enough to reach any sign of civilization. Keeping their distances, they then swung around the wreck like a pair of dividers. One of the men fell into a deep ravine in the dark. He wasn't hurt, but he lost some enthusiasm for exploring.

While this human line of communications extended on one side of the crash, I heard voices from the other side. A rescue party was approaching. I shouted back as loud as I could, but nobody heard me. The party went on by, and the voices dwindled in the distance. At first this near-miss seemed tragic. But then I realized that if they had stumbled across the gasoline-soaked wreckage with their kerosene lanterns, they might have set us all on fire.

Finally, in the cold, gray light of early dawn, at about 7:00, a searching party found us. It took them an hour to cut and pry and loosen the twisted metal that held me. They pulled me out, and I saw myself looking at a camera. Suddenly both camera and photographer disappeared. One of the Eastern boys had pushed the photographer aside, not too gently. Covered with blood and with my eye hanging down on my cheek, I was not very photogenic.

The doctor in the searching party gave me a shot of morphine. It had no effect at all on the pain I was suffering. Dope makes me wilder than a March hare, but the pain was so terrible that I asked for another shot. He gave it to me, and it produced some slight relief.

Members of the searching party guided those who could walk to the road and carried the rest on stretchers. When it came my turn, four men started carrying me to the road. The terrain was rough and the ground was slippery, and every step hurt. Going down the steep side of a ravine, some of my bearers slipped. The stretcher buckled on my broken back and it was all I could do to keep from crying out with the pain.

They carried me on across a little creek and finally reached the road. An ambulance was waiting, but the dead were placed on first. The first ambulance drove off filled with corpses. I asked why. Someone said that state law authorized a $20 fee for transporting a dead body but only $10 for a living one.

It was almost an hour before another ambulance arrived and we were loaded aboard. An Eastern pilot who had been in the searching party rode in the ambulance with me. I must have been a horrible-looking mess, with my eye out of its socket, my face black and blue and the rest of me caked with blood. The pilot suddenly became nauseated from looking at me.

In spite of my condition I couldn't help commenting. "Why are *you* sick?" I asked. "I'm the one who's supposed to be sick."

I was perfectly rational. I felt every bump on the way to town. Our destination was Piedmont Hospital; years before I had anticipated the possibility of accidents and had made arrangements with hospitals all along the route to provide emergency service when, as and if it should be needed. In Atlanta, Piedmont had been chosen.

At the hospital the attendants rolled me into the emergency room. There were only two interns on duty at that hour to care for nine injured passengers. At that point I was too weak to talk, but I knew everything that was going on. One of the interns took a quick look at me and told the attendants to push me out of the way.

"He's more dead than alive," I heard him say. "Let's take care of the live ones."

I was lying there helpless and speechless when a Catholic priest entered the emergency room. I overheard him ask the nurse my religion. If I were a Catholic, of course, he would give me the last rites. The nurse came over and asked me what I was. Suddenly my voice came back.

"I'm a damn Protestant just like ninety percent of the people," I said.

It was not a tactful remark, even under the influence of dope, but it brought results. The head surgeon of the hospital, Doctor Floyd W. McRae, had been called from his home, and he arrived and took over. It was not the first time Doctor McRae had worked on me. He had assisted in my mastoid operation in Paris in 1918.

First he pushed my eyeball back into its socket; then he sewed up the eyelid to keep it there. He didn't want to use an anesthetic, he told me, as it would affect the muscles of the eye and make the replacement more difficult. To hold me still, one of the interns put both hands on my shoulders and pushed down hard. I heard my broken ribs go snap, crackle and pop, and I let out a bellow of profane protest.

Doctor McRae calmly went ahead and finished sewing up the eyelid. I have had good vision in my left eye ever since; it's better than my right one. The crash actually improved my nose. It had been a little off-center, thanks to being broken six times in my life. That time, the seventh, left it perfectly straight.

A full complement of doctors had arrived at the hospital to take care of the injured passengers. Doctor McRae had me rolled into the operating room, where members of his staff and a couple of outside specialists looked me over. They all began arguing about what they could do.

I could tell from the way the surgeons talked that they were all, in their minds, busily sharpening up their scalpels. I was half out of my head with the effects of the dope, and one of the doctors wanted to bore a hole in my skull at the indentation to relieve the pressure.

They also discussed my smashed hip and broken pelvis. The ball of the joint had crushed the socket and ridden up on top of it. My left leg was four inches shorter than my right. There was much discussion of whether they should operate on the hip, set it or leave it alone. Then I heard the calm, assured voice of Floyd McRae.

"Well, gentlemen," he said, "we may let him die on our hands, but we will never kill him."

I popped off again. "Nuts!" I said. "Get me a good osteopath, and I'll be out of this place in three days."

There was no operation.

Adelaide happened to be visiting with friends in Charlotte, North Carolina, at the time. The boys were in school in Asheville, not too far away. The three hastened to Atlanta. Ralph Greene, Eastern's medical chief, came up from Miami and stayed at my bedside day and night.

The next morning Doctor McRae suggested that I be given a little brandy. Brandy was the last thing I wanted, but they mixed up a little in a milk shake and fed it to me anyway. It must have worked, because right away I realized that I was starving.

"Wouldn't you like something else?" Doctor McRae asked.

"You bet I would," I said. "I want a bottle of beer and a ham-and-egg sandwich."

By that time the doc knew better than to argue with me. He sent out for a ham-and-egg sandwich and a bottle of beer. It was a delicious meal.

The lobby of the hospital was crawling with reporters. When Ralph McGill, editor of the Atlanta *Constitution*, called to ask how I was, the doctor told him that I was getting a lot better.

"Why, he just asked for a ham-and-egg sandwich and a Coca-Cola," he added.

That story went out all over the world. The Coca-Cola Company, which has its headquarters in Atlanta, sent up one of their largest coolers to be installed in my room, and it was kept loaded with Cokes.

On Saturday it was decided to put me in a plaster cast in order to let the bones start knitting. "Eddie," Doctor McRae said, "we're going to have to wrap you up. It's going to be painful, as we can't give you an anesthetic."

"Go ahead," I said. "I can take it."

He was right. They had to turn me over as they put on the wet, plaster-impregnated bandages, and the pain was excruciating. But I took it. When they were through, I was in plaster from my chin to my toenails. Only one of my arms was free. A contraption was rigged up over the bed to hold my legs up at an angle, so that the blood would not settle in my feet.

By Sunday morning, I seemed to have improved. Doctor McRae called Adelaide, and they decided that the boys could go back to school. They left at about 8:00 in the morning on the bus.

Two hours later, I suddenly took a turn for the worse. I began to die. I felt the presence of death. I knew that I was going. The sensation was the same as that when I had nearly bled to death following the tonsillectomy back in 1917.

You may have heard that dying is unpleasant, but don't you believe it. Dying is the sweetest, tenderest, most sensuous sensation I have ever experienced. Death comes disguised as a sympathetic friend. All was serene; all was calm. How wonderful it would be simply to float out of this world. It is easy to die. You have to fight to live.

Doctor McRae could see that I was going. He called Adelaide at her hotel and told her to hurry over. She called the state police and asked them to intercept the bus that the boys were on and bring them back to their dying father's bedside. The patrol car, with David and Bill in it, hit 80 and 90 miles an hour. The boys loved it, they admitted later.

The troopers had to stop for gas at a little garage on the outskirts of Atlanta. They told the attendant to hurry up because they were taking Eddie Rickenbacker's boys to his bedside.

"Well, you don't need to hurry anymore," the fellow said. "He died an hour ago. News just came over the radio."

Fortunately, the news was exaggerated, and the troopers brought the boys in so that they could see for themselves.

When they came into the room, I was having a hallucination brought on by the morphine. I thought that I saw the most delicious-looking cherries and grapes hanging from the bar over my head. I asked the boys to pick some of that luscious fruit. David, the older boy, understood that I was not myself, but Bill took me seriously.

"But, Daddy," he said, "I don't see any grapes or cherries." He turned to Adelaide and said, "Mother, is Daddy always going to be nuts like that?"

But that was only a brief moment of comic relief in what was the greatest fight of my life—and *for* my life.

Because I had decided not to die. I recognized that wonderful mellow sensation for what it was, death, and I fought it. I fought death mentally, pushing away the rosy sweet blandishments and actually welcoming back the pain.

There was a radio in the room, and at 7:00 that evening Walter Winchell came on. Suddenly I heard Walter say, in that excited, high-pitched voice of his: "Flash! It is confirmed that Eddie Rickenbacker is dying. He is not expected to live another hour."

That made me furious. I had always considered Walter a good friend of mine. With my good hand, my right hand, I grabbed the nearest thing, the water pitcher, and heaved it at the radio. It hit full center, and they both broke.

I began muttering angrily. Adelaide bent over and figured out what I was trying to say.

"Get on the phone," I told her, "and call the top men at the radio networks. Tell them to make their commentators quit talking like that. They're not helping me any by telling me I'm dead. I'm not dead, and I'm not going to die."

She picked up the telephone immediately. I heard her place the long-distance calls and say just what I had told her to say. It didn't seem strange at all that she had no difficulty locating all the network presidents in their offices at 7:30 Sunday night. She had actually made all three calls into a dead phone, but I was satisfied and dozed off.

The battle continued all night. I was ice cold, and the call of death was appealing, but I kept fighting.

Another night I had a flailing and thrashing fit and tore the oxygen tent down. Adelaide, exhausted, had retired to her room in the hospital for the night, as she stayed at the hospital the first ten days that I was there. Suddenly, she appeared. She had dreamed that I was calling her and had hurried to me. She was able to soothe me, so that the oxygen tent could be replaced.

The next ten days were a continuous fight with the old Grim Reaper. I don't know how many transfusions of whole blood and plasma I received. Time and again I felt myself slipping into that sensuous and beautiful state. How sweet it would have been simply to let go and slip off into that lovely land where there is no pain. But each time I recognized that feeling for just what it was, the calling card of death, and I fought back.

Doctor McRae told me later that he had never had a patient with such determination to live, and he attributed my recovery to that will. To return the compliment, I was glad to have him in my corner.

In some of my hallucinations I thought the doctors and nurses were abusing me. When Doctor McRae would come in on his morning rounds, I would complain bitterly about the cruel treatment I had received. Later I would snap out of it and have to explain to him that I had dreamed the whole thing.

Kept under the influence of dope, I was unable to tell the doctors about my extreme reaction to it. One night, through sheer exhaustion, I slept for five hours straight and woke up refreshed. My mind was clear. I realized what that morphine was doing to me, and I told McRae to discontinue it.

"Eddie," he said, "you won't be able to stand it." Finally

he agreed to withhold it for a period of 24 hours. He warned me that I would regret it.

The pain was horrible. The morphine had indeed reduced it to a degree. But, even as the pain increased, I could feel myself coming back mentally. The drug had been retarding my natural recuperative powers. Free from it, I began to get better immediately.

I didn't want to be encased in the cast anymore. I protested so vehemently and steadily that they finally began reducing it bit by bit. After about six weeks the whole cast was removed.

But all that time, in my smashed left hip, the ball at the upper end of my left thigh was lying on top of the smashed socket. When they thought I could take it, the orthopedic men began pulling my leg back into position. They bored a hole through the thigh bone just above the knee, put a bolt through it and secured a cord to the bolt, in order to pull. A steel brace was placed on my knee to lock it in place.

And, of course, all this time the most excruciating agony had been in my left hand and arm. The dope that brought on the hallucinations gave little relief to the pain resulting from the crushed nerve. Doctor McRae tried putting the arm in a cast, but it hurt with such intensity that I simply gnawed the plaster off with my teeth.

Doctor McRae took a look at the chewed-up mess, shook his head and said, "All right, probably it will be just as well if you don't have it on."

He was right. It wasn't the broken arm that bothered me so much as the paralysis in my hand, which was caused by the crushed elbow. Later I asked Adelaide to bring me a rubber ball, and I kept it in my hand, squeezing it, practically the entire time that I was in the hospital. Gradually this exercise overcame the paralysis.

Doctor McRae estimated that I would be in the hospital for about eight months. I disagreed with him. When the cast was off, I demanded that an osteopath be brought in to start working on me in order to speed recovery. McRae did not disapprove, but the other doctors hardly recognized osteopathy.

I asked for Doctor McRae to come in. "Doctor," I said, "you're going to get me an osteopath. If you don't I'm going to get out of here, get a good osteopath and get better and better. Then I'm going to tell the cockeyed world that the osteopath was the one who cured me. You tell that to your associates."

"I think that will work, Eddie," Doctor McRae said. A few days later an excellent osteopath, Doctor Alexander Dahl, came in; he continued to visit me every day. The treatments were painful, but I knew that they were helping.

Through the best efforts of the combined medical and osteopathic sciences, I improved steadily. One day I saw a little girl, a paralytic, roll down the corridor in a kind of kiddie car. It was a little box on rollers, with a seat inside. I made a rough sketch of it, added a few improvements and had the mechanics in Eastern's Atlanta shops make one up for me. At first I sat in it and pushed it along with my feet; then, slowly, I graduated to standing up inside it and, with its support, taking a few steps. I prowled the corridors of the hospital hour after hour, learning to walk again. Then I graduated to crutches, then to a pair of canes. I walked, walked, walked, exercising my bad leg by the hour.

In my first days in the hospital, I was hardly in a condition to appreciate the tremendous flood of cards, calls, telegrams, letters, flowers and gifts that was pouring in. More than eighteen thousand communications, including some seven thousand telegrams, came in from all over the world. During the first few days an inexhaustible supply of cut flowers and potted plants arrived, and we kept the entire hospital supplied with them. Then Adelaide arranged with the local florists to send them over only on request. I was never without flowers all the time I was in the hospital.

Many of the telegrams, letters and cards were pasted in a giant scrapbook for me to look over later. There were many cablegrams from foreign countries; one was from Ernst

Udet, the German ace. Many of the messages reflected the personalities of their senders. For example:

"KEEP PUNCHING. Bob Considine."

"YOU'LL NEVER KNOW HOW MANY PRAYERS WERE BEING WHISPERED AROUND OUR TOWN THIS MORNING. Bill Corum."

"IF RICK NEEDS BLOOD, I'VE GOT PLENTY OF IT. WILL TAKE FIRST AVAILABLE TRANSPORTATION. Cedric E. Fauntleroy."

"GET UP OUT OF THAT BED. YOU CAN'T DO THIS TO ME. Steve Hannagan."

"I KNOW THE INDOMITABLE RICKENBACKER SPIRIT WILL PULL THROUGH. John Edgar Hoover."

"PLEASE TAKE CARE OF YOURSELF. Fiorello La Guardia."

"GOD BLESS YOU OLD MAN AND TAKE CARE OF YOU. Wendell Willkie."

Two of my visitors, by odd coincidence, were both Catholic clergymen named O'Hara. One was the priest who had inquired about my religion in the emergency room that first day. I told Father O'Hara that I wanted to apologize for my remark that day, and I did so.

The other O'Hara was a dear friend of long standing—Bishop John Francis O'Hara of Buffalo, New York, former president of Notre Dame University. He came down to Atlanta for a personal visit, which I greatly appreciated and enjoyed.

Four months and two days after the crash, I was released, thanks to the wonderful medical and nursing care I received at all times. It exceeded the normal expectations of hospital service. I will always be indebted to the staff of the Piedmont Hospital in Atlanta, Georgia, for its meticulous attention and services. We returned to New York and then took a little cottage on Candlewood Lake in Connecticut. I spent three days a week in town, the other four with my family on the lake. One of the orderlies at the hospital, a giant Negro named Mose, came up and spent the summer. He exercised me twice a day, twisting and turning me with his huge hands. We had a little boat, and I rowed it every day.

The boys and I had a wonderful time together. Bill, who inherited some of my interest in mechanics, had a little motor for a model airplane. We took it to pieces and put it back together again.

I had hoped to be able to return to work full time in the fall, but that program turned out to be too ambitious. I was still crippled and in pain. I needed constant exercise. Rowing the boat had proved to be so beneficial that I began exploring ways to continue it. Eventually I arranged to spend the winter on a houseboat at Marathon in the Florida Keys.

In the meantime, the United States went to war. On December 7, 1941, we were still in New York. I went down to the office that Sunday morning, as I usually did, to write some letters without interruption. The news of the Japanese attack on Pearl Harbor came over the radio. I hurried home, and Adelaide and I followed the news all that day and all that night.

Now there was more reason than ever to get fit again. Adelaide and I hurried to the houseboat in Miami. We also had a smaller boat rigged for deep-sea fishing. Wearing only swimming trunks, I'd go out in the morning and stay out all day, soaking in the salt air and the sun and limbering up my muscles.

The Atlanta crash left several physical mementos. I was still hard and tough, the indestructible Rickenbacker, but my carriage was not as straight, and I walked with a slight but permanent limp because of the severed nerve in my left leg. I found that I couldn't use that foot to disengage the clutch when driving a car. That was easy; I gave up driving. The groove in my temple filled in gradually over the years.

But the crash, with all its immediate pain and permanent disabilities, did have a positive and beneficial result. It brought home to me once again the conviction that surely I was being permitted to continue living for some good purpose. I was being tested for some great opportunity to serve, a privilege that might come at any time. By early spring, I was ready —but for what?

Then one day in March came a call from Washington. It was General H. A. "Hap" Arnold, who was commanding general of the U.S. Army Air Forces. After inquiring about my health and being assured that I was recovered he said: "Eddie, I've got a very important mission for you. I can't tell you over the phone. When can you come to Washington?"

"I'll be there bright and early Monday morning," I said. Though I had no idea what job he had for me, I knew that it would be an important one, one related to the mission of the Air Forces in our fight for freedom. I thanked God for sparing me to fight again for America. War is hell, but sometimes a necessary hell. When it comes, everyone should be proud to give his services unflinchingly to his country.

THIRTEEN

BEFORE WORLD WAR II

Some historians trace the origins of World War II to the rise of Adolf Hitler. Others go further back in time—to the Franco-Prussian War or even to the tribal wars of the Middle Ages. I do not argue with them. All I can say is that I saw the beginning of World War II. It was the gleam in the eyes of a group of German former fighter pilots who told me ruthlessly and arrogantly, one October day in 1922, that Germany was determined to regain her position as a world power, through peace or war.

I was even given the blueprint. It was Hermann Goering, later Hitler's top lieutenant in the Nazi Party and commander of the German Air Force, who told me in his harsh, guttural accent:

> Our whole future is in the air. It is by air power that we are going to recapture the German Empire. To accomplish this we will do three things. First we will teach gliding as a sport to all our young men. Then we will build up a fleet of commercial planes, each easily converted to military operation. Finally we will create the skeleton of a military air force. When the time comes, we will put all three together—and the German Empire will be reborn. We must win through the air.

Goering's remarks did not come as an absolute surprise. Even in those days following the end of World War I, I did not believe that this war had ended all wars. In 1919, in the speeches I made all over the country and in my testimony before Congress, I argued that a reasonable proportion of our military strength should be in air power. As one of the organizers of the American Legion, I was hopeful that those of us who had been through the horrors of war could make our voices heard in favor of keeping America strong as the best means of preventing aggression against it. As chairman of the Aviation Committee of the Legion, it was my duty to do my best to preserve undiminished the air power we had finally developed.

In 1922, after Dan Cupid finally caught up with me, Adelaide and I honeymooned in Europe. We were in Berlin while Germany was in its terrible inflationary period. I remember tipping the floor waiter and the maid at our hotel 50 marks each. Adelaide told me not to be so extravagant. Indeed, only a short time before, those 50 marks would have been worth about $12.50, and the recipients of the tip acted as though I had given them that much. But, when I figured the rate of exchange exactly, I realized that I had given them only about 6 cents apiece and went back to give them more. During that terrible period, money became practically worthless. The German people themselves did not believe what was happening to them.

I saw German children wearing shoes without soles; their emaciated bodies and drawn faces clearly revealed undernourishment. Obviously, German morale, already low, was falling. Under such conditions, people will turn to any glimmer of hope, to any prophet, true or false.

While we were in Berlin, Ernst Udet, who had become the leading German ace after Richthofen was killed, learned that I was there and sought me out. He asked me to come to a dinner with him and some other German pilots of World War I. I naturally accepted. The dinner was held in a secret room under a small restaurant. About a dozen Germans were present. I met them all, but I talked at length with only three, Goering, Udet and Erhardt Milch. All three spoke English quite well. Goering, the professional soldier, then a fine figure of a man, positive and dedicated to the rebirth of the fatherland, was definitely the leader of the group. He had commanded the Flying Circus after Richthofen's death. Udet was short, stocky and jovial. Erhardt Milch was on the slender side. He was dignified and well educated.

Although it was Goering who spelled out the plan, all three of these men, destined to take their places among Germany's top military leaders, were outspoken—at least to me—in their determination to elevate their country again, through force if need be, to a position of world leadership. The conversation was cordial, and we reminisced warmly about the air war, but there was still the ring of *Deutschland Über Alles* in their voices.

At that time, only five years after the Russian Revolution, I believed that the threat to Germany, and ultimately to the world, lay in Bolshevism. I foresaw a German alliance with Russia, Turkey, Japan and, through Japan, possibly China—an alliance that would menace the world. Actually, of course, the revolution came in the form of Hitler's National Socialist Party, but the menace was no less. Later Germany did become an ally of Soviet Russia, during the crucial early days of World War II, and of Japan, during the greater part of the war.

As for the German-Italian Axis, which came much later, Italy in 1922 was in such turmoil that anything could have happened. Adelaide and I continued our trip from Germany into Italy, and we were there when Benito Mussolini and his Black Shirts marched on Rome and took over the government. We were in Naples when he made his first speech there; I remember remarking on his Napoleonic pose.

In 1922 I saw the future course of history as constituting a grave danger to the United States and the Allies. What could be done to alleviate the conditions in Germany that were pushing it to the verge of collapse?

I put a great deal of thought into this question and drew up a plan that, I firmly believed, would, *first,* help Germany back to a healthy economy and, *second,* alleviate the conditions that were pushing the world toward war. Financiers and statesmen, with whom I discussed it, gave it their approval.

In my official presentation of the Rickenbacker Plan for World Peace, I likened Germany to a tramp, out of a job, hungry, poorly clothed and desperate—practically in the gutter. Some might have said that it served the German people right, but I could not feel that way. Without apologizing for Germany's past, I distinguished between the German people, with their ideals and aims, and the Kaiser and his caste, by whom the people had been led into war. German sentiment and aspirations were republican, and I believed that we in America should help those people realize their republican dream. It is not the American way to knock a man down and then keep kicking him. We had administered the necessary licking. It was now in our own interest to lend a hand to lift the German people to their feet again and to help them produce enough for their own needs and a surplus to pay their debts. If we did not come to Germany's aid, I could foresee some kind of dictatorship arising.

In 1922 the Allied war debt to the United States was about $11 billion. It was generally agreed by both bankers and statesmen that to force the war-weary nations of Europe to pay that debt, even if it could be done, would defeat our own ends. The only way that those countries could pay off the debt would be by supereffort and superproductivity at starvation wages. Should they proceed along that path, we would be unable to compete with them for the commerce of the world. Neither could they, under those conditions.

Continued absence of European trade would result in lowered prices, prices inadequate to repay American farmers their production costs and consequently a domestic market insufficient to absorb the output of our factories. Even with the vast hoard of gold in our vaults, we would still have a dominant industry.

The Rickenbacker Plan for World Peace was twofold: First, it provided for reduction of the German indemnity—the amount owed other nations—combined with an extension of terms that would make it possible for her to pay the balance.

Second, it included the loan from United States to Germany of an amount sufficient to meet immediate indemnity payments, stabilize the government, place the currency on a firm basis and rehabilitate the country in general.

This loan would be coupled with the reservation that the money could not be used to build up another military machine. Germany would be required to repay her debt to the Allies out of our loan. This repayment would enable the Allies in turn to repay us. In short, the entire transaction would be merely a matter of bookkeeping; the money need never leave our own country. We would not only collect the $11 billion the Allies owed us, but Germany in her time and turn would also repay with interest.

By enabling Germany to meet her obligations to her archenemy, France, we would in turn enable France to disband her enormous army and use its manpower to economic advantage. For, with American money controlling Germany, there would be no fear that France would invade Germany.

As I wrote in 1922: "At one stroke, we could control the policy of Europe and without the cost of one dollar to our own people. In the place of the almost worthless IOU's of the Allies, which we now hold, we would have a first mortgage on Germany as well."

I took this plan to Washington, but again I was many years too early. The war was over, and no one wanted to think of the grim possibility of another. I prepared a lengthy statement of the plan and gave it to the press. It received good coverage, but the public was not interested.

Looking back on the Rickenbacker Plan for World Peace from the vantage point of some 45 years, I still believe that it would have worked. It is certainly a tragic and inescapable fact that World War II, the most terrible in the history of mankind, did occur. It cost the United States alone $600 billion to fight that war. Had we spent 2 percent of that sum in 1922, we could have changed the course of history. Not only would World War II have been averted, but also its aftermath, the deplorable conditions and problems that we face today in almost every corner of the globe.

Eventually a program basically similar to mine was proposed and put into effect. It was the Marshall Plan, presented in 1947 by General George C. Marshall, then Secretary of State. But it was 25 years too late. By that time, millions had died, and Communism had grown to full stature in many parts of the world. It is still growing. And I am still asking myself why our statesmen ignored my straightforward and comparatively inexpensive solution to the basically simple problem of Germany in 1922? Couldn't they see what was going to happen? I could.

I returned to Germany in 1935, and that time I saw positive proof that, under Hitler, the Germans were building a great war machine. In the meantime I was both preaching and practicing preparedness in the United States, to the extent of my ability.

Right after I came home in 1919, as I have mentioned previously, I was invited to spend several days in Washington testifying before congressional committees on the potential of air power. The congressmen listened attentively, but that was unfortunately no period in which to speak of national defense. Not even America's first air-power strategist, General Billy Mitchell, was able to put across his theories, all later tested in warfare, either to Congress or to the military hierarchy.

Mitchell made a plea for a separate air force; instead, what little air strength remained after World War I was split between the Army, the Navy and the Marines. Mitchell claimed that bombs dropped by airplane could wreck cities and sink ships; Josephus Daniels, Secretary of the Navy, reflected much of the shortsighted thinking of officialdom when he said that he would stand on the deck of a ship while Mitchell was bombing it— "with my hat off." The Air Corps did sink a captured German warship by bombing it (Daniels was not aboard), but little came of that.

Mitchell foresaw the Hawaiian Islands' vulnerability to Japanese bombers twenty years before Pearl Harbor, but the only people who paid any attention to him were the Japanese.

Finally Mitchell's criticism of the general staff for its aviation administration became so vehement that he was charged with insubordination and brought before a court-martial on October 28, 1925. The case continued for almost a month. I was proud to appear as the General's final witness on November 20. Newspaper accounts reported that I was asked what place among the nations the United States stood in aviation and testified that, according to the latest authentic information, six countries were ahead of us in aviation—France, England, Italy, Germany, Russia and Japan. What the reporters did not know was that I had a bitter exchange with members of the court, including Major General Robert Lee Howze, president of the court, Major General Hugh N. Drum and Major General Douglas MacArthur. The controversy became warm, and some intemperate words were spoken.

I spoke in defense of Billy Mitchell whenever and wherever the opportunity presented itself, knowing that my remarks would get back to Washington. They were as follows:

> What were we supposed to do when we went to the front in 1917? We had to take the planes that the French refused to use. Because of the cowardice and stupidity of our own War Department and government authorities, when the Wright brothers went to the government with their new invention, they were refused encouragement and had to turn to France. France saw the possibility.
>
> When we entered the war, we had no aircraft industry. Hundreds of lives of our fliers were sacrificed needlessly by defective planes and obsolete equipment in training camps thousands of miles from the front.
>
> This nation owes General Mitchell a debt of gratitude for daring to speak the truth. He has learned his lesson from the only real teacher—experience. It is pathetic to think that military leaders, in the declining years of their lives, are in such a position that they can, through petty selfishness and envy, destroy a man who has done us the service Mitchell has.

It is a crime against posterity. This nation will pay the price of their selfishness. Not perhaps in this generation, but in that of the boys who are growing up today or their sons.

Unified air service is the life insurance of our national integrity. We have spent $450 million since the war on aircraft, and today you could not scrape together $1 million worth of air matériel in the country. One-tenth of 1 percent of the money now wasted on national defense, if put intelligently into aircraft, would give us some real protection. The Army is helpless without aircraft. So is the Navy. Today we have an Army airfield on one side of the street and a Navy field on the other. Both seek the same thing. Conditions are as bad in the mail service, in the forestry patrol work and everywhere else. If the sons of our government leaders, this generation of so-called "statesmen," could make the rounds of wartime flying fields and look at the graves of men whose lives were a pitiful sacrifice to the same sort of statesmanship in this country twenty years ago, they would not act as they do.

I might as well have been talking to a stone wall. Billy Mitchell was found guilty and dismissed from the service. That was his reward for the great service he had given his country.

A decade after the court-martial, I received word that he was at Doctors Hospital in New York, quite ill. I visited him several times. He was gloomy and depressed. I was out of town on business when I received a wire that he had died.

His body was to be shipped back to his original home in Milwaukee. A few of his old friends escorted his casket to the train. The casket was unloaded at the back end of Grand Central Station, and we carried it through the dark and cold catacombs to the express car. As I was tramping along, holding the casket and hearing the eerie echoes of our footsteps, I felt so bitter, so grief-stricken, so shocked at this ignominious, demeaning end to a brilliant career, that I found the whole episode hard to believe.

Years later, of course, Billy Mitchell's theories were proved and his predictions realized. Had our military hierarchy carried out his recommendations in the years following World War I, we could have had an air force truly worthy of the United States. In my opinion, such an air force would have awed Hitler and Goering to the extent that they would never have started the war.

They knew in 1939 how few planes we had and how little we had accomplished in aeronautical research and development. They were also fully aware of the true situation in England and France.

I took the case for air power directly to the President of the United States, Herbert Hoover. The occasion was propitious: It was the presentation to me of the Congressional Medal of Honor, the country's greatest honor.

The medal was awarded by a special act of Congress. The citation reads as follows:

> *Edward V. Rickenbacker,* Colonel, specialist reserve, then first lieutenant, 94th Aero Squadron, Air Service, American Expeditionary Forces. For conspicuous gallantry and intrepidity above and beyond the call of duty in action against the enemy near Billy, France, September 25, 1918 [the morning of the day I assumed command of the 94th Squadron]. While on a voluntary patrol over the lines Lieutenant Rickenbacker attacked seven enemy planes (five type Fokker protecting two type Halberstadt photographic planes). Disregarding the odds against him he dived on them and shot down one of the Fokkers out of control. He then attacked one of the Halberstadts and sent it down also. Residence at appointment: 1334 East Livingston Avenue, Columbus, Ohio.

The presentation was made at Bolling Field outside Washington on November 6, 1930. General James E. Fechet, chief of the Air Corps, read the citation. When he had finished, President Hoover put the ribbon over my head with the following words:

> Captain Rickenbacker, in the name of the Congress of the United States, I take great pleasure in awarding you the Congressional Medal of Honor, our country's highest decoration for conspicuous gallantry and intrepidity above and beyond the call of duty in action with the enemy. In the stage of development of aviation when the flying of airplanes was a much more hazardous undertaking than it is today, you were achieving victories which made you the universally recognized Ace of Aces of the American forces. Your record is an outstanding one for skill and bravery, and is a source of pride to your comrades and your countrymen. Although this award is somewhat belated I hope that your gratification in receiving this Medal of Honor will be as keen as mine

is in bestowing it to you. May you wear it during many years of happiness and continued usefulness to your country.

I was moved by the President's words, and I could not conceal it:

> Mr. President, I should be ungrateful if I failed to recognize this great honor as a true tribute to my comrades-in-arms, soldiers and sailors, living and dead. In peace and in war they have contributed their share. They have perpetuated the traditions and high ideals of the United States in the air as they have on the land and the sea.

After the presentation, a brief air show was put on by nineteen planes of the new 94th Squadron from Selfridge Field, Michigan, five bombers of the 2nd Bombardment Group from Langley Field, Virginia, and nine observation planes from the 9th Group, Mitchell Field, New York.

Immediately after the presentation of the medal and before the planes arrived, I attempted to put in a word to Mr. Hoover on the importance of a large, independent and unified air service. I had marshaled my arguments and presented them as best I could. His mind, however, was obviously on many other things. It had been only a year since the stock-market crash, and the nation was descending deeper into the Depression. The President was polite and courteous, but his interests were not in military aviation.

It was obvious that the nation's leaders were simply not ready for military preparedness in general, military aviation in particular. If we could not build a mighty aviation industry to produce military planes, I reasoned, then we must develop an aviation industry to build commercial planes. When our government and military leaders finally awoke to the great danger from abroad and the need to rush production of airplanes of all kinds, then at least we would have a base to progress from. That was my major reason for entering the aviation field and staying in it. During my early years in aviation, particularly while I was with Eastern Air Lines, I was offered several positions, chiefly in the automotive and financial fields, at several times the income I was receiving at Eastern. But I believed that, by staying in aviation, I could help to build commercial air transportation, create a need for more airplanes and force the aviation manufacturing industry to grow in order to produce them.

In Germany, in the meantime, the nation's leaders were building a mighty war machine, with full emphasis on military aviation. I returned thirteen years after that dinner with the group of German pilots in 1922.

On August 15, 1935, Will Rogers, the great humorist and a close friend, was killed in a plane crash in Alaska while attempting an around-the-world flight with Wiley Post. I was asked to help organize the Will Rogers Memorial Fund and gladly did so. Coupled with my regular job of trying to run an airline, it was an exhausting job. When the fund was successfully underway, I decided that I needed a change of scenery.

With the valid excuse that I wanted to look at airline operations in Europe, Adelaide and I took a ship for England. When we arrived in London, we had breakfast with Lord Beaverbrook, the influential British publisher, whom I had met in Canada when he was still William Maxwell Aitken. He inquired what I planned to do and my itinerary. I told him, adding that I should be back in London about four weeks later.

"Then will you have dinner with me at our town house when you return?"

"Yes, we would be delighted," I said. I had no idea at that time of the importance of that dinner meeting.

Adelaide and I traveled through England, France, Germany and Italy, riding the airlines of Europe and hoping to learn from their example how to do a better job back home. When we arrived in Germany, we were met by two of the men I had dined with at the little restaurant in 1922—Milch, then the equivalent of what is now our Secretary of Air, and Ernst Udet, then head of design, supply and equipment for German aviation. Udet had visited the United States as a stunt flyer several times since 1922, and we had come to know each other fairly well. We had been playing an interesting little game over the years. He had been trying to pump me on what the United States was doing in military aviation, while I had been trying to pump him about German accomplishments.

When they met us at the airport, both were dressed in full Nazi uniform, complete with shiny sabers. They escorted us to our hotel in a motorcade of gleaming new automobiles. Ernst took me to a special luncheon at the Air Service building. The building itself was a powerful indication of the way that military aviation was going in Germany. It was a block long, and its roof was of solid concrete six feet thick. The entire headquarters was one big bomb shelter.

At the luncheon, Hermann Goering, then president of the Reichstag, joined us for a few minutes.

"Herr Eddie," he said, "do you remember what I told you about the future of our air force when you visited us in 1922?"

"I remember it very clearly," I said.

"Gut," he said, beaming and rubbing his hands together in a characteristic gesture, "now we will show you. Ernst Udet will take you in charge and show you everything that we have been doing."

At that, I too felt like beaming and rubbing my hands together, but I kept a noncommittal, half-doubting look on my face. I knew the characteristics of the "Heinies"; it takes one to know one. I knew that Goering, in his intense national pride, would hold back nothing in order to impress me. I would see what no other outsider in the world had seen.

For the next several days, Udet was my guide as we visited the aviation complex of the new Germany. First, we visited his old squadron, the Richthofen Flying Circus. It was located in a pine forest and so well concealed that I had no idea it existed until suddenly I was right in the middle of it. I had seen camouflage before but nothing like that.

A German squadron at that time had a complement of eighteen fighter planes and pilots. I counted only twelve fighters plus a half-dozen two-seater training planes. I asked Ernst what the trainers were for. He explained fully the way Germany was going about building an air force in absolute violation of the Treaty of Versailles. Udet said:

> With our method of training and expansion, we can't afford to waste gasoline. We can't afford to waste manpower or pilot time. We can't afford to waste materials. We hand-pick every man in the squadron—cooks, clerks, mechanics—and train them as pilots while they are doing their assigned jobs. When a pilot is transferred out of a squadron, we move the next qualified man into his place. When we create a new squadron, we staff it with new pilots from the enlisted ranks along with officers who have already served as pilots in other squadrons.

I also saw, with Udet as my guide, aviation factories turning out both commercial and military planes. Some of those factories were also camouflaged. They contained fascinating new aeronautical developments. I was shown, for instance, a wind tunnel for testing tailspin characteristics of new designs. I had never heard of such a thing before. I saw their newest engines, instruments and designs still on the drawing board.

Udet—and, for that matter, Milch and Goering—made no effort to conceal the reason for this massive aviation program. It was to recapture the glory of the German Empire. If war was necessary to achieve this goal, they were prepared to fight.

Knowing the German mentality, I did not find it at all strange that they were telling me, an American, their plans to lick the world. First, they did not really consider the United States basically an enemy, as they did England and France. Second, whether I was friend or foe, I had a reputation as a combat pilot, and they had a compulsion to awe me with their Teutonic might.

The Germans had little respect for either England or France as a military power. They knew how decadent France had become. They did not have to explain it to me, for I had just left France and seen its condition. Through their discipline, sacrifice and preparation, the Germans honestly believed that they had earned the right to wage war and to win it. They had been pre-

paring while England and France had been dissipating their
wealth and energies.

Though my three acquaintances were in accord on this German destiny, they did not all support Hitler, not by any means.
Udet told me many a time, in both the United States and Germany, that he disagreed with Hitler completely.

Erhardt Milch was no supporter of Hitler. Milch's mother was
Jewish, and by 1935 persecution of the Jews had already begun
in Germany. Milch was such an intelligent and capable airman
that Goering kept him in his high position.

While I was being shown these evidences of German rearmament, at least in aviation, I wondered why I had heard so little
about German military aviation over the years. A partial answer to that question came when Adelaide and I were entertained at an embassy party in Berlin. The air attaché, who should
have been finding out what was going on in his area, proved to
be more interested in the social life of the German élite.

Four weeks after our breakfast with Lord Beaverbrook, Adelaide and I returned to London. On the day of our arrival, Beaverbrook's secretary arrived with an invitation to dinner the
following evening at 8:00 at the Beaverbrook town house. When
we arrived and were introduced to the other guests, I was surprised—though I successfully concealed it—by the number of
important personages assembled. Just about everyone in the
government of Prime Minister Stanley Baldwin was present, except Baldwin himself.

I had not been served my first cocktail before Robert Gilbert
Vansittart, the foreign undersecretary, led me into a corner.

"When are they going to be ready, Captain?" he asked.

"When is who going to be ready?" I asked.

"The Germans," he said impatiently. "When will they be ready
to fight?"

I looked at him a moment and decided to tell him truthfully
what I believed.

"In my opinion, a minimum of three years, but I lean to a
maximum of five years." (I missed by two months.)

"Oh, no, no, no," he said. "Two years at the most!"

His voice was shaking. "You sure as hell are going to get it if you don't conceal your jitters any better from the Germans than you do from me," I thought to myself.

This quick exchange with Vansittart made me realize why Beaverbrook had invited me to dinner. I was to report on the German situation. Following my brief conversation with Vansittart, we all sat down to dinner. Again I was asked for my opinion, and again I gave it: Germany was building a great war machine and would not hesitate to use it if necessary to regain world eminence.

As the dinner progressed, it became clear that, of all those present, only Vansittart believed that the Germans would dare to precipitate another war. All the others disagreed so bluntly and positively that, after only a few minutes of conversation, I realized that it was pointless for me to continue the discussion. "Rickenbacker," I told myself, "just be a country boy. Keep your mouth shut and your ears open, and maybe you'll learn something."

What I learned was that the British leaders of that period were more interested in petty bickering and attempting to keep themselves in power than they were in even learning about German aims, much less preparing to defend against them. At that time in Britain, preparedness was considered warmongering. Winston Churchill, one of the few eminent Britons who believed in preparedness and who made his militant voice heard at every opportunity, was very much in disfavor at the time. So was Anthony Eden. It was a government of compromise and self-delusion. In their internal political fights the English leaders had forgotten the outside world.

When we arrived home, we found the situation in the United States no better. In vain did I attempt to describe to our military leaders the true situation in Germany. My reports were completely at variance with those coming in from our social-climbing lounge lizards, who were too busy going to cocktail parties to do their jobs.

At one conference with several high-ranking Air Corps officers, including my friend Hap Arnold, I attempted to describe in detail the methods by which the Germans were training their pilots. When I said that the Germans were making pilots out of cooks, mechanics, drivers and the like, they refused to believe me.

"Eddie, you're nuts," one of them said. "It can't be done. You can't make qualified pilots out of mechanics."

In vain I pointed out that I myself had been a mechanic, that I had had a most difficult time getting into the Air Service in World War I because I was not a college graduate but that I had managed to do all right. But I was talking to deaf ears. Our military leaders had their own ideas of training, and anything that did not conform to those ideas could not be allowed. I could not awaken them to the danger. They continued on their placid way.

Nor did the American people want to hear of war. For two years the Economic Club of New York had been asking me to address the membership, but I had felt that it was not yet ready to hear what I had to say. In the early part of 1939, however, I decided that, if anyone in the United States would be receptive to the truth, it would be this group of farsighted, intelligent, successful men. In my speech I said that the day would soon come when the United States would be plunged into war whether or not we wanted it. Our participation would not be restricted to money and munitions but, rather, to *men,* money and munitions—"and, gentlemen, I mean millions of men."

During the entire speech, members of the club sat stolidly. Usually when I speak there are interruptions of applause; on that occasion, there was not one. When I had finished and sat down, there was a full ten seconds of silence before a perfunctory round of hand-clapping began.

(Some years later John D. Rockefeller, Jr., asked me to be the guest of honor at a dinner at the Metropolitan Club in New York. About fifty couples were present; Adelaide, of course, accompanied me. After dinner Mr. Rockefeller stood up and made some gracious and complimentary remarks. Referring to that Economic Club dinner, at which he had been present, he said: "I am glad to be able to offer Eddie Rickenbacker my apologies. He was right, and we were wrong.")

Despite the cold reception from government and civilian leaders alike, I never quit working for American preparedness. If I could not obtain government cooperation, then I would have to go at the problem in my own way. If the government would not train large numbers of men for aviation or encourage the establishment of at least potentially greater aircraft production, then it would be up to the commercial airlines to do so. By selling air travel, by increasing both mileage and service, by working constantly to perfect the reliability of commercial aviation, we could establish nuclei of production and training that could be expanded when the need arose.

Even then we received small encouragement from the armed forces. It was the airlines, as I have already recounted, that worked with Don Douglas on the development of the DC-1, the DC-2 and the famous DC-3, or "C-47," as it was known in the military.

When Douglas first started drawing up plans for a larger plane than the DC-3, with the increased payload and dependability that four engines could provide, he attempted to interest the military services in it. He was turned down cold. An Army general asked him, in all seriousness, "but what possible use could the U.S. Army have for a four-engine transport?"

I went to the top brass in the Air Corps, including Hap Arnold, by that time a brigadier general, and told them bluntly that they ought to order one thousand of those planes immediately. They laughed at me, just as they had laughed at Douglas. It was only through the financial support of the airlines that Douglas was able to complete the design and development of his four-engine plane. It was the DC-4, or C-54. Its praises were never sung as loudly as those of the C-47, the "gooney bird" as it was affectionately known, but the C-54, because of its greater capacity, had a large share in winning the war.

My recommendations for achieving air power can be broken down into two proposals, one made in 1925, the other in 1939.

In 1925 I published a far-reaching program for the development of military aviation in the April issue of *Aero Digest,* in which I strongly recommended the unification of all our air activities. The Army, the Navy and to some extent the Marine Corps were proceeding along their own aviation lines without even consulting one another. This duplication resulted in the dissipation of large sums of our preparedness dollars. Between Armistice Day in 1918 and in 1925, $450 million had been spent on military aviation. But, owing in large part to duplication, it would have been difficult to locate $1 million worth of adequate equipment in the country.

In the early 1920s not only the military branches of the government were flying planes but also the Department of Interior, which maintains a flying forest patrol, and the Post Office Department, which flew the airmail until the Air Mail Act of 1925 went into effect. You'd find air installations on either side of the road, each approaching the same problem by its own method. The taxpayer, of course, paid the bill for this extravagance in research and experimental work.

What thought was given to military aviation in those days was usually restricted to its potential as a weapon. I pointed out the value of military air transport. At that time it was estimated that one division could be moved from coast to coast in two weeks by truck or train or in three weeks by ship through the Panama Canal. I stated flatly that the equivalent number of men could be moved from coast to coast by air in 36 hours.

Even when the government was flying the mail, I believed that a great impetus for aeronautical development would come from the commercial airlines. I made the proposal that every city with a population of 25,000 or more establish a municipal airdrome at civic expense. On the official completion of the airdrome, the city would then be officially designated as an airmail station and be connected with the national network of airmail routes. The city would lease the hangars and other field facilities to commercial organizations and private individuals.

This stimulation of the use of the airmail would create a demand for airplanes, which in turn would create great additional activity in the aeronautical engineering field. All this activity would arouse sufficient confidence for private capital to invest increasing amounts in this great new industry. The full scope of this proposal has yet to be realized forty years later, but it did have some influence on commercial aviation in general.

Although my own personal military experience had been in fighter planes, I had been convinced of the strategic value of the bomber ever since I had witnessed the first missions planned and directed by General Mitchell in France in 1918. All through the 1920s and all through the 1930s, when so many of our military and government leaders could not even imagine the potential of this terrible new weapon, I preached, in hundreds of talks, the concept of strategic air warfare with the bomber as the backbone of the Air Force.

In early 1939, six months before World War II began, I made a careful appraisal of the American situation in military aviation for *Collier's Weekly,* at that time the most aviation-conscious of all the major magazines, in which I recommended a fleet of fifty thousand planes.

In 1939 we were tragically unprepared for high-speed production of airplanes of any kind. The aviation industry was producing about 3,700 planes a year, of all types. About 36,000 men were employed in the industry but not steadily; employment was exceedingly spotty. By using the full capacity of airplane-manufacturing facilities and full employment of its manpower, the industry could probably step up to 5,500 planes a year—if that many were ordered.

An adequate training program for future engineers and technicians in the aircraft industry did not exist. Of 26,000 high schools, only five hundred maintained any aviation activity whatever. Pilot training was conducted on a most conservative level. In Germany at that time, for example, there were dozens of schools for aviation instructors alone; we did not have one. We had one aviation research center, at Wilbur Wright Field in Dayton, Ohio; Germany had five.

It was a sad fact but true: judging by the number of planes on hand, in production or capable of being produced; by replacement capability; by the number of aeronautical engineers and technicians working and in training; by the number of pilots and pilot training programs, and by all the other ponderables involved, the United States was at best a fifth- or sixth-rate air power.

Our aircraft industry did not have to remain that far down the list. Although not producing to its full capacity, it was nevertheless a maturely planned industrial organization with thousands of intricate details already in place—plans, jigs, tools, assembly line, materials and supply and a nucleus of trained men. Our aviation industry could borrow from our automotive industry, the most efficient type of high-grade mass production in the world. Development of this same kind of industrial effort, organized and massed for the single objective of large-scale production of airplanes, was the indispensable key to air supremacy.

But how to accomplish this drastic step-up in production? I knew that we would never gain public support for an armaments race, even in 1939. The remedy I proposed was to tie in this large increase with the everyday conditions of American life. The answer would be to utilize the one strategic factor that no other nation had—our immense commerce; we carried on one-half the business of the entire world.

The method: Carry all first-class mail by air. This move would stimulate the immediate production of a fleet of fifty thousand planes.

In 1939 airmail was being picked up at 250 points. By flying all first-class mail, except mail for local and suburban delivery, we could have increased the number of points of call and therefore the number of airports many times over.

In 1939 we were shipping 7 million pounds of express and freight by air. That amount too could have been greatly increased, with a resulting acceleration in all business.

Equally important would be increased training of pilots. Of all the services, land, sea and air, only the Air Corps lacked a nucleus of personnel and the means of training additional pilots. As I pointed out repeatedly in the 1930s, there should have been a West Point of the air. Until the establishment of such an academy (and it was not founded until 1959), an increase in commercial flying would provide an excellent advance-training program for pilots. Three months of transport flying would give military fliers more practical experience than they would gain in a year with the Army or Navy. The vital bomber command in particular would benefit from this training. Military equipment was insufficient and inefficient in comparison to that of our commercial airlines. Transport pilots gained experience not only in flying big planes but also in working with instrumentation, which the Air Corps was only beginning to use.

As history shows, these recommendations ran into opposition from the railroads. Nevertheless, both the specification of a definite number of planes and the suggestion of a means to obtain them stimulated thought and action in the highest government circles. For years I had been the only civilian to utter those thoughts. I had been willing to stand up and be counted. I had been taking my case to the nation, and the press had been coming to me over the years for comment. This plan summed it all up and placed it in the lap of our leaders.

Within a few months, President Roosevelt announced the official recommendation of fifty thousand planes. By that time the war had begun, and Germany had demonstrated the tremendous new potential of aviation in warfare. I proposed the following: 250,000 military airplanes, 500,000 pilots, 1,175,-000 nonflying personnel, 1,000 master airports, 100,000 parachute troops. I recommended that we build an Air Force capable of dominating any place within three thousand miles of the United States—and that included Hawaii. Those figures, astronomical as they seemed at the time, were underestimates; the United States built more than three hundred thousand airplanes in World War II.

Those airplanes helped to win the war. I believe that my actions and words had some influence in producing them more quickly and more efficiently. But I am also convinced that, had our nation's leaders only listened to me earlier, the entire war could have been prevented. One billion dollars invested in air power during the 5-year period from 1935 to 1940 would have given us an air force capable of deterring both Germany and Japan. Hitler would never have dared to begin hostilities had the American military potential been, in 1939, a fraction of what it was by 1945.

Aviation, instead of the tremendous destructive force that it proved to be, could have meant peace to the world. From the days of World War I to the present moment, I have proclaimed that aviation will someday tie the peoples of the world together; provide commercial, political and social intercourse among them and enable them to understand one another. Then, instead of being the most deadly weapon God ever let man create, the airplane will become truly the Angel of Peace He intended it to be.

FOURTEEN

TO WAR AGAIN

While we in America were blinded by our ideals, mistaking dreams of peace for reality, foolishly believing that the unsound peace terms of World War I had ended large-scale conflict forever, the Axis powers were driving relentlessly onward in their determination to rule the world.

In August 1939, Adelaide, the two boys and I enjoyed a delightful family vacation in Europe. David was fourteen years old that summer, Bill eleven. We spent several days in Germany, where I visited again with my old friend Ernst Udet, by then in charge of all aircraft production for the Luftwaffe. We all saw the new, confident, belligerent spirit of the Third Reich. Then we went on to Norway, where we had leased a sturdy little ketch, complete with crew, for a trip along the Norwegian coast. It was a peaceful, interesting little cruise, and we all relished every minute of it. At the completion of the cruise we planned to visit Finland and then come home on the Polish liner *Batory*. We had reservations from Helsinki to New York. We were met in Oslo, however, by Hjalmar Riiser-Larsen, a good friend who was in charge of the Norway division of the Scandinavian Air Service. Riiser, as he was called, advised us to head for home immediately.

"The Germans are going to move into Poland any day now," he said, looking down at us from his six-foot-six height. "All hell is going to break loose."

Riiser, an excellent pilot and former explorer, was not the kind to exaggerate. We took his advice.

Instead of going to Helsinki therefore, we took a plane for London, from where I had reservations to fly home. David and Bill had never seen Paris, and I thought that there was a tragic possibility that, if they did not see it then, they might never again see it as it was then. I knew what the German bombers could do. So I suggested that they and Adelaide stay in Europe, take a good look at Paris then board the *Batory* at Cherbourg.

The boys did see Paris, but they saw more than that. They saw the beginning of a war. In the last ten days of August, Hitler signed a nonaggression pact with Russia, then demanded the Polish corridor, which separated Germany and East Prussia. Refugees began pouring out of Middle Europe into France and from Paris toward the coast. France declared national mobilization of all military services, which tied up all transportation. Adelaide and the boys had to hire a Paris taxicab in order to get to Cherbourg. They handled their baggage themselves.

The *Batory* was late arriving in Cherbourg, and there was a great press of refugees seeking passage. There were some tense moments when it looked as though the three Rickenbackers might be left at the dock, but fortunately their tickets were honored, although their staterooms had been assigned to others. Adelaide made such an uproar that they finally gave her the cabin originally reserved for her, but the boys had to sleep in an inside cabin.

The ship sailed on August 28. While it was at sea Hitler

invaded Poland, bombing Warsaw and other cities, and Great Britain and France declared war on Germany. A British liner was torpedoed off the coast of Scotland, and there were many submarine scares on the *Batory*. In the meantime, in New York, I was frantically trying to find out where the ship was and when it would arrive, but no one could tell me. Finally I made a transatlantic call to a friend in Scotland Yard, who informed me confidentially that the *Batory* was blacked out and proceeding from St. John's, Newfoundland, under destroyer escort. It finally docked in New York on September 5. I found my wife and boys tired from the constant strain and eager to get off the crowded ship and onto the shores of the good old U.S.A.

During the rest of 1939 and all of 1940, I was busy building Eastern Air Lines for the role I knew that we, and all forms of transportation, would be called upon to play in the crucial years ahead. I continued to speak, exhorting the people and their leaders to greater efforts. I declined active participation in the armed forces at that time. I had canceled my commission as a colonel in the Specialist Reserve in 1934, in protest against the legalized murder of the young Army pilots sent out to fly the airmail at the time of the cancellation of the airmail contracts.

I strongly believed that those of us who had expertise in production and management of essential industries should remain civilians. When my old friend Bill Knudsen, president of General Motors, was brought to Washington and made a 3-star general in charge of military production, I made a special trip to Washington to see him. "If you take this commission, you'll be through, Bill," I told him. "Your usefulness to the country will be cut in half."

Knudsen served his country well as a lieutenant general, but I still believe that he could have done a better job as an unfettered civilian.

Perhaps if I had been in uniform I might have been somewhere else on February 27, 1941, when the airplane crash near Atlanta laid me up for over a year. It was the early part of March 1942, when I was still recuperating from those injuries in Florida, that I received the call from General Hap Arnold summoning me to Washington for an important specific mission. I entered his office on the following Monday morning.

"I'm concerned about the reports I'm getting from combat groups in training, Eddie," Hap said. "I'm told that they are indifferent, that they haven't got the punch they need to do the job they're being prepared for. I want you to go out and talk to these boys, inspire them, put some fire in them. And while you're there, I want you to look around and see what our problems are."

It was the kind of mission I had been hoping for. "I'll be ready to go in ten days," I said eagerly. "The boys are coming down for Easter and . . ."

"Eddie," Arnold interrupted me, "some of these units will be on the way overseas in ten days. If you don't go right away, there's no point in your going at all. The situation is that serious."

"I'll go right away, General," I said.

My companions on the tour were to be General Frank O'D. "Monk" Hunter, a fellow pilot in the 94th Squadron in World War I, and Colonel Hans Christian Adamson, a reservist who would handle our press relations. General Hunter had broken his back in a crash a few months before and planned to take his doctor along with him. I realized that the trip would be a strain on my battered body, still not completely healed from the Atlanta crash, and I took along a masseur. That's the way we started out on March 10, 1942—two battered old retreads attended by a doctor and a masseur going out to inspire young fighter pilots headed for combat.

But, like all old warhorses, once we had the bits in our teeth, we gave our attendants trouble keeping up with us. I found that, with the help of a cane, I could get along fine at the air bases. It was when I stopped moving around, either at the end of the day or in flight between bases, that my body would stiffen up. Then my masseur would take over and get me mobile and comparatively limber again.

We spent several hours at each base, talking, observing, analyzing and trying to inspire the kids. We visited both pursuit and bomber units. We visited a unit in Tampa, Florida, on March 10, a Tuesday; one in Savannah, Georgia, on March 11; groups in Florence and Columbia, South Carolina, on Thursday; units in Tallahassee on Friday, and others in New Orleans on Saturday. Sunday, March 15, we took off so that I could write Hap a full report on our week's activities.

By that time we had shaken down the procedure to an efficient operation. After talking with the leaders of the outfit, I would limp out and talk to the rest of the personnel, particularly the pilots. My job was to share with them the combat experience and psychology that I had learned and developed in combat in World War I and in my subsequent experience with aviation. With each group I talked from an hour and a quarter to two hours. Some days I would talk seven or eight hours, and it was high-pressure selling. Frequently the commanding officer would introduce me as captain or colonel, and I would begin by pointing out that I was not Captain Rickenbacker or Colonel Rickenbacker but plain old Buck Private Rickenbacker. That always broke the ice. Then I would talk about some of the equipment we had to fly with in World War I, the Nieuports that could not come out of steep dives without shedding the linen on their upper wings, planes with no armor whatever, little 30-caliber machine guns that jammed.

"You guys are lucky," I would say. "You've got something to fight with."

Frequently, we would have brief question-and-answer periods. "Don't tell me what's right," I would say. "Tell me what's wrong."

Partly from the answers to these questions, partly from an indefinable attitude that I could sense, the root of the problem quickly became clear to me. There was nothing wrong with those boys. They were America's best: keen, alert, inspired, enthusiastic, fit. They craved action.

But instead of putting in the long hard days that their energies and desires demanded, they were undergoing severely curtailed training. They wanted to give it all they had, but we were not letting them.

Why? There was not enough equipment. It was not only the shortage of planes. The obstacles lay in the entire complex of maintenance. Parts of planes and engines wear out and are damaged in use, and they must be constantly repaired or replaced. But there were not enough parts and equipment in inventory at any base I visited. Nor was there an efficient distribution system by which the necessary equipment could be quickly delivered from the manufacturers. Requisitions would go into supply, and it might be days, even weeks, before the necessary part or parts arrived.

Even if there had been an efficiently planned distributive operation, the transportation pipeline was in no condition to keep the items moving. The Air Corps was supplying itself by ground transportation, primarily railroads, and by March 1942 the nation's railroads were already overtaxed. The first groups I visited were located in the southeastern states, but they were flying planes that, for the most part, were made on the West Coast. Filling requisitions was a matter of weeks. As a result, planes were grounded for weeks at a time for want of parts—and there were not enough planes in the first place.

There was also a shortage of guns and ammunition. I remembered well the importance of target practice from my own early experience. I had found learning to shoot accurately as difficult as learning to fly. The weapons of World War II were more complicated and required more training and practice. Again, owing to lack of equipment, pilots of pursuit ships and gunners of bombers were not receiving enough training, and they knew it.

The natural griping of young men with nothing else to do was the feedback that General Arnold had been getting. Though I never delivered a stock speech to any of the units, I did take to ending my talks with this thought: "I know what your problems are, and I just want you to be a little patient, because I think I can help cure them."

After visiting only six groups, I was able to make a preliminary, but comprehensive, report to Hap Arnold on my findings. The problems were, first, not enough flying time; second, not enough gunnery practice both on the ground and in the air; third, insufficient maintenance personnel; fourth, scarcity of parts and delays in getting them to the field units; fifth, lack of standardization and insufficient training in the use of the extremely complicated gun turrets on bombing planes.

My suggestions:

1. Training and more training, which requires men and equipment and instructors, is essential. Effort should be put forth to start selecting boys from 16 years up who are pilot possibilities and give them a thorough ground training in high schools and colleges. Such a program would shorten the period of actual combat training and give you much better men.

2. Immediate action on the lack of gun ranges for ground work, as well as target practice in the air.

3. A determined effort should be made to multiply the training schools, give all the airline maintenance bases an opportunity to finish off these trainees with a three-month course. Concentrate on the key maintenance men of the automobile industry throughout the country, who are now available due to the shutting down of the automotive industry. For quick action you've got several hundred good maintenance inspectors on multi-motored aircraft in the CAB who could be many more times effective in the armed services than they are trying to police the airlines. . .

4. The scarcity of good supply men, stock routing men, is very serious. Key men in automobile factories and the distributors and agencies throughout the United States could well be utilized for these purposes.

5. Standardization and simplification of gun turrets.

I found different improvable areas at each group. In Tallahassee, for example, I spoke to a squadron of Negro pilots who were still enlisted men. As I wrote Hap, "They are a grand bunch of kids and great pilots, but something should be done immediately to commission them, they are deserving of it." This suggestion was acted upon quickly, and the nation had a new group of second lieutenants.

We continued on, visiting units across the southern tier of states. At Long Beach, California, I visited my old squadron, the 94th. "Now I feel at home again," I told them.

This is my outfit. There are new names, new faces, but the same old tradition. And I know that you will do the job. I want you men to exceed the achievements of the old 94th with your accomplishments. I want you to live in the tradition of your squadron, the first American unit to shoot down an enemy plane in World War I, and we brought down the last one, too. Many changes have been made. We were the first U.S. squadron out. We flew with 100-horsepower planes. You have more than 2,400 horsepower in these planes. We fired two small machine guns. One of your P-38s has more fire power than our whole squadron. These modern pieces of equipment, plus your traditional teamwork, will keep the 94th on top. I know. God bless you all.

One of the complaints of the kids in the 94th was about their insignia. For some technical reason, the adjutant general's office had ruled that the good old hat-in-the-ring insignia could not be used. That red, white and blue stovepipe hat had great historical significance, and the boys wanted it back. I took this matter up directly with General Arnold, and the order came down immediately restoring the hat-in-the-ring to the 94th Squadron. As a matter of fact, in an official letter of commendation, which I prize, dated April 12, 1942, the

General closed with the good news about the 94th. The letter in its entirety reads as follows:

War Department
Headquarters of the Army Air Force
Washington

April 12, 1942

Dear Eddie:

This is an opportunity that I have long wanted to publicly commend you for the valuable work that you have done in forwarding the interests of the Army Air Force.

Your recent epic trip throughout the entire length and breadth of the United States was an inspiration to us all in the way you overcame the handicap recently imposed upon you by your serious accident in Atlanta, Georgia, on February 27, 1941.

The speed and energy that you put into this mission demonstrates that your devotion is of the highest quality.

Your talks were straight to the point and were a source of greatest inspiration to our young pilots and constituted a most valuable contribution to the building up of the morale and efficiency of our various widespread units.

Your magnificent record during the last war has been splendidly carried on in this fine piece of work that you have just finished, and we all salute you.

The Uncle Sam's Hat-in-the-Ring insignia of the 94th Pursuit Squadron which you commanded with such distinction during the first world war is now being returned to that unit.

With my best wishes for a long and useful life, I am,

Very truly yours,

H. H. Arnold,
Lieutenant General, U.S.A.
Commanding General,
Army Air Forces

We talked with 41 groups in as many states in 32 days, finishing up on April 13 at Mitchell Field, Long Island. Then I hurried down to Washington to make my final report to Hap Arnold. For years I had been pleading for an orderly buildup of aviation. Now we were at war, producing combat planes but giving no thought to air transport. I had been in Don Douglas' office one day in 1940 when he received a call from Robert T. Patterson, then Undersecretary of War. Patterson actually threatened to send troops to take over the factory if Don did not stop building transports.

"When will they be here?" Don asked quietly. "They can have it any time."

Patterson backtracked. And Don, thank God, continued to manufacture transport planes.

In Washington I went directly to Arnold's office. "Hap," I said, "cut off the telephones. I want three hours of your uninterrupted attention."

"That's impossible, Eddie," he said. "I want to hear what you have to say, but you've got to be quicker than that."

"Hap, you're the head man of this outfit," I said. "If you won't listen to me, then there's no sense in my continuing my efforts to be of help to you."

"All of my generals are here right now," he said. "They've come in from all over the country for a conference. You go on in and talk to them."

"I've been all over the country talking to them," I said. "I want you there, too. Unless you go in with me and listen to what I have to say, then there is no point of my carrying on. I'll walk out right now, and we'll forget about the whole thing."

And I meant it.

We entered the conference room at 11:00 A.M. A group of generals was already there. We did not break for lunch; sandwiches and coffee were brought in. We all, and that included General Arnold, stayed in that room until 6:00 that evening. I began by outlining the situation as I had found it: Replacement parts were not getting to the bases, planes were sitting idle on the ground and men who needed and wanted training were sitting on the ground along with them.

First, you need to set up a perpetual inventory system to get these parts distributed efficiently and swiftly. Get hold of Chrysler or General Motors or Ford, and tell them to give you the best parts men they've got to set up this perpetual inventory for you. I don't think you'll have any trouble getting the men or establishing the system.

And then you'll have to develop an *air* transportation system to get these parts and other necessary equipment to the men who need them. I suggest that you call in the operators of all the nation's airlines. When you get these operators together, tell them the truth about just how bad the situation is. Ask their cooperation in turning over to the Air Corps a certain number of their airplanes—cargo carriers and passenger planes—complete with crews. Speaking on behalf of Eastern Air Lines, I hereby pledge any part or all of our fleet. This will be the nucleus of a military air transportation system which is already long past due.

The officers in that room that day were combat-oriented and could not have cared less about hauling carburetors and fan belts. But by 6:00 they had come to realize that, without those spare parts delivered efficiently and swiftly by air, the combat wings would suffer. They bought the program.

Hap Arnold informed me that my recommendations had been read with interest by Secretary of War Henry L. Stimson, a powerful influence in Washington. "The Old Man," as Hap referred to him with respect, had ordered Hap to call a meeting of his department heads to expedite my recommendations. They were thus being developed on two levels. A meeting of all the major airline executives was called in Washington. Arnold started to outline the program, then spotted me and broke into his own talk.

"There's no use my standing here talking with Eddie Rickenbacker in the room," he said. "Come on up here, Rick, and tell them the whole story. You've been everywhere, and you know more about this than I do. Take over."

I stood up and limped to the front of the room. "All right," I began bluntly, "first thing I've got to say is that all of you guys get rid of the chisels that you've got in your pockets. I know. You brought a pocketful of them down here so that you could chisel your way out of doing things that you're going to have to do whether you like it or not. This is the time when you're going to have to think about your country first and your airline second. Because if your country doesn't win this war, you won't have any airline."

At that meeting we worked out complete details and contracts by which the civilian airlines leased half their fleets to the government. The services of pilots, mechanics and men from every phase of airline operation (weather, dispatching, management) were made available to the Air Corps.

In June of that year, 1942, the existing Ferry Command, whose mission was strictly to deliver planes from factory to base, was expanded, renamed the "Air Transport Command" and assigned the mission of air transport. The ATC grew to a complement of thousands of planes flying millions of tons of supplies, matériel and personnel, including returning the wounded to hospitals back home during World War II. It later became the Military Air Transport Service, one of the most important branches of the Air Force.

Six weeks after I had returned from the mission and made my first report to Arnold, he called me into his office again.

"We're getting a tremendous amount of criticism from many quarters," he began. "It comes from the press, congressmen, so-called 'aviation experts' and from the parents of our airmen. We're being criticized for our training program, for our leadership but most of all for our planes. Look at this file—here are hundreds of letters which we have received from mothers and fathers accusing us of sending their sons to doom in inferior equipment.

"All we can say is what anyone would expect us to say—that we're doing the best we can. However, I wonder if someone of your stature, someone the public knows and trusts, would tell the truth about our planes, if that would not dispel some of this doubt and anxiety. You've been out in the field, you've seen the planes on the bases, you've seen them being manufactured in the factories and you've flown in them. Would you take on the assignment of telling the American people the truth about the Air Corps, and especially its planes, training and leadership?"

"Will you give me access to the facts with reference to the equipment and access to the truth from all sources?" I asked.

"Certainly," he replied.

"Then I'll be glad to take on the job," I said.

Specific criticisms centered for the most part on our pursuit planes, specifically the P-40 and P-38 (Lightning) and the B-17 bomber (Flying Fortress).

I had some specific knowledge of all these planes and of the conflicting philosophies behind much of the controversy. With this personal knowledge as background, I began my own research program with confidential, trustworthy information furnished by the Air Corps and by men who had flown our planes in combat. When I was sure that I could speak positively and hearteningly of the situation, I arranged for a series of three reports to the nation to be given in the East, the Midwest and the Far West, each broadcast by NBC on a national hookup. In each talk I made a straightforward presentation of the background of the controversy, the rumors and the facts.

In the early days of the war, there was a great deal of talk about the alleged superiority of the Japanese Zero. The American plane that faced it most often was the P-40, a sturdy ship that had undergone seven successive stages of improvement and was at that point known technically as the "P-40-F." I said in my Midwestern talk, given before an audience of radio technicians and broadcast over NBC:

> The P-40 has seen more combat than any of our other fighters. How does it compare with the Japanese Zero? The Zero is an excellent climber. It is very maneuverable. In these two respects, it surpasses the P-40, but only in these two. The P-40-F has more firepower, heavier guns, and carries more ammunition than the Zero. The P-40-F has protected gasoline tanks. The Zero has

none. American incendiary bullets turn it into a flaming coffin. To all of these factors, add our superior training of the flight crews, and you will see why our P-40s destroy the Zeroes better than two for one.

Yes, the Japs have added armor to their latest Zeroes. They've toughened them up—but at a definite loss in climbing and speed maneuverability. But, we still knock them down. In Japan, it's a great thing to fly and die for your country. In America, it's a great thing to fight and live for your country—to fight another day.

On the other side of the world American fighters were being critically compared with the British Spitfire, which, it was claimed, was lighter and more maneuverable. Well, the Spitfire was indeed a fine fighter plane. It was designed to defend the skies over England against German bombers, and for that mission it was superb.

Why did we not copy the Spitfire? Because we were building planes for a different purpose. Our plans called for us to take the offensive. At last our military establishment was beginning to heed the words of Billy Mitchell, kept alive by a small core of dedicated airmen within the Air Corps. It was our plan to send our bombers over enemy territory escorted by protecting fighters. Those fighters needed longer ranges and heavier armor than the swift but purely defensive Spitfires, and they were the planes we were building.

Another criticism was aimed at one of those fighters specifically, the P-38, and at fighters in general. It arose from British loyalty to the Mosquito, a twin-engine plane built of plywood. It was being manufactured in Canada and was cheap and easy to build. It could reach an altitude of about 25,000 feet, but it could not do much else, as it was virtually defenseless. By 1942, however, it was bug-free, whereas our P-38, the plane to which it was compared, still required some modifications. The P-38's potential was enormously greater than that of the Mosquito; it was a first-class fighter in every respect. It was capable of reaching 35,000 feet of altitude and of inflicting severe damage on anything else that could climb up there with it.

The P-47, or Thunderbolt, was just beginning to come off our assembly lines. It too was a powerful, sturdy ship—and it had a ceiling of forty thousand feet. The secret of those high-altitude planes was the turbosupercharger, developed by American aviation engineers. The Mosquito reached its altitude at a sacrifice of armor and firepower; our new planes were reaching greater heights with full offensive and defensive capabilities. There was no comparison.

Our B-17 bomber, the Flying Fortress, has often been called "The plane that won the war." The American bombing philosophy was to knock out strategic targets with pinpoint accuracy in the daytime, when the target was visible. This goal required an excellent bombsight, which we had, and a heavily armored plane with great firepower that could also carry a reasonable load of bombs at high altitudes. Such a plane was the B-17, and to some extent the B-24. The B-29, or Superfort, was to come later.

The British philosophy favored saturation bombing, rather than the pinpointing of precise targets. The British flew at night. For their purpose, lower-flying, slower planes with less firepower were adequate. As the war went on, the Royal Air Force and the American Bomber Command resolved their differences and dovetailed their operations so that Germany was under bombardment practically around the clock. But in the early days of the war, the zealous advocates of each system refused to listen to the others. When the British flew the B-17 it was according to their philosophy, not the one for which the plane had been built. Naturally, under those conditions, it did not show up well. For our purposes it was superb. In my West Coast speech I told about one of these Flying Fortresses:

Its crew named it "Alex the Swoose." It is not the latest model. It was built three years ago. It fought in the Philippines and then flew to Australia. Next Alex the Swoose attacked the Japs at Davao at Palembang and in Macassar Strait. It has limped successfully out of battle on three engines—on two engines. This Flying Fortress once made a crash landing in Australia. It has taken off from mud flats in Java. It has returned home with so many bullet holes in the fuselage and wings that it looked like a screen door. Yet after all of those battles this Flying Fortress had enough stamina and speed left to fly from Australia to Honolulu. About five thousand miles in less than thirty hours. A world record. The facts speak for themselves. The quality built into that plane by American men and women aircraft workers did not let our fliers down.

I did not restrict these speeches, of course, to mere defense of certain planes. I discussed all the planes that I could talk about freely at that time and said that what we needed was not criticism but more effort and support from everyone on the home front.

"Just remember, Hitler, Mussolini and Tojo," I concluded the West Coast address, which was carried worldwide, "the only things that really count are the hard-boiled facts. Don't draw any comfort from those who try to tell you that our bombers cannot range far afield with heavy loads, that our fighter planes cannot rise in equal combat against our enemies, that our aircraft production is limping along. The facts are America is pushing ahead in every effort to win the war. If you have any doubts that we will win it, you are in for a rude awakening, Hitler, and that goes for you, too, Mussolini and Tojo."

The press covered these talks extensively, and I hammered home the same theme in interviews wherever I went. Many of the so-called "experts" quietly shut up and crawled away. The response from the American people, particularly the parents of boys in the Air Corps, was overwhelming and rewarding. As hundreds said, in letters, wires, telephone calls and personal conversation, at last they knew the truth and were grateful for the relief it gave them.

FIFTEEN

MISSION TO ENGLAND

War Department
Washington, D.C.

September 14, 1942

Dear Captain Rickenbacker:

This spring you did a magnificent job in evaluating the fighting spirit and training of our men in the Army Forces. I am writing you at this time to ask if you would undertake to go to England and visit the various Army Air Forces stations in the bomber and fighter commands, as a continuation of your tour of inspection in March and April.

I am, of course, fully aware of the high-spirited confidence and efficiency of the AAF air and ground crews. Nevertheless, my interest in our Army airmen overseas is so deep that I would welcome a firsthand report by a non-military observer on how they are getting along.

No one could be better equipped to undertake this mission than you, not only because of your distinguished aviation record and profound aviation knowledge, but also because of your clear and sympathetic understanding of human problems in military aviation. I am certain that your visit itself will serve as a welcome message from home.

Therefore, if you accept this assignment, as I hope you will, I am happy to authorize you to proceed to England and visit the various AAF stations. On your return to this country, you would report to me directly.

Awaiting your early and favorable reply, I remain,

Sincerely yours

(signed) Henry L. Stimson,
Secretary of War

To Whom It May Concern:

The bearer of this letter, Captain Edward V. Rickenbacker, will visit the stations and installations of the Army Air Forces in the British Isles for such purposes as he will explain to you in person.

Captain Rickenbacker, in this capacity, as Special Consultant to the Secretary of War, is to receive every possible assistance in the performance of his special duties, by all commanders concerned, and he is to be provided with such transportation both ground and air as he may need and such accommodations as may be available under the circumstances.

(signed) Henry L. Stimson,
Secretary of War

Commanders to whom I showed this sweeping communication raised their eyebrows as they read it. This blanket order actually gave me the authority to command them to assist me in my mission.

The two communications added to the weight of the responsibility that was resting more and more heavily on my shoulders. I had long had great respect for Secretary of War Stimson, and it was increased by observing the deferential attitude toward him on the part of General Arnold and other high-ranking officers. The tremendous responsibility Secretary Stimson placed on me made me all the more proud and eager to carry out my missions, yet at the same time I realized that one small mistake on my part might be compounded into a large one. I enthusiastically accepted the opportunity to serve, at the same time reminding myself to be constantly careful not to go overboard in my observations and recommendations.

In addition to the duties set forth in the letter of instructions was a verbal order from Secretary Stimson personally. When General Arnold had first asked me to tour the United States bases, he had requested me to keep my eyes and ears open for any hint of subversive activity. Any suspicion that I might have should not be put on paper but, rather, reported to him verbally. When Secretary Stimson called me in to discuss my serving as his eyes and ears over the world, he too gave me this additional duty. He expressed it in his final words to me before I left for England:

> Whatever you observe or hear along these lines, please do not write it down. Rather, report it verbally to me, and to me alone. Don't breathe a word of these final instructions to anyone, Eddie, because we must never let anyone suspect that you are doing intelligence work for me. To everyone but you and me, your duty is to evaluate the aviation progress and equipment of the enemy, our allies, and ourselves.

This extra, ultrasensitive assignment had a special personal significance. A peculiar incident had occurred in New York some time before. Bob Considine, the well-known journalist and my good friend, who was then with the New York *Mirror*, had interviewed me on the types of planes and weapons that we would be seeing as World War II progressed. One of my predictions was that we would harness the power of the atom, thus producing a bomb destructive beyond anyone's wildest imagination.

The first edition of the *Mirror* had hardly appeared when the editor received a telephone call ordering the paper to stop the press and pull out the story. A deluge of grim-lipped government and military officials poured down on both Bob Considine and me. They all demanded to know where I had received my information. All I could say was that I was interested in science, that I knew many scientists and that the possible development of an atomic bomb had been a natural topic of conversation. I admitted to the officers who came to see me that I had been completely wrong in referring to a potential weapon of such importance. My only excuse was that Bob Considine was a master when it came to worming information out of people.

At that time the Manhattan Project, the supersecret agency that did develop the atomic bomb, was just getting underway. Only a few men in the government hierarchy knew about it— plus, of course, the Russian spy network. I learned later from a source in military intelligence that, following the brief appearance of that one story in one edition, the Russians increased intelligence and espionage activities in the United States.

The combination of that one lapse and the great trust placed in me by the Secretary of War resulted in what might have been an oversecretiveness in my reports for the Secretary of War. I made lengthy reports to him in writing, and, although they were confidential at the time, they have long since been cleared for publication. What I reported to Secretary Stimson and General Arnold verbally, however, will not be revealed here or as long as I live. Neither Stimson nor Arnold ever made public mention of my confidential verbal reports to them, either during their lifetimes or in material published after their deaths. I can only follow their precedent.

I undertook these missions, incidentally, at a salary of $1 a year and paid my own expenses. Following the successful tour of the United States bases, I was offered a commission as brigadier general by both Arnold and Stimson. I refused. They raised the offer to a major generalship, but I still declined.

"No, sir," I said. "When I return from these missions, I want to be able to pound the table, point to the facts and insist on what I believe to be the most efficient way of doing things. I have had all the honors a man can get in uniform. Now let me serve as a civilian, where I can do the most good."

I never even thought of trying to figure out how much the missions cost me financially. Fortunately, Eastern Air Lines was by then organized on a firm and dependable basis and could get along without me for periods of time. Between assignments, I worked twice as hard and twice as long to make my absences possible. Air transportation was a vital service during the war years. After turning over half our planes and an even greater percentage of our personnel to the government, we at Eastern still carried more passengers than ever before.

As for the work, time, discomfort and danger involved in my missions, I never considered them. I had learned in the aftereffects of the Atlanta crash that travel is my life. I have worked hard and lived under pressure since I was a boy; I always have, and I always will. My personal reason for going on these missions, indeed the foundation of my life, can be summed up in one sentence: *Men grow only in proportion to the service they render their fellow men and women.*

Again Hans Adamson went with me as my aide. In the United States he had done an excellent job in arranging press coverage, but in England, as we were traveling in the strictest secrecy, he did the opposite. Not one mention of my presence in England was made, not one interview given, not one photograph taken during the entire visit.

The English mission could be broken down into two parts: a survey of the conduct of the air war in general and evaluation of our equipment and personnel in particular.

In order to appraise the conduct of the war, I talked with British leaders, including the great Prime Minister Sir Winston Churchill himself, my old friend Lord Beaverbrook and several ministers of the government. Our ambassador to Great Britain, John Gilbert Winant, was of great help. My friendship with Gil dated back to World War I, when he had landed his sputtering two-place Spad at the 94th Squadron's field and asked if anybody could check his engine. I found the trouble and fixed it myself. Now he had an opportunity to return the favor, and he did a wonderful job. Our country was fortunate to have a man like Gil Winant representing it in London at such a crucial time in world history.

My contacts with the leaders of the Royal Air Force were particularly rewarding. Though England still suffered from sporadic bombing raids, the terrible period of nightly bombardments was far enough in the past to enable us to analyze the Battle of Britain objectively. Churchill had not yet said "never in the field of human conflict has so much been owed by so many to so few," but we knew that it was so.

One of those "few" was Air Marshal Sir Hugh Dowding, the quiet, thoughtful man who had, years before, analyzed the coming German attack and organized the only possible means of thwarting it. I had seen the preparation for the Battle of Britain being made in both Germany and England in 1939. The Germans were concentrating their aircraft production on the short-range bomber known as the "Stuka." It was obvious that the plane had but one purpose, to bomb England. The Germans risked everything on their belief that they could knock England out quickly with unescorted swarms of poorly armored and poorly defended bombers.

Britain too put all her eggs in one basket: the short-range, rapid-climbing, swift fighter plane.

As Dowding and I talked, I could see the battle shaping up in my mind. The Germans sent over fleets of Stukas one hundred, even two hundred, at a time, in the most devastating air onslaught in history up to that time. English pilots, pink-cheeked fellows like those I had seen in 1916 at the training field in London, rose up to meet them in their Spitfires and Hurricanes. They flew to the point of exhaustion, and many gave their lives. In the meantime, the British people were holding on with that unique, incredible stamina, facing nightly air raids, a starvation diet and the cold of winter but still producing and maintaining planes. The credit for inspirational leadership must go to Winston Churchill, the man of the hour. But credit for the foresight to create the only force capable of holding back that merciless attack must go to Hugh Dowding.

As we talked, I thought of something that even Sir Hugh

did not know. In 1939 in Germany, Ernst Udet had told me
that he had recommended a different type of bomber force. His
idea was to build larger planes capable of carrying heavier
loads longer distances, with strong fighter escorts. The valiant
English pilots and their swift little planes would have had to
break through a screen of fighters to reach their targets.

What would have been the course of history had Udet's
recommendations been adopted? The world will never know.
Udet told me that it was Hermann Goering himself who decided against his proposal. After the failure of the Battle of
Britain, Udet killed himself.

I had long wanted to meet Air Marshal Sir Hugh Trenchard,
whose career and philosophy of air power closely paralleled
those of our own General Billy Mitchell. He was out of England,
but he left for me a copy of a secret report that he had made to
the Air Ministry. The depth of his strategic thinking and his
vision of air power as it could be were incorporated in this
forward-looking communication. His first point was a plea that
we—the United Kingdom and the United States—try not to go
down two roads at once, thus permitting our air power to be
inextricably tangled in large schemes and protracted operations of two-dimensional warfare. His second point, the local
projection of Mitchell's thinking into World War II, was that
air power alone could win the war in Europe. His carefully
reasoned contention was that simple: we could win the war
through air power, without an invasion, without landing one
man on the Continent of Europe. As his plan was not followed, I will not devote any more space to his cogent arguments. I did pass on his notes to Mr. Stimson with the "urgent
recommendation that they be given the serious attention they
deserve."

The current state of the air war and its immediate future
I discussed with Air Marshal Arthur T. Harris of the Bomber
Command. The British were then taking the air offensive,
sending their heavy bombers on night bombing raids over
Germany. Harris reported great damage to industrial areas

and to the morale of the enemy. The English air strategy was to drop tremendous bombs in the general area of the specified target from low-flying bombers in night raids. Even if the target were only partially damaged, the heavy bombs hitting around it would do great damage to civilian morale.

Even Harris, the most outspoken of the night-raid adherents, was beginning to see, however, some merit in the high-altitude, precision daylight bombing that our B-17 made possible. By combining the two principles, the Allies achieved round-the-clock bombing of Germany.

I had visited Harris at one of the airfields outside London. It so happened that the Prime Minister was at the same field that morning on an inspection tour. He greeted me cordially and asked me to ride back to London with him. We had lunch together at 10 Downing Street. Several other government officials were there, and the discussion continued into the afternoon.

Churchill was extremely knowledgeable on every phase of the war. The British had staged their largest air raid of the war on May 30, plastering Cologne with bombs from more than one thousand planes. Churchill was still talking about it. Intelligence reports said that the Germans had been forced to evacuate approximately two hundred thousand people from Cologne after the raid, and Churchill used this fact to show the effect of bombing on German morale. But he was also aware of smaller technicalities. At that time the supercharger on the B-17 and B-24 emitted a bright orange flame, plainly visible at night. Churchill knew about it.

"Would it not be possible to control this flame?" he asked me. I assured him that something could be done and would be done—and it was.

Churchill's two main concerns were controlling the German submarines and stepping up the bombing of Germany. As some guests left and others came in, I heard him repeat one sentence several times. It was "Give me another thousand heavy bombers and two hundred more destroyers, and, while I won't promise to change the trend of the war, I will promise to shorten it."

The most productive results of my mission to England came from inspections and conversations on the airfields. One day, at a field in southern England, I watched a mock combat between an American P-38 and a captured Focke-Wulf 190 flown by a British pilot. A group of pilots, both English and American, was also watching, and we commented on the action like spectators at a football game.

The English pilot, I learned, had had a great deal of combat experience, whereas the American had had none. Even so, the P-38 was clearly superior to the Focke-Wulf. It had greater power and could climb faster. Had the combat been real, the inexperienced pilot in the P-38 would have blasted his opponent out of the sky. There was that much difference in the two planes.

When the two men came down, we all gathered to hear their comments. They verified and augmented what I had seen: this P-38, which had not yet been flown in combat, was clearly superior to the best plane the Germans had in the skies at that time.

This one episode was worth the trip to England. At that time the P-38 was still under heavy criticism. It was unusual in appearance, with twin engines and twin booms. Its critics outnumbered its supporters because no one really knew exactly what the plane could do. Well, now I knew. I made a full report on it to Hap Arnold and Secretary Stimson. Arnold told me later that I did more than any man living to keep the P-38 in the Air Corps. It served us well.

Another plane I saw impressed me even more. It was an English plane, but it was no Spitfire or Hurricane. It had been made in the United States. Through my friendship with E. H. "Dutch" Kindelberger of North American Aviation, with which I had been connected when it was known as the Fokker Aircraft Company, I had heard the story of this mystery plane some time before. North American had been making training planes for the British, who were well pleased with their performance. In 1940 the RAF asked Kindelberger to build them a pursuit ship similar to the P-40, and he proceeded to do just that. He told me that it was the best plane in the sky.

In England I saw it and talked with pilots who had flown it. They agreed with its maker. I had never heard such enthusiasm for an airplane. I looked at it, and it was beautiful. Its clean lines promised the performance that men who had flown it told me it was capable of. Even equipped with an Allison 1,450-horsepower engine, compared to the Focke-Wulf's 1,700 horsepower, it outperformed the German plane.

It was the P-51, the Mustang. Had it gone through the regular channels and been subjected to the standard tests at our experimental station at Wright Field, it never would have gotten through the red tape. After it was in production, thanks to the English orders, the Air Corps bought a few. But we did not know what we had.

But after seeing it and discussing it with men who had flown it, I was positive that it was the best fighter plane in the sky.

And it could be even better. The Rolls-Royce people in England had produced the Merlin engine capable of 1,600 horsepower. What a combination! At that time the ship was being sent over with the 1,450-horsepower engine. I recommended that only the frame be shipped and that the Merlin be installed in England, which was done.

I do not believe that any plane in history has had a more loyal and enthusiastic group of rooters than the Mustang had. On my return to the United States, incidentally, I visited the Allison factory to persuade them to step up their 1,450-horsepower engine. The Allison engineers did step it up to 1,750 horsepower, with no increase in weight, which was a remarkable achievement. It was that combination—P-51 plus the Allison 1,750-horsepower engine—that made the Mustang the ruler of the skies until the jet fighters took over.

I recommended several improvements on our fighter planes. The P-38, for example, had blind spots not only on each side where the twin engines were but also in the rear. Great changes had taken place between the time I had flown in combat and 1942, but one factor remained constant: the pilot had to keep looking behind him to make sure that no one was sneaking up from the rear. I recommended that the rear vision be improved, and it was.

The English pilot who had flown the captured Focke-Wulf 190 in mock combat pointed out to me the great superiority of the Focke-Wulf controls. The Germans had automated and simplified them. Our planes were too complicated. When a man is fighting for his life in the sky, he does not want to have to fiddle with a lot of gadgets on the instrument panel. I recommended that our controls be automated and simplified.

Other recommendations affected the P-39, the A-20 and the B-26. My work with the B-17 bomber was much more comprehensive, however. In the fall of 1942, Major General "Tooey" Spaatz's 8th Air Force, with Brigadier General Ira C. Eaker in charge of his bombers, was beginning to carry the air war to the Germans. Morale was high from top to bottom. Our men had a great job to do, and they were doing it.

But still there were complaints. I had long discussions with unit commanders, attended briefing sessions, talked things over with pilots and crews and came to the conclusion that many of the complaints were justified. The B-17 was basically the great plane I had been saying it was, but it could be made better. When I had completed my investigation and analyzed my findings, I found that I had listed 21 separate criticisms of the B-17 and 17 separate recommendations for improvements. Some of them, though technical, may be of general interest.

My first criticism read, "The center of gravity is too far aft." The big ship had undergone so many modifications and additions that the center had shifted, with a resulting loss of 10 to 12 miles an hour.

"The oxygen supply is insufficient." A definite number of

oxygen bottles had been assigned to each plane at the beginning, but as missions grew longer, the amount of oxygen was not increased. It was an important oversight. I also found out that our oxygen masks were inferior. Under certain conditions, they would actually freeze to the wearers' faces. Masks used by the British and the Germans were lined with chamois skin and were far superior. British flying clothing was also superior; I recommended the use of similar lightweight, electrically heated clothes.

"Lack of armor plate under the pilot and navigator section and in front of the instrument panel." Years before I had placed a stove lid under the seat in my Spad. Here was the same problem all over again.

"Position of guns at waist stations too close to each other." When I sat in the waist gunner's seat and simulated firing at a moving target, I would bump into the other gunner. Gunners also needed chin rests to help sight their guns. Empty cartridges were spewing out into the air, with resulting damage to planes following in close formation. I recommended a catcher for the cartridges. Gun turrets were freezing at high altitudes. More electrical power was needed to heat them.

"More firepower." German fighters could hover out of range of our guns and reach us with theirs. Strangely, the gun in the nose was fixed. The pilot had to aim the whole ship at the target. That gun should have been flexible.

All these criticisms and recommendations led to a major one: It should not be necessary to send Rickenbacker all the way to England to find out that planes are out of balance or that gunners bump into each other. One of my strong recommendations was therefore that representatives of the manufacturers visit the proper commands for a week at a time at regular intervals, in order to keep up with the rapid changes that take place in combat.

I also recommended the development of a heavily armored airplane with tremendous firepower, a flying battleship that would escort bombers on their missions. A few models of flying battleships were subsequently made and tested, but the idea was overdone. They were too heavy and slow to keep up with the planes that they were to protect.

Several recommendations were made in regard to personnel. After fifty missions a pilot or crew member should be sent home for a rest and to pass on his knowledge to other men in training.

While in England I naturally paid my respects to the commander of the European theater, Lieutenant General Dwight D. Eisenhower. His headquarters was in a state of anticipation and excitement. In a month's time the greatest invasion in history, in North Africa, would take place. The plans were complete. In order to make sure that one set of plans would reach Washington, three were sent. One went by a United States cruiser, another was sent by special courier and I carried the third. I left England on October 11, flying home by way of Ireland, Iceland, Greenland and Canada. The plans for the African invasion were turned in to Secretary Stimson, along with my complete report, on October 13, 1942.

SIXTEEN

LOST AT SEA

The Secretary of War must have been pleased with my performance as both consultant and courier, for on the day after my return from England he issued orders sending me to the South Pacific Theater with the same basic directive. In addition, I was entrusted with a message from Secretary Stimson to General Douglas MacArthur, a message of such sensitivity that it could not be put on paper. It was given to me orally by Secretary Stimson himself, and I memorized it, in order to be able to pass it on to General MacArthur the same way.

Again Hans Adamson accompanied me as my military aide. We left New York on the night of October 17, just six days after returning from the United Kingdom. I visited my mother, who was living with my brother Dewey and his wife in Los Angeles, on the 18th, and the next day Hans and I boarded a Pan American Sikorsky Clipper in San Francisco bound for Hawaii. It was a pleasant, 15-hour flight, and, though I twisted and turned regularly to keep from stiffening up, I nevertheless arrived in Honolulu sufficiently refreshed to put in a day's work inspecting the

Air Force units in the area. Brigadier General William L. Lynd, who commanded Hickam Field, promised to have a plane ready at 10:30 P.M. to take us on to General MacArthur's headquarters at Port Moresby, New Guinea.

That night Lynd picked Hans and me up and drove us to Hickam Field himself. He was giving us a B-17-D for the mission, he said, with an experienced crew from the Ferry Command.

After that buildup, I was a little surprised, on arriving at Hickam Field, to find that my pilot was a Texan with a goatee and high-heeled cowboy boots. But there wasn't much for me to do but go aboard.

Later I was to come to know these men better than they knew themselves, but that night the introductions were brusque, on a last-name-only basis.

The pilot was Captain William T. Cherry, Jr., who had flown with American Airlines as a copilot. The copilot was First Lieutenant James C. Whittaker. He seemed a little old for a copilot; I figured him to be about forty. He had about 1,500 hours in small planes to his credit.

The navigator was First Lieutenant John J. De Angelis. He was small and wiry, with dark skin and black hair.

The radio operator, Sergeant James W. Reynolds, was a slender young man who seemed experienced, competent and confident. Private John F. Bartek was the mechanic, a red-headed, freckle-faced kid who had been out of mechanical school only about three months and had little experience on Flying Fortresses.

There was one other passenger, a young crew chief who had just been discharged from the hospital in Hawaii and was on his way back to join his unit in Australia. He had had a serious case of jaundice, as well as an appendectomy. When I was introduced to him, I didn't hear his last name and asked him to repeat it.

"Oh, just call me 'Alex,' sir," he said. "Nobody can pronounce my last name."

His full name was Alexander T. Kaczmarczyk, and I was happy to call him "Alex."

Cherry taxied the big bomber out onto the runway, revved up each engine for a final test, received the green light from the tower and proceeded to take off. The plane was halfway down the runway, building up speed, when a tire blew out. The plane lunged to the left, heading for the hangars. Cherry did a good job of swinging it back onto the runway and throttled back. We were headed straight for the bay. Cherry waited until the last second, permitting the speed to decrease, then, at the end of the runway, cut the rudder hard to the left and swung the tail around in a violent ground loop. We came to a screeching halt, but it saved us from plunging into the bay. The plane was in no shape to continue, and a truck came out and towed us back to the hangar.

As we climbed out of the plane, Cherry gave me a big grin and said: "We got more of these planes, Captain. The crew and I will stand by until another one is ready."

"Well, it had better not be like the first," I thought.

General Lynd was full of apologies and drove us back to his quarters. Shortly after midnight, another Fortress was ready for us. Our bags and a dozen sacks of high-priority mail destined for different headquarters en route had already been placed on board, plus two cots for Adamson and myself. The crew and Sergeant Alex were also on board. I hung my cane over my left arm and climbed aboard too. That time the plane took off smoothly.

When we were airborne I went up to the cockpit to visit with the crew. It was a beautiful night. A three-quarter moon shone down over high, thin clouds onto the plane and the great Pacific beneath us.

"What's the weather like ahead?" I asked Cherry.

"Like this, all the way," he said. "I expect an uneventful flight."

We discussed our first destination, Canton Island, 1,800 miles southwest of Hawaii. I had never heard of it before. Having crossed the Atlantic only a week before, I found it difficult to get

used to the enormous distances in the Pacific. We had flown
fifteen hours from San Francisco to Hawaii, and now we were
beginning our second, 10-hour leg to this tiny dot in the Phoenix
Islands, one-third of the way to Australia. At Canton we would
refuel, then continue southward to Suva in the Fiji Islands, New
Caledonia in the Loyalty group and Brisbane on the east coast
of Australia. From there we would go north to Port Moresby.
There was an obvious reason for the circuitous route; the Japanese controlled the area on a straight line between Hawaii and
New Guinea.

After an hour's quiet chat in the dimly lit cockpit over the
moonlit sea, I stood up, stretched and walked back to my cot in
the tail of the plane. It was cold at that altitude. I was wearing a
leather jacket over my new suit. I threw the Burberry I'd bought
in London over me and added a blanket. I was still cold, and the
stiffness that was a consequence of the Atlanta crash set in to
make for an uncomfortable night. In his cot, Hans was sleeping
like a log.

Daybreak came, and I had an excuse to get up. There were
sweet rolls for breakfast, with thermos jugs of orange juice and
coffee. Up in the cabin Cherry said our estimated time of arrival
at Canton was 9:30 A.M. He was perfectly at ease. At 8:30 he
put the big plane into a shallow descent and leveled off at one
thousand feet. We all looked ahead, waiting for the island, about
8 miles long by 4 miles wide, to come into view.

A dozen times in the next two hours one of us in the cockpit
would sit upright and lean forward, eyes squinting, as a dark
spot would come into view on the surface of the great expanse of
ocean before us. It would always turn out to be only the shadow
of a cloud. At 10:15 I asked Cherry how much gas he had.

"A little over four hours," he said.

I was beginning to suspect that something was wrong. Could
it be possible that we had overshot the island?

"How much tail wind are we supposed to have?" I asked.

"About ten miles," Cherry said.

At best that was but a reasonable guess. There were certainly no weather stations beneath us. Nor was there anything by which I could gauge our speed, just the interminable Pacific. But I still had a feeling that we had more than a 10-mile-an-hour tail wind and consequently were flying faster than we thought. Sometime later I happened to meet the navigator of a plane that had left Hickam Field for Canton only an hour before we had. He too had been given the 10-mile-an-hour forecast, but after shooting the stars he had figured, as I had, that the actual velocity was greater. He had taken this difference into consideration and, after landing at Canton, had proved that the tail wind was really about 31 miles an hour.

"I believe we've overshot the island," I told Cherry. "I think we ought to get cross bearings in order to find out just exactly where we are."

Sergeant Reynolds, the radioman, got busy, raised Canton Island and asked for a bearing. The Canton radio operator replied that he did not have the necessary equipment. It turned out later that the equipment had been on the island for several weeks but had never been uncrated.

The only other American outpost anywhere near us was Palmyra Island, roughly midway between Canton and Honolulu. It, too, is just a dot in the Pacific. Reynolds roused the station at Palmyra and asked them to send out a continuing radio signal from which they would get a bearing. In the meantime, we flew on.

All we saw were shadows on the sea. By now we all had "island eyes," as they call it in the Pacific. Any shadow looks like an island.

I'd been lost in the air before, but never over such a vast expanse. The ocean seemed endless. Our charts showed other small islands and island groups, but we saw none of them. To the northwest of Canton was Howland Island, the destination of the famous aviatrix Amelia Earhart's round-the-world flight in 1937. She and her navigator Fred Noonan had been trying to find that tiny atoll when they disappeared, never to be seen again. There has always been a persistent rumor that they fell into the hands of the Japanese, but I have always doubted it.

Some five hundred miles west of Canton were the Gilbert Islands, of which Tarawa is one. We hoped that we weren't that far off course; the Gilberts were in the hands of the Japanese.

By then it was obvious to all of us that we were in grave danger. De Angelis, the young navigator, was naturally on the defensive. He shot the sun with his octant and gave Cherry another course. Thirty minutes later he made another reading and changed the course he had given only a half-hour before. He simply couldn't figure out what was wrong. Then it occurred to him that the instrument, which was assigned to him personally, had been damaged when the first B-17 ground-looped back at Hickam Field. If that were true, every reading he had made had been erroneous. We could be hundreds of miles off course in either direction.

The radio station on Palmyra broke in with the suggestion that we climb to five thousand feet and circle for thirty minutes, sending out a radio signal, while they took a bearing. We did. They supplied us with a compass course, which meant nothing; we could be on it, yet a thousand miles below or above the island. Nevertheless, we let down through the cloud layer and lined up on the new course, which took us west. We flew on, at better than three miles a minute, but all we saw was water and more water.

"Get on that radio and tell Canton to start firing antiaircraft shells into the air," I told Sergeant Reynolds. "Tell them to time their shells so that they burst at seven thousand feet, above the cloud level. We'll keep a look out. Ask them if they have planes they can send up."

Reynolds got busy with his key. "They answer affirmative," he cried.

In the meantime I had suggested to Captain Cherry that he box the compass, an old maritime-navigation operation. We would go west for one hour, then turn north for an hour, then east, then south. But I knew that the gas would not hold out for all four legs.

Canton reported that the shells were being fired and the planes were taking off. We saw nothing. We were running on the leanest possible gasoline mixture. Cherry cut the two outboard engines in order to save more gas. The clouds began to thin out, and he climbed higher in order to be able to see a greater area. But there was no land, no ship, as far as all our eyes could see.

"One hour's fuel remaining," Cherry said.

I wrote a message to that effect and passed it over to Sergeant Reynolds. That was the last word anyone heard from us.

"Send out an SOS," Cherry told Reynolds. The sergeant began banging the key. Again, again and again. But there was no answer, no acknowledgment. Wherever we were, no American could hear us.

That meant that, even if we made a successful crash landing on the water, nobody would know which way to look for us.

"This was a hell of a fine place to start from," I told Adamson.

It was time to start lightening the ship. Every ounce would count. Cherry would have to bring that big Fortress down gently, hitting the surface at the precise instant. Otherwise it would go straight down with all of us in it or break in two.

Alex and I went back to the tail. We pried open the bottom hatch and began throwing everything we could move overboard. First went all that high-priority mail. Out went the cots complete with blankets, along with my Burberry coat and the beautiful suitcase that the Eastern employees had given me for Christmas two years before. Out went my briefcase, containing most important papers. I carried my orders in my billfold in my breast pocket. I had taken three handsome handkerchiefs, which Adelaide had bought for me in Paris, out of the suitcase and stuck them in a pocket. I broke out a couple of cartons of cigarettes, put three packs in my pocket and passed the rest around. I patted my upper left-hand pocket. That's where I have always kept the crucifix that my little friend gave me in 1917.

We kept back a small hoard of rations and filled several thermos bottles with water from the main tank.

"Eddie," Hans Adamson said, "don't you think we'd better drink all the water we can hold right now, before we leave the ship?"

"No, I don't," I said. "I think we'll need it more later."

As Adamson remarked later, that was probably the worst piece of advice he had ever been given in his life.

Two or three thermos bottles were filled with coffee. Alex dumped half a can of condensed milk into one of the bottles. "I've got to have plenty of cream in my coffee," he explained.

The thermos bottles, with a metal box containing emergency rations, were carefully placed on the deck in the radio compartment. From this compartment a hatch opens overhead to the top of the ship, where we planned to make our exit.

The plane was equipped with three life rafts. Two of them were described as "five-man" rafts. They were stored in compartments on either side of the plane and would be automatically released by pulling the proper levers in the cockpit. This task was assigned to Bartek.

A two-man raft was stored in the radio compartment. It was placed with the small pile of rations under the hatch.

Places were assigned in the three rafts. Cherry, Whittaker and Reynolds took one of the five-man rafts, and Adamson, Bartek and I took the other. De Angelis and Alex, both small men, were assigned to the two-man raft.

Most of the men took off their shoes, and some even took off their pants to make it easier to swim. I remained fully clothed, including the high-topped shoes that I had to wear because of the injuries in the Atlanta crash. We were all wearing what we called "Mae Wests," those big yellow life preservers, each inflated by a carbon-dioxide cartridge, and I figured that mine would keep me floating, shoes and all. I even kept my cane.

We knew that we would hit with a jar. In the cockpit, of course, Cherry and Whittaker were strapped into their seats. Sergeant Bartek stood behind Whittaker, his hands on the raft-release levers. Sergeant Reynolds would remain at his desk until the last second, sending the SOS that would never be heard.

We had held back two mattresses. Adamson sat on the floor of the plane and braced his back against one mattress. De Angelis used the other. Alex chose to squat behind Sergeant Reynolds. I took a seat on the right-hand side of the plane and held a parachute in front of me.

Time was running out. How long would we have in the plane after Cherry landed it? Would it remain afloat for thirty seconds, sixty seconds or no seconds at all? I made a last-minute check of my possessions. I stuffed a map in my shirt, put a chocolate bar in my pocket and, on a sudden hunch, grabbed a 60-foot rope and wrapped it around my waist.

Nothing more remained to be done. It was time to sit down. I looked up at the hatch through which we hoped to make our escape. It was locked tight. Alex and I loosened it so that it would not be jammed in the crash.

We all took our places. I could feel the nose go down as Cherry put the plane into a long glide. We were all silent. There was no panic. Someone asked, "How much longer?" I could see out. The ocean was coming closer. As we came down, I saw that a long heavy swell was running. It was going to be a rough landing.

"Not yet, not yet," I said. Still we descended. Cherry was bringing the plane down parallel to the swell. He would land in the trough, using the swell to reduce speed. It would take split-second timing.

One of the engines fluttered and died. That marked the beginning of the end. "Hold on!" I shouted. "Here it comes!"

The other engine died. We were in sudden silence. No one spoke. The sound of Reynolds continuing to bang out his distress call filled the plane.

Crash! It was louder than thunder, louder than the crash at Atlanta. A heavy piece of equipment in the tail of the plane broke loose and crashed into the compartment with us. Pieces ricocheted around like shrapnel. Just as I was coming out of the daze resulting from the first crash, a second one came. Cherry had let the tail down first, then the fuselage. The plane stopped quickly.

The window beside me was broken, and the green Pacific Ocean poured in. The hatch we had loosened was ripped off, and a gaping hole showed above us: more water. But the plane remained afloat. Bill Cherry, goatee, cowboy boots and all, had brought it down perfectly.

In the noise and confusion, I did not know whether I was hurt or not. A quick check proved that I was a little shaken up, but, thanks to the seat belt and the parachute in front of my face, I was all right. Some of the others were not so fortunate. The impact had whipped Adamson's head forward, straining his neck and back. Reynolds, pounding his key to the very moment of impact, had been thrown forward against the radio panel. Blood was streaming from a slash across his nose.

"The rafts are loose," Bartek called. The water was rising fast in the plane. Cherry and Whittaker came wading toward us. "Go ahead," they shouted to Adamson and me. We were the passengers. Clutching my cane with one hand and boosted by the crew, I stepped up on the arm of the seat, reached up to the hatch, grabbed hold and pulled myself up while the others shoved from below. I clambered out on the wing. Seawater was just barely sloshing over it. Bartek was already there—he had crawled out the forward hatch—and he helped me pull the others up through the hatch.

I saw red stains in the green ocean. Bartek's hand was dripping blood. The two rafts that he had released were floating, but the line of one of them had become tangled. Trying to get it loose, he had ripped his fingers on a piece of jagged metal.

Cherry, Whittaker and Reynolds got into their raft and pushed off. Adamson was in great pain and almost immobilized. Bartek and I held the raft steady so that he could slide down the wing into it. The swells were fully twelve feet high, and the plane was wallowing. But we got Adamson aboard, and Bartek and I slid in after him.

De Angelis and Alex had to inflate their raft. De Angelis got in without mishap, but when Alex crawled in the raft capsized in the swell and threw them both into the ocean. They clung to it and somehow, even in the heavy swell, managed to get it upright. De Angelis pulled himself up, but Alex had a harder time. He swallowed a great deal of seawater.

A strong breeze was blowing, and it pushed all three rafts away from the ship. It was still floating, but low in the water.

"Who's got the water?" somebody shouted.

I looked in our raft. Adamson and Bartek shook their heads. There was no water on our raft. And there was no water on any other raft either. Nor was there the ration box, nor even Alex's thermos bottle of coffee with cream. We had piled those things so carefully under the hatch and had then gone off and left them there in the confusion.

"We're going to need that water," somebody said. "Let's go back and get it."

"Don't be a fool. That plane's going to sink any second."

"It's been up for at least three minutes. Why shouldn't it stay up another three minutes more?"

"You'd never find the water and the rations anyway. They're all sloshing around underwater."

"Anybody who's in that plane when she goes down will go right down to the bottom with it."

And so we decided not to try to get the water and rations out of the plane. That was another mistake. The big ship stayed afloat for almost six minutes. Then, slowly, the tail swung up and poised gracefully for a split second, and the ship went down. I looked at my watch. It said 2:36 P.M., Honolulu time.

Our raft was half full of water, and I started to bail with my faithful old gray hat. Adelaide had threatened a dozen times to throw it away; well, it certainly proved itself in those first few minutes. My cane, which I had so carefully brought into the raft with me, I now realized was completely useless. I looked at it for a moment, then threw it overboard.

"The good Lord forgot to teach me how to walk on water with it," I explained to my raftmates.

Whoever determined the dimensions of that so-called five-man raft had midgets in mind. The over-all length was nine feet, the width five, including the doughnut-like roll that held us up. The inside dimensions were 6 feet 9 inches by 2 feet 4 inches. Adamson was tall and heavy, weighing more than two hundred pounds. I was not as heavy but taller. Bartek was not quite as tall. How could the three of us possibly fit into this wet, narrow area? To make things more difficult, the raft had two canvas seats running horizontally across it. It was impossible to sit on them in that heavy swell. The center of gravity was too high. The survival kit in the raft contained a knife, and we used it to cut out the canvas seats.

Adamson was in agony, and we gave him the place of honor. He lay lengthwise. I was at the other end, sitting crosswise in the bottom, my knees over the roll. Bartek was catercornered, his head toward Adamson, his feet behind my back.

Cherry, Whittaker and Reynolds had worked out a somewhat similar arrangement in their raft. None was seriously injured, and it was a little easier for them. De Angelis and Alex had an impossible situation. They found that the least uncomfortable position was facing each other, with each man's legs over the other man's shoulders. Alex was gagging and retching. The saltwater he had swallowed was all coming up.

Each raft had a pair of broken-down aluminum paddles, which we could put together. Paddling that clumsy raft through the heavy swell would have been difficult even from a normal position. Lying down, it was practically impossible. The strong wind and the high seas were pushing our three rafts apart. We somehow managed to paddle them together. I unwrapped the line from around my waist. Cherry made one end of it fast to the hand line around the roll of his raft. As captain of the ship, he would occupy the lead raft. Ours was tied on next, about twenty feet astern. Then came the 2-man raft, another twenty feet behind.

Many criticisms of this arrangement were voiced as the day wore on. As the swells pushed us together, then pulled us apart, the ropes would loosen, then tauten and jerk the rafts unmercifully. It was painful and uncomfortable. But we were together. It was important for us to be together. Together we could all help one another. I could foresee that such help was going to be needed.

As we drifted away from the spot where the plane had gone down, I noticed dark shadows in the water. Then an ominous triangular fin broke the surface. We had company, and I hoped that they hadn't come for dinner. They were sharks. Long, ugly, evil-looking monsters, they may have been attracted by the smell of blood from Bartek's cut hand. We saw their dark shapes in the water around us, but they seemed willing to keep their distance.

Riding up and down on 12-foot swells is almost guaranteed to produce seasickness. I had developed an immunity to motion sickness in the skies over France in World War I, but the others were not so fortunate.

Pulling our rafts together, we checked our supplies. Cherry had four small oranges. Alex had half a dozen chocolate bars, and I had one. The saltwater had already turned them into green mush, and we threw them away. That left the oranges. We decided to hoard them. Saltwater had worked its way into every pack of cigarettes we had. I warned everyone about drinking saltwater. "Saltwater will kill you," I told them all. "No matter how thirsty you get, don't touch a drop."

I was worried about the danger of sunburn too, but it was too late. Most of the men had left their caps on board the plane, along with their shoes. Bartek wore only a one-piece jumper; Reynolds had no pants. The two pilots were in much better shape; each had his leather jacket. I had a leather jacket too, along with a brand-new blue tropical-weight business suit, complete with necktie and vest, and my old gray hat. Adamson had on his uniform and his cap.

We all poked through the equipment that came with the rafts.

Each raft had a patching kit. There were two hand pumps for bailing and for keeping the air pressure up. We had two collapsible bailing buckets, two sheath knives, a compass and a pair of pliers. There was also a first-aid kit and a Very pistol with eighteen flares. Cherry and Adamson each had his service revolver. I had my map of the Pacific. Reynolds came up with two fishing lines, complete with hooks, but there was no bait.

Night came on. A cold mist settled on the sea. A three-quarter moon arose, shining weakly through the mist. Though we were practically straddling the equator, it was miserably cold. The seas were still running high and splashed on us. We were wet through.

Though I considered myself pretty lucky to be able to get around as well as I did, I still had a few traces of discomfort from the Atlanta crash. One was the stiffness, the numbness, the poor circulation. I was in the habit of turning over many times during the night. Now I had to lie in one uncomfortable position without moving all night long. It was agony. If anyone had told me the day before that I'd be able to stay in one position for a whole hour, much less an entire night, in wet clothes and a cold mist, I would have said he was crazy.

But I had no choice. I simply had to lie there and take it. It was a matter of survival. But, even as I heard Hans Adamson groaning softly in his sleep and little Alex still giving a dry heave every now and then, I realized that the worst part of the ordeal for me would be the enforced immobility. My suffering, in short, was going to be in my head.

But not one of the other seven men would ever know it. With the exception of Adamson, who was handicapped by his injury, I was the senior member of the group. I was also more experienced; it was not the first time that I had faced death. We did not know where we were, and no one else did either. We were the only ones in the whole world who knew we were alive. It might be days, even weeks, before we were picked up. It might be never. There would be long grueling days ahead, days of excessive sun and excessive cold, days without food or water.

The seven men bobbing with me in these crowded rafts made up a typical cross section of young American manhood. They had their strengths, and they had their weaknesses. Somebody was going to have to hold them together, and that somebody would have to be me.

I set up a system of two-hour watches, to assure that someone would be awake and observant at all times. It would take keen eyes on the part of the searchers to see these three little rafts on the surface of the ocean. At night, should we hear the sound of a plane overhead or see the lights of a ship, we should be ready to signal immediately with our flares.

"Hey, everybody," I called. "I've got a hundred dollars for the first man to sight land, a plane or a ship."

The offer sounds a little silly now, but it did perk up the men's spirits for a while and gave them something to talk about.

During the night, I felt a bump on the thin rubberized canvas bottom of the raft. Another bump, another. Something was splashing in the water around the raft. Then I knew what it was, and my heart rose in my throat. Sharks! They were coming up underneath the raft. But what were they trying to do? It would be difficult for them to bite through it. I thanked the good Lord that they weren't swordfish. But their rough scaly hides could still tear the material, perhaps rip out the bottom. It was a terrifying thought.

The bumps continued all through that long, cold, miserable night. The ocean was still rough, and water splashed on us constantly. Even with my suit, shoes, socks and leather jacket, I was colder than I had ever been in my life. The gray mist around us began to brighten, slowly, slowly, and we all responded to the promise of dawn. But the fulfillment of that promise was hours in coming. The sun was high in the east before it broke through the mist, then dissipated it and finally began warming our chilled bones.

As soon as it became light, I began watching the sharks. Why had they bumped the raft? One of them, I noticed, a gray cylinder ten feet long, had a discoloration on his head. It was some kind of leech about six inches long. The shark had obviously been trying to rub it off. Under other conditions I might have sympathized.

Breakfast time. Cherry brought out his four oranges. After several minutes' discussion, it was finally determined that we would stretch them over a period of eight days. We would eat one of them now and save the rest for alternate days.

I was honored with the twofold duty of dividing the first and serving as custodian of the other three. We had pulled our rafts together, and seven pairs of eyes were on me as I took one of the sheath knives and prepared to cut the orange into eight equal parts. I knew that, if any man received a piece even infinitesimally smaller than the rest, it might have serious repercussions. No skilled diamond cutter ever examined a precious stone with greater concentration.

I made the decision to cut it in half crosswise, along the line of its equator, cut each half in two, then bisect each of the four pieces. I used the roll of my raft for a table and carefully made the incision, as the other seven men watched intently. The pieces were as nearly equal in size as anyone could expect. One piece might conceivably have been a little smaller than the others; I took it. Then we ate. One man would nibble at his piece; another would squeeze it into his mouth. Everyone ate seeds, pulp, skin and all, except Cherry and me. We saved our pieces of peel to use as bait.

We had seen fish other than sharks swimming around us. Even a raw fish would taste pretty good. Each of us carefully cut a sliver of orange peel, carefully placed it on the hook and carefully dropped the baited hook in the sea.

The fish paid no attention to it whatever.

The wind that had splashed us during the night had subsided completely with the dawn. The ocean smoothed out and became glassy. Our rafts were motionless, with the lines slack. The sun began to beat down. As it climbed higher and higher above us and not a breath of breeze stirred, it began to burn into us, through us.

Again I was comparatively fortunate. The clothes that had protected me to some degree during the night continued to protect me during the day. Time and again I would fill my gray hat with water, then slap it back on my head. I passed out the three large handkerchiefs I'd brought. Folded bandit fashion across the nose they protected the lower part of the face. Men who had shirts used them in the same way.

There was no way to hide from the blistering rays of the sun. Poor Reynolds, who had chosen to strip down to his shorts, was in the worst predicament. I could almost see his skin becoming pink, then red, then blistering. The cut across his nose remained open, oozing blood. He would wash it off, but more would come. It would dry over the lower part of his face in an ugly brown crust.

Bartek's cut hand also refused to heal. Two of his fingers were slashed to the bone. I took the first-aid kit and dabbed iodine on the wound, but it was impossible for him to protect his hand completely from the salt water. The iodine would wash away, and the salt would eat into the open flesh.

Salt was everywhere. It dried in a white, grainy crust that covered everybody and everything.

Where were we? Everyone had a different idea, based on some degree of reasoning or on just a hunch. Cherry and I were of the opinion that our final legs of boxing the compass had taken us to a position north and west of Canton Island. I pulled out my map, and we consulted it together. If our theory was correct, and we later proved that it was, the nearest land was the Japanese-held Gilbert Archipelago four or five hundred miles away.

I felt sure that some current was running. It could have been taking us west, right into the hands of the Japanese, or south and east toward American-held islands. But, even if we came close to an island, we might not see it from our position on the surface. After all, we had not seen one single sign of land from the air. We could all be dead before the current, if there was any, brought us to land.

Should we send up flares? If we were near the Japanese, calling attention to ourselves would be suicide. The consensus was to take the chance.

"We have eighteen flares," Cherry said. "If we send up three a night they will last us six days."

"That's a good idea," I said. "Suppose we send up the first just after nightfall, the second about midnight and the third just before dawn."

This prospect at least gave us something to look forward to. But the long day passed slowly. The sun blazed down on us, and its rays were reflected from the sea. The constant glare burned into our eyes. It had a hypnotic effect, and we fell into a kind of stupor. Hours went by in which nothing was said. We did not have the energy or interest to converse.

Nightfall came. The duty and honor of firing the flares belonged to Captain Cherry. He carefully loaded the long cylinder in the Very pistol. He pointed the barrel to the sky. We heard the sharp report, saw the flash of fire in the darkness and then looked skyward to see the flare burst into light. Nothing happened. The shell was a dud.

Cherry tried again. This time the flare burst, but it was not as bright as I had anticipated. It burned for a few seconds, then went out. It did us no good.

After more debate, we determined to fire the third flare of the night at midnight. That time, as we all peered up into the night, the flare suddenly burst into a brilliant red ball of flame. Suspended from its parachute, it hung over us for what seemed an eternity—perhaps ninety seconds. It illuminated our entire world—raft, men and sea—with an eerie, eye-hurting light. Surely any ship or plane, friend or foe, would have seen it. When it finally went out, leaving us in a night that was blacker than it had been before, we could not help hoping that keen eyes had spotted the flare and had marked its course—and that rescue was on the way. Our spirits were higher, our conversation enthusiastic, even gay. But as the night went on and no plane was heard overheard, no ship loomed on the moonlit horizon, our spirits dropped again.

We continued the flare operation each night. After the first two nights, when there had been too many duds, we finally arrived at the decision to fire one a night at about midnight. We followed this procedure, but the good ones lasted only a few nights, and no one ever saw them.

At least the empty cartridges served a purpose. They were about six inches long and an inch and a half in diameter. Even though there was no water, we all had to urinate at normal intervals. We would not stand up in the rafts, so we used the empty cartridges to urinate in, emptying them over the side.

The next several days and nights merged into agony. The dead calm continued. The sea was glassy, and our rafts floated listlessly on its gently undulating surface. The sun beat down. We couldn't escape it. It burned the skins of the men red, then blistered them and left them raw and bleeding. Again and again I'd fill my hat with water and pull it down over my head, down to my ears. But still, even with that protection, I felt the burning rays of the sun. To those like Reynolds the entire day was torture. The restricting confines of the raft made everything ten times worse. We were all in constant physical contact with one another. The slightest move made by any of us rubbed a sore spot on another man, perhaps two other men.

Alex and De Angelis were the worst off. Their standard position was with De Angelis' legs over Alex's shoulders and Alex's legs under De Angelis' arms or vice versa. Sitting in this cramped position under the equatorial sun demanded some relief. An alternative was to sit back to back, with their legs dangling in the water. Sometimes De Angelis would lie on his back, and Alex would sit on his chest. De Angelis developed a tan, but Alex's skin burned and peeled off in patches.

We were already scared, depressed and in anguish. When the thoughtless motion of a companion raked raw flesh, it was natural to explode into irritation and anger. We all said things that we were sorry for later.

We could not possibly keep the rafts bailed out, and sores resulted from the constant exposure to salt water. They began with an itchy red rash. The rash turned into hard, red bumps, more painful than boils. Pus formed, the heads broke and we were left with running sores that would not heal.

As we blistered, all around us was that cool green water. No one even considered going into it at first; the menacing dark shapes circling around us were hardly inviting. But such was the power of the sun that, as the heat grew stronger, fear of the sharks grew less. Finally, in the height of the midday heat, Whittaker said, "Oh, what the hell," and gingerly let himself down in the water outside his raft. We all held our breath, but the sharks ignored him completely.

Cherry went over next. Finally everyone except Adamson and me tried it. It was by no means a complete relief. The salt water stung the blistered spots and the sores and softened the skin so that the sun could burn it even more when they got out.

For me the nights were worse than the days. At least in the daytime, we could see one another. At night when the cold mist settled down over us, we were alone. With my acute sense of responsibility, I could never relax. No matter who was on watch, I was afraid that he might doze off. I would constantly whisper to him through the mist. The fact that, with all my vigilance, there was never anything to see or hear, no ships, no planes, no breakers pounding on the shores of an island, was beside the point. We had to keep hoping; we had to keep looking. We could not give up.

We were cold. We were afraid. We huddled together for warmth, even though the contact was painful to our burned skin. We pulled our rafts together for additional companionship. We talked about where we might be, how long it would take our searchers to find us, whether we would be found by ship or by plane. I did my best to stimulate such conversation, to keep hope alive. When the mist lightened and we could see the stars, we talked about the constellations. The friendly, familiar North Star was low in the heavens at that latitude. Hans had been with the

Hayden Planetarium in New York for many years, and he gave us interesting lectures on the heavens, illustrated by the stars above us. Though he was in poor condition, I kept him talking for his own benefit, as well as for all the rest of us.

But eventually the conversation, the camaraderie, would die down. The gentle rocking of the rafts; the quiet slurp, slurp of the water; the fatigue of nervous tension would lull the men to sleep. I would lie there stiff, numb, awake and unable to move. Lying motionless in the cold mist was the hardest thing I have ever done. The effort was all in my mind; I had to keep control of myself.

During the long, lonely nights I began to see things. Above me would float forms both beautiful and sinister. They were the shapes of lovely women, of animals, of all sorts of things. They were formed, of course, by the combination of moonlight and clouds. Adamson explained the phenomenon to me and assured me that he saw them too, that they were there for all the world to see. But I still found them eerie.

We divided the second orange on the fourth morning; it was the only food or drink that we had had. Again Cherry and I tried to catch fish with pieces of orange peel. The fish were right there, sleek and luscious-looking, but they had no interest in orange peels.

On the fifth day, we decided that it would be better to eat the third orange. The decision was made primarily for the benefit of those who were sick. Alex was the worst off. He had not fully recovered from his ailments when he boarded the plane. He cried out piteously for water. It was only after I berated him soundly for complaining that I learned that he had a disease something like trench mouth, which was eating at his lips and gums. I did not learn for another couple of days that at night he was drinking seawater. De Angelis awakened to find him leaning over the edge, gulping the seawater down. No wonder the boy cried out for water during the day; salt water has been known to drive men mad with thirst. We could see Alex growing weaker and weaker. I knew that he couldn't last. He huddled to himself, reciting the "Hail Mary."

He was in love with a girl back home, and he had her picture in his wallet. He would sit and look at that picture, talk to it, pray over it. In the daytime he lay broiling in the sun. At night he was so cold that his whole body shook. We could all see him shaking. But there was nothing we could do for him.

We ate the last orange on the sixth day. Much of the juice had evaporated, and it was beginning to rot. From the point of view of physical deterioration, it would have been pointless to keep it any longer. Still, eating it was a mistake. That last wrinkled orange had been a symbol, something to look forward to. Now there was nothing.

Almost immediately some of the men began suffering pangs of hunger so strong that they could not be controlled. They began to talk about food and drink. Each man had his own peculiar desire. Cherry wanted chocolate ice cream. Reynolds mused out loud about the quantities of soft drinks that he was going to consume during the rest of his life. They talked about the California fruit-juice stands that advertised all you could drink for a nickel.

As the talk went on, suddenly a familiar taste became actually present in my mouth. When I was first working for the Duesenbergs back in Des Moines, my daily lunch had consisted solely of a chocolate malted milk shake with an egg in it. I hadn't had a chocolate malted milk shake for perhaps 25 years. Now I wanted one so badly that I could literally taste it. I felt the cold, thick, sweet sensation in my mouth. My tongue moved involuntarily, and I swallowed. But there was nothing there.

It was necessary to divert this talk to more positive channels. Bartek had brought a small New Testament with him, and he occasionally took it out of his pocket and read it. As I've explained, I've always been fully conscious of the existence of a Great Power above. I learned to pray at my mother's knee, and I had never gone to sleep at night without first getting on my knees and praying. But my religion had always been a quiet, personal thing. I had not worshiped formally since Sunday-school days. Now, for the first time in all those years, I realized that I should share my faith with others and help them to find strength through God.

One morning I suggested that we pull the rafts together and have a prayer meeting. Some of us were religious, some not. Adamson and Whittaker made no secret of their lack of religion, but I insisted that they participate. Bartek read a passage from his New Testament, then passed it on. Each man read a passage. For some of us it was the first time, yet every man leafed through the little book to find something to fit the occasion. The 23rd Psalm, which was included in it, was particularly fitting. Under the baking sun on the limitless Pacific, I found a new meaning, a new beauty in its familiar words. Someone else found a passage in the Gospel According to St. Matthew, Chapter 6, Verses 31–34, which also struck home. It read as follows:

> Therefore take no thought, saying, What shall we eat? or, What shall we drink? or, Wherewithal shall we be clothed?
> . . . For your heavenly Father knoweth that ye have need of all these things. But seek ye first the kingdom of God, and his righteousness; and all these things shall be added unto you.
> Take therefore no thought for the morrow: for the morrow shall take thought for the things of itself. Sufficient unto the day *is* the evil thereof.

Our little prayer meetings were held twice a day, morning and evening, and each concluded with a prayer uttered by one of us. The words were often halting, the grammar frequently imperfect, but the feeling was sincere. After our little meetings we'd sing hymns. Two of our favorites were "Lead Kindly Light" and "Onward Christian Soldiers." We didn't know all the words, but we did the best we could. I encouraged the singing, and, when some of the men began to lose interest and faith, I'd sing louder, keeping time on the side of the raft, exhorting them all to join me. I never lost faith, not once, but it was sometimes necessary for me to rekindle faith in others.

Some of the men began to think, for the first time in their lives, of what would happen to them when they went to meet their

Maker. We all realized that, at some time in our past, we had been tested and found wanting. We had all made mistakes. Now the time had come to talk about those mistakes, to confess our sins and omissions, to think about and articulate our hopes and fears and ambitions and desires—the meanings of our lives. No one held anything back. We laid bare our innermost secrets, our sins. I came to know those men—indeed we all came to know one another—better than they knew themselves. But everything that was said in those long, frank, intimate conversations was completely confidential and will never be revealed.

There were some cynics and unbelievers among us. But not after the eighth day. For it was on that day that a small miracle occurred.

Cherry read the service that afternoon, and we finished with a prayer for deliverance and a hymn of praise. There was some talk, but it tapered off in the oppressive heat. With my hat pulled down over my eyes to keep out some of the glare, I dozed off.

Something landed on my head. I knew that it was a sea gull. I don't know how I knew; I just knew.

Everyone else knew too. No one said a word, but, peering out from under my hat brim without moving my head, I could see the expressions on their faces. They were staring at that gull. The gull meant food—if I could catch it.

Slowly, gradually, a fraction of an inch at a time, I began moving my right hand up to my hat. Slowly, slowly. I felt that I was shaking all over, but it must have been my imagination, for the bird remained. My hand was up to the level of my hat brim. The temptation was great to make a sudden grab, but I couldn't take the chance. I didn't know just exactly where the bird was. I brought my open hand closer and closer to where I felt the bird should be, and then, when I sensed the presence of the gull, I closed my hand. The bird's legs were in it.

It took about one second to wring the gull's neck. It did not take much longer to defeather it. Then I cut it into eight equal pieces, with seven pairs of eyes watching intently. The raw meat was dark, sinewy, tough, fishy—and delicious. We chewed it slowly, bones and all.

That was only the first course. I had held back the intestines to use for bait. Cherry weighted his line with Whittaker's ring and dropped the baited hook overboard. Something hit the bait immediately, and Cherry pulled it in. It was a small mackerel, about twelve inches long. I threw my line out and landed a small sea bass. Then I set to work to carve up the mackerel. It too was delicious, much more so than the gull. The flesh was cool and moist; it seemed to satisfy our thirst as well as our hunger. As with the gull, we chewed up the bones and swallowed them.

To our shrunken stomachs, this 2-course meal was a surfeit. Our spirits rose. Even the two sickest individuals, Alex and Hans, ate their portions and seemed to improve. All because of one little gull hundreds of miles from land. There was not a one of us who was not aware of the fact that our gull had appeared just after we had finished our prayer service.

Some may call it a coincidence. I call it a gift from heaven.

After eight days of scorching calm, with not a drop of fresh water, that night it began to look like rain. We worked out elaborate plans to catch every drop we could. Each raft had a bailing bucket that we could use to store water. The flares had been packed in canvas covers, which we had saved. We would use them as reservoirs. To catch the rain we could spread out articles of clothing and, when they were soaked, wring them out into the reservoirs.

I dozed off about midnight, then came awake with a bang. Strong gusts of wind were churning up the ocean. The rafts were bobbing up and down, jerking against the lines that held us together. The moon and stars were totally obscured, and the night was pitch-black, illuminated only by flashes of lightning. I smelled rain. We were all alert and ready for it. We removed the clothes we intended to use for wringing cloths—Adamson even took off his shorts—and had them ready.

An hour went by, another and another. Scattered drops of rain fell. I leaned my head back, opened my mouth and let the cool sweet water land on my face, my lips, my tongue. Nothing has ever tasted so good, before or since.

But we had been merely brushed by the edge of the squall and received only a few drops. Off in the distance I could see a heavier blackness, spitting lightning, and recognized it for the shadow of the squall. "It's over there!" I shouted. "Let's go to it. Grab your paddles."

Our craft still had two aluminum paddles. Cherry's raft had only one; Whittaker had lost the other trying to harpoon a fish. De Angelis and Alex had two, but Alex was not capable of much effort. Paddling was awkward and difficult for all of us, but we tried nevertheless, and the bulky rafts did indeed move through the water. Added to my physical effort were my prayers. As we paddled toward the squall, I asked God to help us.

And we did catch it. We paddled right into it. The wind tossed us about. Waves lifted us, dropped us, broke on us. Bright, frightening flashes of lightning etched us momentarily against the wall of darkness. Thunder cracked in the peculiar echoless reports of a storm at sea. We were all shouting: "Over here! Rain! This way! Rain! Rain!"

Then—"Hey! We've broken loose! Help! Help!"

The cry came from De Angelis. The little raft had broken loose. Our raft was the closest, and Bartek and I started paddling after it. Cherry's raft followed.

The small raft was hard to see in the blackness, and De Angelis' cries were hard to hear in the gusts of wind. I thought we'd lost them. But a breaking wave furnished a white background, and there was the raft silhouetted against it. We caught up and secured the line in the darkness.

We were in the midst of the squall. Rain fell, not in drops, but in sheets. It was a wonderful feeling, being rained on. The pure, distilled water washed away the encrusted salt and bathed the sores and wounds. But I luxuriated in it for only a moment. It was necessary to start collecting it.

First I had to rinse out both the wringing cloths and the reservoirs. The cool water stimulated Adamson to the point at which he could be of some help, and he and Bartek passed me the soaked articles of clothing for me to wring. Getting all the salt out required several soakings and wringings. The wind howled, the waves threw us up and down, the lightning and thunder were all around us, but we kept working.

A strong jerk twisted our raft around. I looked in the direction whence it came just in time to see Cherry's raft tip over completely. My immediate fear was for Reynolds, the weakest of the three, but the next flash of lightning showed three heads by the capsized raft. They were holding onto the hand lines. Bartek and I pulled the raft toward us, hand over hand. Determined men who won't give up can do anything, and Cherry, Whittaker and Reynolds proved it that wild night by helping us right the raft, then helping each other climb back in.

The three men were saved. They'd clung to their oar. But the flares and the Very pistol were gone. So was the bailing bucket. It was a double loss, for I had to lend Cherry mine for him to bail out the raft. Precious time, which meant precious water, was lost. While he bailed, the rest of us filled our own bodies, by wringing the wet cloths into our mouths. When Cherry had his raft reasonably well bailed out, he gave me back the bucket, and I gave him our cartridge cover. Then we set to work filling both.

Wringing out the cloths broke the skin on my burned and blistered hands, and they started bleeding in a dozen places, but I hardly noticed it. The goal was to fill that bucket. When the squall left us and the wind and the rain shut off as though by a switch, we had accumulated about a quart and a half in the bucket. We had all managed to get a reasonable amount of pure water in us. De Angelis and Alex, having nothing to use as storage, had occupied themselves the whole time by wringing out their shirts into their mouths.

But we were still in a terrible state of dehydration. We pulled the rafts together and held a council. What should we do with the water we had? We knew from past experience that on this expanse of ocean eight days might pass without rainfall. The decision was to portion it out on the most conservative basis. After much discussion we arrived at the figure of one half-jigger a man per day. And we all wanted our shares then. Without further discussion I poured what I considered to be a half-ounce from the bucket into the empty cartridge case and handed it to Alex. He drank. I repeated that process seven times. The last serving was for me. Though it was only enough to half-fill a jigger, I sipped it slowly and savored it. It was indeed the sweetest water in the world. It tasted better than even a chocolate malted egg milk shake.

The next day we ate the fish and had our ration of water. But things became bleak again. We entered another dry period. The only fish we caught was a small shark. I cut him up and served him, but, hungry and thirsty as we were, none of us could stomach that tough, rancid meat. I forced myself to continue chewing on a piece if only for the liquid, but I gagged on it. Sharks carried away our lines before we could catch any more edible fish.

There had not been enough food and drink to keep Alex's condition from growing worse. For his and Adamson's benefit we voted to increase the water ration to two jiggers a day, then three. But he was failing fast. We all felt so sorry for the poor burned, shivering kid. I suggested that he and Bartek change positions, in hopes that Alex would rest better in our bigger raft. Transferring his semiconscious body was not easy.

That night, when the cold came on and his shivering started, I cuddled him against me as a mother would a child, trying to give him some of the warmth from my own body, sharing the protection of the leather jacket. He stopped shivering and seemed to go to sleep. From time to time he would mutter in Polish, talking to his mother and his girl, but he did seem to get some rest. We passed two nights that way, but before the third night came he asked to be put back in the little raft. Later that night I heard a long sigh and then silence. Our little sergeant was suffering no more.

The presence of death was so strong that the other men awakened too. They all knew that Alex was dead. There were still several hours before dawn, and I insisted on waiting for light before we made any decision. It was a dreadful night. Gusts of wind swept across us. All three rafts, but particularly the smaller one bearing the dead body, leaped and dived in the waves. De Angelis had to lie there with Alex's cold body lying across him.

Dawn came. We pulled the three rafts together. We were all fully aware of the awesome responsibility that was on us; we could not consign the body of our friend to the sea if there was even a spark of life within him. I felt his wrist for several moments; it was cold and lifeless, and I could feel no pulse. I put my ear against his chest; there was no heartbeat. I insisted that Cherry and Whittaker, as the two senior officers, also examine the body. They did, and they agreed with me that Alex was dead. The examination was probably superfluous, as rigor mortis had already begun to set in, but we wanted to make sure.

Even after we had agreed that Alex was dead, we hesitated to perform our next duty. Captain Cherry removed his identification tags and his wallet to return them to his family. We removed the clothes from the emaciated, burned body, and then we hesitated again. But at last, as gently as possible, we rolled the remains of Alex Kaczmarczyk over the side. But it was as if Alex did not want to leave us. The body did not sink but floated face down along with us. We paddled away and left him there.

Sometime after Alex died, Bartek asked De Angelis if he would trade places with him. A little game of musical rafts resulted; Bartek took the small raft, De Angelis joined his fellow officers, Cherry and Whittaker, and Reynolds came in with Adamson and me.

We were in the midst of another spell of doldrums. The sun blistered down. De Angelis and Whittaker had developed a resistance to the sun, but the rest of us were still in agony.

If anyone was slated to go after Alex, I knew that it would be Hans Adamson, my closest and dearest friend of all those in the rafts. The pain of his wrenched back was with him constantly. His saltwater sores were the worst of all. A fair-skinned Dane, he had not become tanned and hardened to the sun. His face, arms, hands, legs and feet were masses of red pulp. The paralysis was spreading over his body. Though we didn't know it, he was developing lobar pneumonia and other serious ailments brought on by starvation. His eyes were bloodshot and swollen. Most of the time he was neither awake nor asleep but in a pain-wracked stupor. I shared his suffering. Watching this fine man deteriorate before my eyes was as painful to me as my own physical problems.

One night I was awakened from a doze by a strange movement of the raft. It had shifted weight. Hans was not pressing against me. I jerked up with a start. He was gone. Then I saw something in the water, and my hand whipped out toward it. It was Adamson's head. I had him by the shoulder. He was almost a dead weight, and it was all I could do to hang onto him, much less pull him onto the raft.

I called to Cherry and Whittaker, and they came to my aid. Together we finally hauled the sick man back on board. Nothing was said that night. With daylight, Hans seemed to return to his senses. He realized that he had let himself become discouraged and disconsolate. He was sorry. In a brave, pathetic gesture, he pulled back his burned lips in what was meant to be a smile and stuck out his red, throbbing hand for me to shake.

My response was one of the most difficult actions I have ever taken in my life. It was doubly difficult because I really didn't know how much longer Hans had to live. He might die with this, his last, memory of me. But I steeled myself. I had to get through to this man somehow.

"I don't shake hands with your kind," I said, deliberately making my voice cold and harsh. "If you want to shake hands, you've got to prove yourself first."

He pulled back his hand and said nothing more. I knew that he was thinking, analyzing himself, determining whether to live or die. I believe that it was at that point that he decided to live. But he was still the weakest and the sickest, and I knew that he would be the next to go. Reynolds would be next, then Bartek. De Angelis and Cherry were about on a par as far as survival quality went. Whittaker had a physical and mental toughness that would keep him alive to the very last.

There was no doubt in my mind that I would outlast them all. I had been there before. From suffering comes experience, and I had had my share of both.

Less than two years before I had lain in a hospital bed for four months, thinking about life and fighting death. I realized that those four months had been a test and a preparation for this most demanding of all my adventures. More than anyone else in those three rafts, more than all of them combined, I had faced death and had learned from those encounters the meaning of life, the meaning of God, the meaning of the Golden Rule.

It was clear to me that God had had a purpose in keeping me alive. It was to help the others, to bring them through. I had been saved to serve. It was an awesome responsibility, but I accepted it gladly and proudly.

I did not forget that I myself still had a mission to perform and a message to deliver to General MacArthur.

In the days that followed the feast of the sea gull and the rain squall, everyone's spirits drooped lower and lower. Having experienced one small miracle, they all expected another, and, when it was not immediately forthcoming, they became discouraged and despondent, some more than others. I'm afraid that some of them would really have preferred simply to give up and lie there baking in the sun, waiting to die.

But I wouldn't permit that to happen. I continued the nightly prayer meetings and insisted that we continue trying to raise our cracked voices in song. I used every trick I knew on them. To some I spoke with encouragement; I was as soft and gentle as a mother. But others required stronger medicine. I rode them; I tore them to pieces; I struck at every raw nerve in their bodies.

One of the men screamed back at me, "Rickenbacker, you're the meanest, most cantankerous so and so that ever lived!"

I smiled inside. I had proved that there was still some fight left in that man. If he could snarl back at me, he could snarl back at death.

I learned later that several of the boys swore an oath that they would continue living for the pleasure of burying me at sea. I wish I had known it at the time. I'd have been even more pleased with my efforts to keep them going.

Occasionally, gulls flew overhead, but none landed. The two guns had long since corroded into uselessness and been thrown away. The fish were all around us, but we couldn't catch them. I got my hands on a small shark, but he got away.

Of all our watches, only Whittaker's continued to work. With it we were able to determine that the sun was rising a little later in the morning, which could mean only that we were drifting in a westerly direction. But Cherry and I were convinced that we were north and west of both the sea and air lanes. We were drifting in the wrong direction. We tried to paddle, but we simply didn't have the strength.

The little squalls that raced across the surface of the ocean seemed always to be going to the southeast. When we saw one, we would paddle in its direction, hoping to be blown along with it as we collected water. Sometimes it worked. One night we didn't have to paddle; several squalls passed right over us. "Rain, rain," we cried, like excited children. We worked all night long, laying out our clothes and squeezing them into the bucket.

In his raft Cherry was using a compartment of his Mae West as a reservoir. He trapped about as much as I. We went back to water rations of two jiggers a day. I worried about leaving the water in the open bailing bucket. We didn't want a drop to evaporate. I was wearing a Mae West too, and I suggested using one of its compartments as a container for the water. Adamson and Reynolds agreed, and I began the long, tedious operation of transferring the water from the bucket to the Mae West. The only way to do it was to take a mouthful of water from the bailing bucket, then force it by means of a long tube down into the compartment. Every eye was fixed on me. If my Adam's apple had jumped once, they'd probably have thrown me overboard.

Sharks were sticking with us. One night a school of mackerel came swimming by. The sharks went wild feeding on the smaller fish. The mackerel were trying to escape, even leaping into the air. One fell into Cherry's raft, one into mine. We ate one the next day, the other the day after. Tiny fingerlings, like freshwater minnows, gathered around the rafts, their noses against the sides. With perfect timing and a little luck, those of us who were still in good shape—Cherry, Whittaker, De Angelis and I—could catch them. We shared them with the others. They were cool, moist and crunchy.

Before dawn one morning I dozed off and found myself on a beautiful island. An old friend had a luxurious home there. He gave us a delicious breakfast, with large frosty pitchers of orange juice, grapefruit juice, pineapple juice, apple juice and grape juice. He had a telephone, and after breakfast I planned to place a direct call to Secretary Stimson.

And then I woke up.

Every night I had that dream. And every morning I would awaken, look around me and realize with horror and astonishment that I was not in that lovely home on that beautiful island drinking those fruit juices after all, but right back on the raft, lost in the Pacific.

Eastern Air Lines had taken out a million-dollar life insurance policy on me. Several companies had gone in together on it, and it had come through only a couple of months before the Atlanta crash. Insurance-company doctors had descended on the hospital like vultures to look me over. Well, they sure weren't coming to look me over here. I cackled out loud at the thought.

Nineteen days. Afternoon. Rough sea. I happened to be looking over at Cherry's raft when I saw him freeze in an attitude of alertness, head cocked, looking toward the southeastern horizon.

"Plane," he cried. "I hear a plane."

I heard it too. I strained my eyes in its direction but saw only a black squall about five miles away. Suddenly, out of the squall, came a plane, flying low and fast. It was a single-engine pontoon job, and it was heading away from us. It could have been either American or Japanese, but we didn't think of that. We started shouting and waving. Bartek was in my raft that day, and I held him about the knees so that he could stand up. He waved his arms and shouted until he fell down exhausted. The plane flew on and disappeared.

The pilot had obviously not seen us. Our throats were sore from screaming. Then came the emotional letdown. Some of the men were dangerously close to the breaking point; the combination of sudden hope and crushing disappointment was too much for them. Some actually sobbed.

"Cut that out!" I shouted at them, adding some choice profanity to shock them. "That's the best thing that's happened to us. Where there's one plane there must be more. Don't give up now!"

Hopes became high again. That plane had to come from somewhere. We chatted about it all night long. Two more planes of the same type appeared the next day. They didn't see us. The following day there were two pairs of planes in the morning but no more the rest of the day. Down went our spirits. We knew now that we were difficult to see. Our little rafts were just specks against the ocean, particularly when the whitecaps were breaking. The afternoon passed and all the next day. No more planes. Perhaps we had drifted through a string of islands without knowing it and were out of patrol range again.

Cherry came up with what I thought was a wild idea. He wanted to take the small raft and paddle off alone. I thought it would be most unwise. Three rafts bunched together would be easier to see than one. And how would he know which way to go? But he was determined. All I could do was to give in and wish him good luck. De Angelis gave him the little raft, and Cherry paddled off.

Then Whittaker and De Angelis wanted to go. Again I disapproved. Poor Reynolds was lying unconscious in the raft with them, and I didn't think it was fair to him. But they went. By nightfall both rafts were out of sight. I was alone with Adamson and Bartek. Neither of them was in any condition to know what was going on. I had to hold their heads up to pour their allotments of water down their throats.

It was a long night. The next day, Friday, November 13, was a scorcher. Twenty-four days on the open sea. I kept a constant lookout, but the three of us, two unconscious men and I, seemed to be alone in the world. Not even a sea gull was in the sky. Late that afternoon I felt Bartek pulling at my shirt. I had dozed off; he had awakened.

"Listen, Captain—planes!"

Two of them. Adamson and Bartek were too weak to stand up themselves or to steady me if I did. But we had to make some sign to show we were alive. I swept my old gray hat back and forth over my head. The planes, low over the water, passed by us and kept on going. This time even I felt despair. It was getting late in the day. I didn't know if my companions could stand another night.

Half an hour later I heard the planes again. They were coming out of the sun and were heading directly for us. They went right over us. The three of us screamed at them hysterically. I waved and waved.

And this time the pilot saw us. I saw him see us. He was smiling and waving. It was a Navy plane. God bless the Navy. I kept on waving my hat. I wanted them to know that we were alive.

The first plane made a full circle around the raft, then set off after the other. About three-quarters of an hour later, the two planes came back. One plane remained overhead circling, while the other returned to the base. I kept waving my hat for more than three hours. I don't know how in the world I was able to continue so long.

Darkness was approaching. The plane kept circling. I kept waving. The pilot fired two flares, a white one and a red one. In the distance I saw lights blinking; the pilot had signaled a boat. Now that the boat had our bearings, the pilot came down and made a marvelous landing on the choppy sea. He taxied to within a few yards of us, then shut off the engine. I paddled the raft to the plane and grabbed the pontoon. The radioman came down to give me a hand, then the pilot.

They were the finest-looking young men I had ever seen. I was proud to be an American like them. The pilot was Lieutenant William F. Eadie of Evanston, Illinois, and the radioman was L. H. Boutte, from Abbeville, Louisiana.

"There's a PT boat on its way," Eadie said, "but I'm afraid to show another light. There might be Japs around. I'd suggest we taxi into the base. It's about forty miles."

"Let's go," I said.

"All the rest have been found," Eadie said. We were the last. We were southwest of the Ellice Islands, a full five hundred miles southwest of Canton. We had drifted through the Ellice chain during the night. The next island group was another five hundred miles away across the open sea. The base to which Eadie was referring was the island of Funafuti in the Ellice group.

Before we boarded the plane we finished off the water in the Mae West. We'd made a deal: Adamson and Bartek got all the water in one compartment of the Mae West, water we knew to be sweet. There was twice as much water in the other compartment, but it contained some salt. Adamson and Bartek had about a pint apiece. My share was twice as much and salty, but I drank it.

There was no question that Adamson was the sickest of the three of us. The two Navy men hoisted him into the cockpit. That left no room for Bartek and me. "You fellows are going too," Eadie said. "On the wing."

They lifted Bartek up to the wing, set him down with his feet over the leading edge and tied him on. They tied me to the left wing in the same way. As they were working, I was saying things like "Thank God" and "God bless the Navy," and I meant every word.

We taxied over the ocean. A PT boat emerged from the darkness; its skipper, Eadie and I discussed what to do next. I recommended that Adamson continue on in the plane, rather than be hauled out and loaded on the boat. Bartek and I were untied and transferred. The crew cheered as we were helped on board. They brought out bedrolls and blankets. Bartek lay down and went to sleep instantly, but I was too excited.

They gave me a mug of hot beef broth, which, a little later, caused me to have my first bowel movement in 24 days. After the broth I asked for water, and I drank four mugs full, one right after the other. The skipper thought I was drinking too much, so I switched from water to pineapple juice, two cups full.

At the base a smaller boat came alongside, and we were transferred to it and taken ashore. The men carried us on stretchers to the hospital. The route lay under beautiful palm trees through which the moon was shining. The night air was warm. What a lovely evening!

The hospital was one little room. They started undressing us. Our clothes actually fell to pieces. We were washed off, our sores were treated and we were put to bed. Adamson was given an immediate transfusion of plasma, and he and Bartek slept. But I wanted water. The medical officer, a Colonel Fuller, told me that I could have two ounces every two hours.

"I want it in a bucket," I growled, "not a medicine dropper."

I was as badly off that first night on shore as I had been any night on the raft. My throat cried out for water. I imagine that the salt in the tainted water had something to do with it. About 11:00 P.M. I called the hospital attendant over.

"You must be tired and sleepy," I said. "We're all right now, so you go on to bed. Just put that jug of water by the bed, and I'll drink it according to instructions."

Within one hour that jug was empty.

My burns and saltwater ulcers, though treated, actually hurt worse than they had ever hurt on the raft. Finally I went to sleep and dreamed the same old dream about the beautiful island.

When I saw myself in the mirror the next day I was horrified by my appearance. On my sunken cheeks was a dirty brown beard about an inch and a half long, with a drooping Chinese moustache. I knew that sooner or later the photographers would come swarming, and I didn't want that face in the mirror to be splashed across newspaper pages. We found someone who had a pair of clippers—he was a pharmacist's mate and a Harvard graduate—and he gave me a haircut on the face. Then he shaved me with a straight razor. "First time I ever did this," he mentioned while he was doing it.

I have regretted that foolish and vain impulse ever since. I'd give my shirt to have a picture of the way I looked that day. I may not have been a pretty sight, but I was an interesting one.

From 180 pounds I had gone down to 126. Adamson and Cherry, both heavier than I, had each lost 55 pounds. Jim Reynolds had lost 40 pounds, but he had started out with only 130. He was an emaciated wreck. Reynolds, Whittaker and De Angelis had been picked up off a small island. Cherry had been spotted by a plane and picked up by a PT boat.

Two doctors who had flown in from Samoa decided to fly all of us, except Bartek and Reynolds, to a larger hospital at Pago Pago on the island of Tutuila, American Samoa. They were too sick to be moved until later. As for Hans Adamson, who was the worst off of all, the doctors thought that the superior treatment he would receive at Samoa was worth the risk of moving him. As Hans' friend, I agreed with that decision. I did not think that he should be left alone.

At the large base hospital in Samoa, Cherry, Whittaker, De Angelis and I recovered quickly. Bartek and Reynolds also started to mend. Adamson, however, remained in critical condition. The sulfa he was given for pneumonia caused a dangerous reaction in his bloodstream. It took three transfusions of whole blood to pull him through that crisis.

In the meantime I had advised Secretary Stimson that I would be able to continue the mission. Hap Arnold, in a warm message, promised to send a plane when I was ready. I drank fruit juices by the gallon, ate everything in sight and put twenty pounds back on in two weeks. I kept busy touring the interesting island in a jeep that the Army lent me.

On Sunday I rounded up my gang, and we went to church in

the Quonset hut that served as a chapel. Catholic services were at 9:00, Protestant services at 10:00. We all sat through both.

Several men stationed at Pago Pago had hometown newspapers and showed them to me. I hadn't seen my name in such big black headlines since I was winning auto races back in the Teens. Some editorial-page cartoons had me lost forever, like that of my friend Burris Jenkins, Jr., of the New York *Journal-American*. It was captioned, "End of the Roaring Road?" I tore it out of the paper, wrote "Hell, No!" across it and sent it back to Burris. The paper printed it.

C. D. Batchelor's cartoon in the New York *Daily News* showed a black wreath floating on the waves and was captioned "So Long, Eddie." The *News* also ran an editorial, entitled "Good-Bye Rickenbacker," on the same page (a week after we'd gone down), which practically buried me. Not every man gets to read his own obituary, and the *News* editorial was most complimentary. It concluded: "If we've lost Rickenbacker we've lost one of our best flying men and one of our best men."

My heart went out to Adelaide and the boys. When I was first reported missing, the reporters went to see her. News stories described her as fighting back tears but declaring: "Eddie will turn up. He's too old to get lost in an airplane now."

"That's typical of Adelaide," I thought.

I learned later that both Stimson and Arnold had kept in personal contact with her. It was her determined urging that had led them to continue the search. Hap had called early Saturday morning, November 14, and told her that I was found.

Several papers had brought out extras. I chuckled at what I was called in the purple prose of the lead paragraphs. The International News Service: "The Death-Cheating Pioneer of the World's Air Lanes." The Associated Press: "The Man Who Always Comes Back" and "Iron-man Eddie." The United Press: "That Indestructible Man of Aviation."

There'd be a warm reception awaiting me when I came home, but in the meantime I had a mission to finish. At sunrise on December 1, I climbed aboard a B-24 converted for transport duty, and we were off. Continuing on over the vast expanse of the Pacific, I was perfectly at ease. My only concern was about meeting General MacArthur. The last time that I had seen him had been at the court-martial of General Billy Mitchell. We had disagreed vigorously and had said some unpleasant things to each other. I couldn't help wondering what kind of reception he would give me.

I had several days to think about it as I stopped in at several bases on the way to Australia. Our schedule had been arranged so that I could fly by night, sleeping in the comfortable cot and sleeping bag placed on board for me, and work by day. I resolved to keep a mental armor plate about me at all times to prevent me from saying anything derogatory or argumentative, regardless of what he might say.

In Australia I learned that General MacArthur refused to permit me to come to Port Moresby in an unarmed plane. A B-17, bristling with firepower and flown by a combat crew, came down to pick me up. We landed on a metal strip in the hills. At the end of the runway, a group of men was waiting. One of them stood out from the rest; with that familiar cap and dramatic stance it was MacArthur himself. I started toward him, and he met me halfway.

"God, Eddie, I'm glad to see you," he said and threw his arms around me. There went my armor plate.

I delivered my oral message. Though I remember every word of it to this day, I shall not repeat it. Stimson and MacArthur took it with them to the grave, and so shall I.

I spent the weekend with MacArthur as his houseguest. It was not luxurious living. His headquarters consisted of a frame shack and an outhouse. MacArthur was interested not in comfort but in winning a war. He was up each morning at 6:00 A.M., and he worked until past midnight during the three days that I was with him.

Only at dinner did he relax. At one of those leisurely meals, he himself brought up his early opposition to air power. "You know, Eddie," he said, "I probably did the American Air Forces

more harm than any man living when I was chief of staff by re-
fusing to believe in the future of the airplane as a weapon of
war. I am now doing everything I can to make amends for that
great mistake."

One of MacArthur's staff officers, Colonel C. A. Willoughby,
looked familiar, but I did not place his name. Then it came to
me. He had been one of my fellow officers at the flying school
at Issoudun in World War I, but then his name had been "Wiedenbach."

Port Moresby was a bombed-out ruin of a city in the
center of a cloud of swirling red dust. I visited airports in the
area and found them to be mere strips hacked out of the jungle.
Only in the direst emergency would I have permitted Eastern Air
Lines' most experienced pilot to attempt to land one of our
airliners on such a strip. Yet young men with shiny wings straight
from the United States were using these short and narrow run-
ways and thinking nothing of it.

In the hellhole of New Guinea an idea struck me. Suppose our
civilian leaders back home, especially those men concerned with
labor and war production, could be brought to this godforsaken
spot to spend one day living the way our boys in uniform lived
all the time. I bet things would soon be different back home.
That germ of a thought was expanded and compounded a few
days later, after I had returned to Australia and came back in
a northerly direction to the Solomon Islands. For I found myself on Guadalcanal.

Guadalcanal! Later in the war the Guadalcanal operation was
to be dwarfed by bigger and bloodier island battles. In December 1942, however, that tropical island slaughterhouse was the
epitome of the American war effort in the South Pacific. It was
difficult to see how men could even exist under such conditions,
much less carry on the highly skilled warfare of the twentieth
century. We had to contend with an almost constant downpour,
mud, tropical diseases and vermin.

And all purely to gain a miserable little airstrip from which
to carry on the most difficult air war imaginable. From that

strip our planes went out on missions that would last ten to
twelve hours, all through enemy-held air. They were subject to
attack all the way out and all the way back. And when they got
back, *if* they got back, the quarters to which they returned were
steamy wet tents set in acres of mud and clouds of malarial mos-
quitoes.

Yet everywhere I went and among all the men I talked to, the
overwhelming desire was not to get out of this tropical swamp
but rather to have more equipment, more guns, more ammunition, more planes, in order to complete the job they had come
to do.

And that's where I came to the positive conclusion that, if
only we could take the troops out of these foxholes and hellholes all over the world, send them back home to work in the
war factories of the nation and dispatch the factory workers to
fill their places in the wet and the filth and disease-ridden areas
facing Japanese soldiers, then production would be increased,
even doubled, within thirty days.

I said so, not as a person opposed to labor or labor unions.
I have been a laboring man myself, and I have enjoyed good
relations with honest unions. I simply meant that, if the workers
on the home front could be exposed to what our boys on the
fighting fronts were going through, they'd think no more of
strikes and overtime pay and featherbedding and would devote
all their energies to winning the war through production. That
was the message I resolved to take home with me.

And then I was headed home. I arrived back on Samoa on
Friday, December 11, after eleven days of hard going, day and
night. I hoped to be able to take Hans Adamson home with me,
but I learned that his troubles were continuing. A lung abscess
had developed and had required an operation. He was in bad
shape. His doctors and I held a conference, and we agreed that
to take him with me in his present condition would be dangerous,
but to leave him behind would be a crushing blow. I had one
more inspection trip to make, on the neighboring isle of Upolu.
I went in to see Hans that night.

"I'm going to spend Saturday and Sunday on Upolu," I told him, "and will leave here at midnight Monday for Christmas Island and Hawaii. The doctors tell me that if you buck up and develop a positive attitude you'll be able to go with me. If not, you'll probably have to stay here another two or three months and go back home by hospital boat."

Then I played my trump card. I knew Hans' devotion to his wife Helen, and that afternoon I had been arranging a little communications project. "If you come with me to Hawaii," I said, "There's a possibility that you may be able to talk with Helen by telephone Tuesday night."

I left him to think that over. When I returned from Upolu on Monday, I found Hans lying there with a great big smile. The doctors said that he had shown tremendous improvement and that he could go. I broke the news to him.

"Thank God," Hans breathed. "Thank God."

"Thank God is right," I said, remembering back to those early days on the raft when Adamson professed not to be religious. "God has been riding with you all these many days, and now He has you well in hand. You'd better thank Him."

All the others had gone home except Jimmy Reynolds. He was still skin and bones but on the mend, and I took him too. Commander John Durkin, their doctor, came along to take care of them both. We refueled at Christmas Island and arrived at Hickam Field at 5:00 P.M. Monday. An ambulance met us and took Hans to the hospital. The telephone call with Helen in Washington was set up for the next evening. Hans and his wife spoke for at least fifteen minutes. It was such a tremendous stimulant that the doctors said that he could leave that night. We took off at 10:00 P.M. and arrived at Oakland, California, the next morning. Jimmy Reynolds' mother and father were there to greet him and take him home with them, and it was one of the tenderest reunions I have ever witnessed.

With everyone else taken care of, I thought I would like to hear the voice of my own beloved. I put in a long distance call home. The New York operator came on the line with the news that the number had been disconnected. "Eddie doesn't live here any more," she said with a laugh. I didn't find it so funny.

I called the manager of the California Telephone Company, who in turn called the manager of the apartment house in New York where we lived. He explained that our number had been changed because so many calls had come in and gave him the correct number. When I finally reached Adelaide on the phone, I was choked up so badly that I could hardly speak, but finally it came out: "I hope you will never have to go through such an ordeal again."

After Hans had had a 24-hour rest, we moved on to Los Angeles. My brother Dewey brought my mother to the airport, and we had a nice long visit. She had never given up hope, she told me, all during those 24 days. It was a wonderful reunion, for Mother has always been the greatest inspiration in my life.

With a stop in San Antonio, Texas, we arrived in Washington at the time I had notified Hap Arnold that I would be there: 9:00 A.M. Saturday, December 19. Adelaide, Dave and Bill were there to meet me, along with Hap Arnold and a welcoming group of officers. I saw them as I came down the steps. Suddenly Bill, the youngest, broke out of the waiting group and ran to me. I bent over, and he threw his arms around me.

"Oh, Daddy, I'm so happy to see you again," he cried. I couldn't say a word.

Then on to the office of the Secretary of War. Secretary Stimson greeted me warmly. I had given no interviews, and the outer office was swarming with correspondents. Secretary Stimson asked them in and said:

> Gentlemen, I promised you the other day that I would produce Captain Rickenbacker, and I told you that, as soon as he came to me, I would bring him in to see you. He is back, and I think there is more of him here than went away. I'm sure of it, and I know that you will want to see and hear him, and, while this is merely a preliminary talk, because he is just off the plane and he is coming back again, I bring him here because I want to keep my promise that you would see him at once. Captain Rickenbacker, the chair is yours.

He stood up and waved me to his own chair behind the big desk. I sat down, and he moved back. Flashbulbs popped, and the reporters burst into applause. I started talking and told the whole story of the ordeal in more or less complete detail. I told of our suffering, and I told how God had answered our prayers. I told how our brave little Sergeant Alex had died and of the eventual rescue. The rescue, I said at the press conference, came on the 21st day. That was the way I had figured it. The press accepted that figure. In the book I later wrote about the experience, *Seven Came Through,* I used the figure 21 days. It wasn't until later that I began to figure it out and realized that we had been on the expanse of the Pacific for a total of 24 days.

I wound up my talk with a brief account of the continuation of my mission and a description of the conditions I had found. I concluded:

One thing we need above everything else is more and more of everything. After seeing these boys in the air and on the ground, working as they are, twenty-four hours the clock around in the most unbelievable living conditions, I have come to the conclusion that if you brought our combat troops back to America overnight, put them into the factories and transfer the present war workers out into their position, you would have production doubled in thirty days. I mean that!

If only we could get the American people to realize that by even a small amount of additional effort they can increase production of planes, ships and equipment, and get to our fighters their supplies, ammunition, guns, gasoline—we will have served a great purpose!

Objections to rationing of rubber and gasoline seem so insignificant and ridiculous when we see what those boys haven't got! I cannot help but think of the fact that the old rubber in an old rubber tire was sufficient to make up two or three of the type of rafts that we were in. If people only knew that the saving of one old rubber tire makes it possible to produce one of those rafts which might be responsible, as it has been in our case, for saving seven men, they might take it more seriously. They might not worry so much about whether they had their automobiles on weekends or whether they had to walk or ride the streetcar or subway. Those of us on the home front must remember that we are three thousand to six thousand miles away from all of those hellholes of fire. It is difficult for a man to imagine what our boys are doing without seeing. With all the security and comforts of home we are enjoying, I hope that we will resolve to do much better.

I hope that the trip, and whatever hardships we had to accept or endure, may prove to be a lesson to our people back home and a stimulus to drive them on to greater things because, without their effort and the material they are producing, our boys can't do the job they are so willing and anxious to do in the four corners of the world.

I have been talking a long time, Mr. Secretary. I am very grateful.

After lunch with the Secretary of War, we went home to New York where Mayor La Guardia and other old friends met us. More press conferences, and then finally I went home with my family.

The entire nation, it seemed, wanted me to tell the story in my own voice, either in person or on the radio. On my first Sunday home, December 20, I spoke to the nation on all the major networks from my apartment in New York. I begged my listeners to give more and more effort "because you can never approximate the sacrifices our men are making on the battlefront for you and me.

"If I can only help you understand that," I concluded, "then I will be able to enjoy the first Sunday afternoon I have spent at home in many, many weeks."

Christmas was coming. It was good to know that the mission was over. Once again, I had faced the Grim Reaper and had not only bested him myself but had also brought six others through with me. All was well. I resolved to complete my report to Secretary Stimson after Christmas.

But it was not yet all over. At 10:00 Christmas Eve the phone rang. It was Helen Adamson calling from Walter Reed Hospital in Washington. "Hans is dying!" she cried.

"Let me talk to his doctor," I said. Helen brought the colonel in charge to the phone. He confirmed Helen's fears that Hans was in a dangerous condition.

"Would my presence help any?" I asked.

"It can't do any harm, and it might do some good," he said.

"I'll be there by midnight," I said.

I hurried to La Guardia Airport and was fortunate in getting a plane out almost immediately. I arrived in Washington shortly before midnight and went directly to the hospital. Hans was indeed in terrible shape. I pulled up a chair by the side of his bed and started talking to him. The boys on the raft would not have recognized me that night. The old tough Rickenbacker was gone. What was said that night was between Hans and me, but I pleaded with him to live. I did my best to inspire him to live, and I prevailed upon him to join me in prayer, asking God's help for him to live.

After about an hour and a half, the doctors came in and asked me to leave so that he could go to sleep. I went back to the Washington airport, caught a late plane to New York and arrived home about 5:00 A.M.

After Christmas breakfast and the opening of the presents, I called the hospital. Hans was better, much better. I couldn't help choking up over the phone, as indeed I am choking up right now as I recall it. Hans did recover and went on to live a useful and happy life. And so, on Christmas Day, the ordeal ended. Seven had come through, and I was sure that little Alex too was among friends and at home in heaven.

SEVENTEEN

AFTERMATH OF AN ORDEAL

He who does most, lives most. He who lives most, gives most.

It had never occurred to any of us out there on the Pacific that our suffering would result, directly and indirectly, in many measurable benefits to the nation and to the world.

First and most obvious, of course, was the improvement of ferrying operations in the South Pacific. Even before I was able to put my criticisms and recommendations for their correction into the hands of Secretary Stimson, many improvements had already been put into effect. It was our situation that forced quick action. My recommendations encompassed many areas of radio and communications, coordination among the services, proper briefing and the keeping of proper logs. Those improvements, most of which were in effect ninety days after we went down, saved an inestimable number of men, planes and tons of cargo from our fate or worse. They reached their destinations safely in order to contribute to victory.

Bill Cherry was ordered to Washington to work directly with the designers of completely new survival equipment. I unbur-

Mother and Brother Dewey read the good news

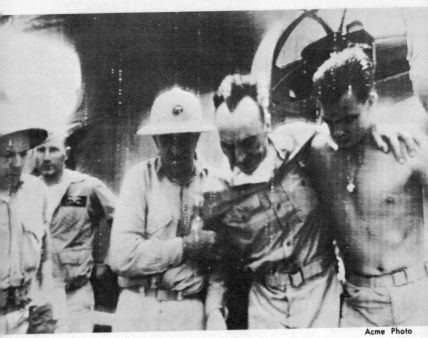

Acme Photo

Author being helped ashore after the rescue

First real meal in 24 days

Acme Photo

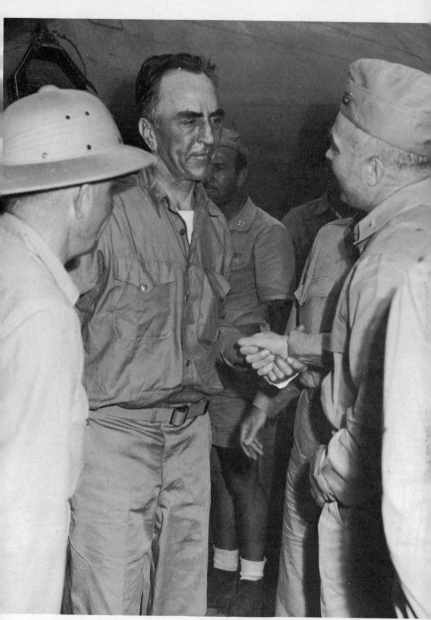

Greeting on arrival at Pago Pago, American Samoa

Arrival in Washington; being greeted by Mrs. Rickenbacker and sons

General H. H. "Hap" Arnold congratulates the author on his return

Welcomed back to New York by Mayor Fiorello La Guardia

U.S. Army Signal Corps

Reporting to nation on national radio hookup from author's home in New York City

Finally reporting to Secretary of War, Henry L. Stimson

dened myself to Secretary Stimson about several suggested improvements in life rafts, beginning with the obvious recommendation that they be made wider and longer. Another was that each raft be supplied with a sheet of appropriate material that could be used as a sail, as a shield against the sun and as a rain catcher. Emergency supplies should include liquids and concentrated food, vitamins, sedatives, first-aid kit, rubber patches and waterproof glue, flares and Very pistols, a large jackknife, fishing tackle and appropriate bait, *all enclosed in absolutely watertight containers.*

Later the Air Force proudly demonstrated one of the new rafts to me. It was equipped with radio, chemical water distillers capable of drawing one and one-half quarts from the sea daily, hermetically sealed rations, sedatives, fishing tackle and other necessities. The new rafts, I was told, were referred to as "Rickenbackers."

"I could live for three months on one of these and come back in good condition," I said.

The chemical water distiller grew out of a separate personal campaign. You have to go without drinking water to realize how delicious this ordinary liquid can be. Ever since my rescue, I have drunk several glasses of water a day for the sheer enjoyment of it.

I gathered a group of scientists and implored them to seek a practical means of desalinating seawater. The immediate result was the development by the Navy of a pill that would make a small quantity of saltwater potable. The small distillation apparatus, which became standard equipment in all life rafts, followed. Interest has steadily grown until today some of the United States' largest corporations are developing and building plants to take the salt out of seawater.

Water is our greatest life-giving natural resource. It is God's gift to man. We must make use of it. The development of nuclear power, the nearest thing to perpetual motion, is making desalination possible on a scale I never dreamed of back in 1943. It will affect the entire population of the world. There is not enough hard money in the world to raise the standard of living of the world's peoples 5 percent in ten years. But by desalinating water from the great oceans we can, without building huge reservoirs and inundating more land, irrigate the deserts and feed half a billion more people. With irrigation from the oceans we can create great wealth.

The Pacific experience has also resulted, at least indirectly, in a helping hand in time of need for thousands of dependents of deceased airmen. After my press conference in Stimson's office, I visited with Hap Arnold. He happened to mention that he and Mrs. Arnold were planning to create an Air Force Aid Society to help the widows and children of airmen killed in action. At the time Mrs. Arnold had raised about $500.

I was already beginning to receive offers from newspapers, magazines and book publishers for the story of our ordeal on the Pacific. My intention was to turn the information over to the Secretary of War and let him dispose of it as he saw fit. After all, it happened while part of my expenses was being paid by the American taxpayers. But what Hap Arnold told me changed my mind.

"I'll sell the story to the highest bidder and donate every penny of whatever I receive to the Air Force Aid Society," I promised him.

Later in New York, I met with Henry Luce of *Time* and *Life* and his associates; I received a bid of $25,000 for the story. It would run in three issues, *Life*'s first serial. In addition, Henry promised to give me a full page to explain the importance of the Air Force Aid Society and solicit contributions.

I dictated the story during the next week. Henry gave me his certified check for $25,000. It was a far greater thrill to give it than to receive it, for I shall never forget the look on Eleanor Arnold's face when I presented Luce's check to her for the Society.

Doubleday & Company published *Seven Came Through* in book form. I donated my royalties and Doubleday its profits to the Air Force Aid Society. The book has never been out of print and has consequently brought in many more thousands of dollars to the Society.

The aviation industry contributed several hundred thousand dollars. The trustees insisted that I become president of the Society, and I have served in this capacity ever since. At this writing, the fund is worth about $25 million. In addition to disbursements to widows and children, the Society supports and administers the Hap Arnold Educational Fund, which makes it possible for a thousand boys and girls, children of Air Force parents, to attend college each year. The Air Force Aid Society has done a world of good, and it was our getting lost on the Pacific that got it off the ground.

Souvenirs of the Pacific ordeal kept popping up over the years. Years later a Marine colonel presented me with the bailing bucket, which had washed ashore on Funafuti. I turned it over to the Air Force Museum in Dayton, Ohio, along with the shoes I had worn, which were in surprisingly good condition, and my old gray hat.

I had resolved that some day I would put my foot on Canton Island. The opportunity came in 1962 when Adelaide and I were returning from an extensive trip through the Orient. Pan American Airways graciously permitted the Pago Pago-Hawaii flight to land on Canton.

As soon as the plane came to a stop, I hurried down the steps and stamped my foot on the sandy soil. "After twenty years," I said, "I finally found you."

I spent an hour on Canton, now a tracking station for the space program and an emergency refueling stop. If in 1942 it had had one-tenth of one percent of all the electronic equipment that is located on the island today, we'd never have missed it.

The aftermath of the Pacific ordeal led to a suggestion that I had never before considered: that I run for public office. In Ohio, my home state, both Democratic and Republican leaders suggested that I run for senator. Several newspapers carried editorials proposing that a new Cabinet position, Secretary of Air, be created and that I assume the office.

Captain Joseph Medill Patterson, publisher of the New York *Daily News* and a powerful behind-the-scenes figure in both New York and national politics, invited me to come to lunch with him and his wife Mary one day. We had hardly sat down when Mrs. Patterson leaned toward me.

"Eddie," she said, "a group of well-known people has asked us to urge you to consider running for the Presidency of the United States."

"Thank you for this great honor, Mary," I said, "but I couldn't possibly consider it. Even if I were qualified for the job, I wouldn't have a chance of being elected. I'm too controversial a figure to be elected, and you know it."

While I was having lunch with the Pattersons, incidentally, C. D. Batchelor, the *Daily News* cartoonist, came in with a large original under his arm. It was the cartoon that he had drawn while I was lost at sea, the one in which he had precipitously finished me off, entitled, "So Long Eddie." He took a black grease pencil out of his pocket, wrote "Beg Pardon, Eddie" across it in big black letters and presented it to me.

The feeling I expressed to the Pattersons remained my position on seeking public office. I felt that I could serve my country much better as a private citizen who happened to have the ear of the people. Later I was named chairman of the National Policy Committee of the High School Victory Corps. It was a job to my liking. Its goal was to enable 6.5 million high-school students to participate in the war effort and to prepare themselves for future service on the battlefield or production line during the last few years in high school. I traveled about the country speaking to these youngsters—boys and girls—and urging them to serve. I received a heartwarming response. I've always felt close to American youth, and in this way I could serve both them and their country.

Of all the changes brought about by those 24 days on the Pacific, one of the greatest was in me. As I remarked, I had always been quietly religious, although there were probably quite a few of my cronies who did not realize it. After our deliverance, which I attribute directly to the providence of the Lord above, I no longer had any hesitancy about expressing my true feelings.

Ray Tucker, the columnist, wrote: "Rickenbacker has become an evangelist without knowing it. There is an unworldly gleam in his eyes and a quaver in his voice these days."

Ray was wrong in only one respect: *I knew*. From the time of the Pacific ordeal, my faith in God was an active, open part of my life.

My full report on the Pacific mission went into Secretary Stimson on January 25, 1943. One recommendation in the emerging field of military transport might have some interest today:

> The ever changing technique in aerial warfare demands that engineers think in terms of designing artillery, automobiles, tractors and airplane parts with the idea of disassembling and reassembling them quickly for transportation by air. The day will come when all cargo and weapons will be transported and will have to be by equally fast cargo planes to keep us with the combat planes in any maneuvers or moving from one place to another.

Twenty-five years later this prediction is becoming a reality.

Less than three months after I had submitted that report, I was summoned to Washington again. Stimson and Arnold had another mission for me. And, from the broad hint that Stimson gave me, I could gather that this one might well be the most interesting of all.

EIGHTEEN

RUSSIAN MISSION

War Department
Washington

To Whom It May Concern:

The bearer of this letter, Captain Edward V. Rickenbacker, will visit the stations and installations of the Army Air Forces in the North Africa, European Theatre, U.S.A. Forces in the Middle East, U.S.A. Forces in India, Burma and China, European Theatre, *and any other areas he may deem necessary for such purposes as he will explain to you in person.*

Captain Rickenbacker, in his capacity as Special Consultant to the Secretary of War, is to receive every possible assistance in the performance of his special duties by all commanders concerned, and he is to be provided with such transportation, both ground and air as he may need and such accommodations as are available.

(signed) Henry L. Stimson
Secretary of War

I have italicized the nineteen key words in those sweeping orders, nineteen words with a meaning that the Secretary did not want put on paper. The phrase "any other areas" referred, in the Secretary's mind and mine, to that huge, enigmatic land that even then was behind an iron curtain, our ally Russia. Few Americans were being permitted to enter Russia in those days. It may have seemed effrontery or naïveté on my part to think that I, as outspoken an anti-Communist as existed in the United States and a citizen very much on the outs with the administration in power, should even consider the possibility of entering Russia. Yet I had hopes not only of going in but also of seeing and hearing enough to make the trip worthwhile.

Early in April 1943, I went to see Secretary Stimson to tell him that, if he wanted me to continue as his special consultant, I was ready to go. After my return from the Pacific in December, I spent three months traveling across the continent, speaking to hundreds of thousands of factory workers, inspiring greater effort on their part. Actually I spent about two weeks at home. That was all the rest I needed.

Stimson gave me an ambitious assignment. By 1943 our military operations were truly worldwide. We went to the large map on the wall of his office and looked at the location of Army Air Forces units. His finger traced the path I would take: from Miami to the West Indies; to Natal, Brazil, the easternmost point of South America; across the Atlantic to Dakar, the westernmost point of Africa; up the coast to Algiers, where General Eisenhower was directing the North Africa campaign; then east along the Mediterranean coast of Africa to Cairo, Egypt, and Abadan and Tehran in Iran, the gateway to Russia through which Lend-Lease supplies were pouring; on eastward to India; and via the airlift over the Himalayan Mountains to China, which was the sole means of supplying the Chinese armies and our own Air Force units fighting the Japanese in that section of the world.

"Mr. Secretary," I said, "if I'm going to be in China, why not arrange an invitation for me to go into Russia through the back door? I know there's a lot you'd like to know about Russia, and General Marshall and General Arnold would too."

"That's a good idea," he said. "You're certainly right about our wanting to know more than we do know about Russian activities. I'll take the matter up with the Secretary of State at the Cabinet meeting tomorrow and let you know his reaction."

The next day, following the Cabinet meeting, he called me at my hotel. In his quiet, unexcited voice, he said, "Eddie, I'd like to see you when you have time."

"My time is your time, Mr. Secretary," I said. "When would you like me to be there?"

"The sooner the better," he said.

"I'll be there in fifteen minutes," I said.

In his office Stimson told me that he had indeed taken the matter up with Cordell Hull, the Secretary of State. Hull had said that the only possible way to get an invitation for me from Russia would be for President Roosevelt to ask Premier Stalin personally. And, Stimson went on wryly, Hull had expressed the opinion that, in view of the personalities involved, he didn't think the President would be interested.

"I agree with him completely," I said. There wasn't much else that I could say. I had publicly criticized the Roosevelt administration for its handling of the war in the Pacific and its involvement with organized labor.

But I had by no means given up the idea of visiting Russia. If our Department of State was not interested in what a trained observer with a background of aeronautical knowledge might turn up in Russia, then I knew another governmental agency that certainly should be—the Lend-Lease administration. Lend-Lease was the program, inaugurated in March 1941, by which America became the arsenal of democracy, sending military supplies to all nations fighting the Axis. Equipment was pouring into Russia; the total value of goods and services Russia received during the war amounted to $11 billion. Aircraft and aircraft engines alone amounted to $1.5 billion.

The director of the Lend-Lease program was Edward R. Stettinius, Jr., who had left United States Steel to take this position with the government. I knew him well. I suggested that we meet in a place where there was no danger of unseen listening devices picking up our conversation. He agreed to come to my suite at the Hotel Carlton.

As I had anticipated, Stettinius was very much interested in my looking into the Lend-Lease situation in Russia. He had a representative there, General Philip R. Faymonville, but it was obvious that Faymonville saw only what he was permitted to see. Ed agreed to do anything that he could to help me get into Russia.

"Here's what you can do," I told him. "You can personally make an appointment for me with both the Soviet ambassador and the official receiver for Lend-Lease equipment for Russia. How about it?"

"I'll be glad to, Eddie," he said.

"Good," I said. "Wait until I've been out of town a few days, then call me in New York and let me know what luck you had. Now there's one other thing. Mr. Stimson will arrange for someone to check my passport through the State Department and have my passport validated for all the countries I intend to visit. You must know someone over there who could just casually happen to stamp Soviet Union in it, too—but not a word to anyone."

"I can handle that, too," he said. About a week later, Stettinius called me in New York.

"Eddie," he said, "you have an appointment at 12:00 noon, April 25, with General Belyaev, the Russian Lend-Lease representative here. You ought to get along well with him. He is an officer in the Russian Air Force and speaks good English. At 1:00 P.M. you have an appointment with the Russian ambassador, Maxim Litvinov. Do you know him?"

"I have met him and respect him," I said. "I believe that he is one Russian who is truly desirous of world peace. I appreciate this greatly, Ed. I hope that something will come of it."

I spent the morning of the 25th visiting with Secretary Stimson and making last-minute preparations for the trip; my scheduled departure was two days off. At the meeting I was entrusted with another message of such sensitivity that it could not be written down. It was for the ears of General Joseph W. "Vinegar Joe" Stilwell, commanding the China-Burma-India theater.

At 12:00 sharp I was in the office of Major General Alexander Ivanovich Belyaev, chairman of the Soviet Purchasing Commission. I told him that I planned to investigate American air units from here to China, advising them on technical details. Russia was receiving and using hundreds of American planes, particularly the P-40 and P-39 fighters and A-20 attack planes. I was thoroughly familiar with those models, I told him, and I sincerely believed that I could help his people get the most out of them.

General Belyaev had obviously been receiving reports of difficulties with American equipment. "We would be delighted to have you come to Russia," he said. "I will cable my government today."

"I have an appointment with your ambassador in a half-hour," I said, "and I intend to discuss the matter with him, too. Perhaps it would be wiser to let him make the initial request, and you get the military to endorse it."

"That would indeed be the best way to handle it," he said. He paused a moment, then went on. "By the way, Captain, the Russian ambassador in China is a very good friend of mine. His name is A. S. Paniushkin. You will see him when you get to Chungking. Would you mind taking a letter to him from me?"

"I'd be glad to," I said, without batting an eye. I'd trade a favor for a favor any day, I thought. To my amazement, he produced a manila envelope already prepared, addressed and with sealing wax all over it. I took it, shook hands and left.

At the Russian embassy, I was escorted into Litvinov's office immediately. He was at a desk in the far corner of the room, and he immediately stood up and came prancing across the room to meet me. He was a little man, with small hands and small feet. He grabbed my hand, pumped it up and down and said, "Captain, I'm glad to see you in the flesh again!"

He motioned to a large leather chair by his desk and asked about the Pacific episode. I told the whole story as briefly as I could. When I finished, he said, "Thank God for your rescue."

I thought all Russians were atheists, but if he wanted to thank God for my rescue I concurred all the way. Then we got down to business. I told him why I believed that a visit to Russia by me would benefit the Soviet Union and the war against Hitler.

Then Litvinov looked me straight in the eye. "I will cable the Foreign Minister, Vyacheslav Molotov, immediately," he said. "The answer may not be forthcoming for a few days. Where will I be able to reach you?"

"I will be at General Eisenhower's headquarters in Algiers in about a week," I said.

"I will cable you there," he said.

I was almost positive that the cable would be waiting for me and that the answer would be affirmative. Belyaev and Litvinov had told me so in the eye language. For many years, I had been a student of this universal language and considered myself fairly proficient at it. The Russians, I had learned that day and would rediscover later, are past masters of the eye language.

The voice, even facial expressions, may speak falsely, but the eyes speak the truth. When I shake hands with a man, I look him in the eye. His handshake may be firm and his greeting may be warm, but if his eyes look away, fail to meet mine or even flicker momentarily I know that there is something wrong somewhere. If I ask a person a question and his eyes flicker before or during his answer, I suspect the truth of that answer. Few men, in short, can control their eyes when their voices are not telling the truth.

Both the general and the ambassador, however, had looked me full in the eye without the tiniest flicker of reservation or indecision. When Litvinov said that he would cable me in Algiers, his eyes were telling me that he meant it.

I left Washington the next day for Miami, where the trip would officially begin. With me was General William P. Nuckols of the U.S. Air Force, my military aide. General Hap Arnold made a special effort to wish me Godspeed. "Eddie, you're taking a hell of a long trip over a hell of a lot of big country," he said, looking at me with a special intensity.

Adelaide met me in Miami. So did Doctor Alexander Dahl,

the Atlanta osteopath who had done me so much good after I had been smashed up in the airplane crash two years before. I'd been having a little trouble—stiffness, numbness, lack of circulation—and I thought that Doctor Dahl would be able to keep me physically ready for the hard work that lay ahead. He was delighted to make the trip. At my request, the War Department appointed him "special consultant on military morale" and arranged for him to accompany me.

It occurred to me that I would be visiting with the wives of military and governmental leaders of the countries I was going to visit. I asked Adelaide what they would appreciate the most.

She replied unhesitatingly, "nylon stockings." At the time they were not available for love or money, but friendship was a different matter. I called an old friend in North Carolina, and he had a shipment en route that day. In addition, Adelaide obtained for me three dozen sets of compacts, each with an extra carton of powder, and three dozen lipsticks, each with an extra unit. In Miami, it occurred to me that I had nothing for the children. I gave Adelaide a $50 bill and asked her to buy all the spearmint chewing gum that she could find at the commissary. She came back with a footlocker full. We were ready to travel.

The Air Force had assigned me a C-87, a B-24 modified for transport service, which I would pick up in Africa. For the first part of our trip, therefore, Dahl and I boarded a C-54, along with several military passengers. We stopped at the Air Force base at Puerto Rico, then continued on.

Flying along the northeast coast of South America, the crew told me that it was one of our most dangerous runs. Beneath us lay the interminable jungle, a sea of green, with no landmarks for hundreds of miles. There were few radio aids. Though it was thousands of miles from the fighting fronts, weather reports and other advice were given in a code that some of our young and inexperienced pilots did not always read correctly. As a result of this confusion, we had lost many planes and men along the route, and when they went down in that jungle they were lost forever. When we stopped in Belém, Brazil, for fuel, I radioed Hap Arnold suggesting that there be fewer restrictions and more air aids on the route and that, because of the heavy losses, whatever was to be done, be done quickly. I learned later that Hap had taken immediate action.

During the flight across the Atlantic from Natal to Dakar, Doctor Dahl gave me a treatment and loosened my joints and muscles up again. As far as we knew, it was the first time an osteopath had practiced his profession two miles up over the open sea.

My first small chill of apprehension came on the flight from Dakar to Marrakech, Morocco, some 1,500 miles over the vast Sahara, in a C-47. (I was to pick up my C-87 at Cairo.) If I had my choice between 24 days on the Sahara and 24 days on the Pacific, I'd take the Pacific all over again. At both Dakar and Marrakech, as at all major stations, American personnel were assembled so that I could talk to them and hear their problems. At those stations, far from the front, there was some discontent because our boys felt that they were not contributing their full measure to the war effort. I talked to them at length about other bases that I had visited, from the States to the combat zones, and assured them that their participation was of great importance in the over-all war effort.

At Casablanca I visited several installations, including an enormous assembly line for fighter planes, and spoke to a group of about ten thousand young replacements on the way to the fighting front. There was also a large aviation installation at Oran on the north coast of Algeria. From Oran it was only a short hop to Algiers, the center of the combined American and British operations in North Africa.

On landing in Algiers, our plane was met by a colonel, a captain and a sergeant, all three of whom conducted me immediately to General Eisenhower's headquarters in the St. George Hotel. They were not unpleasant, but neither were they very communicative. I wondered what I had done now. At headquarters, Major General Walter Bedell Smith, Ike's chief of staff, relieved some of my worry by greeting me in a friendly fashion. He asked to see my orders from the Secretary of War, commented on their comprehensiveness, then motioned to the door.

"Go on in," he said. "The old man's getting a haircut."

I entered, and there was Ike with a barber. He told me to make myself at home. When the barber had finished and departed, Ike strode to his desk, picked up a piece of paper, shoved it under my nose and said, "What in hell does this mean?"

It was a communication from Ambassador Litvinov in Washington. I read it carefully. It said that Molotov had assented to my visiting the Soviet Union and that I should report to the Russian ambassador on arrival in Chungking.

Eisenhower was looking at me intently, almost belligerently, waiting for an answer to his question. I put my finger to my lips.

"Shhh," I told the commanding general with a straight face. "That's a military secret."

I had to laugh at his expression. After exacting from him a promise to keep the matter secret, I told him the whole story. As I expected, he told me fervently that he would cooperate in any way, as he himself would be vitally interested in any information that I could bring back from that great question mark, the Soviet Union.

"There's a big favor you can do me, General," I said. "A major in your intelligence section is an old friend of mine, a fellow pilot in World War I. His name is Alden Sherry. I would greatly appreciate it if you would assign him to me for this mission. He's a clever, inquisitive sort of chap, and he would be of great help to me."

"You can have him," Eisenhower said. "And I wish you luck on your mission."

Sherry was stationed at Constantine, two hundred miles to the east. In the meantime, I had plenty of work to do in Algiers. The North African campaign was a pilot's paradise with the exception of the poor P-39 pilots, who were forced to attack at low altitudes, where the Germans outperformed them badly. The morale among the P-39 pilots was zero.

In the early days in North Africa, when things had been tougher, combat crews had been promised home leave on completion of 25 missions, or 200 hours of combat service. Many pilots now had that number of missions, but the high command realized that it simply could not spare them from the successful prosecution of the campaign.

I suggested that I might be able to alleviate this problem to some degree. My mission called for me to visit all Air Force units. I proposed that, in connection with these visits, I speak to the members of all combat units and lay the facts on the line. The brass was happy to hand me this hot potato, and I immediately went to work. In one week I covered twenty-four groups, in one day visiting six groups that were stationed close together.

"Victory here in North Africa is only a steppingstone to the bigger job to be done across the Mediterranean in Europe," I told them. "In my opinion Germany is not going to be cracked before the fall of 1944, if then. You can't go now, men. The fight is just beginning."

I was brutally frank, but I could afford to be. I was a civilian. All the men there knew my attitude toward the Air Force, that my sympathies were with them. As several of them told me later, they didn't like what I had to say, but they were glad that there was someone who had the guts to tell them the truth.

Lieutenant General James H. "Jimmy" Doolittle and I were having dinner at his hotel in Algiers when the Germans staged a bombing raid. We stepped onto the balcony to watch the fireworks. I have never seen so much antiaircraft activity. An enemy plane burst into flames.

"This stuff they're shooting up there has got to come down," Jimmy said and went inside, but I insisted on staying out to see the fun. The next morning I found two chunks of heat-blued metal where I'd been standing.

I picked up Sherry at Constantine. He was eager to come along. One of the units that I was scheduled to meet was the 57th Fighter Group in the Constantine area. Sherry said that he could take us to it. We flew northward up the coast. After flying for several miles without finding the fighter group, we flew southward and landed at an English field to ask directions. The commanding officer, an angry, red-faced colonel, came up and demanded at the top of his voice just what were we bloody blighters doing flying over behind the German lines in an unarmed C-47? He said that we were leaving a trail of flak behind us in the sky.

If we had found any kind of airport, we'd have landed, thinking it was the 57th. And we would have wound up as prisoners of war. I looked at Sherry. The same memory passed through our minds: that time in France in 1918 when he had almost taken us behind the German lines. It was the second time that he'd almost gotten me captured by the Germans.

In the area, I visited with many well-known personages of World War II, including Generals Eisenhower and Smith; British Air Marshal Sir Arthur W. Tedder, one of the most capable and brilliant airmen I ever met; my old friend Tooey Spaatz, who was serving as Tedder's deputy, and Generals Elwood R. "Pete" Quesada, Jimmy Doolittle, George E. Stratemeyer and Lewis H. Brereton.

I found my discussions with these great leaders interesting and informative, but it was my visits with the combat units in the field that were the most rewarding. I felt at home whenever I was with them because wherever I went I was greeted with a flashing smile and a "Hello, Captain Eddie!"

Over and over again I listened to those young men tell me how their love for America and their appreciation for the American ideology had been strengthened by the great contrast in the conditions they found overseas. They expressed hearty approval of my campaign against the labor racketeers, and many said that they had actually written me letters cheering me on. I had not received those letters, and I wondered if they had been stopped by military censorship.

There was a marked difference between the thinking of those men and of the men I had served with back in World War I. In 1918 we were caught up in a great adventure, with the emphasis on thrills and excitement. In 1943 there was a sense of dedication and obligation to win this war and to preserve freedom, liberty, opportunity, comfort and standard of living for present and for future generations.

Most of the men were willing to stay and fight it out until the enemy was destroyed. Though these boys were doing their best, they were haggard with exhaustion. There were not enough reserve pilots and combat crews. My recommendation for increased numbers of relief pilots and crews was eventually approved by the high command.

Even in war there is time for fun. When we finally found the 57th Fighter Group, I talked with the boys until midnight, then spent the night with them. When I turned in, there on the cot was a rubber raft.

"We thought you'd be more comfortable on something you were used to," the CO said with a wry grin. Then they all roared. The next morning they pulled the raft out on the desert, put a couple of captured German machine guns in it and insisted that I climb in while everyone crowded around and took a picture of Rickenbacker on a raft in the desert.

The 94th Squadron, named after my old World War I unit, was in North Africa. Before leaving the United States, I had had a jeweler in New York make up insignia pins with the hat-in-the-ring motif and had persuaded Hap Arnold to approve them. I took them with me when I visited my old squadron and handed them out at dinner.

From Constantine we flew over Tunis and the Libyan desert, viewing with awe the wreckage strewn over the desert by the retreating Germans, to Benghazi, Libya, and then to Cairo, Egypt. The Air Corps supply depot, built in the desert just outside Cairo, was so large that it took me three days to go through it. There were thousands of American soldier-mechanics, building, repairing or overhauling engines, aircraft and motor vehicles. They had built a steel mill and a foundry, and they even had a lens-grinding operation.

We also had a large hospital in Cairo. It was filled with patients, many of whom, the cream of American youth, were maimed and wrecked for life. I tried to give them a word of cheer to keep their spirits alive, reminding those who were worst off that they would soon be taken home.

While I was in Cairo, I called on our consul general, who invited me to lunch with him. Maxim Litvinov and General Patrick J. Hurley, who had been Secretary of War under President Hoover and was now ambassador-at-large to the Middle East with headquarters at Cairo, were also there.

Pat Hurley told me that he had been in Brazil at the time I had crashed in Atlanta. He had heard a report that I had been killed, and that evening at a small gathering, he went on, he had proposed a toast to a departed friend. One toast led to another. The next morning he learned that I was still alive and that his headache was unnecessary.

Then came the time when I was lost in the Pacific. Hurley was in Moscow. After ten days, he was convinced that I was dead and again put on a kind of absentee wake, complete with vodka. Again a headache.

Not long after that he returned to Washington. Groggy and tired from the long trip, he stepped out on the ramp, and there he saw an emaciated apparition.

"I blinked and looked again," Hurley said, his eyes twinkling, "and then I thought, 'My God, this pilot has landed me in hell— there's Rickenbacker.'"

Later he abruptly asked, "Are you going to run for the Presidency in 1944?" I gave him the same answer that I had given to Cap and Mary Patterson: "No!" He persisted, and then his interest became clear: He wanted to be my running mate for the Vice-Presidency! We might not have made a bad team at that. Hurley had an enormous fund, in gold, to dispense among the North African tribesmen as he saw fit. I laughingly commented that he could easily have set aside a few million as a campaign fund.

As we parted at the conclusion of the luncheon, Litvinov said that he was looking forward to having lunch with me in Moscow.

The C-87 that I had been promised was waiting for us at Cairo. The pilot was Captain William F. Richmond, formerly of

Northwest Airlines and a good man. He had a full crew consisting of copilot, navigator, engineer and radio operator. This new 4-motor luxury plane carried us over the Suez Canal; over Jerusalem, Bethlehem, Jericho and the biblical cities whose names I had learned in Sunday school, and on over Iraq to Abadan, Iran, at the head of the Persian Gulf.

At Abadan a large plant had been constructed to assemble P-39s, P-40s, A-20s and Spitfires. The heat was unbearable; it reached as high as 130 degrees in the sun at noon. It was impossible to produce in such heat; the men worked in shifts, from 4:00 A.M. to 7:00 A.M. and from 3:00 P.M. to 8:00 P.M. Planes assembled there were flown north across Iran to Tehran, up the Caspian Sea to Russia and eventually to the front. I found morale poor and production low because two service squadrons had been transferred to North Africa, leaving a serious manpower shortage. I sent off an immediate evaluation of the situation, with a recommendation that more personnel be sent in. As these very planes embodied recommendations that I had made previously, I had hopes that this one would be carried out, and it was.

Karachi, India (now in Pakistan), was the next stop when we arrived May 21. This remote city, halfway around the world, was the crossroads of the Air Transport Command routes. We proceeded on to New Delhi.

I found India most depressing. People were existing in the most deplorable conditions imaginable, in squalor, filth and stench. Such abject misery could result only from exploitation of the many by the few. I felt that such people could hardly be ready for independence.

At Pandepeshar I had the honor of decorating thirty officers and enlisted men of the 7th Bomber Group with newly arrived Distinguished Flying Crosses. We visited two other units in the same general area, then moved on to Calcutta. It was so hot that touching the exterior of the plane actually seared the hands. Several fighter squadrons were located in the Brahmaputra Valley running northeast of Calcutta toward China. The squadrons protected the airlift over the Himalayan Mountains. Groups of cargo planes were scattered through the area, and I visited all of them. Morale was low, and so was tonnage at the time of my visit. Twenty-six transports had been lost in the previous six months. Living conditions were intolerable, and over all management was not too good.

I noted several recommendations for improvement. Command changes were later made, and the Hump airlift over high mountains and enemy-held terrain became the first great proving ground for military air transportation.

As our plane was unarmed, we were not permitted to take it over the Hump. We made the trip in an armed C-87, crossing at nineteen thousand feet.

We landed at Kunming. I talked with the boys of a fighter squadron there, then proceeded to another airport just thirty minutes away. As we landed on one runway, a total of forty thousand Chinese men, women and children were building another runway—by hand. They were actually cracking large stones into small pieces with hand hammers and placing them, piece by piece, into the foundation laid for the runway.

Using Kunming as a base, I flew to several Air Force units in southeast China. At Chengtu we followed by radio the activities of a squadron of B-24s on a bombing mission with fighter escort. They were jumped by a pack of Japanese Zeros. Suddenly one of the American boys screamed, "I got him!" and we all let out a cheer.

For the rest of our travels in China, we were assigned a C-47. The pilot was Captain Al Novak, formerly a senior pilot with Eastern Air Lines. I appreciated having an experienced man assigned to us in this far-off land, especially after hearing a hushed-up story about General Arnold. His plane had gotten lost flying the Hump and had flown over Japanese-held territory in China before making it back to Kunming, four and a half hours overdue. So that was the significance of his parting remark when I was leaving Washington: "Eddie, you're taking a hell of a long trip over a hell of a lot of big country!"

Coming into Chungking I was again glad that we had Al Novak. The landing strip had been cut out of the side of a hill. It was only about two hundred feet wide, with the cut on one side and a hundred-foot drop to the river on the other side. The approach is between two hills so close together that you'd think the wing tips would touch. But Novak brought us down smoothly and safely.

In Chungking I asked our acting ambassador, George Achinson, to make an appointment for me with the Russian ambassador.

"He called a week ago and asked me when you were going to arrive," Achinson said.

Achinson was looking at me closely, and I didn't blame him. The Russians knew more about my plans than our own Department of State did.

Now a serious hitch developed. General Stilwell was not in China. I would have to go back to New Delhi to see him. Then I could proceed to Tehran and enter Russia through there.

At 10:00 the next morning, I called on the Russian ambassador, A. S. Paniushkin, an enthusiastic individual who greeted me effusively in good English. He was about 38 years old and had formerly been an artillery officer. We got along fine. He promised to wire the Russian ambassador at Tehran and assured me that I'd have no trouble there. Within fifteen minutes he had validated my passport and those of General Nuckols, Alden Sherry, Doctor Dahl and the crew.

"I always thought of aviators as a fast-working lot," I told him, "but you artillery officers are even faster. I expected the visas to take a day or two."

"Perhaps there is a reason," he said with a smile. He produced a letter and showed me the signature. I recognized it as Molotov's. Paniushkin translated it for me. It said to show me every courtesy and consideration and to expedite the visas.

Paniushkin asked me to return to the embassy the next day to see the Russian documentary film on the battle of Stalingrad, which had just arrived. On the way, I stopped to have tea with

Madame Sun Yat-sen, widow of the founder of the Chinese Republic and one of the three famous American-educated daughters of Charley Jones Soong, a wealthy Shanghai publisher who had also been educated in the United States. One of her sisters had married the current Chinese leader, Generalissimo Chiang Kai-shek, the other H. H. Kung, banker and finance minister.

Madame Sun's idea of "tea" turned out to be vodka and champagne. I found her attractive and alert, with a good sense of humor, but definitely leaning to the left. She was later to become Deputy Chairman of the government of Communist China. Our session was rewarding and informative. We went on to the Russian embassy together.

After the film, which was most interesting, Ambassador Paniushkin whispered an invitation to both of us to stay on with a few other guests for a buffet supper. I soon had occasion to learn a Russian phrase, *do dna,* which means "Bottoms up!" After several *do dnas,* I sent Major Sherry back to our quarters for presents for the ladies—the compacts, lipsticks and nylon hose I'd brought from the States. They went over in a big way.

The situation among the American forces in China was not as carefree. Neither General Claire L. Chennault, commanding the Air Force in China, nor General Stilwell could get along with General Clayton Bissell, who commanded the 10th Air Force in India. Furthermore, Stilwell's contempt for the Chinese leader, Generalissimo Chiang Kai-shek, was well known; he publicly referred to him as "Peanut." To make a clean sweep of it, Stilwell didn't like the British in the area either.

Everyone was playing his own little political game. Chennault, for example, would go to Chiang or to Madame Chiang, who was almost as powerful. They in turn would go to President Roosevelt, who would usually decide for Chiang. I was glad to leave China. Not long after that, incidentally, Bissell was relieved, and George Stratemeyer, a strong and capable general, was sent in to command the Air Force in both China and India, with Chennault as his deputy; Stratemeyer, in turn, served as deputy to Stilwell. This move straightened out the situation to some degree.

A major problem in China was the simple fact that we were there. Differences between the United States and China and between Americans and Chinese were so great that bridging the gap seemed hopeless. I liked the Chinese people, a cheerful and industrious lot. But the upper strata were preying upon the masses and robbing us blind. The United States was pouring men, money and material into China to help the Chinese fight off the oppressors, but the Chinese were taking advantage of us at every turn.

The house that General Stilwell occupied was leased from T. V. Soong, brother of Madame Chiang Kai-shek and Chinese ambassador to the United States. It was an attractive house, which in America would be in the $25,000-$30,000 price range. In China it surely could have been replaced for $15,000. Yet we were leasing it for $50,000 a year—in gold. And I know from personal experience that it was infested with bedbugs.

At breakfast with a high Chinese official one morning, I asked him to explain the workings of the black market in Chinese yen to me. His explanation didn't make sense, and I later found out the reason why: He was up to his ears in the black market himself.

A provincial governor and prominent member of the Generalissimo's staff was known to be selling tungsten to the Japanese.

I could cite many such instances. I believed that we should help the Chinese fight the Japanese, but I also thought that we should follow up our money with a closer inspection of who was receiving it and for what it was being used. Too much of the money we were pouring into China was enriching the already rich, rather than prosecuting the war or helping the Chinese masses.

Flying back over the Hump to India in an armed C-87, we took the low-level route over Japanese-occupied territory and flew over several Japanese airports at the bend of the Salween River between China and Burma. I went back to the 50-caliber machine gun in the tail of the plane and fired several shots down at one of the fields as a farewell gesture. About halfway over the Hump, the captain invited me up to the cockpit to listen to the Japanese on the radio. At the time they were singing silly songs and jamming the frequency. But they had been known to give false instructions and lure inexperienced pilots to their deaths.

We picked up the C-87 assigned to me at Jorhat, where it was 130 degrees in the sun, and proceeded to New Delhi. Stilwell and I met for breakfast at 6:30 A.M. at his headquarters. Vinegar Joe was bitter. Roosevelt had refused to listen to his difficulties with Chiang Kai-shek. After a 2½-hour conference, during which I delivered my secret message, we drove back to the airport together. Stilwell was leaving for China at 10:00 A.M.; I was taking off in the opposite direction at the same hour.

That night we stopped in Karachi, where I talked to the station personnel for about an hour, and pushed on toward Tehran early in the morning. I was impatient; this trip was taking too long. After a quick look at the map, I ordered the pilot to proceed to Tehran in a straight line, across the mountains of Pakistan and the rugged plateau of Iran. That could have been a mistake. At Tehran I learned that we were the first to fly over that desolate region, and we may well have been the last.

General Donald H. Connolly, commanding the Persian Gulf Service Command, consisting of forty thousand Americans along the supply line from the Persian Gulf to the Caspian Sea, had formerly been the liaison officer between the Air Force and the Civil Aeronautics Board, and I knew him well. We buzzed the city before landing, and, sure enough, within a few minutes Don arrived with two or three staff members. He had heard that I was in Asia and correctly assumed that the plane was mine.

His operation was surely one of the most efficient in the world. He had rebuilt both the railroads and the highways from Abadan to Tehran and the docks on the Tigris River, where thousands of tons of war material were passing to the Russian front each and every day.

Connolly was doing such a tremendous job that I thought surely he deserved a trip to Russia to see what was happening to all those supplies. When I visited the Russian ambassador, a former newspaper publisher about forty years old, I requested a visa for General Connolly and his aide.

I was constantly being entertained and constantly being asked questions. At one function, the Turkish ambassador asked what role his country should play in the war. I said that, in my opinion, Turkey should permit us to establish air bases in that country. In answer to another question, I said that I would like to see bases in Eastern Siberia, from which we could bomb Japan.

It never occurred to me that this informal discussion could possibly cause all the trouble it did later.

I had heard of the Russian characteristic of saying neither "no" nor "yes" but waiting. General George C. Marshall, Chief of Staff of the United States Army, and General Arnold had been kept waiting and had never visited Russia. Now it was happening to me.

But I was convinced, from what I had read in Litvinov's eyes, that I would be welcome in Russia. The delay could be due only to the addition of Connolly and his aide to the party. I had no choice but to sacrifice them.

But we had to save face. I asked Don to arrange a hurried visit to Cairo. The Russian ambassador was respectfully asked to withdraw the request for Connolly's visa, as he had been hastily summoned to Cairo.

The following evening at 7:30 our visas were delivered. We could leave the next morning. It was tough news for Don Connolly. "Well, at least I know now where I stand," he said.

At 6:00 A.M., July 19, 1943, our C-87 took off from the field at Tehran and headed toward Russia. The crew was augmented by a Russian navigator and radio operator, two hard-eyed individuals who were obviously members of the secret police. Also on board were several cases of a good brand of vodka. I wondered about taking vodka to Moscow—it was like taking bourbon to Kentucky!—but the bottles only cost a dollar and a quarter apiece, and I couldn't get too badly hurt.

We climbed to about fourteen thousand feet and went through a pass in the Elburz Mountains. Once through the pass, we found ourselves over green and beautiful countryside. At last we were en route to our destination, and our spirits rose.

Proceeding up the western shore of the Caspian Sea we passed over Grozny, the farthest point of the German advance, and saw the trenches and tank traps beneath us. At Astrakhan, where the mighty Volga flows into the Caspian, the many deltas and channels reminded me of the mouth of the Mississippi below New Orleans. The country beneath us was green farmland.

We landed at Kuibyshev shortly after 1:00 P.M. It had served as the capital of Russia while Moscow was under siege. All the embassies had moved there, and some of the American staff still remained. Several Russian officers and the bewildered American chargé d'affaires, Warwick Perkins, met us at the airport. The Russians had known we were coming for weeks; the American embassy had just been notified.

The fields on either side of the highway seemed to be bursting with grain, and the Russians said that indeed they were anticipating a bumper crop. The people seemed strong and healthy. Everywhere we looked women were working, and working hard, at heavy labor.

That night Perkins took us to an opera. I noticed two familiar faces in the audience. I had seen them before at the airport.

"Why are they shadowing me this closely?" I asked Perkins.

"They're not spying on you so much as protecting you," he said. "They don't want anything to happen to you which would cause the government any embarrassment."

We spent the night in the embassy. As I was getting up next morning, Sherry came dashing into my room yelling, "My God, Eddie, we have a flush toilet!" It was the first one we had seen in weeks.

We took a twisting path to Moscow next morning, following our Russian navigator's instructions in detail to avoid the fluid front line beneath us. The countryside was much like that of our own Middle West. In the villages houses lined the roads. Behind each house was a beautiful little garden plot. Perkins had told me that it was the only way the government could obtain additional food production. When the people came home after working all day at the cooperative farm, they had no desire to put in any more work for the state. The government leased them these plots of five-eighths of an acre, with the stipulation that the land must be cultivated only after working hours. Each family could have 95 percent of all it could grow, to eat or to sell as it saw fit.

This small free-enterprise system contributed much to the food supply of Russia. What interested me was that it was closer to free enterprise than to Communism. It was the first evidence that I saw of the beginning of Russia's slow, but marked, shift away from pure Communism.

On landing in Moscow, we were met by a group of high-ranking Russian officers and three confused-looking Americans, Admiral William H. Standley, our ambassador; his military attaché, General Joseph A. Michela, and the naval attaché, Admiral Jack H. Duncan. Standley came running up to me and whispered, "What in the hell are you doing here, Eddie?" He had been notified of my arrival just thirty minutes before and had hastily called the two attachés together to come out and meet me. All I had time to say, before the Russian officers came up to greet us was, "It's a military secret!"

When we were alone, I explained my mission to him. He and the other members of the embassy whom I took into my confidence did not believe that the Russians would permit me to see or hear anything. General Faymonville, head of our Lend-Lease mission in Russia, joined the meeting and seemed to be of the same opinion. I did not think that Faymonville had seen very much himself. I had memorized a long list of things that I wanted to do—visit several different types of war-production factories, including aviation, see the defenses of Moscow and talk with both the commanding officers and the pilots flying the planes, visit the front—figuring that if I did only a percentage of these things I would be fortunate.

I spent the rest of the day driving around the city, seeing the sights. It was truly the face of a nation at war. The people had a purposeful air. There was no shopping; only those stores distributing the most vital consumer goods were open. Some of the closed stores displayed papier-mâché imitations of what they would sell if they had it. The butcher shop, for example, had some very realistic imitation sausages in the window.

The next morning General Michela came to my room with a cablegram from Secretary Stimson. It was shocking, amazing. In it Stimson said that he had been advised by the British and Turkish ministers at Tehran that, first, I was trying to talk Turkey into giving us air bases; second, I was attempting to obtain information on the Siberian front, and, third, I had stated that I was representing the President of the United States. Stimson recommended that I leave Russia immediately and await further orders at Tehran.

All this trouble, of course, grew out of the conversation I had had with the Turkish ambassador. Also involved was the intense American-British rivalry in Tehran, resulting from Don Connolly's forcible and successful operation of his command. I had reason to believe that it was the British who had deliberately misrepresented the facts.

I immediately replied to the Secretary by cable telling him exactly what information I had requested from the Russians through our embassy and that anything they had heard contrary to these facts was a dastardly lie. I said that I believed that I could finish the mission in two weeks. Admiral Standley supplemented my cable with one of his own, insisting that I be permitted to stay and finish the job I had started so well.

I realized that tremendous pressures were being placed on Stimson. The situation was compounded by the fact that, of all the news services, only TASS, the Russian agency, had ignored my request for strict secrecy and had broken in the United States the story that I was in Moscow. The left-wing press immediately began screaming to high heaven—what was labor-baiting Ricken-backer doing in the People's Democracy?

But I stayed in Moscow. Things were going too well for me to give up. Standley took me to a ceremony in the Kremlin at which twenty American Distinguished Service Medals were presented to heroes of the Russian Air Force and twenty American Navy Crosses were presented to heroes of the Russian Navy. Maxim Litvinov, who had returned to Russia with a heart condition, was at the ceremony, and so was Foreign Minister Molotov himself. Litvinov came over to welcome me to Russia and to make good his promise to invite me to lunch.

We met in a beautiful mansion in Moscow, which was used for entertaining foreign guests. Molotov was present, and so was Marshal Georgi Zhukov, Chief of Staff of the Russian Army. Litvinov himself served as our interpreter.

The dining room was magnificent. The table linen was white as snow, and the service was of solid gold.

"Have you ever lost any of this through the activity of souvenir hunters?" I asked Litvinov, gesturing at the gold service.

He looked directly at me, smiled and said, "Not up to now."

Luncheon consisted of fresh caviar, black bread and rich butter and cold fish, all washed down with vodka.

"What is it that you wish to do here and what do you wish to see?" Molotov asked me through Litvinov.

I methodically ticked my list off as Litvinov wrote down each request and Molotov and Zhukov watched. Neither showed any signs of understanding what I was saying. When I had finished, however, Molotov looked at me and spoke. Litvinov translated.

"The captain, of course, has his interpreter with him?"

"No, sir," I said, "I don't. I came here to learn what problems you are having with American aviation equipment and to try to help you surmount them. If I had brought along an interpreter, he wouldn't know any more than I do. What I want you to do, Mr. Molotov, is to give me a man who is a good pilot and a good aeronautical engineer and who also speaks English well enough so that we will be able to understand each other."

There was an immediate flash in Molotov's eyes. He said a few words to Litvinov, and Litvinov nodded.

"The Foreign Minister has asked me to arrange with the military to show you whatever it is you want to see, and to answer your questions promptly and honestly," he said. "You will hear from me as soon as the war office has made the arrangements and found an interpreter for you."

"Thank you," I said calmly. Inside I was shouting with joy. That bit about the interpreter had been the clincher. I knew by means of the old eye language that I would see much of what I wanted to see. We had made a deal.

I celebrated by going out to the plane, loading up a truckload of C-rations, a dozen cartons of cigarettes and four dozen cases of vodka and taking them down to the Metropole Hotel, where the news correspondents were staying. "Here," I said, "spread these around."

Taking vodka to Moscow had not been such a bad idea after all. Even diplomats were strictly rationed to one bottle a month, at $10 in gold.

Though things were shaping up well as far as the Russian government was concerned, I still seemed to be in the doghouse with my own. A cablegram from the Department of State, addressed to me at Tehran, told me to stay there until I heard from the War Department. They obviously thought I had returned to Tehran like a good boy. Finally Secretary Stimson cabled to the effect that he believed my statements and that I should stay on and finish all that I was able to do. He concluded with warm reassurances.

The call I was waiting for came at 11:00 P.M. I was to be at the headquarters of the Russian Air Force at 6:00 A.M. I was there on the dot. A young Russian captain named Smolazov, a handsome 6-footer disabled for combat service, was waiting for me. He spoke English better than I did. I asked him a few questions about aeronautics, and it was obvious that he was a good engineer.

We drove to the headquarters of the Moscow defense command, where a mysterious colonel joined us. I never did find out who he was or what he wanted. He pretended not to understand English, but his eyes gave him away. Smolazov took us to the command post, deep underground. The commander of the operation was waiting for us. Smolazov was about to introduce me when the commander took a second look, rushed over, threw his arms around me and cried, "Ah, Eddie!"

What a coincidence! I even had old friends in Russia. The commander was Andrei Youmachev. He had been the copilot on the Russian single-engine plane that had flown over the North Pole from Moscow to San Jacinto, California, in July 1937. I had been asked to entertain the pilot and copilot when they came through New York, and I did, in real American fashion and for a solid week. Now here was the commander of one of the most sensitive military operations in Russia, pounding me on the back and pumping my hand. I couldn't have asked for a better stamp of approval.

After our reunion, I asked Andrei my most important question: "Why are the Germans bombing locations as far as five hundred miles behind Moscow but not Moscow itself?"

Andrei smiled. "I will show you," he said. He handed me a stop watch. "When I telephone, you push."

He picked up a telephone on his desk and bellowed a command into it. I pushed the button on the stop watch.

"Now come quick," he said. We hurried up to an observation post. There was not a plane in the sky. Suddenly, they began to appear—American P-39s. In 39 seconds I had counted one hundred of them. Andrei beamed at me. There was my answer.

Back in the command post, he showed me the locations of air bases around Moscow on a large wall map. They were strategically placed in three concentric rings. Andrei called for his staff car and took us first to one of the bases in the outside ring. At that base a squadron of planes sat at the end of the runway, engines running, pilots at the controls, radios tuned in to headquarters. Each pilot served a 4-hour tour of duty.

It was from this and other bases in the outside ring that the planes I saw in the air over Moscow had come. At the second circle of bases the pilots sat in the planes, but the engines weren't running. They were started and warmed up once an hour to keep them ready. These planes would be about ten seconds behind the outer circle. At the inner-circle base we visited, the pilots were gathered in a heated tent. The planes were just outside and were warmed up every two hours.

"Commander," I said in admiration, "now I understand thoroughly why the Germans do not attempt to bomb Moscow."

Back at headquarters, he showed me on another map where the antiaircraft artillery defenses were located. The city bristled with them like a porcupine. He insisted on driving us to several of these emplacements too. He obviously wanted to convince me that these batteries were not simply marks on a map but the real thing.

As we drove around, we discussed every phase of the operation. I talked at length with the pilots at the bases. The pilots had learned to fly on Russian aircraft, of course, and, as far as the American planes were concerned, they were more or less self-taught. I was able to pass on to them a great deal of information that I had garnered in my previous missions and that would enable them to improve their handling of these planes. Pilots and engineers both could see that these technical improvements would mean a great deal to the Russian Air Force.

After a long, cold day, Andrei said, "Now we will have lunch." The dining room was underground. Andrei's staff was already seated. Even the military operated on the strange Russian schedule: late breakfast, midday snack, lunch at 6:00 and dinner at midnight or later.

A bottle of vodka was on the table. The mysterious colonel filled our tulip-shaped glasses to the brim, about two ounces, and said, "To the great American Air Force!"

I stood, acknowledged the toast, took a sip of vodka, and sat down.

Do dna, do dna! he roared. I knew what that meant—bottoms up! Every eye in the room was on me. I was a foreigner, an imperialist and a capitalist, but I was also an airman, and I was being challenged by this colonel who unquestionably also represented the NKVD. I didn't have much choice but to stand up again, raise my glass and gulp it down. Incidentally, I don't like vodka. Give me bourbon any day. Vodka has no taste—it's liquid fire.

"Rickenbacker," I thought, "you'd better go on the offensive." I took the bottle, filled his glass to the brim and said, "To the great Red Air Force!"

It was *do dna* all over again. Out of the corner of my eye, I saw that my interpreter was cheating. Andrei, seated next to me, nudged me with his elbow and said, "Eat, eat."

I took a slice of thick bread, spread about an eighth of an inch of butter on it and about a quarter of an inch of caviar on top of that and ate. In the meantime, the colonel was proposing another round. He wasn't fooling me. The idea was to get me plastered and loose-tongued so that I'd talk carelessly on the drive back to the embassy. The younger officers were looking on with sympathy. They knew what that liquid dynamite could do.

We drank another toast and another. Now everyone was cheating except the colonel and me. I was fighting the alcohol mentally, fighting to keep it out of my bloodstream, fighting to keep a clear head. As lunch concluded, the colonel began to talk loudly and roar with laughter. I filled his glass for the seventh time. He looked at it, then suddenly his face went slack. He slid off his chair and under the table.

The Air Force officers leaped to their feet, yelling like a bunch of kids, and waved their napkins over their heads. The underdog had triumphed!

Lunch was over, and I had sense enough to go home. As I left, two rosy-cheeked young women, both of them in uniform, came running up and presented me with a beautiful bouquet of wild flowers, freshly picked. Andrei and I again gave each other a big bear hug. Smolazov and I began the ride back to the embassy. He made a couple of leading remarks, but I thought I'd better keep quiet.

At the embassy, Admiral Standley and members of his staff were awake, eager to hear my account of the day's activities. I walked in with a bouquet of flowers in each hand. I presented them to Standley.

"Put these in water, Admiral," I said. "I'm going to bed before you have to put me there." I made it to bed and collapsed. I slept fourteen hours without twitching an eyebrow. In the morning I was a little groggy, but otherwise I felt fine.

Standley, Michela and Duncan were amazed and quietly elated at my account of the day's activities. No American had ever seen so much before. Much of what I had picked up, when properly evaluated and interpreted, would be of great value to our war planners back home. The Russian pilots, for example, had told me that there had been a marked decrease in the quality of the German pilots in the past six months. That was important. It could mean that the Germans were running out of trained pilots, or it could mean that they were transferring them to the western front.

Standley had received, in a sealed diplomatic pouch, several questions from General Marshall and General Arnold to pass on to me. It was obvious that any information I could pick up concerning the true situation on the Russian front, both on the ground and in the air, would be of vital importance to our own top-level plans for the prosecution of the war.

This, remember, was in June 1943. The Germans were still five hundred miles deep into Russia, and every indication showed that they planned to continue the offensive. They had made two frontal assaults on Moscow and had been beaten back. Would they take the offensive again? If so, when? Would they be successful? Would the Russians retreat, hold or mount a counteroffensive?

Forthright reports on these questions were not being made available to us. The War Department could not be positive of any action the Russians might take. If they collapsed, as in 1917, or signed a separate peace, several German armies would be released to resist us in the west. Or did the Russians have the capability and the determination to carry the war on to Germany?

On the most immediate question, it was Standley's opinion that the next German offensive would not be until fall. But Russian military officials, from Marshal Zhukov down, told me that the Germans were preparing to mount the offensive almost immediately.

Zhukov told me that the Germans were concentrating troops and armor in the Orel sector, two hundred miles south of Moscow. "We've already stopped two of their frontal attacks on Moscow, and now they are thinking of going around to the south and coming in the back door," he said.

"What will you do?" I asked.

"If they attack, we will defend," Zhukov said. "If they do not attack until winter comes, then we will and will tear them to shreds."

His eyes bored into mine. I believed him completely.

Three of the ranking generals of the Russian Air Force, in a conference in which we discussed primarily technical improvements in American aircraft, backed up Zhukov's statements. They were beginning to achieve air superiority. They were confident and determined.

Why were the Russians so frank with me? After a pleasant supper with the three Russian generals, I was bold enough to ask them why.

"There are two kinds of foreigners whom we entertain," one of them said. "One kind is those we must, the other, those we like. You happen to fall in the latter category."

Late one night I received word to report to the airport in the morning. Smolazov and I were going to the Orel sector. A Lend-Lease DC-3 was assigned to us.

"We will provide an escort of five Yak fighters for you all the way," the commanding general of the base said. I did not think it necessary to burn up gasoline and put wear and tear on planes and pilots to escort me to Orel, and I told the general so.

"If something happened to you," the general said softly, "what do you think would happen to me?"

We flew southward at less than one hundred feet. Shelled-out ruins of farmhouses were beneath us, but even near the front the farms were well tilled. I saw tank traps and gun emplacements by the thousands and great concentrations of troops. Eighty minutes from Moscow our pilot put the plane down at a well-camouflaged airport. We picked up a Russian officer and took off immediately. Smolazov explained that our new passenger was a special navigator familiar with the location of the fields at the front. They were so well camouflaged that our own pilot and navigator would never be able to find them. In about twenty minutes we made another turn, and again I was barely able to determine that there was a field beneath us. We landed.

It was the headquarters of an air regiment flying Douglas A-20 twin-engine light bombers. The colonel of the regiment was named Bousilov. He escorted me into his headquarters, where a group of pilots and engineering officers was waiting.

I spoke at length on the A-20's flying characteristics, and I could tell, from the enlightened expressions on the faces of the pilots, that I was giving answers to questions that they did not have sufficient experience with this plane to formulate.

The engineers and maintenance men had questions too, most of which I was able to answer. Before leaving the base, I made a quick inspection of two of the planes. They were clean and well cared for, proving the Russians' respect for this American equipment.

We flew on to another well camouflaged base, and I repeated the performance there. It was the headquarters of the Air Force commander of the Orel sector, Major General I. D. Antoshkin. On his chest were a medal proclaiming him to be a hero of the Soviet Union and an American Distinguished Flying Cross. He was one of the twenty men who had received the award in the Kremlin; he remembered my presence at the ceremony and was obviously proud of the honor.

After I had finished the technical discussion with the pilots and maintenance men, it was Russian lunchtime, and the General personally escorted me to a T-shaped table. There on the table were the inevitable bottle of vodka and the tulip-shaped glasses. Antoshkin looked at me slyly.

"I understand the captain is quite a vodka drinker," he said through the interpreter.

"Oh, my God, here we go again," I thought. The Russian grapevine was working fast. "Just ordinary," I said, watching him fill my glass.

We had a few drinks, but it did not develop into a contest, and the heavy bread and oily butter enabled me to keep my head. It was a delightful meal with frank conversation. The General said that the Germans had decreased the number of operational planes in that sector from approximately 2,700 to fewer than 2,000. I made a careful note of that figure. They could have gone nowhere else but to the western front. Antoshkin went on to say frankly that the Russians had three thousand planes on the entire front but that this number did not represent great superiority over the German Air Force. He admitted that they were unable to use their equipment as fully as the Germans did.

"We have a surprise for you," the General said after lunch. "There's a Cossack division located near us, and they have agreed to send over a troupe of entertainers to put on a show for us this evening."

Not long after, a bus drove up with the entertainers. They were soldiers who performed in addition to their regular duties. The show they put on would have been a success anywhere in the world. The band played one American selection for me. It was "Beer-Barrel Polka," one of my favorites, and the Russians played it very well.

Twilight was deepening, and I wondered about the lights. What a nice target we would make. The show ended soon after, and the General invited the troupe and all the rest of us in for supper. At 2:00 A.M. Smolazov and I were driven to our billet, a partially wrecked barn—the farmhouse was completely gone —in which two cots had been set up with white sheets. A rosy-cheeked girl soldier was waiting for us and served a midnight snack on a well set table by candlelight.

At 7:00 A.M. we were back at the airport. The General was affable and clear-eyed and took us into breakfast. The moment we sat down, he filled our glasses with vodka—at 7:00 A.M.!

"Is it customary in Russia," I asked cautiously, "to absorb this much vodka and still perform flying duties satisfactorily?"

"Oh, there's a great deal of difference between Americans and Russians," the General said.

After some more banter, the General finally broke down and confessed that the front lines were fogged in and that no one was flying that morning.

When I left, Antoshkin presented me with three bottles of vodka and the tulip-shaped glass from which I had been drinking. "Drink to us when you return to America," Antoshkin said.

"I will, and gladly," I said. "Furthermore, I will get my family to join me, and I'll send you a photograph of it."

My next stop was with another group of A-20s, then a group of P-39s, or "Bell Airacobras." The P-39 pilots were outspoken in their appreciation of our planes. One of them had shot down a total of 27 Focke-Wulfs and Messerschmitts.

During the day, as we flew from field to field, I saw great concentrations of men, tanks, artillery and equipment of all kinds on the western front. Every patch of woods held quantities of troops.

That night we returned to our barn five miles east of Kursk. Suddenly during the night the earth began shaking. Smolazov and I ran out to see what was going on. To the west the sky was lit up with shell bursts. Artillery blended into one steady deafening blast. We hurried to Antoshkin's headquarters and were admitted to his underground war room.

"The Germans have attacked!" he cried excitedly. "Let them come. We'll stop them and chase them all the way back to Berlin!"

I almost forgot to answer. I couldn't believe my eyes. On the wall, plain to see, was a complete map of the entire front line, with the location of every major unit plainly indicated by markers in the universal military language.

I made some remark to the General, while I concentrated with all my power on memorizing what I saw on the map. It never occurred to me that the Germans might have broken through the lines, which were only five miles distant, and could have been enveloping us at that moment.

I stood there, trying to look casual, and memorized that map. The Germans did break through at Belgorod on the southern flank, 75 miles away. But at Kursk and Orel, about the same distance to the north, the Russians held. In the Kremlin that night, I learned later, the decision was made to counterattack and to continue attacking.

Despite the beginning of the all-out German offensive, the Russians were perfectly content for me to continue with my mission. The following morning I visited, among other units, a squadron of Stormovik planes. I could not see too much of them at that time, as they were busy doing what they were designed to do, but I was extremely impressed. The Stormovik had an outstanding design for a specific purpose, the destruction of tanks, railroad engines and small craft. It was the only armored attack plane in the world. The pilots told me that, a few nights before, they had found a German tank column gathering fifteen miles behind the front and had disorganized it completely. It was one of the reasons why the German offensive was stopped.

Smolazov and I returned to Moscow late that afternoon. The fighter escort was overhead. General Michela met us at the airport, and, after I had given my hearty thanks to everyone and said good-bye, we hurried to Michela's apartment. Admiral Standley came over, and I gave him a verbal report of everything that I had seen and heard. One of his secretaries took it down in shorthand. I described in detail the map I had seen of the front lines and the location of the military symbols on it.

The moment that I finished, Standley was on his feet. "This information must go to Washington without delay," he said. "Eddie, we've got to get you on a plane for Tehran *now!* Tonight!"

"No, Admiral," I said, "that would be suicide on my part. I'd never reach Tehran. They're still suspicious of me; they watch everything I do. Besides, I haven't finished here. I'd like to suggest that you have this prepared in code, put it in a diplomatic pouch and send it to Tehran by courier tomorrow. Arrange to have a fast plane waiting in Tehran to speed it to Washington."

He finally agreed, and the material was sent on to Washington the next day. It included not only troop dispositions but also my observations and opinions. I stated my conviction that the Russian Army, with its enlightened leadership and its fanatical determination to achieve total victory, would never quit fighting, would never sign a separate peace, until the enemy had been totally destroyed.

I had come to know the Russians. I liked them as people. They had lost two-fifths of their productive capacity, two-fifths of their land. Five million of their soldiers had been killed or wounded. Fifteen million civilians, men, women and children, had also been killed, had starved to death or had died of disease in the occupied areas; another 10 million had died from starvation, neglect and lack of medical supplies in Russian-held territory. It was impossible to think that these people would accept such losses without retaliation, without complete dedication to total victory.

I was convinced that the Red Army and the Red Air Force were growing stronger every day. The military leadership was excellent. Russia's military forces were no longer a Communist rabble without discipline or order. They comprised a capable military machine, and I was convinced that they would fight to the very gates of Berlin.

Apparently my visit to an aircraft factory, the only request still not granted, was not going to come through. I made routine preparations to leave the next day. After warm good-byes all around, we took off. Twenty miles out of Moscow, oil began pouring out of the number three engine. The only thing we could do was turn around and go back. The engine was completely shot.

Members of the embassy staff and correspondents said that it would take anywhere from six weeks to three months to obtain another one, but I didn't believe that for a moment. I arranged for Nuckols to go to Cairo for one. In the meantime, the delay worked to my advantage, for I was given permission to go through the famous Stormovik plant in Moscow.

I was being escorted through the factory by the top men when the chief test pilot came along. He took a look at me, then exclaimed "Hello, Eddie" and gave me a bear hug. It was Mikhail Gromov, the pilot of the over-the-pole plane, whom I had entertained in New York back in 1937. He poured out a burst of Russian at my escorts, which I assumed to be an account of the time that I had shown him in New York, and from then on the factory was mine. I believe that every question I asked was answered frankly and freely.

Of the employees, 67 percent were women, and 25 percent were boys as young as ten years old. At eighteen, every male in the Soviet Union was inducted into the armed forces. The rest of the employees were technicians with highly specialized skills. Women were doing the hardest, heaviest tasks and also precision work.

I was interested in how labor unions operated in the workers' paradise. The managing director gave a short laugh and said: "We are the union. We have no problems."

Employees worked eight hours a day, six days a week, plus three hours a day overtime at time and a half, which was compulsory when necessary for everybody but women with children.

I was surprised to learn that payment was on the incentive plan, on a piecework basis. "What kind of Communism is *that?*" I wondered. Again and again I had seen evidence that Russia was becoming less Communistic. The Communists we had in America would have been most disagreeably surprised to realize the true state of affairs, and as for the Russians themselves the feeling was mutual. Many of those with whom I talked spoke in contemptuous terms of our party members.

Great privilege was given in Russia to the skilled and the producers. All was not equal, not by any means. Rewards were given in food, in clothing, in living quarters, in prestige. In the Stormovik plant, for example, and in another plant that I visited, the criteria for incentive payments were both quality and quantity. For exceptional work, bonuses were paid in more food of higher quality and in better living accommodations.

I asked about absenteeism and had great difficulty explaining the word. I finally said, "What do you do when an employee gets drunk on vodka on Sunday and doesn't show up for work on Monday morning?"

"Ah," said the managing director. "If an employee is twenty minutes late, he is reprimanded. For absenteeism an employee is tried by a court of his fellow employees, and if guilty his wages are cut. If it happened again, the food ration would be cut, and if it ever became flagrant, the employee would be automatically fired."

That meant that he would lose his ration card and go on the bread line. I had seen the bread line—old people, people who could not produce, standing in line at 4:00 in the morning to get a piece of black bread each. The Russians were ruthless when it came to the distribution of their limited food supply. It went only to those who were producing. And that's why the word "absenteeism" was not known in the Soviet Union.

The Stormovik itself was beautifully designed. It was a low-wing monoplane, completely protected by armor. It had tremendous firepower. Its .37-millimeter cannon-fired shells would penetrate the three-inch armor plate of the Tiger tank, Germany's largest and best. Gromov took me to the firing range pit so that I could see how the cannon was synchronized and tested. I sat in the gunner's seat while Gromov fired the gun. He warned me to put my fingers over my ears, but, as it was, when he turned loose those cannon, they almost jolted my eyeteeth loose.

The plane also carried a four-inch rocket under each wing, and I asked Gromov to fire one. He did, and the resulting explosion tore half the pit away.

Gromov took me for a 30-minute demonstration ride, in which

he banked the plane vertically, dived, pulled it up into a stall and performed every other maneuver that either of us could think of—all at an altitude of not more than five hundred feet. I was impressed all right, but there were moments when I wished myself safely back on the ground.

Discussing the evolution of the plane at lunch, with my friends' tongues loosened a bit by the inevitable vodka, I learned that this plane was designed to break down a tank attack before it could begin.

"When you are fighting with large numbers of tanks, they must be organized into a tank formation at least twelve hours before they start for the front line," Gromov explained. "We sought to find a weapon which could jump over the front and reach the tank assembly area twelve to fifteen miles behind the lines. This is the result. By breaking up the organization of the ranks far behind the lines, even those which escape and reach the front are easy prey to the artillery and antitank guns."

The German attack at Kursk had been even greater than we had realized that night, I was told at the Stormovik plant. More German tanks were involved in that offensive than in any other battle in the war. Yet they made no advance beyond the Russian lines. Hundreds and hundreds of them were smashed, first by the Stormoviks behind the lines and then by the antitank guns at the front, which took care of the demoralized stragglers.

I was so impressed by the success of this tank-busting plane that, in my report to the Secretary of War, I recommended that a general review be made of our tank strategy and tactics. Fortunately, however, we never met one in combat. The British tried to emulate its success by equipping a Hurricane single-engine fighter plane with two 40-millimeter cannon. They neglected to armor the plane, however, and it was an easy prey to machine-gunfire and light antiaircraft fire from the ground. It was never successful.

Waiting for the engine gave us the opportunity to spend a pleasant weekend at a *dacha,* or country lodge, on the river. Two of the officers on Michela's staff had rented it, and they invited their Russian secretaries and Doctor Dahl and me to join them. The girls picked wild strawberries for us and later went swimming in the nude. They maintained that everyone did it and that no one thought anything of it one way or the other. I couldn't help noticing that all the girls I saw swimming in the river were using the backstroke.

While we were enjoying dinner that night, an old woman covered with rags and carrying an emaciated child came to the door to beg for food. I gave her a glass of vodka for a stimulant, then saw to it that both she and the child were given plenty to eat. As she sobbed out her gratitude, she told us that she had not heard from her husband, a soldier, for three years. She could not contribute to the war effort because she had to take care of the child, and, as a result, she received no support from the government. And she was not an old woman after all; she said that she was only 27.

After she left, with her handbag full of scraps, the two Russian secretaries criticized me bitterly for wasting food on someone who could not contribute to the war effort. I thought their heartlessness sickening and told them so. But I'm afraid that their attitude was all too typical of the younger generation of Russians to whom victory was everything.

Driving home at night we saw another example of this psychology. A convoy of several hundred ambulances passed us, bringing the wounded back from the front. I was told that the Russians deliberately moved their wounded at night, both to leave the roads free for troop movements in the daytime and to conceal the numbers of wounded from the civilians.

In the meantime, General Nuckols had secured an engine in Cairo and had brought it back to Moscow. The Russian crew installed it overnight, which would have been an excellent performance even in the best equipped depot in the United States. The captain of the crew had been doing a good job all along, and I wanted to reward him specifically. One of the most desired objects in Russia was a watch. I arranged to buy a good one in the black market, but I had to be careful about presenting it, as he could not accept a gift from a foreigner. I put it under the rear seat in the cabin of the plane and then called him to come and see what the trouble with the seat was. I raised the cushion and showed him the watch. He almost collapsed with gratitude then and there, but he recovered quickly, said, "I will fix it," in a loud voice, got some tools and went back into the airplane alone. The watch disappeared.

Again we said our farewells. Admiral Standley got up at 4:30 in the morning to see us off.

"You've seen more and heard more in Russia in two months than all the experts combined," he told me. "Good-bye and good luck."

Four hours out of Moscow an escort of five Yak fighters suddenly appeared and escorted us to Stalingrad. I had received permission to fly low over the city, or rather over what was left of the city. Where once half a million people had lived, there was not a single roof visible on any building. There were two large salvage dumps of German airplanes, one about two blocks long. There were literally acres of burned-out tanks, both Russian and German. I could not help thinking that, if any of the cities of the United States had been destroyed to such an extent, there would be more interest in eliminating slow-downs, featherbedding, strikes and absenteeism.

The five fighters escorted us back out of range of any German planes, then went ahead, turned and executed a farewell dip in formation. It was a grand gesture, a final and heartwarming good-bye.

Though certainly there could be no doubt of my opposition to Communism, nevertheless I had come to realize that the Russian people deserved our understanding if no more. They had had a rough time in the twentieth century. There was no question that oppression had existed under the rulership of the czars. Russia had suffered devastating defeats in the Russo-Japanese War of 1904 and in World War I, losing hundreds of thousands of men. More hundreds of thousands were lost in the revolution and the civil war that followed.

Then came the period of consolidation, Communism at its worst. No one was safe from informants, from the dread knock on the door in the night. Those opposing the Communist leadership during those years were ruthlessly eliminated. A fear complex developed and a distrust of all foreigners and of one another. And after all, we were one of the last nations to recognize the Soviet Union.

The war with Finland proved to the Russian leadership the inferiority of its military arm. It tried to stay out of World War II by making a treaty with Hitler. The leaders hoped that Germany would weaken itself against the Allies and that Russia would thus become the dominant force on the Continent. They also hoped for time to rebuild the Russian army, war industry and equipment. But the Germans attacked with a force and a brutality that swept them to the gates of Moscow. There the Russians held, and their attitude changed to determination and confidence.

But Russia remained suspicious of the Allies in general and of Americans in particular—and again with reason. We had opposed all Russia's actions for a generation. When we became Allies against Germany, we were still suspect. The vast amounts of Lend-Lease supplies that we promised did not come through immediately. The Russians thought that we should open a second front on the Continent as early as 1942. We wisely delayed until there was reason to believe that it would be successful, but Russia was still impatient. In short, we could hardly expect Russia to have unlimited confidence in us.

In Tehran I was assured by the embassy that the situation growing out of my conversation with the Turkish ambassador had been cleared up completely. We flew to Cairo, stopped overnight, then went on to Marrakech. There we were warned that the flight to England might entail some danger. German planes operating out of bases in western France had shot down several British transport planes flying between North Africa and England. To circumvent them, our flight plan called for us to fly directly west from Marrakech to a point about five hundred miles out in the Atlantic Ocean, then to proceed north toward Ireland, keeping well off the coast of Portugal and Spain.

As fog tended to hang over Land's End until 10:00 A.M., we were advised to delay our takeoff until about 2:00 A.M. the following day. We were taken to a lovely home in Marrakech, in order to snatch a few hours' sleep. I was given the bed that President Roosevelt had slept in on his way home from the Casablanca conference. That bed was about the only thing the two of us ever had in common.

We left Marrakech at exactly 2:00 A.M. on a beautiful night and proceeded on our planned course. At ten thousand feet, we found ourselves between two layers of overcast. I went up and sat in the cockpit with the pilot and copilot. Should an enemy plane have appeared, we would have dived into the sheltering cloud cover beneath us. We had been warned at Marrakech that the Germans were monitoring our radio frequencies, and we maintained radio silence. After a long flight, we suddenly flew out from under the overcast into the bright sunlight, and there ahead of us was the unmistakable green loveliness of southern England.

Great changes had taken place in the air war over the Continent since my visit to the United Kingdom the year before. Visiting with the commanders and staffs of both American and British commands, I was shown photographs of the utter, horrifying devastation caused by our bombing raids. I visited with several American units, had dinner with my old friend Lord Beaverbrook at his country place and conferred with Averell Harriman, Lend-Lease representative in Britain, and Ambassador Gil Winant.

I discussed my visit to Russia at great length with Gil. He was so interested that he called a friend in British intelligence. As a result, I was invited to meet with top officers of that hush-hush operation. I talked for about two hours on the situation as I had seen it in Russia, then volunteered to answer truthfully any and all questions, pertinent or impertinent. To my surprise, this period lasted only about fifteen minutes before the questions were exhausted.

"We in America have never before needed a comprehensive international intelligence system," I said, "and our ignorance in these matters is at least understandable. But you British have been involved in international intrigue, particularly with your neighbors on the Continent, for centuries. Bearing that in mind, Gentlemen, I must say that I am shocked to realize how little you know about your own ally, Russia."

There was silence for a moment. Then the presiding officer got to his feet, pounded the table with his fist and said: "I concur with everything Captain Rickenbacker has told us here today. We're going to have to reorganize and start all over." He later repeated these sentiments in a personal letter.

Word of this meeting reached Prime Minister Churchill. He sent me an invitation through Winant to come to lunch at Chequers, Churchill's country estate.

"I suppose he wants me to talk about Russia," I said to Gil.

"I think so," Gil replied.

"All right, I'll be there," I said and began organizing my thoughts for the discussion.

The Prime Minister's car picked me up at the Savoy Hotel. It appeared to be European-royalty day at Chequers, with all the deposed kings and queens of the Continent present. After a pleasant luncheon, Churchill and I moved outside and sat under a large oak tree. He asked me about Russia, but, when I started to give him my observations, he interrupted me in a bantering tone, questioning my statements as though I had been sold a bill of goods.

"Mr. Prime Minister," I said, "you invited me here, and I was pleased to come. If you don't care to listen to what I have to report, then I would really prefer to leave, for I am behind schedule and have plenty to do. And if you aren't busy, you ought to be, as I would imagine you'd have plenty to do too."

"Oh, I'm sorry, so sorry," he said. "Please do continue."

I did, and this time he listened attentively. I concluded by imploring him to work for a better understanding between him and Roosevelt on the one hand and Stalin on the other. I recommended that Britain and the United States be realistic with Stalin and establish a firm and just agreement before the war was ended, with positive understanding and respect on all sides.

"If this isn't done," I said, "Russia will demand ten times more after the war than she will ask for today. By sincerely holding out the olive branch of peace today, you will get credit on the books of history for eliminating the possibility of another great war within the next 25 years."

Discussing other areas of the war, Churchill said that, when victory in Europe was secure, he would send his armies to the Pacific to give the Americans abundant help against the Japanese.

"Mr. Churchill," I said, "when the Germans capitulate, the English people will be through with war. You will probably no longer be prime minister."

It is sad, but that is exactly what did happen.

Winant also wanted to arrange a meeting for me with Roosevelt. I said that I would bet two to one that Roosevelt would not agree to any such meeting, but Winant insisted on sending a cable recommending it. He showed me the cable; it was a positive statement of the importance of the information I had and almost begged the President to see me. I didn't think anything would come of it, but I was willing to wait and see.

We were all beginning to be a little weary. Doctor Dahl, in particular, was growing homesick. The mission had begun on April 27; it was now August. I had promised Secretary Stimson that my next mission for him would be to the Aleutian Islands, and I wanted a little time at my desk, running the airline, before heading out again. We were all happy, therefore, when, on August 4 at 8:00 A.M., we boarded our C-87 and left Britain for Reykjavik, Iceland. In Iceland I inspected our excellent new fighter base and Air Transport Command facilities.

The next morning we left for Greenland, which was also on my inspection tour. The weather was terrible, and we were unable to establish radio contact with Greenland. I told the crew to change course and head for Labrador. The head winds were so strong that Bill Richmond brought the plane down to barely five hundred feet above the water. The waves were gigantic, and I could almost feel that ice-cold water. Then the radio station at Greenland came in loud and clear and advised us that the weather there was fine.

We headed back again for Greenland, passing over icebergs by the dozen, flew up a long fjord with sheer walls on each side, bucking a 50-mile-an-hour wind, and came in on the landing strip, which ran uphill. We spent two days in that barren, rugged country, waiting for the wind to die down. One of the morale problems that I found there resulted from the fact that the commander was a teetotaler and had closed the bar down tight. If ever there was a place where a man would benefit from a reasonable amount of body-warming beer or whiskey, that was it. I made a note in my little book, and conditions were changed shortly thereafter.

At 3:00 A.M. August 7, I was awakened with word that the wind had abated. Without stopping to wash or shave, we all dashed to the mess hall, ate a good breakfast and took off for home. We stopped at Gander, Newfoundland, for fuel and a lunch of sardines and crackers. On the last leg to the United States, ten thousand feet up, I stripped, took a sponge bath and shaved. Then I took over the controls and flew the ship for about two hours. Beautiful New England was beneath us. As I looked down at the countryside, I appreciated more than ever that here was a land truly worth fighting for.

It was Saturday afternoon, and in Long Island Sound hundreds of sailboats were in the water, and tens of thousands of people were on the beaches. Coming from Russia and the all-out dedication of its people to fighting and working for their homeland, I was saddened by the complacency and indifference I saw below.

We landed at La Guardia Airport at 4:20 P.M. I had not been able to notify Adelaide in advance, of course, as our flight was under censorship. Before going home I had a job to do. On my travels, I had accumulated from men along the way a tremendous number of souvenirs, many of great value, to be sent to their wives, mothers and sweethearts. In Iceland I had borrowed three huge mail sacks to pack these souvenirs in. As it was Saturday afternoon and the post office was closed, I persuaded the commanding officer at La Guardia to give me a special truck to take the mail home with me. A captain and a sergeant were detailed to go along.

Adelaide was surprised to see me walk in, and the surprise was compounded by the captain and the sergeant carrying the mail bags.

On Monday I had an Eastern Air Lines truck pick them up and take them to our shipping department. Each one of the several hundred items was repacked and sent to the designated recipient. Every single package arrived safely at its destination.

To recapitulate this mission quickly, I had flown 55,000 miles halfway around the world and back to visit our own Air Force installations and those in Russia. The trip had lasted three months and seven days. I had talked to approximately three hundred thousand American troops, the great majority of them members of combat units made up of heavy, medium and light bombers and fighters.

My reports had been coming in to the Secretary of War, and action was being progressively taken on the more urgent recommendations. I turned in a complete report to him after my return home, of course, and visited with our military and civilian leaders to discuss many issues personally. Direct action was taken on many of the recommendations; on others I merely planted seeds. For example, it was my belief that the next ambassador to Russia should also be a military man, as was Admiral Standley. I expressed this point of view, with my reasons for it, to Ed Stettinius. After he became Secretary of State and Standley retired, Stettinius sent one of our most capable generals, Walter Bedell Smith, to Moscow as ambassador.

Roosevelt, of course, did not even have the courtesy to reply to Gil Winant's cable urging him to see me. After ten days had passed, I cabled Gil one single word: "no." He knew what that meant.

While I was in Russia, Adelaide had sent word to me that our older boy David had joined the U.S. Marines. I had cabled him my congratulations and promised to visit him at training camp on my return to the States. Waiting for me was a somewhat humorous request from him that I please, please *not* come to see him at boot camp. It seemed that the name Rickenbacker was more a hindrance than a help. The public information officer was always calling him out to have his picture taken with visiting VIPs, but the tough Marine drill instructor could not have cared less what his name was and made things twice as tough for him on his return. I saw his point and stayed away. I was very proud that, in spite of this handicap, David completed his training and went on to serve with distinction in the Pacific.

He was therefore unable to participate in the toast that I had promised General Antoshkin that my family and I would drink to his health on my return to the States. Bill, on summer vacation from Asheville School in North Carolina, joined his mother and me in the toast to our friends fighting for freedom thousands of miles away on the eastern front. I called in a photographer, who snapped us in both serious and gagged-up poses and sent the photographs along with a letter to General Antoshkin. He responded, and we had a pleasant correspondence.

After the excitement of the Russian mission, my tour of the Aleutian Islands, our coldest and dreariest military front, may seem somewhat anticlimactic today. In 1943, however, the Aleutians were of great importance. It was necessary for us to remain on those islands to keep the Japanese off. Most of the islands, of course, were much closer to Japan than to the continental United States. I covered the major bases all the way out to the westernmost island of Attu, inspected them, talked with the personnel and made my report.

This mission also included stops at the bases at which we transferred Lend-Lease planes to Russia. At Great Falls, Montana, one of the American officers, Major George Racey Jordan, took me aside and informed me that he had seen what seemed to be shipments of uranium on board planes en route to Russia. At that time, two years before the atom bomb was dropped, it was a top secret—or supposed to be.

I shared Jordan's concern over this shocking lapse of security. When I returned to Washington, I informed Secretary Stimson of what Jordan had told me and shown me. Stimson said that he had heard about it too but had been unable to do anything about it.

No wonder the Russians developed the atomic bomb so quickly. After the war, Jordan wrote a book about this delivery of atomic secrets to the Soviet Union and appeared before Congress. Much of the press, however, ridiculed his assertions, and no positive action was ever taken. I have good reason to believe with Major Jordan, however, that our atomic secrets may have been deliberately given away to Russia.

Following my return from the Aleutians, Gil Winant, who was back in the States, asked if he could try one more time to persuade Roosevelt to listen to my observations on Russia.

"Please, Gil," I said, "don't try it again. I would have seen him before, out of respect for the office of the President of the United States and because I believe I had something important to tell him, but I wouldn't see him now if he asked me."

And so my observations on the Soviet Union and recommendations for dealing with this vast country were never carried by me personally to the President.

If they had been, they might never have been considered or applied. But the fact remains that, owing to a unique and fortuitous set of circumstances, I was able to see more in Russia and talk more frankly with that country's political and military leaders than could all the official emissaries, both British and American, sent to Russia during that period.

I strongly believed that Roosevelt and Churchill could and should get together and negotiate with Stalin, with both understanding and strength. I believed that positive concessions should

be made but that they should be based on justice, not on any
effort to buy Stalin off. I believed that Stalin would listen and
meet us halfway.

But we did not negotiate from strength, and Stalin, wily and
suspicious, got the better of us at the conference table. As a
result, today there is a divided Germany, and Berlin is one hundred miles within the Communist sphere, with a wall running
through the middle of it.

NINETEEN

THE POSTWAR PERIOD

While the United States was winning a war overseas, our Eastern Air Lines family and I were waging our own personal and corporate war back home against inefficiency, shortages of equipment and personnel and the inevitable bureaucracy. For years we had been the only airline to operate without dependence upon the taxpayer's dollar in the form of subsidies, the only airline to show an honest profit. During the war all airlines had more customers than they could carry. Some of our competitors spent money almost for the sake of spending it, but we at Eastern continued our frugal, conservative, dependable management. In a sense we were penalized; we were the only airline to pay an excess profits tax.

We paid many millions to the government during that period, and some of our people felt that we were being taxed unduly.

"Take it easy," I told them. "The day will come when the situation will reverse itself, and we will be the beneficiary of the excess profits tax. It is forcing us to be even more exacting, to watch our expenditures even more minutely. Not one of our competitors is saddled with this excess profits tax, and they're getting mighty careless in their methods of handling money. Someday this tax will be removed, and, while the others are adjusting, we will continue on in our tried and true way and come out ahead."

The war years were demanding. Despite having given the government one-half of our fleet and the personnel required to maintain it, we actually, our operating figures showed, flew more miles and carried more customers as the war continued. When it was over, ironically enough, we, the first airline to volunteer our equipment, were the last to get it back. But still we showed a more favorable balance sheet than anyone else in the industry.

But we couldn't stand still. As I have often said, it only takes a little more thinking to figure out how you can do a better job. To do a better job, we needed better equipment. Through my association with Lockheed Aircraft Company, which built the P-38, I learned of its new design for a transport plane, the Constellation.

Howard Hughes of TWA had originally gone to Lockheed in search of a plane that would carry 44 to 46 people nonstop from New York to London. Hall Hibbard, Lockheed's chief engineer, beginning with a clean sheet of paper, laid out a completely new design, a plane conceived, designed and built as a new transport airliner, an entity in itself. It used the new, more powerful Wright engine, and the design of the plane was oriented to this new power source. The plane had a short takeoff; in fact, you couldn't keep it on the ground. Open up the throttle, and it would pull itself into the air. The Constellation's performance exceeded even Hughes' specifications, for the production model carried a payload of 85 passengers with seating arrangements of two and three.

I hated to tell my old friend Don Douglas that we were leaving him. It would be the first time that we would buy a plane not built by Douglas. I thought, however, that Don's new plane, the DC-6, was only a stretched-out DC-4, with all the weaknesses and inefficiencies of such a production.

Hughes and TWA had put $1.5 million into the development of the new plane and had the exclusive rights. Hughes didn't want to let us in.

"Howard," I said, "are you sure you want to be the only airline using this new plane? If you had an accident with it—and as long as anything moves, an accident is possible—it would have an adverse effect on your line exclusively. But, if we flew this plane too, then any repercussions would be spread out."

Hughes agreed to let us purchase ten Constellations at $2 million each. I arranged with a group of bankers to borrow the money. I have always looked up to Alfred P. Sloan, Jr., and I went to him for his opinion. He looked at my balance sheet and approved my action.

"We borrowed $100 million for General Motors at two and a half percent interest yesterday," he said. "What rate are you paying?"

"One and one-half percent," I said.

He was silent for a moment. "Maybe you'd better come over to General Motors and do our borrowing for us," he said.

At that meeting, Mr. Sloan graciously brought up the subject of jet engines. When I had returned from overseas in August 1943, the two of us had had luncheon in his small private dining room. I suggested that he send Charles F. Kettering, GM vice-president and general manager of the research laboratories, with a few other engineers over to England to the Rolls-Royce people to investigate the jet engine, the engine of the future for both military and commercial use. I could tell by the twinkle in his eye that Mr. Sloan thought that I was being overoptimistic, but he did send Kettering and the others to look into it.

As a direct result, he told me that day, Allison had gotten off to a great start in the production of the jet engine and would manufacture more jet engines that year, 1946, than all the other engine manufacturers in the United States put together. Mr. Sloan also said that, if people had told him a year before that GM wouldn't make a profit in 1946, he would have said that they were crazy, but GM still was not going to make a profit that year. I was quietly proud that Eastern *was* going to be in the black.

We received our first Constellation in May 1947. On May 17, with Captain Dick Merrill at the controls, it took off from Los Angeles for Miami and crossed the Miami tower 6 hours, 54 minutes and 57 seconds later, a new record.

We were the first line to fly the Constellation, and we accepted our responsibility for helping to make it a serviceable plane. Our maintenance department made up a list of weaknesses, or "bugs," in the new plane, with a description of how we had repaired each one temporarily and our recommendation for a permanent fix to be handled by the factory for all future models. A group of Eastern people, including Charles Froesch, vice-president and chief engineer; Ambrose Chabot, vice-president in charge of maintenance; several of their assistants, and me, went out to Burbank to discuss the Constellation's problems with Lockheed. Robert E. Gross, the president, was there, along with Hall Hibbard and the production men.

So were the subcontractors, one of whom grew a little angry when I called the ball bearing he was using a piece of junk. He said that the bearing was the best he could obtain in that postwar period of transition. I asked him if he had a purchasing agent. He said "yes" and pointed to him.

"If he was really a purchasing agent," I said, "he'd have had sense enough to go over the catalogues of all the companies manufacturing ball bearings and pick out the ones he could use. Then he'd get a list of customers who had bought these ball bearings over the years, and he'd find tens of thousands of excellent bearings sitting on shelves all over the country."

Within a week the company had bought enough ball bearings at reduced prices to last them several years.

Bob Gross said that it would be impossible to make all the modifications. The company couldn't afford to wait for its money.

"That's exactly the point," I said. "You give us your best project engineer, two good toolmakers and a draftsman, and we'll show them right there on the plane just what needs to be done and how to do it. The draftsman will make a sketch of the new part. The toolmakers will make it themselves, then and there, without going through the engineering department. If it proves out, we'll make enough for all the planes you have on order. And we'll have those airplanes out of here, all changes made, in six weeks."

After two weeks' time, working twelve to fifteen hours a day every day, we had proved every one of the new parts. Eastern spent $1 million advertising and promoting the Constellation. Airline executives came from all over the world to see it in action. Within six months, Lockheed had deposits on more than one hundred Constellations. Bob Gross, in his gratitude, admitted that we had saved the company; it had been on the verge of bankruptcy.

A few years later, I was visiting the Lockheed plant, and Bob told me of his new plans for the Super-Constellation. In order to save money, he was going to build it with a straight, stovepipe-shaped fuselage, rather than retaining that beautiful "Connie" configuration, and make other money-saving changes. Bob said that he didn't think Lockheed could sell enough planes to warrant putting any more money into its design.

"I'll make a deal with you," I said. "If you incorporate the changes we recommend, I'll give you an order for twelve of them tomorrow, with a substantial deposit. And, for every plane that you sell over twenty, you give me a rebate on the planes I will buy in the next two years."

Gross agreed. The plane that resulted was an excellent one, and operators, governments and military services the world over bought it. About three hundred were made and sold, but I stopped collecting rebates after fifty—and several million dollars.

During those years, we were using the aging DC-3 for the short hauls. We investigated the twin-engine Martin 202, made by my friend Glenn Martin, and found a weakness in the attachment of the wing to the fuselage. I told Glenn that the day would come when he would change that design but that I was afraid he would kill a lot of people first. A 202 did have a very bad crash caused by this weakness.

Glenn strengthened the ships already in service and brought out a new design called the 404, which was acceptable. TWA contracted to buy 25, and Eastern took 35 with an option on 25 more. Eastern put up a deposit of $11 million and TWA $7.5 million.

Even with that much money on hand, the Martin company was having financial pains. The Korean hostilities had broken out, and the Air Force and the Navy wanted a great deal of additional equipment. Martin tripled his payroll but had a great deal of turnover because of poor management. Suddenly the company was worse than broke. It had gone through Eastern's money, TWA's money, a loan from the Navy Department and a large loan from the Reconstruction Finance Corporation. Laurance Rockefeller, a member of our board of directors, and I went to see Stuart Symington, head of the Reconstruction Finance Corporation, and tried to persuade him to advance Martin more funds. Symington refused.

I put in a call to Charles E. Wilson, formerly president of General Electric and then Director of the Office of Defense Mobilization. He said to come over right away. He heard the story, let out a blast at Symington for failure to act, then promised to see what he could do. He called a meeting of all those involved and called on me to state my case.

I had the facts, figures, history and details of the transaction. At that time, Martin had somewhere in the neighborhood of forty thousand people on the payroll and no money in the bank to meet that payroll. But, if the company were thrown into bankruptcy, we would all be losers, for no planes would be delivered to anyone. Eastern would be out $11 million, and we were not large enough to stand such a loss. We too would go into the hands of receivers. TWA, the Navy, the RFC and the three banks would also lose, and no one would gain. Still Symington wanted to close it down. Wilson took him outside. Ten minutes later they came back.

"The Navy," Wilson said, "has agreed to advance the next payroll, and in the meantime we hope to work out a plan to refinance the Martin Corporation."

That mastermind of aviation finance, William Barclay Harding of Smith, Barney and Company, together with the bankers, worked out a refinancing program. Glenn stepped down from his position as president, chairman of the board and chief executive officer, and George Bunker, a very able individual who was then president of a subsidiary of the Pullman Company in Chicago, came in to head the newly reorganized Martin Corporation. He did a wonderful job and put the company back on its feet. TWA and Eastern received their planes, which served us well for many years and brought in good prices when we sold them, and everything ended happily.

From the Super-Constellation, we went to the Lockheed Electra, a turboprop plane and a new design. I practically commuted to Burbank to sit in with the Lockheed people in the early stages. Key men from our engineering, radio, engine and maintenance departments also contributed to the design.

We agreed to take 40 Electras, and American Airlines agreed to buy 25. When the plane was ready, it did not quite come up to the specifications. I was satisfied with it, because I knew that, with more powerful engines, the deficiencies would be eliminated. American, however, threatened to cancel its order.

The Lockheed people became frightened and lightened the plane by 1,600 pounds in order to meet the specifications. Then it was my turn to become frightened. In my experience, a new plane always requires some strengthening, which means adding weight rather than taking it away. When our planes were delivered, we tested them thoroughly and added reinforcements in certain areas amounting to six hundred pounds. We placed the plane in service, and it performed beautifully.

Other lines too bought and used the Electra. Then came a series of crashes involving Electras and causing great loss of life. Representatives of the government, the airlines and the factory all investigated the crashes, seeking the cause, but it remained a

RICKENBACKER

mystery for months. Eastern also lost an Electra, but the cause was known. On takeoff at Boston, the plane ran into a flock of starlings, which suffocated two of the engines. In the meantime, we had reduced the cruising speed of our Electras one hundred miles an hour. The Civil Aeronautics Authority ordered all airlines to do the same.

The cause of the crashes was finally pinpointed as a harmonic vibration where the wing joined the fuselage. The metal became fatigued, and the wing snapped off.

All Electras were grounded and returned to the factory. Lockheed had to put back the reinforcements, which strengthened the pods holding the engines to the wing and which had been removed to save weight. The Electra became a very effective plane.

When I first became associated with Eastern Air Lines, we were a small outfit, with a payroll of less than $1 million a year. Most of the personnel knew one another. The heads of the different departments would get together once a month in New York, talk things over for a day and then go back home.

As we grew, we began to have quarterly meetings in different cities. They were called off during the war. But, when the war was over and our employees began coming back, increasing the number from approximately 3,400 in 1944 to more than 6,700 in 1946, I began to realize that the bigger the army, the farther the generals are from the doughboys and the more chances there are of error. What I had to do was put the generals and privates all in the same trench, so that everybody would know what was going on.

To do so, I set up in 1946 what we called "boards of directors." The first, called the "advisory board," was composed of all the officers of the company—president and vice-presidents—who made up the first echelon of management and all the major department heads who formed the second echelon.

The third echelon of management was composed of the station managers, city traffic and sales managers and other men out in the field with comparable positions. We called it the "field board of directors." Many had come up from menial jobs. I wanted to encourage their desire and capacity for growth and educate them in management at the same time.

Our first meeting was held in New York City in the spring of 1946. We met at 8:00 in the morning, took an hour off for lunch and came back after dinner for an evening session. Every one of the four hundred men present had to bring in a detailed report on his operation, including at least one recommendation for the entire system. A copy of each report was sent to me prior to the meeting. I read every one of the reports, rising at 3:00 some mornings that week to do so, and made notations in the margins. Each man would have to stand up and read his report, and each quickly learned to look over my shoulder at my copy to see how often and when he was going to be interrupted.

Each meeting was a kind of controlled free-for-all. Questions could be asked and criticisms made at any time. I wanted everyone to learn to think on his feet. Some of the men were so nervous as they read their reports that they actually shook while they stood before the microphone. I'd give those men a good hard rap on the leg, and it would settle them down immediately.

There was one iron-clad rule: all controversy had to be forgotten when the meeting ended. I set a precedent for that right off the bat by making a couple of recommendations that would not work, letting myself be proved wrong and accepting it in good grace. As far as I know, no one ever realized that I was deliberately setting up straw men so that they could be knocked down.

It was a highly stimulating week. We finished with a dinner Friday night, and the thought suddenly struck me as I looked around and saw our first, second and third echelons of management—"Who the devil is running the airline?" The answer, of course, was the assistants to the men present. That in itself was good. For that week, each assistant had no one to turn to. He was the boss, and he had to make his own decisions. And that week everything went even more smoothly than usual.

But it also meant that those assistants should be exposed to management, just as their bosses were. The junior board of directors, consisting of all assistant managers, both city and station, and the foremen and chief mechanics in the maintenance department throughout the system, was set up and the first meeting held August 19, 1947, in Miami.

One of our most interesting case histories involved a chief mechanic, a member of the junior board. He was a farm boy who stuttered badly. His backwoods parents had been too poor to let him finish even grade school, and he had had to make his way in the world without education. It was agony for him to give his report.

I encouraged him and sent him to a voice teacher. He became able to deliver an intelligent report with only a modicum of stuttering. On the job you could call on him at any time of the day or night, and he'd be there, cheerful and efficient. He worked his way up the ladder to a responsible position and gave his three children the advantages that he had never had.

We had separate meetings, one for the advisory and field boards and one for the advisory and junior boards, in the spring before the summer schedule went into effect and in the fall before the winter schedule came back. Anyone was welcome, any representative from any other airline here or abroad or from any other business. I boasted, and I believed it completely, that any one of our fourth-echelon employees who had attended staff meetings for five years or more knew more about Eastern Airlines than the president of any other airline knew about his own.

One year we happened to have a rash of baggage trouble. People were complaining bitterly about the loss of their baggage. About that time, the spring meeting was held in Miami. As the men arrived, they were told that their baggage would be placed in their rooms. Instead, I had it all locked up overnight. There they were for the meeting next morning, unshaven, teeth unbrushed, wearing dirty shirts. There was no sign of the baggage all day. That night it was delivered, with a great pounding on all the doors, at 3:00 A.M.

Left to right, front row, Senator Charles L. McNary, Oregon; Senator Walter F. Geor
Georgia; Eddie Rickenbacker; Senator Millard E. Tydings, Maryland; standing, Sena
Kenneth McKellar, Tennessee; Senator Pat McCarran, Nevada; Senator Harry F. By
Virginia; Senator Alben W. Barkley, Kentucky

Left to right in front are Eddie Rickenbacker, Quentin Reynolds and Wendell Willk
top left to right, Lieutenant Colonel Larry McPhail, former Dodger boss; Sid Merc
baseball writer, and Elmer Davis, chief of the Office of War Information

With Donald Douglas, Sr.

With World II ace Major Richard I. Bong

With Kate Smith and the Kilgallens

With Henry and Edsel Ford, and Lawrence P. "Larry" Fisher, President, Cadillac Division of General Motors

On Russian Front with General Antoshkin and Lieutenant Archangelski

Drinking toast to the Russian success with vodka, a gift from the Russian Front

Author's name written in Russian and Hat-in-the-Ring painted on his plane by Russians n Moscow, 1943

In the Kremlin at medal presentation—Ambassador Standley at far left; Molotov, second from left; Russian
Ambassador Litvinov, far right

With Lieutenant General Leslie R. Groves, who headed the Manhattan Project

With Babe Ruth, James Farley and Al Smith—1943

Del Ankers

With Fleet Admiral William Leahy

Flying into the future—the Bell Rocket Belt

In Algeria with Generals Tooey Spaatz, left, and Jimmy Doolittle, right

Speaking to the troops in the Aleutian Islands—1943

Marine Honor Guard at American Embassy, Tokyo, Japan—1962

With Bernard "Barney" Gimbel

MR. BERNARD G
50ᵀᴴ MILLION PA
ON
EASTER
AIR
LINES
JAN. 10, 196

Speaking to the troops in India —1943

In Chungking, China—1943

Building runway in China— 1943

...ceiving honorary degree at commencement exercises, University of Miami—1962

*...ment dinner at "21" Club—left to right, George Champion, Chairman of the
..., Chase Manhattan Bank; Floyd D. Hall, new President, Eastern Air Lines,
...and son, David Rickenbacker*

Mrs. Adelaide Frost Rickenbacker

With secretary—Marguerite H. Shepherd—1963

Eastern Air Lines

Beverly Griffith

With Senator Barry Goldwater at Wings Club—November, 1962

Irwin Dribben

With mother, brothers and sisters

David E. Rickenbacker and family

William F. Rickenbacker and family

Charlie Preston Studios

At the opening session that day, I said, "Now you guys know how the customer feels when you mishandle his piece of baggage."

It made an impression on them, all right. It improved the baggage situation too. And the story of how the boss locked up his employees' baggage spread through every airline in the world.

That is the way we ran our airline, the way we developed our people. Thanks to that system you found all throughout Eastern Air Lines responsible, articulate executives who began at the very bottom. Here's a letter, for example, written to me by a foreman who had to quit work because of illness.

Dear Captain Eddie:

I want to tell you that these past nine years have been the happiest years of my life. Everybody both in high position or low has been kind and cooperative and I want to thank you all.

How I remember my first job, the very unsightly restroom in the DC-3 after a rather rough trip. What a wonderful thing to remember that a perfect stranger to all as I was can, in nine short years, advance from a toilet cleaner to a responsible position and be accepted as a junior board member of Eastern Air Lines.

Please tell the boys for me that all they need in order to advance in Eastern Air Lines is to be interested and loyal to their jobs.

I'm not going to try to thank you for all your kindness to me because I could not put it into words, so with a big tear, I am yours,

Sincerely,

Henry J. B. Skern,
Foreman, Building and
Construction

This Eastern training system was covered extensively by management magazines, and many other industries adopted it. Its success, however, depends upon one ingredient. If the top man doesn't work at it, it isn't worth a damn. If I hadn't read and made notes on those four hundred reports four times a year, on top of all the other reports I had to read and assimilate, our meetings would not have meant much. As the 1,600 reports came from every operation on the line, I had to be familiar with every operation in order to be able to tear the report to pieces or to congratulate the author. But then, that is all simply a projection to the final stage of the responsibility of leadership.

The leader must set the example. I've always been punctual, always ahead of time, all the way back to school days. Punctuality is vital to an airline. I could hardly raise hell with a gang about punctuality without getting there first myself.

We now had over one hundred stations. Although one year I did visit every single station, talking not only with the Eastern personnel but also with the community VIPs, I never wanted to do it again. I continued to visit several stations a year, but the management meetings, with their detailed reports, gave such a clear picture of each station that personal inspections were no longer necessary.

Knowing every phase of the operation enabled me to move in and discuss our problems, either as the boss or as an interested co-worker, in every department. An interesting example occurred in the maintenance department in Miami. A Wright TC-18 engine was giving us trouble.

We couldn't figure out what was wrong with it. Tony Pitisci, who was in charge of engine overhaul, was working on the problem himself. I was also interested. For one thing, it was my job to be interested; for another, I was intrigued by the mechanical problems.

When we disassembled the engine, we could find nothing wrong with any individual part. My eye happened to fall on a gear about the size of a saucer. Something about it wasn't right.

"How many teeth is this thing supposed to have?" I asked Tony.

He checked the blueprint. "Forty-five," he said.

"Then here's your trouble," I said, handing him the gear. "It's got forty-six."

That was the talk of the shop that day and for weeks after— for years after, as a matter of fact, for on my retirement from

Eastern I was presented with that very same gear, mounted on a bronze plaque, with the inscription:

To
Captain Eddie Rickenbacker
on your retirement

As a memento, this is the gear that was removed in 1953 from the Wright TC-18 engine on which you helped solve the problem. This gear had one tooth too damned many.

From the Maintenance Department—Tony.

Eastern thus maintained its position as the most prosperous operator in the entire industry in the years following the war. Having proved that airlines could be run without subsidy, I was galled by the spendthrift methods of some other airlines, supported through subsidy by the people of the United States. It was infuriating. If we could make a profit for our stockholders, why couldn't other operators at least break even?

In May 1949, I wrote a letter to Senator Edwin C. Johnson, chairman of the Senate Commerce Committee. In that letter I named five domestic airlines—National, Delta, Capital, Chicago and Southern, and Colonial—and said

Eastern Air Lines, Incorporated, hereby offers to operate the entire domestic system of any one or more of the five above-mentioned air carriers at a non-subsidy rate. According to my calculations, the five above-named air carriers carried 2,701,000 ton-miles of mail in the above-mentioned areas in 1948 and received an average of $4.45 per ton-mile for doing it, aggregating $12,077,000 received from the government by them in 1948.

We were operating profitably at 60 to 65 cents a ton-mile. I therefore offered to carry those 2,701,000 tons of mail for a fee of $1,676,000, thus saving the taxpayers $10,401,000.

But the other lines did not accept this generous offer.

Man did not learn to fly without paying a price, and in the early days flying was indeed dangerous and daring. During the 1930s and the war years, billions of air miles were flown, and airline travel became a reliable means of transportation. Note that word "reliable." I've never liked to use the word "safe," for nothing that moves can be 100 percent safe.

We demonstrated reliability in many ways. Whenever we went into a new city, we would put on an inaugural ceremony and fly groups of community leaders over the town and to other points on the line. As a Shriner, I knew of the great work the organization does for crippled children, and we cooperated with the Shrine in several cities to give the youngsters airplane rides. We would arrange for the children to be taken from the hospitals to the airfields in fire engines and trucks; then we would give them rides over the cities.

How would we expose even more children, the passengers of tomorrow, to the thrill and reliability of air transportation? We couldn't possibly take them all for rides. Beverly Griffith, our genial, roly-poly public-relations director, came up with an idea: give the schoolteachers rides.

The first educators' airlift was operated in Charlotte, North Carolina. We started at 8:00 in the morning one Saturday and made 27 separate flights over the city, giving 743 teachers rides. The next Saturday we took up 523 county teachers on thirteen flights. I found it amazing that, in a progressive city like Charlotte 68 percent of the educators of children, the coming generation, had never flown before. Naturally, when teachers are given airplane rides, they're going to talk about flying to their pupils. Some fifty thousand children in and around Charlotte heard about the pleasures of flying on Eastern Air Lines, and surely a good many took the message home to their parents.

The educators' airlift was repeated in every medium and large city on our system. It took two years to complete. We carried a total of 107,500 schoolteachers, who enlightened over 2,150,000 pupils on air transportation.

It was the type of program that Bev Griffith, one of the most beloved members of the Eastern family, loved to put on. Bev and I have enjoyed a friendship that goes back to 1913, when he was a movie cameraman and I was a racing driver. Over the years, he served as manager of the Fox Film Company in Mexico, Italy, Spain and then in China, doing an outstanding job wherever he worked. We always kept in touch.

During the early days of Eastern Air Lines, he dropped in to see me one afternoon. "Captain," he said, "I've had all of China that I can stomach. I want to go to work for you."

I had nothing open. The very next day our public-relations man, who was from California, gave notice, as he wanted to go back home. When Bev Griffith came in a few days later, I told him that I had a job for him. "You're our new director of public relations," I told Bev.

"My God," he said, "I don't know anything about public relations."

"That's all you've been doing since you were a cameraman," I said. "You'll get along all right."

And he did. He was one of the hardest workers in the company, and he had more good ideas than anybody else, including me. He rode the planes all night and worked all day, just as I did, visiting with people in the communities we served and putting over his promotional ideas. Bev's only problem was his appetite. He'd eat as many as five meals a day. He was about 5 feet 10 inches tall and weighed close to 270 pounds. I sent him to Doctor Floyd McRae in Atlanta, who told him that, if he didn't quit eating so much, he'd wind up with diabetes and have to take a needle each morning. That scared Bev into dieting down to 180 pounds and staying there. At the age of 79, he is still going strong, still full of ideas and still loyal to Eastern Air Lines and me.

I only wish that I could pay fitting tribute to all the thousands of members of the Eastern family who contributed in such great measure to the success of Eastern Air Lines. Some of the members of the team I would like to single out are the late Paul Brattain, vice-president in charge of traffic and sales; Sidney Shannon, who had been with the line since its earliest days and was vice-president in charge of operations; M. M. "Jack" Frost, vice-president and executive assistant to the chairman of the board; Captain John Halliburton, vice-president of all Flight Operations and an extremely capable individual; the late Leslie Arnold, one of the Army round-the-world fliers in 1924, vice-president in charge of all our property; Charles Froesch, vice-president in charge of engineering and a brilliant one; Joseph H. Brock, vice-president in charge of purchasing and later in charge of personnel; Ambrose Chabot, vice-president in charge of maintenance; Thomas F. Armstrong, vice-president in charge of finance, who also served as president; Don McRae, in charge of all communications; General Joseph George, chief meteorologist and one of the most capable in America; Johnny Ray, one of the earliest pioneers in aeronautical mechanics, who was in charge of engine overhaul; J. S. "Tony" Pitisci, a student of Johnny's who succeeded him.

Many of our most faithful and productive workers at Eastern came to us as a result of my interest in disabled veterans, particularly amputees, during and after the war. Lawson General Hospital in Atlanta was devoted exclusively to the care and rehabilitation of amputees, and I visited it often, trying to cheer the boys up. Our personnel department made an analysis of our job classifications, and we found that 90 percent of the positions in Eastern Air Lines could be filled by amputees. That included my job too.

One day a nurse asked me if I would talk with a young man who had just come in from the war zone. He had lost a foot. He was pretty low.

I talked with him and made him see that there were still plenty of jobs that he could do on a wooden foot. He came into my New York office to see me when he was on furlough, still on crutches. After a long talk, he stood up to go, then blurted out a question: "Why are you paying so much attention to us amputees?"

"Sit down," I said. I told him how from my own suffering I had gained experience and compassion. All I wanted was for young men who had sacrificed so much for their country to realize that they could lead rich, happy, productive lives.

When I had finished, he grinned. "You know, Captain," he said, "I'm a helluva lot better off than you are. I'll get used to my wooden foot, but you've got to carry that lame leg of yours for the rest of your life."

"That's the spirit!" I said.

When he was discharged from the Army, he went to work for Eastern selling air transportation and worked his way up to station manager. Then he went into business for himself as an insurance agent. To take some of the pressure off, I promised him that he'd always have a job waiting. He did well.

Our success with disabled veterans, particularly amputees, proved to other industries that these men were worthy of their hire. In my trips about the country, I pleaded their cause with industrialists and businessmen, not on the basis of charity but rather on the basis of good business—these men could produce. One of Eastern Air Lines' most significant honors was the award bestowed upon it by the American Legion "for conspicuous service in providing employment for disabled veterans."

From my earliest days with Eastern, I had had four major expansion areas in mind. They were Puerto Rico, Canada, Mexico, and the southern transcontinental route.

Puerto Rico came first. The four-engine DC-4s had made it possible for us to fly directly from New York to Miami, which means flying over the water for several hundred miles, which gave us experience in overwater flights. I had long envisaged a great amount of traffic between the continental United States and San Juan, the major city of the island. Puerto Rico had more population than it could support, and it had to go somewhere.

I felt that the entire Caribbean area was ready to bloom. Puerto Rico, an American possession, centrally located and populous, was its logical heart. The route was open to competition, as Pan American was the only operator to San Juan.

Eastern applied for and was granted both the New York-San Juan route and the Miami-San Juan route. Then came the job of convincing the American people that Puerto Rico was an

American possession and in the Atlantic Ocean, rather than in the Pacific. We published full-page advertisements, including large maps.

From the beginning, the run was profitable, and today San Juan is the crossroads of the Caribbean area and the West Indies.

We reached Canada and Bermuda by purchasing Colonial Airlines, which had routes from New York to Montreal and Ottawa in Canada and to Bermuda. Later, we gave Colonial's local service in New York and New England to Mohawk Airlines.

The Mexico City route was another natural. There was a large, colorful foreign land to the south, our neighbor on the same continent, with a common boundary yet requiring a journey of several days to reach its capital. After World War II, we opened up a route from New Orleans to Mexico City, but it was still a long way from New York.

In the meantime, I was becoming more interested in all our neighbors to the south. In 1949, with a group of newspapermen, Eastern officials and Arthur Godfrey, the popular radio personality, I took a 31-day tour through Latin America in one of our Constellations. We visited San Juan, Puerto Rico; Belém, São Paulo and Rio de Janeiro, Brazil; Montevideo, Uruguay; Buenos Aires, Argentina; Santiago, Chile (where we were caught in a revolution); Barranquilla, Cartagena and Bogotá, Colombia; Lima, Peru; Caracas, Venezuela; Balboa, Canal Zone, and Mexico City. We met with the heads of government, prominent industrialists, airline operators and other important groups. We were welcomed with open arms. I believe we left some goodwill wherever we stopped. We brought back some pertinent information on how to increase the friendly cooperation among all the nations of the New World.

With the advent of jet planes and their great range, a nonstop New York-Mexico City flight became possible. There would be plenty of potential in both tourist and commercial travelers.

The Mexican government, however, didn't want us to come in with a nonstop jet flight. I made a dozen visits to Mexico, conferring with President Adolfo López Mateos, but I didn't get anywhere. Then I had an inspiration.

We had several jets, Douglas DC-8s, on order. We could let Mexico have one of them at cost. Eastern could train their crews, take care of service and maintenance of their plane at our facilities in New York, charging them on an hourly basis, and permit them to draw upon our inventory of parts. We would also maintain service equipment in Mexico City and let them use our expensive equipment, like trucks and tractors, on a rental basis. All they'd need, in short, would be the plane, which we would buy for them two years before they could, and their own crews, which we would train.

I spent several days in Mexico working out the program. It was translated into Spanish and printed. López Mateos and I then conferred for two hours. I suggested that he think it over and stood up to go, picking up the printed agreement.

"No!" the President said, reaching out for the paper. "I will keep it!"

We completed the deal at the next meeting. Under its terms the Mexicans had practically no worries and no expenses other than those for plane and crew. We maintained the plane, fueled it, put the passengers on it and dispatched it. We thus set up and maintained our own competition. But, in exchange, Eastern won permission to fly our own ships into Mexico City, and there was plenty of business for both of us.

Long before we added these new routes, I had been working on the most ambitious of them all, the southern transcontinental route across the states from Florida to California.

So much interest was generated that hearings were held in Miami, Houston, Los Angeles and Washington. Representatives of the communities, states and regions involved; other airlines and transportation companies; trade associations—all showed up to speak their piece. Millions of words were spoken, taken down and printed.

The CAB's decision was a conglomeration of combinations and interchanges. TWA was awarded the route from California to Amarillo, Texas; Braniff from Amarillo to Houston and Eastern from Houston to Miami. Braniff did not have any transcontinental equipment.

We didn't like the decision, but we went ahead and tried to make it work. An arrangement was made between TWA and Eastern to alternate with each other's planes from California to Florida. We rented Braniff's trackage from Amarillo to Houston, giving one-plane service between California and Florida. We took full-page newspaper advertisements in the communities involved, announcing the route, and flew a Super-Constellation with a group of VIPs from each major city from Miami to California, promoting the new run.

I was actually on my feet before a meeting in Los Angeles when I received a call from Washington. National Airlines, prompted by American, had obtained a court order staying the CAB from allocating the route on the basis that no interchange had been specifically mentioned in evidence at any of the official hearings.

After many more months of argument and delays, the CAB gave the California-Amarillo run to TWA, Amarillo-Houston to Braniff—and terminated it there on the basis that there wasn't any need for service from Houston to Miami!

Operating on an interchange basis only two-thirds of the way across the continent, TWA and Braniff suffered heavy losses and were permitted by the CAB to give it up. More hearings were held all along the line. I was still fighting for it. After many more months, another conglomeration was created. Continental Airlines was given the route from Houston to the West Coast. National was permitted a continuation of its Miami-Houston route to the West Coast. Delta was awarded the run from Dallas to the West Coast and up to San Francisco. Eastern, after conceiving, planning and fighting for the southern transcontinental route, was given only a portion of it, from Dallas to New Orleans, Tampa and Miami. Of course, we could not compete with Delta and National, which offered single-plane service from coast to coast. Thanks to bureaucracy, we thus wound up frozen out of the route I had conceived and pioneered for the previous 25 years.

Other pioneering moves had produced better results. Our pre-war relocation in Miami looked better and better as the years went by. After the war, a war-production plant and large acreage became available near the city. I learned that the price was $700,000. Under Federal regulations, the city or state had first call on it, but neither had that much money. I took the whole proposition to my board of directors, and they authorized me to give the money to the City of Miami to buy the property. The city built a fine new airport on the acreage and gave us a long-term lease on the plant at a reasonable figure. Eastern's investment in Miami grew to $150 million.

For years I had been watching the local people busily collecting money from the tourists during a few months in the middle of winter, then closing up everything and going back to sleep for another several months. I thought Florida could well be a year-round resort center. I hammered away at this theme and finally persuaded the hotels and resort businesses to stay open during the summer months, provided that Eastern would promote summer travel to Florida.

In 1949 we spent $1.5 million on that promotion, the largest, most expensive and most energetic travel campaign ever put on by the airline industry. We had great response. Our planes were full, hotels were full, restaurants were full and the beaches were full. From then on, Florida was a year-round resort.

Florida was also the scene of one of my most appreciated honors. I look back with great pride to November 10, 1947, the day of the opening of the four-mile Rickenbacker Causeway between Miami and Virginia and Biscayne Keys.

The acceptance of New York as the center of world air travel is unquestioned today, I am sure. Yet there was a bitter period of several months in 1952 when there was an immediate danger that all three of the major airports serving the city would be shut down or their use curtailed.

My part in the fight to save New York's three airports began with a telephone call in the middle of the night while I was spending a few days at my ranch in Texas, eighty miles north-west of San Antonio. When my telephone rang at 3:30 A.M., I began steeling myself for a possible blow before I picked up the receiver. No one ever called after midnight with good news; it was always bad.

I don't even know how I heard the phone ring that night. It was downstairs, and I was upstairs asleep. Yet I did hear it and shuffled downstairs to answer. It was Sheppy, my secretary, and the news was bad. A plane, not one of ours, had crashed in Eliza-beth, New Jersey. Twenty-eight passengers and members of the crew had been killed, and, in addition, four apartment dwellers in Elizabeth were dead. Hundreds of people in the area had been scared almost out of their senses.

"They've closed Newark Airport," Sheppy was saying. "We're moving everything over to Idlewild. We're in tents."

That was in February 1952. We were not operating out of Idlewild—now John F. Kennedy International Airport—at that time. We had no hangar and no facilities there.

"I'll be there as soon as I can," I told Sheppy and hung up.

Texas was no place for the chief executive officer of an airline when that airline and the entire aviation industry were in trouble in New York, several hours away.

I hastily dressed. I could get a plane to New York sooner from Houston, three hundred miles to the east, than from San Antonio, and one of the ranch employees drove me there. While I was en route, I thought of our problems. At that time 65 percent of Eastern's New York operations and all our New York mainte-nance were carried on at Newark Airport. We had some flights out of La Guardia Airport and had been negotiating with the Port of New York Authority to put in service out of Idlewild, but Newark was our base. Now, all within one hour, the entire airport was closed and locked up. It was the peak of our season. It couldn't have happened at a worse time.

The crash was the third serious one in the Newark-Elizabeth

area in the previous few months. More than one hundred passengers and crew members and ten residents of the area had been killed. Hysteria was building up. I had learned never, *never* to underestimate the power of hysteria. The newspapers would unquestionably run scare headlines, whip up more anger and emotionalism and use the situation as a circulation getter. The airlines were in grave danger not only of losing Newark permanently but also of being pushed out of La Guardia and Idlewild. The thought may sound ridiculous today, but in February 1952 the situation was explosive. In addition to the danger of airplane crashes, the noise of planes taking off and landing over residential areas was an important issue.

I arrived in New York just in time to attend an emergency meeting called by the New York Port Authority and attended by airline operators, government officials and other interested parties. Howard Cullman, chairman of the Authority, called on each of those attending for ideas. No one else had much to say, perhaps because no one else had been thinking about it for three hundred miles in an automobile and from Houston in a plane. But I had a program all worked out. I stood up and gave it, bing, bing, bing.

And so I was appointed chairman of a 15-man committee to save the three airports. It later became the National Air Transport Coordinating Committee, made up of presidents of the airlines involved and representatives of the CAB, CAA and other government officials. Influences were pulling in all directions. We had the basic outline I had drawn up to begin with, however, and, by hammering away at it day and night, we were able to come up with a comprehensive seven-point program.

In justice to the people who complained about the noise, we did work out many procedures that we had never thought of before to reduce the noise in the areas around the airports.

In the meantime, Eastern was losing $1.5 million in revenue a month. The gasoline problems at Idlewild alone cost us $25,000 more a month than at Newark and overtime and employee transportation another $50,000. But it was heartening the way the gang stuck with us. Much of our work was carried on outside or under canvas.

We were out of Newark for almost a year. But we maintained steady public relations pressure in the proper places, and eventually the saner elements of the community became vocal; the airport was reopened, and New York air traffic became normal again.

Those busy months did have one beneficial result. After serving as chairman of the committee that preserved all three airports, I found it much easier to deal with the Authority, under whose jurisdiction all three airports come.

Like all major operators, we began to consider the potential of jet-powered planes. I was privileged to fly the prototype of the first American jet in production, the Boeing 707, for a few minutes, and it was a thrilling experience. The directors of Eastern Air Lines were holding our meeting at Los Angeles, and the Boeing Company sent the plane to take us to Seattle so that they could show us around their factory.

I couldn't help recalling that it used to take me thirty-six hours to go from Los Angeles to Seattle by train—and there we were doing it in three hours and a fraction. Our directors shared my thrill at participating in this demonstration of progress. Actually flying the smooth, vibrationless giant enhanced my appreciation of it. My one criticism was that the fuselage was too narrow. The Boeing people accepted the suggestion, and every model they have built to the date of this writing has maintained the width I recommended.

Though we were impressed by the plane, we did not consider buying it at that time. Our planes were giving excellent economical service; to replace them with far more expensive jets seemed unwise. But, eventually, competition forced us to do just that. I told both Boeing and Douglas, one of whom would get the Eastern Air Lines contract, that I would insist on two things, a noise suppressor and a reverser. The jet engines made so much noise that I felt it essential to make some effort to suppress the sound as much as possible. The reverser would be a mechanism on the end of each jet engine that would act in the same capacity as reversing the propeller on piston planes. Additional braking power would be needed, as much on these huge new jets as on propeller-powered planes. Douglas was noncommittal about both, but the Boeing people took the attitude that, having built more jet bombers and jet tankers than anyone else in the world, they didn't need my advice.

I had also been arguing with both companies about the large deposit each insisted that the airline put up. It meant that the airline had to borrow money to finance the manufacturer's production. I insisted that, if Eastern had to put up a deposit, at least the manufacturer should pay interest on it.

The final answer of the Boeing group was a refusal to pay interest on the deposit. That afternoon, a Sunday, Don Douglas came in and agreed to pay us 3.5 percent interest on our deposit.

"And now," I said, "how about the noise suppressor and the reverser?"

Don sighed. "I don't know whether we can give them to you or not, Rick, but you can bet your life we'll try."

"That's enough for me," I said. Don and his engineers did try, and they were successful.

In the early 1950s, Hall Hibbard, the chief engineer for Lockheed, had designed a jet transport with four engines in the tail of the ship. It made a lot of sense to me, but no other operator would go along with it, and Lockheed gave it up. Had the company continued, it would have dominated the jet production of the world, for, from the mid-1960s on, nearly every jet design has had the engines in the tail.

Though we never bought any, Eastern was also interested in the British turboprop and jet planes, both of which were in production before their American counterparts. I rode in the prototype of the Viscount, manufactured by the Vickers Aircraft Corporation, made several suggestions for improvements and modifications and predicted they'd sell up to five hundred of them, and they did. The Viscount, unfortunately, because of insufficient range and capacity was not an efficient plane for American operation.

The first commercial jet was the four-engine Comet, built by De Havilland in England. The De Havilland management invited Eastern's top executives over to take a look at it. We climbed to about forty thousand feet and flew around over England. It was an amazingly smooth and comfortable ride. I visited in the cockpit, then strolled back toward the tail. Halfway down the aisle, I suddenly stopped short. I couldn't believe what I was seeing. The sides of the plane seemed to be moving in and out like an accordion. I pushed my finger up against the side. I could feel it.

It scared the living daylights out of me. Sooner or later that metal would fatigue and crack. At forty thousand feet, the pressurized cabin would explode like a toy balloon.

As casually as I could, I went back to the cockpit, tapped our host on the shoulder and said quietly: "I think we've seen everything we want to see. And we have an appointment, and we're about thirty minutes late now. So we'd like to go back, but please don't hurry on our account. Take your time going down."

How I maintained my composure, I'll never know. I swore to myself, and later to my fellow Eastern executives, that never again would we all fly together in that type of plane. We could have lost the entire top management in one accident.

On the ground, I talked to De Havilland's engineers, even the directors of the company. They refused to believe me. Three Comets crashed before the cause was determined. The fuselage had exploded, just as I had feared it would. The Comet crashes were a great blow to British prestige. From my personal experience with the plane, I was able to warn American manufacturers about this accordion weakness, and steps were taken to prevent it.

The serving of food aloft has long been a headache. I'm as much to blame for it as any operator, but I never believed in the extremes to which we all went. I naturally resented the CAB's permitting other airlines to duplicate the routes we had pioneered, particularly when they had to be subsidized by the taxpayers' money. National Airlines, in 1949, was paid $3.74 a ton-mile to haul mail between New York and Miami; we were paid 66 cents a ton-mile—one-fifth as much.

When National and Delta Airlines began serving filet mignon on competing routes, we were forced to serve it too. Those filets mignons cost us an extra $15,000 a month. It wasn't long before we began receiving complaints about them. Our flight crews and our regular commuters actually got sick of filet mignon.

Don't believe for one moment that the luscious meals served aloft are free. The money has to come from somewhere. When the CAB was subsidizing our competitors, it came from the taxpayers. On nonsubsidized lines it comes from the passengers, one way or the other.

I protested so loudly against serving so-called "free" meals in flight during wartime that the CAB called a special meeting on it. I pointed out that the custom was ridiculous. Do clothing stores give away ties with shirts? Do shoe stores give away socks with shoes?

One of the operators arguing against me said, "Why, even if you charged, you'd only collect about half of what it costs you to serve these meals."

"That's a stupid objection to make," I snapped. "You'd be fifty percent better off than you are now, wouldn't you?"

We didn't believe in giving away liquor, either. Alcohol doesn't belong on an airplane. We finally had to begin serving drinks aloft to keep up with our competitors. I attempted to persuade all operators to go along with us and to charge for liquor as an industry-wide policy, but only our direct competition agreed. Transcontinental and international operators refused, but they will join the rest of us some day.

We also set a limit of two drinks to a passenger. But I am still not in favor of serving alcohol on planes. And, as for serving meals, I predict that airlines will eventually charge the passenger directly for the food he eats, rather than falsely labeling it "free" and adding the cost of food to your ticket whether you eat it or not.

In 1953 Thomas F. Armstrong, our vice-president in charge of finance, was made president, and I moved up to chairmanship of the board and remained as chief executive officer.

During my 25-year stewardship of Eastern Air Lines, we were never in red ink, we always showed a profit, we never took a nickel of the taxpayers' money in subsidy and we paid our stockholders reasonable dividends over the years, the first domestic airline to do so. During the postwar years, when all the other lines were in red ink and were running to the Civil Aeronautics Board for more routes and more of the taxpayers' money in subsidies, the Board would point to Eastern Air Lines as a profitable company and suggest that the other airlines emulate our example.

At the same time, the Board continually permitted other airlines to fly routes duplicating Eastern's, setting up additional competition to the extent that Eastern became the most duplicated airline in the world. Take the New York-Washington run, for example, which Eastern pioneered and developed. We encouraged passenger travel in many ways. One was the merry-go-round service, which we set up in 1937 and which was operated with twenty round trips daily, flying empty or full. Everyone making the 80-minute flight between New York and Washington was eligible for membership in the 80-Minute Man Club with a lapel button to prove it. It was a mark of prestige. The club held an annual dinner, attended by several hundred members, and a gold card was awarded to the one who had had the most flights that year.

The merry-go-round was the forerunner of the popular shuttle service established April 30, 1961. By that time, there were nine airlines operating between Washington and New York. How could any one line show a profit in such a situation? Imagine the chaotic state, the lack of service that would result if there were nine separate telephone companies in New York or Washington, nine utility companies, nine water companies. They'd all go broke before they got started. Yet that was the situation Eastern faced at that time: eight other competitors between two cities.

The same fundamental philosophy on the part of the CAB

affected every other part of the Eastern system. I have never held that there should be no government regulation whatever. But I do deplore the trend toward more and more bureaucracy, more and more governmental control, that has marked the course of government since Roosevelt and the New Deal. It is taking America in the wrong direction.

As I neared the age of seventy, I became so disgusted with this trend toward socialism that I felt like stepping out of the airline business completely, provided that we could find the right type of executive to take over from me. Some of our directors felt that Eastern should have a younger chief executive officer, to which I agreed. Malcolm A. MacIntyre, a brilliant lawyer but a man inexperienced in airline operation, took over as president and chief executive officer on October 1, 1959. I remained as director and chairman of the board.

A difficult period followed. The airline industry was entering the jet era, with its attendant pains. To keep up with the Joneses, we had to replace perfectly good piston-powered and turboprop airliners with the expensive new jets. An internal power struggle between the pilots and the flight engineers caused a strike that affected us adversely. Eastern was in debt and losing more money every day.

A complete new financial setup had to be worked out and new financing arranged. Again, Bill Harding, by then senior partner and chairman of the board of Smith, Barney and Company, helped us out.

Floyd B. Hall, the solid, dependable, hard-driving senior vice-president and systems general manager of Trans World Airlines, headed a new management team, which took over the operation on December 16, 1963. I assisted him wherever I could. From his past experience and knowledge, I assumed that Hall and his new team would be on the right track. In 1964 and 1965, the Eastern Air Lines family once more showed what a determined group of Americans can do. Through hard work and dedication, they brought the company out of the red and into the black again.

It has been my good fortune, from the time Eastern Air Lines became a separate entity in 1938, to have been associated with a board of directors that should be recognized for its dedication, cooperation and loyalty. I shall always remember all its members and their support and understanding.

On December 31, 1963, I retired from active management and from the board of directors. I was 73 years old. There were many more things in this old world that I wished to do and see, and I could not do them while putting in seven days a week running an airline.

Before closing this chapter, I think that some reflections are in order. There is no more inspiring example of the opportunities that are offered, in such great abundance and in every direction by this free-enterprise system of ours, than the story of aviation. In my life span, the airplane has been developed from a primitive little machine, capable of staying aloft only a few seconds and covering only a few feet, into a great airliner of the sky, which flies across the continents and around the globe at the speed of sound itself. In a single generation, the airplane has superseded all forms of earthbound transportation.

Fantastic as our past progress has been, however, I am confident that the aviation industry will make more progress in the next decade than we were able to achieve in the past half-century. The sky is no longer the limit. We're already reaching out into the universe.

It seems only yesterday, in 1934, that Eastern Air Lines was a struggling little company pioneering in a new and untried field. It became a giant in the industry. We built it through hard work, dedication and faith in the future of America.

This kind of faith in the future of America is being expressed everywhere you look. It is based upon the one eternal truth on which our nation is founded. The future promises that men and women, free to dream and free to work to make their dreams come true, can accomplish anything. There can be no limit to the creative imagination with which a beneficent God has endowed mankind.

I cannot help but remember the many heartaches my mother endured in attempting to keep together our family of seven after the passing of my father. With the help of the three oldest children, Mary, William and me, she managed to keep the wolf from the door until the younger ones, Emma, Louis, Dewey and Albert, were able to do their share. Thanks to our early training, we all became good American citizens. Mary became Mrs. Joseph A. Pflaum; Emma, Mrs. Ralph Hanson. Of the boys, Louis and Albert remained bachelors.

Through the years, I tried to fulfill the promise I had made to Mother after my father's death, that I would assist my brothers and sisters to the best of my ability. During Mother's last illness, when she was 82 years old, I brought the whole family together. She was pleased to see us all happy and healthy. Her last days were content. In the ensuing years, I am sorry to say, William and Dewey have passed away.

As I approached the age of 65, the usual retirement age for Eastern's employees, I began thinking it would be nice to have a small ranch in Texas to retire to. I bought one, a 2,700-acre spread—that's small in Texas—with a large, comfortable house on it. The former owner had imported eight different species of deer from abroad. They were running wild in an enclosed preserve and were wonderful to observe.

Several factors had influenced me to buy the ranch. Dave, my older boy, had been graduated from Hamilton College in New York and was married to a fine young lady, the former Patricia Ann Bowne of Utica, New York. Adelaide and I brought them to the ranch with us, and Dave, who practically ran the place, developed both physically and mentally.

Bill, after having been graduated from Harvard University, had joined the Air Force and was in training as a flying cadet, first at San Antonio, then at Lubbock, Texas. He'd spend Saturdays and Sundays with us and would frequently drive over from San Antonio for dinner. We all had many happy hours together.

Though we enjoyed the ranch for a while, its appeal was not as permanent as I had hoped it would be. Adelaide, eighty miles away from her friends in San Antonio, was frequently lonely. Bill had been graduated, had won his wings and was in Korea, serving in an extremely dangerous capacity with the famous Gypsy Squadron. Dave and Patty were happy, but they too were ready to return to New York.

One day a special committee of the Alamo Area Council Boy Scouts of America in San Antonio, consisting of approximately eighteen thousand Boy Scouts, came by the ranch. They were looking at properties, for their little summer camp was woefully inadequate. The chairman of the committee liked our ranch, but he knew that it would be far too expensive.

A day or two went by, and the president of the Alamo Area Council, Harold D. Herndon, called me about it.

"Fasten your seat belt because I'm going to give you a shock," I said. "Mrs. Rickenbacker and I have decided to give the Boy Scouts part of the ranch, including the ranchhouse, the deer, the equipment, and the stock. And it won't cost you a penny, because you need it more than we do."

There was a long pause. "I want to have you say that to my face," he said.

"I'd be delighted to," I said. He drove out that afternoon, and I repeated our offer. The Council accepted it and bought the balance of the ranch for a very nominal sum.

Adelaide and I then bought a home in Miami, Florida. We commuted to New York, where we had always maintained a hotel apartment, for about three years. The Florida climate did not agree with her, however, and we sold the Miami house and made New York City our permanent residence.

Bill, on his discharge from the Air Force, came back to New York in 1955 and became interested in investments. I gave him the names of a number of my friends down on Wall Street and told him to go around and introduce himself, visit with them and let me know which one he would like to join if the opportunity were available. He chose Smith, Barney and Company and within a year was in charge of the aviation-research department. Then he decided that he could be of better service to the smaller investor and struck out in business for himself. He took a small office in nearby Tarrytown and began building a list of clients. Bill married a childhood sweetheart, Alexandra Harriman Leys of Yonkers, and they are living happily with their two sons, James and Thomas, in Briarcliff Manor, New York.

Bill was inherently in love with writing, however. He is an excellent writer, with a vocabulary larger than the English dictionary. He is also a gifted pianist and a scratch golfer. Bill met William F. Buckley, Jr., the publisher of *National Review,* an outstanding and conservative monthly magazine, and joined the staff. He rose quickly to be a senior editor. His book *Wooden Nickels,* an excellent analysis of the current silver situation, has done very well.

Dave and Patty returned to New York in 1957 and Dave emulated Bill's job-seeking experience. Dave chose the United States Trust Company, one of the oldest in the world, which manages accounts with a value of $8 billion. He was given every opportunity to learn the business and, being a steady, capable and intelligent young man, he became assistant to an officer in charge of many of these funds. He and Patty bought a home in Upper Montclair, New Jersey, and have three children, Brian, Marcia and Nancy.

Dave and Bill are both examples of firm and loving upbringing in a Christian home. As I have been on the go so much of my life, much of the credit for their success in adult life must go to Adelaide, their mother. I appreciate her great love and understanding all the more when I think of all the evenings and weekends—and even months—she has had to spend alone as I traveled the country and the world to achieve success and to serve my country.

We always tried to teach the boys by example. When Dave was one year old I began saving pennies. I have never spent, given away or lost a penny since 1925. When Bill was born, I split the penny account equally. The boys saw their money increasing from hundreds of dollars to thousands of dollars, penny by penny. It was an excellent lesson in thrift, and they are both doing the same for their children.

The boys have always appreciated what they had. When they were youngsters and we went out together, I'd point out crippled or impoverished people on the street and remind them that, to paraphrase the famous quotation, "There, but for the grace of God, may be you."

I pointed out drunks and told the boys to look at them and analyze them.

Not that I advocate either teetotalism for the individual or prohibition for the nation. Far from it, I believe that the national prohibition foisted upon the country in 1918, when the soldiers were overseas and could not vote against it, was a horrible mistake and one of the major causes of the lawlessness that exists in the United States today. During Prohibition, children saw their parents and their parents' friends scorning the law, drinking bootleg whiskey and bathtub gin at home and getting drunk and screaming and fighting in front of them. It could not help but leave scars on the developing youngsters who have grown up to become the parents of today's youth.

After World War II, there was a tremendous increase in the sale of automobiles. Today many high-school boys and girls must have their own cars or ride in those of their contemporaries, rather than walking and developing their bodies. Car pools and school buses deprive younger children of this greatest of all physical exercise. Youngsters today are spending a great deal more time away from their homes, away from the influence of their parents, than before. Parents themselves go out to parties and shows, leaving their children at home with baby-sitters who can hardly be expected to exert a strong moral influence on children temporarily deserted by their own parents. And, whether the parents are home or away, the television set blasts out its themes of violence and lawlessness.

Over it all hangs the stultifying influence of big government and the big-brother philosophy in Washington. This so-called "security" nullifies the basic American values and the incentives that are actually stimulated by insecurity. The more that is done for the individual, the less he does for himself. Self-reliance, ambition and determination, all those natural human traits that were common in the pioneering days and that made this country great, are being softened, even eliminated, in America today.

What a change has taken place in the world! My dear mother, after my father's death, raised seven children on a mere fraction of what people earn today. Mother cooked three hot meals a day, washed and ironed all the clothes for all the family by hand, kept a spick-and-span house and always had the time to advise, encourage and inspire us. Comparing the home life of today with the home life I enjoyed as a youngster, I cannot help but shudder at the thought of the coming generation and of what America will be like in 25 years.

In the postwar years, I continued to be active in the service of my country when presented with the opportunity.

In 1954 I received a telephone call from Herbert Hoover, our former President. He had been asked by President Harry S Truman to serve as chairman of the Commission on Organization of the Executive Branch of the Government. The Hoover Commission, as it was known, made exhaustive studies and produced many recommendations for the improvement of our governmental operation, many of which were followed.

"One of the projects of my Commission will be to form a task force to investigate all of our intelligence services," Mr. Hoover said. "That includes the intelligence sections of the Army, Navy, Marine Corps, Air Force and Central Intelligence Administration, here and abroad. I would greatly appreciate it, Eddie, if you would take the directorship of that task force."

After thanking Mr. Hoover for his trust in me, I had to decline the directorship. I could not take the time just then to give the project the attention it deserved. I recommended, instead, that General Mark Clark be asked to serve as director, with me as his deputy.

In a few days Mr. Hoover called back to say that the General had accepted the directorship and would be getting in touch with me. General Clark and I met and set up a working schedule. He knew the Pacific, and I was familiar with western Europe, so we agreed that each of us would take half the task force and cover the section he knew best. Then we would get together, pool our information and make our report.

I regret that I cannot give a full account of the investigations in western Europe. One of the reasons I was asked to serve was that I had proved in the past my ability to take on a sensitive mission and keep my mouth shut. What we saw was as exciting and as fascinating as any television espionage show. We visited Germany, France, Switzerland, Italy and England, investigating both American intelligence operations and those of the host countries. Through one-way glass mirrors we observed defectors, suspects and spies, some of them double agents, being interrogated by our operatives. There was a great deal of dirty work on both sides. To witness some of the operations required real cloak-and-dagger procedures.

As we proceeded through Europe, we were booked into hotels by an agent who preceded us. When we checked into a hotel, it was standard operating procedure for the communications expert who accompanied us to check every room for concealed listening devices.

In Italy, where the Communists form one of the major political parties, we discussed the situation at length with our ambassador, Mrs. Clare Boothe Luce. It is no secret that the CIA can dispense huge sums of money without answering to anyone but the President, and our conversations with Mrs. Luce on this topic were most helpful. Indeed, in every country our ambassadors and military representatives cooperated with us to the fullest degree. As a private citizen I think I am free to say that, of all our intelligence operations, that of the U.S. Army was the most efficiently run at that time.

Back in the United States, General Clark and his group met with our group. I was surprised at how closely our notes compared. We were not impressed with the over-all effectiveness of our intelligence operations. The task force made its report, recommending several major changes in intelligence operations, but I am afraid that the interdepartmental rivalries and jealousies that prevail in Washington resulted in its being shelved. When John McCone became director of the CIA in 1961, his superior administrative ability was responsible for a great deal of improvement in that agency.

Ever since I had returned from France in 1919 and plunged into a speaking tour, I've been doing a great deal of public speaking. In April 1961, I began a new chapter in my public-address experience.

Since the early days of the Roosevelt administration, I had been observing our country steadily becoming a socialized welfare state. I was bitterly opposed to this trend, but I was hesitant about standing up on my hind legs and stating my views and the reasons for them. I was afraid that the general public had not had the time to assimilate what was happening to the country and would not understand what I was talking about.

In the early part of 1961, I was invited by the Chicago Economic Club, one of the strongest economic clubs in the country, to address its annual dinner meeting. I had frankly stalled the Chicago group for some time, because I did not believe that even this knowledgeable assembly would appreciate what I had to say. This time, however, I agreed to speak, and I resolved to say what was really on my mind. I prepared what I believed to be a challenging, aggressive speech, and I gave its message in the title: "Conservatism Must Face Up to Liberalism."

It was a miserable evening, with snow and sleet, and, driving over to the Palmer House on icy streets, I steeled myself not to be disappointed by the size of the crowd. As I walked into the banquet hall, I could hardly believe my eyes. It was packed. More than one thousand men and women were present; about 95 percent were men. The fact that so many people would brave the terrible weather to hear me speak was in itself a great inspiration.

I cannot reprint the speech in its entirety here; it lasted well over an hour. I was told later that the number of times I was interrupted by applause totaled 24 and that the standing ovation at its close lasted four minutes. I began by declaring that the liberals were no longer firmly in the saddle, that the winds had shifted, that conservatives were rising up across the land, finding new strength in their old convictions, making their voices heard and winning at the polls. Modern liberals had forsaken the original meaning of the word. Instead of advocating freedom, they were striving to pile up the power of government in Washington. It was the conservatives who must take individual freedom as their battle cry and resist the steady encroachment of Federal power.

I delivered an all-out attack on the Federal income tax, recommending that we take the government out of competition with private enterprise and eliminate the billions of dollars in expenditures annually being poured down a rathole. I suggested a national lottery to increase revenue without taxation.

Now New Hampshire and New York State have them, and before many more years pass many more states will join them. Why not a national lottery now?

Chicago papers carried the speech in great detail—the Chicago *Tribune* devoted three columns on the front page to it—and the wire services carried excerpts across the nation. A blizzard of mail poured in, with every letter requesting a copy. I had the speech printed in pamphlet form and mailed out more than fifty thousand copies at my own expense. Hundreds of requests came in for me to speak. I addressed numerous groups around the country during the rest of that year and in the years that followed.

Before that time, I had never considered receiving an honorarium. Most of my appearances had been connected with aviation in general and Eastern Air Lines in particular, except, of course, for those appeals to the American people made during the war. For this speech, however, organizations began offering honorariums of from $300 to $1,000.

I had long been contributing to eight youth organizations. They constituted my favorite philanthropy, as the only real thing you can leave behind when the Grim Reaper calls is potential men. These clubs were dedicated to developing a patriotic spirit, the initiative that is so essential to all Americans and religious faith. And so I began accepting honorariums with the proviso that every penny would be divided equally among these eight clubs. Since that time, each club has received several thousand dollars as its share. The recipients are The Boys' Athletic League, New York; Boys' Club of New York; Children's Village of Dobbs Ferry, New York; Madison Square Boys' Club, New York; Boys' Clubs of America, New York; Big Brothers of America, Philadelphia; Gramercy Boys' Club, New York, and Greater New York Councils, Boy Scouts of America.

Making a speech or even saying a few words is, in short, a complex operation. As in practically every other activity in life, the difference between doing it well and doing it badly is a little thought on the subject.

Whenever I talk to women's groups, I speak bluntly, for women control 65 percent of the wealth of this nation. There are more widows in the United States than in any other nation because their husbands have worked themselves to death prematurely in order to leave those widows annuities, trust funds, savings accounts, insurance policies and pension funds.

Most of this money is in fixed income. It can't grow, but it can decrease. I remind my women listeners of this fact and point out to them that they have to protect themselves and their incomes. They're endangered by inflation, among other threats to their economic well-being, and I tell them that they must understand inflation in order to resist it.

Women frequently come up to me after a speech and say, "Captain Rickenbacker, you frighten me."

"That's just what I meant to do," I say. "I want to frighten you into doing something."

"But I'm just one woman," they'll say. "What can I do?"

"You can read and become informed," I say. "You can discuss issues over the back fence, in your homes and apartments. You can join your voice with others."

For it is only through the concerted action of an informed, concerned and militant people that we can halt this trend to socialism and the welfare state and put these United States back on the right road again.

TWENTY

THE FUTURE

For the past forty years, I have been venturing to predict some of the developments that the future will bring. These predictions have never been imaginative prophecies so much as projections of current knowledge. I have always been interested in the world around me and have sought to add to my store of information about it. Looking ahead is a part of living.

Yet my descriptions of many of the phenomena that we accept as almost commonplace today, especially in the field of transportation—multi-engined airliners, transoceanic air service, military aircraft capable of high altitudes and wide ranges, helicopters, multi-lane highways bypassing towns and cities—were considered by some of my listeners to be the outpourings of an unbalanced mind.

When I first began projecting the present into the future many years ago, my main interest was in transportation, particularly aerial transportation. Today, following many decades of exposure to other areas of scientific interest and bearing in mind the possibility that some will consider me to have overstepped the bounds of rationality, I intend to extend these predictions into the realm of civilization itself.

I have lived through five wars, counting the so-called "police action" in Korea and the fighting in Vietnam as separate phases of the Cold War, which is actually hotter than Hades. In previous chapters, I have described my official missions to Europe, North Africa, the Middle East, India, China, Russia and the Pacific. Since the war I have made fact-finding visits to the remaining major areas of the world, to South America, Central and South Africa and the Orient—Japan, Okinawa, Taiwan, Southeast Asia, Australia and New Zealand. Some of my predictions, based on knowledge acquired on these trips and in continuing research at home, will be controversial.

Let me repeat once again that they are projections of current actual situations and trends and that I do not necessarily support them; they are what I foresee, not what I wish for. If some of my direct prophecies do not materialize, so much the better.

In air transportation, the next step will be the breakthrough from the supersonic speeds of the present and near future— 2,000 to 4,000 miles per hour. Through the use of ramjet engines, which will go into operation after the plane has reached a speed of 1,500 miles per hour, utilizing the force of air pressure, airplanes will travel at speeds of 3,000 to 5,000 miles per hour. Rocket power will produce speeds as high as 25,000 miles per hour. At first rockets will carry only mail, in the timeworn pattern of development of new vehicles, but they will eventually carry passengers.

I remember the jeers that once followed any proposal that man fly nonstop from New York to London—and later the incredulous looks at the prediction that flying time from New York to London could be cut to six hours, the current duration. But within the next fifty years, through rocket power, the flying time to London will be less than a quarter of an hour.

Ten years ago, when an experimental engineer told me that we would have the supersonic transport, or SST, by 1968, I said that 1978 would be a better estimate. Before the SST becomes commercially economical, we shall see the 500-passenger plane become a reality. Then will come the 1,000-passenger plane. It will be so expensive to buy and operate that it will be purchased and flown cooperatively by a group of airlines. It will change the whole concept of terminal design and service. Imagine the problems if half a dozen of these planes landed within an hour and discharged six thousand passengers, all trying to make their way through the corridors and lobbies, claim their baggage and find taxicabs. The airline industry simply must adjust to this new concept.

These huge planes will also bring about a great increase in air freight. Transoceanic shipping companies will be forced to go into air freight.

Forty years ago I predicted that building heights in downtown areas would someday be made uniform and that streets would be bridged over, making the heart of every city a heliport. Elevators would take passenger-commuters, mail and cargo from the rooftops to the street level. That was before the helicopter was invented; I have lived to see and use helicopter travel from airports to mid-city heliports.

The day will arrive, sooner than most people realize, when anyone can have his own helicopter. A device called the "rocket flying belt," which will lift and propel an individual through the air at 60 miles per hour, has passed the preliminary experimental stage and is being perfected for military use. In my opinion, the rocket belt will go through a sporting stage, furnishing excitement and exhilaration to hobbyists, as in the early days of motoring. Within the next fifty years, however, with the development of nuclear power and with safety devices designed especially for its use, the rocket belt will become a routine means of individual transportation.

The development of electronic devices and controls will make the operation of aircraft independent of the weather. It will be unnecessary for the human hand to touch the controls. Within only a few years it will be routine for aircraft to make scheduled stops in rain, fog or snow—and even in strong winds short of hurricanes and violent storms. Indeed, some day we shall not only be able to ignore the weather; we shall control it.

Advancements in aviation will combine to place great traffic pressure on airports and ground facilities, necessitating changes and expansion. Localities—towns as well as cities—with the most complete facilities and services will harvest the fruits of air transportation. No longer need an area be dependent on land or water transportation for growth and prosperity. Any hamlet has the potential to be a port of call on the vast ocean of air on whose shores every man lives. Where localities seize this potential, new boom areas will mushroom all over the world.

When we break through the problems of nuclear power—and we shall—a huge airship will be able to remain aloft for a year or more on a bucketful of fuel, both in motion through the envelope of air surrounding the earth and in orbit beyond it. Such ships will serve as mother ships, with smaller aircraft rising from points below to transfer or take off passengers. American military ships, staying aloft a year or more, will serve as a perpetual peace patrol from which all points on the world beneath can be observed. Should any nation threaten world peace, it could be destroyed.

Huge platforms will orbit the earth to serve as launching pads for ships to the other planets and whatever lies beyond the solar system. These platforms will be essential to the self-preservation of the human race, for whoever controls the immediate area around our planet will also control the universe, militarily, economically and culturally. A shuttle service will be operated from earth to these orbiting way stations, delivering passengers and personnel, mail and express to be dispatched by rocket ship to other planets.

As for the spaceships themselves, within the next half-century they will become commonplace for interplanetary travel. Each will have comfortable accommodations for fifty or more passengers. Using power derived from nuclear energy, they will develop speeds of up to 25,000 miles per hour or better and will have practically unlimited ranges. They will be like self-sustaining planets in themselves.

The creation of these complexities and of even greater wonders requires no greater intelligence than our own God-given capacity. Our progress in aviation and in space travel is limited only by the boundaries of human imagination. We have reached only the noon hour in this area of advancement.

The very existence of aviation is proof that man, given the will, has the capacity to accomplish deeds that seem impossible. We shall never be able to shorten geographical distance between two points, but through aviation we have decreased the time required to cover that distance. Through our aeronautical advancement, for example, we have shrunk the globe. We shall continue to shrink it, in terms of time, and, through extension of this concept into space, we shall shrink the universe.

These new developments in the field of air transportation can, in the hands of men of goodwill, provide the one instrument that can forever eliminate the barriers of time and distance and, as a consequence, the barriers of ignorance and misunderstanding, which, since the dawn of civilization, have set men apart and against one another. As the world becomes progressively smaller, people of all nationalities, of all areas of the world, will possess the means of meeting and understanding all other people, thus eliminating the petty hates and jealousies, born in ignorance, which breed human conflict. I still believe, as I have been saying for forty years, that, instead of being the most deadly weapon that God ever let man create, the airplane—and its successors—will truly become the angel of peace that He intended it to be.

Though our most dramatic progress in the field of transportation in the years ahead will unquestionably be in the air and its extension, space, man will still continue to travel on the surface of the earth. Great strides will be made in all forms of modern transportation, both over land and over sea. Progress in ocean vessels will not stop. Ships will ride on cushions of air and will be much larger and faster than they are today. Speeds over the surface of the ocean will eventually reach 100 to 150 miles per hour, and the great size of future ships will make for greater economy in the transportation of passengers, mail, express and freight.

Greater improvements will also be made in land transportation. Development of the monorail system, similar to that used at the 1963 Seattle World's Fair, will increase the speed and efficiency of travel between the hearts of cities and their suburbs, including airports. Over longer distances, the development of the vacuum tube will make it possible to travel at speeds of 500 to 1,000 miles per hour on land. By straightening the curves of the existing railroad systems, we shall be able to use them in vacuum-tube transportation—and their stations and yards as well. Computer controls will eliminate the possibility of human error, thus providing great reliability at these high speeds. Of course there will be problems, but human beings have the built-in capacity to make the necessary scientific breakthroughs.

The mass-transportation systems of the future will not supplant the automobile. Until small aircraft for individual and family use become practical in both price and safety and the drag of gravity is eliminated by science, people will continue to use automobiles in their short hauls, traveling when and as they choose with their families, at no additional cost.

But, though we shall use automobiles for generations to come, they will not remain the same. Automotive power plants will progress from the piston engines of today to turbines and then to jet-type engines producing greater power at less weight and cost. Turbines, which consume all fuel completely, will come into use just in time. At the rate we are going, current combustion engines would otherwise smother the world in gasoline vapor.

The day will come when the vast reservoirs of oil from which we derive our current automotive fuel will be exhausted; coal fields will also be depleted because of the tremendous use of coal gas and coal dust. This exhaustion of resources will necessitate breakthroughs in the potential of nuclear power. All major forms of transportation, including the family automobile, will someday utilize this source of energy.

Through improved design, braking devices, control systems and highways, automobiles will travel at speeds of more than 100 miles per hour with far greater safety than we have today at speeds of 50 miles per hour.

In the meantime, in the very near future, much more stringent restrictions will be placed on the individual operators of motor vehicles. The current and increasing slaughter and injury on the highways must be curtailed. Drastic and rigid regulations will accompany the privilege to operate motor vehicles. A driver's license will be issued only to those physically and mentally capable. Abuses of the privilege to drive will result in the immediate and irrevocable loss of that privilege.

Driver training will be scientifically administered and universally required. For thirty years in the air transportation industry we have used simulators to train pilots and develop their flying skills. Simulators will also be used universally in the training and licensing of automobile drivers. New drivers will be able to handle vehicles with competence before they ever venture onto the highways. It is a wide-open field, incidentally; millions will be made in the manufacture of simulators for this purpose in the next few years.

Rather than continuing the costly exploitation of land—which could be used far more efficiently in other ways—for the construction of new highways, we shall add additional levels to existing thoroughfares. Some day our road builders will realize the advantages of using existing railway rights of way for vehicular travel through the simple means of constructing new levels above them. The railroads will benefit by the additional income.

Great strides will be made in the field of electronics and communications. An interesting and productive use of television will be the instantaneous registration of signatures in banking houses all over the world. Today billions of dollars—and francs, marks, pounds and other major monetary units—are in enforced idleness while in transit. All banks will have two-way television providing immediate exchange of credit on televised signatures.

Money currently tied up in surface or air transportation will be released into the working capital of the world.

Transfer of both raw materials and finished products of all kinds will be expedited through the use of television. As a small but dramatic example, take the fashion industry. Today buyers attend fashion shows, place their orders and, weeks later when the articles arrive, keep them in inventory to display to their customers. Imagine instead a system in which a customer in Los Angeles observes by television a fashion show in New York or Paris and informs the saleslady of her selection immediately. The order is flashed electronically to the manufacturer and the garment placed on a plane for delivery the next morning. (By rocket, it could be available for wear that night.)

This system can be applied to practically any product or even to the raw material from which that product is manufactured. It would eliminate the great expense of maintaining an inventory, both on hand and in transit. In the case of many products it would eliminate the hazard of obsolescence caused by new developments, improvements or changes in design. The release of billions of dollars lying idle in inventory would be effected.

Having already prefaced these predictions with the recollection that some in the past were considered the products of an unbalanced mind, I shall state without further apology that a major communications breakthrough will occur in the field of extrasensory perception. Serious research work is being conducted in the field of parapsychology. I have had personal experience in extrasensory perception. I have recounted how, during World War I, I saw in a vision the midair collision of two planes flown by Alexander Bruce and my dear friend Walter Smyth and knew that both had been killed.

On the night of February 27, 1965, I awakened from a vivid dream. I remember it clearly. In this dream, my brother Bill telephoned me from his home in Detroit.

"Things are going from bad to worse, Eddie," he said. His voice was unmistakable. "I am not going to stay here very long. I wish you'd come out and see me—the sooner the better. I'd like to have a last word with you and thank you for what you have done for me and my family."

I awakened and started to call him, but I decided against it for fear that it would excite his family. Later that day I received an actual telephone call. Bill had died suddenly. At the funeral his wife Margaret told me that, just before Bill passed away, he said that he wanted to call me and ask me to come to him so that he could say something to me. I know both from my own experiences and from reading about substantiated cases that messages can be sent telepathically.

Is it not possible that all the words, all the thoughts of mankind since the dawn of the human race are still in existence somewhere in the ether? We can transmit impulses electronically through the atmosphere, even into space, and receive them and understand them. Someday I believe that we shall be able to receive and understand the mental impulses that have emanated from the minds of men over the past millennia. They are there; it is only a question of tuning in on them. Someday we shall penetrate this secret and fathom all the great mysteries of mankind, including that of our very origins.

To return to the physical sciences, I have already discussed the future of desalination of seawater, a process in whose origin I had some personal influence following my 24-day experience afloat on the Pacific Ocean. Fresh water distilled from seawater through nuclear energy will be piped directly from the oceans to arid sections of our country and will result in the reclamation of millions of idle acres. It will enable us to increase the production of our own food supply, and we shall be able to feed half a billion people within our own borders. The extension of this potential to the rest of the world will mean that no human being, man, woman or child, will ever again lack food to eat. When that day comes, it will mean that no man will ever again be driven or inveigled by tyrants into aggressive acts through hunger.

More than water can be drawn from the vast oceans of the world. When we learn to control the process of nuclear fusion, through which today we can generate the awesome destructive force of the hydrogen bomb, we shall be able to draw upon the seas for an unlimited power supply. For every five thousand atoms of hydrogen in the sea, there is one atom of deuterium, the fuel required for nuclear fusion. Harnessing this power will make the seas our source of supply. We shall be able to mine the seas of every chemical element, every metal known to man, and harvest them for never-ending sustenance. The sciences of physics and oceanography, both in their infancy, will combine to transform the seas, which comprise seven-tenths of the earth's surface with depths of up to seven miles, into a bountiful source yielding inestimable volumes.

But, until that utopian day arrives, I foresee increasing trouble, misery and starvation in the world. There is not enough wealth in existence, including hard money, precious metals and precious stones, to raise the standard of living of the proliferating hordes of people in Asia, Africa and South America by a paltry 5 percent in ten years. Indeed, within that ten-year period, the population would increase by 15 percent at the present rate, and the people would all be worse off than they were before. The only answer is birth control. It is inevitable that contraception, in one of several forms, will eventually be used by a great majority of people in the world, including people of all religions, in the next quarter of a century. But I do not believe that in that period of time it will restrict the population increase enough to enable the foodstuffs of the world to go around.

In the meantime, the United States is vainly attempting to solve the problems of the world through foreign aid. Billions and billions of dollars of the wealth that we Americans have produced and created through our free-enterprise system have been poured into all parts of this planet, with little beneficial result. Our give-away policy can only develop new dictators, many of them Communists and socialists, in the receiving countries. As we cannot dictate how our money must be spent but must deal government to government, our so-called "foreign aid" acts as an incentive to the dissidents in each country to overthrow the current government and climb on the gravy train themselves. Our give-away program during the last twenty years has caused more governments to fall through revolution and more assassinations of heads of state around the world than occurred during the previous century.

Even if foreign aid were more efficiently administered, even if our billions enabled the peoples of the world to sit back and let Uncle Sam feed them, I still maintain that it would do more harm than good. For it is through insecurity and hardship that all living things on this planet develop and progress. In the animal kingdom, we find that the more rugged the environment and the greater the dangers, the stronger are the creatures who survive. Place wild animals in a zoo and give them artificial security, and they invariably deteriorate physically and mentally. The hardships I have endured in my lifetime, though I admit that I would not want to live them over again, nevertheless proved to be of ultimate benefit, and I became a better man through them.

If foreign aid is designed to stem the tide of Communism, then it is failing miserably. We face a dark, ruthless, ideological competition, and we cannot win by the more lavish bestowal of material wealth on anyone and everyone who will accept it. We fail to make the vital point that the money, the food and the equipment we send out are simply the by-products of our free-enterprise system. The world is indeed sick, and it needs our help, but by far the best medicine we have to offer is the old-fashioned American formula of hard work, thrift and willingness to aid our deserving but less fortunate neighbors. It is the only sure cure for the economic ills of mankind.

On my travels through the Orient in 1962, I was informed by authorities with whom I spoke that the grand design of the leaders of Communist China was to infiltrate, guerrilla fashion, into the so-called "rural" areas of the world—Asia, Africa and Latin America. Since then the speeches and writings of leading Chinese spokesmen have confirmed this information. Teng Chen, Mayor of Peking and a member of the Politburo, for example, speaking at the 45th anniversary of the founding of the Indonesian Communist party in Jakarta, said, "To win victory in the world revolution, the proletariat must attach great importance to revolutions in Asia, Africa and Latin America—that is, to revolutions in the world's rural areas, and there is no other path."

This statement clearly promises at least another half-century of war of one kind or another somewhere in the world. Currently the fighting is in Vietnam, as the direct result of the failure of our diplomatic strategy and services. But, regardless of the outcome there, the fighting will continue somewhere on and off for many years to come.

The obvious solution in Southeast Asia is for us—the Westerners, the white men—to get out of there. I do not mean immediately, nor do I mean that we should leave the area a vacuum into which Chinese Communism could and would pour. Rather, I believe that this entire part of the world should become, with our blessing and its willing acceptance, part of the sphere of influence of the Japanese. I say so after careful thought based on my own personal visit to Japan and that part of the world and on information received from influential and knowledgeable Japanese friends.

The people of Asia do not like, trust or understand the white man, in spite of the blood we shed and the dollars we spend in what we maintain is their behalf. But the Japanese and the other Asian peoples do understand each other. Furthermore, Japan has become the most Westernized of all the Asian countries. It has made great strides in the past century and has made serious mistakes, from which it has profited. The Japanese have proved themselves capable of great industrial development and, I am certain, are now ready to take their place as one of the world's great leaders—not through conquest, as attempted before, but through energy, intelligence and a new sense of responsibility.

Today Japan is a nation of 100 million people; some well-informed observers believe that the number is actually much higher. The Japanese live in an area the size of California, which is already beginning to groan about overpopulation with only 20 million residents on a far greater acreage of arable land. Japan is bursting at the seams; its people must go somewhere. It would be to the advantage of the Western world to release those Pacific islands over which we have control to Japan. We have no use for them; they are remote, many are uninhabited and barren and they do not lend themselves to our agricultural methods. But the industrious Japanese, who work seventy and eighty hours a week coaxing a living out of their rocky soil, would prosper on those islands. They would benefit as individuals and as a nation. With those islands to pioneer and to relieve the pressure of a growing population, Japan would find a new stability and national security. I believe that, in such a situation, Japan and the United States could become and remain partners sharing mutual trade, objectives, security and respect.

This arrangement would postpone the inevitable, giving us time to cement our budding friendship with this rising nation and giving Japan time to take on more of our Western ways and ideologies. We must face the fact that Japan is destined to be, with America and Russia, one of the great powers. As the years pass, Japan must inevitably look more and more to the west, to China. When I was in Japan in 1962, I could see the handwriting on the wall. There across the water, is this tremendous country, with large areas still under-populated, capable of producing a surplus of agricultural supplies and raw materials and needing manufactured goods of the kind that Japan turns out in both quality and quantity. Despite the bloody war with China that Japan started—and current ideological differences—there is nevertheless a great cultural affinity between the two countries. They share the same form of written language, the same religion and of course the same racial heritage. I was not surprised to see trade between the two countries increase, and it will continue to do so.

The danger to the United States and to the Western world lies in the obvious possibility of a weakened and overpopulated Japan being absorbed by the huge Communist sponge on the mainland. A large Communist Party has grown up in Japan since the war, a party larger by far than in Russia before its revolution. It would be a natural development for Japan, under pressure from forces without and within, to leave the free-enterprise system in order to join and eventually lead the Communist bloc currently dominated by Red China.

If that should happen, most grievous consequences would follow. If we lose our friendship and alliance with Japan, we shall lose our last major influential connection with the nonwhite world. The loss of all Asia will follow almost automatically. A Japanese and Chinese alliance will include within its orbit, more or less peaceably, the yellow and brown peoples of the world.

The Africans will follow. The Chinese began moving into Africa a decade ago. During my African tour in 1964, I saw first-hand evidence of their presence in numbers. Should there be an alliance between Communist China and Japan, all Africa south of the Sahara will fall quickly under their influence.

From my own personal observation of central and southern Africa, I believe that there is only one equally unhappy alternative to this grim future. Africans seem far from ready to govern themselves. It may be that, instead of achieving unity under Communism, the black peoples of Africa will revert to the tribalism that prevailed before the white man came. In that case, this great dark continent will disintegrate into one bloody battleground of tribes warring with one another as they did in centuries past. Under those circumstances the great mass of black people would not endanger the rest of the world—as it would if it were united under Communism.

But, in any event, within fifty years, the white-dominated countries of Africa—South Africa, Rhodesia, Angola—will be no more. No white people will remain in central and southern Africa.

For I am positive in my belief that the world is today and will increasingly become divided, not so much by communist and capitalist ideologies as by color. The yellow, brown and black peoples of the world despise and reject the white man.

They are resentful of his color, of his larger individual size, of what is to them his overbearing nature and superiority, of his ignorance of and lack of understanding of their cultures.

It is my firm opinion that the rivalry of color will supplant the current rivalry of ideology. It will pit the whites against the non-whites.

Geographically, this prospect will mean that North America, most of South America, Western Europe and, yes, Russia will be united against the rest of the world. My readers may wonder that I consider our current implacable enemy in the Cold War, Russia, a potential future ally. I do not find it hard to visualize. I can see Russia coming down our highway with a free-enterprise system in the not-too-distant future. I noted the Russian tendency in this direction in 1943, and all indications are that it is increasing.

If this tendency toward alliance does not develop, the United States and Russia will continue in their state of armed neutrality as far as a global conflict is concerned. If it had not been for the atomic power each possesses, we would have been at each other's throats long ago; the standoff will continue.

Although I see no hope for the pockets of whites in the areas dominated by the nonwhite races, I believe that here in the United States people of color will remain loyal to their mother country, the United States. Negro Americans, Japanese Americans and Chinese Americans, in short, will continue to be Americans like the rest of us in this melting pot. A possible alternative could conceivably come about if the Negroes within our boundaries continue to proliferate to the extent that they outnumber the whites.

I realize that this picture of worldwide racial strife is a forbidding picture indeed, but I can only repeat that I am not advocating it. I am merely projecting the situation in the world today.

I hope and pray that the future course of history that current trends suggest may be altered for the benefit and preservation of all mankind. Our future could be so rich, so rewarding. Our own surging economy is but an indication of its great potential. Science is increasing the productivity of man continuously, magically adding to his ability to produce more and more of the things that aid and benefit increasing numbers of people everywhere.

Opportunities? They are stored in abundance wherever we look. They are waiting to be tapped by anyone with imagination, imagination backed by faith in our freedom of enterprise and fortified by the courage to try.

Our problem then is how we can keep our nation on the right highway. We must do so, not only to recover the time that we have lost, but also to speed the promise of the glorious future that we may still achieve. Our survival as a free people and the freedom of generations to come depend upon our ability to reestablish the eternal truths and principles upon which our beloved country was founded—and upon our willingness to demonstrate them in our personal and political lives and in our relations with the peoples of all nations.

To give the world the leadership it needs, to lead the world out of the current chaos and confusion, the United States does not need any new world-shaking discoveries in political science. We need to follow only one course, and it is so clearly marked that our failure to recognize it is frightening. To create harmony among nations and restore dignity to man, we need only to rediscover for ourselves the principles of the American way of life that have been tried and proved over nearly two tumultuous centuries.

Rediscover them first, practice them at home and then preach them to all of our friends and associates throughout the world. We have the greatest opportunity ever afforded mankind to sell this concept of freedom to the world. I'm convinced that, if each and every one of us would renew his faith in the principles of our freedom and would use the highly developed talent for merchandising our principles that we use to sell our products, our country would remain strong spiritually as well as physically. No power for evil could ever prevail against us. Freedom, once more, would be the hope instead of the despair of mankind.

The release of initiative and enterprise made possible by popular self-government ultimately generates disintegrating forces from within. Again and again, after freedom has brought opportunity and some degree of plenty, the competent become selfish, luxury-loving and complacent; the incompetent and the unfortunate grow envious and covetous, and all three groups turn aside from the hard road to freedom to worship the golden calf of economic security.

The historical cycle seems to move from bondage to spiritual faith, from spiritual faith to courage, from courage to liberty, from liberty to abundance, from abundance to selfishness, from selfishness to apathy, from apathy to dependence and from dependence back to bondage once more. But we are not yet in bondage. We still have some liberty left. We are at war to preserve that liberty.

It is not old-fashioned to wave and love the flag of our country or to worship God in heaven. Let us acknowledge and be grateful for the blessings of freedom that God has given us. Let us dedicate our lives to the perpetuation of the American principles of freedom with confidence. Let us stop and analyze ourselves to find out what life means to us.

I want nothing further in material value or personal prestige— no power, no wealth, no political plums. But I do pray that this exhortation in the name of freedom and liberty will spread into every nook and cranny of this land of ours for the benefit of future generations.

Let us therefore pray every night for the strength and guidance to inspire in others the gratitude, the love, the dedication that we owe our beloved country for the sake of our posterity.

Then, and only then, can we say when the candle of life burns low—Thank God, I have given my best to the land that has given so much to me.

DEGREES RECEIVED

Doctor of Aeronautical Science	Pennsylvania Military College, Chester, Pennsylvania, June 7, 1938
Doctor of Aeronautical Science	John Brown University, Siloam Springs, Arkansas, May 24, 1940
Doctor of Science in Aviation	The University of Miami, Coral Gables, Florida, May 26, 1941
Doctor of Science	The University of Tampa, Tampa, Florida, June 9, 1942
Doctor of Humane Letters	University Foundation and American Theological Seminary, Wilmington, Delaware, June 25, 1943
Doctor of Science	Westminster College, New Wilmington, Pennsylvania, May 20, 1944

Doctor of Laws	Oklahoma City University, Oklahoma City, Oklahoma, February 18, 1944
Doctor of Laws	Capital University, Columbus, Ohio, July 31, 1945
Doctor of Engineering	Lehigh University, Bethlehem, Pennsylvania, February 1, 1948
Doctor of Laws	The College of South Jersey, Camden, New Jersey, June 11, 1948
Doctor of Science	Lafayette College, Easton, Pennsylvania, November 1, 1952
Doctor of Science	The Citadel, Charleston, South Carolina, June 12, 1954
Doctor of Laws	Hamilton College, Clinton, New York, June 3, 1956
Doctor of Laws	William Jewell College, St. Joseph, Missouri, November 8, 1962
American Educational Award for 1943	Associated Exhibitors of the National Education Association, February 29, 1944

CITATIONS AND MEDALS

Congressional Medal of Honor — World War I and citation — medal with ribbon and two rosettes and chest ribbon
United States Distinguished Service Cross Citation — April 29, 1918, Baussant, France

United States Distinguished Service Cross Citation—May 17, 1918, Rochecourt, France

United States Distinguished Service Cross Citation—May 22, 1918, St. Mihiel, France

United States Distinguished Service Cross Citation—May 28, 1918, Bois Raté, France

United States Distinguished Service Cross Citation—May 30, 1918, Jaulny, France

United States Distinguished Service Cross Citation—September 14, 1918, Ville Waville, France

United States Distinguished Service Cross Citation—September 15, 1918, Bois de Waville, France

United States Distinguished Service Cross Citation—September 25, 1918, Billy, France

United States Distinguished Service Cross Citation—September 26, 1918, Billy, France

United States Distinguished Service Medal with 9 oak leaf clusters on ribbon representing 9 citations above

American Expeditionary Forces, Distinguished Service Cross Citation—April 29, 1918, Baussant and medal

United States Certificate of Merit—World War II and medal

American Order Association Nationale des Croix de Guerre

Member of National Advisory Committee for Aeronautics, Certificate, November, 1953 to November, 1957

Life Membership Certificate, Los Angeles Lodge No. 99. Benevolent Protective Order of Elks—June 22, 1919

33rd Degree—Honorary Member of Supreme Council Sovereign Grand Inspectors General—Ancient Accepted Scottish Rite—September 28, 1949—Valley of Detroit

Boy Scouts Silver Beaver with ribbon—1942

Boy Scouts Silver Buffalo with ribbon—1944

Mackay Aviation Trophy Medal

Novus Ardo Seculorum Gold Medal with ribbon

Gold Merit Award Medal with ribbon—Veterans of Foreign Wars

Gold Medal National Society of Sons of American Revolution for Good Citizenship

American Legion Wall Street Post 1217 Gold Medal with ribbon

Benjamin Franklin Society — Poor Richard Achievement Gold Medal

General "Hap" Henry Arnold Aviation Award Gold Medal

Eastern Air Lines Gold Medal for Service to Air Transportation Outside the Line of Duty with ribbon

Gold Aviation Award Medal with striped ribbon and bar

Veterans Committee People to People Award Medal for Distinguished Service

Silver Cigarette Case given by Ernst Udet with Richthofen's and other German Aces' signatures

Alaska — 49th State — Gold Medal

Iron World War II Invasion Dollar in the Philippines

Freedom Foundation Award Gold Medal

Small Gold Medal Par Avion

U. S. Service Medal

FRENCH CITATIONS AND MEDALS

République Française Croix de Guerre — May 9, 1918 citation and medal

Citation A L'Ordre de L'Armée, France — May 9, 1918 and medal

République Française Croix de Guerre — November 30, 1918 citation and medal

A L'Ordre de L'Armée — Croix de Guerre — November 30, 1918 citation and medal

A L'Ordre de L'Armée — Croix de Guerre — November 8, 1919 citation and medal

Association Nationale des Croix de Guerre

Ordre National de La Légion D'Honneur — December 18, 1918, France, citation and medal

Medal Ligue Aéronautique of France, Ecole de Cazaux Tir
     Aérien
Marshal Foch Medal with ribbon
There are additional dozens of less important awards

INDEX

SIGNAL CORPS, UNITED STATES ARMY
The following message was received at Radio Station WTJ in CODE
Headquarters Hawaiian Department, Fort Shafter, T. H.

Copy No. _____

For _____ C/S

CRS-M/C

No. _____

ACTION COPY

SECRET PRIORITY

WAR 86   PRTY   WASHINGTON DC NOV 182002Z   NOV 1942

COMMANDING GENERAL

                HAWAIIAN DEPT   FTSHAFTER TH

1404-18TH PRIORITY   I AM PLEASED BEYOND MEASURE THAT YOUR

SINGULAR ADVENTURE WAS SO HAPPILY CONCLUDED PERIOD TO EMMONS FOR ADAMSON

PERIOD THE SAFETY OF YOU AND YOUR COMPANIONS AND THE COURAGE AND

FORTITUDE THROUGH WHICH YOU ATTAINED IT IS AN INSPIRATION TO ALL AMERIC-

ANS PD EVERY MEMBER OF THE ARMY SHARES MY PRIDE THAT NO RPT NO OBSTACLE

OR HARDSHIP COULD OVERCOME YOU DETERMINATION TO SUCCESSFULLY CONCLUDE

YOUR MISSION

            MARSHALL

SENT BY SEC TT

AT 182300Z NOV 1942

BY GL ECD BY WBC

ACTION COMPLETED RETURN TO AGO	INITIALS	DECODED BY: LT G LAWSON 182245Z NOV 1942

The making of an exact copy of this message is forbidden. Only such extracts as are absolutely
necessary will be made and marked SECRET - ~~CONFIDENTIAL~~ ~~RESTRICTED~~. This copy will be
safeguarded with the greatest care and will be returned to the Classified Records Section, AGO.
NOTE: See AR 380-5 for handling of messages of this classification.

	Act	Inf		Act	Inf		Act	Inf		Act	Inf		Act	Inf		Act	Inf
D/C			G-3			AG Off			DOO			HSAC			Surg		
C/S	✓		G-4			Misc			DQM			IG			WBO		
DC/SO			AS/TC	✓		MRU			DR&SSO			JA			7 AF		
CG SOS			AG APO			C/Art			DXO			OMG					
G-1			C&A			Chap			Eng			PM					
G-2 FE			CRS			Chem			Fin			Scho Bk					
G-2 RE			Enl			DC&PC			HAAC			Sig O			File		

Form H. D. No. 1398 (Revised)
4231 Honolulu O 10-20-42 10M   P5

COMPLETE RACING

Los Angeles Times

LIBERTY UNDER THE LAW • TRUE INDUSTRIAL FREEDOM

Picto

VOL. LXI   Three Parts—34 Pages   ★★★   SATURDAY MORNING, OCTOBER 24, 1942.   DAILY

RICKENBACKER'S PLANE MISSIN

First Lady Met by Sovereigns in London — Ace Vanishes

Pacific Starter Noted

Hope Not for Stimson Flying Fort

A ROYAL WELCOME—Flying to England to visit U.S. forces and study British women's war endeavors, Mrs. Franklin D. Roosevelt, wife of the President, was greeted today (Friday) by King George and Queen Elizabeth. Mrs. Owen Culp Hardy, head of Waacs, accompanied First Lady.

MISSING IN PACIFIC—Capt. Eddie V. Rickenbacker, America's greatest air ace of World War I, is reported by Army to be overdue in flight from Hawaiian Islands.

Guadalcanal Marines Repulse New Japanese 'Feeler' Attack

Red Planes Bomb Nazi Destroyer

NEW YORK, Oct. 23 (AP)—The British radio today broadcast a Moscow dispatch saying that Russian planes damaged a German destroyer in the Black Sea during an attack on a concentration of enemy warships.

The R.B.C. quoted another dispatch from the Russian Army newspaper Red Star as saying Soviet fliers had cut an important Nazi supply line near the occupied Black Sea port of Novorossisk.

Genoa Reels From R.A.F. Raid; New Attack on Italy Indicated

LONDON, Oct. 23 (AP)—Genoa trembled and feared last night under the R.A.F.'s heaviest "blockbuster" bombs and French and Swiss radio dispatches reported of the air open last night in undisclosed another attack on Italian soil.

The Paris and Vichy and the Swiss (Switzerland) stations were of the air in quick succession and Queen there obviously to raise morale by comforting the wounded and homeless.

British and Canadian bombers and fighters.

RICKENBACKER

oston Evening Globe

Copyright, 1942, by the Globe Newspaper Co.
SDAY, NOV. 14, 1942 24 PAGES—THREE CENTS In New England

FOUND ALIVE

"GREAT INDESTRUCTIBLE"

ALIVE AND IN GOOD CONDITION—Capt. Eddie Rickenbacker rescued after
life raft in Pacific.

e Lauds
istence
escuers

ORK, Nov. 14 (UP)—
to Rickenbacker ex-
er thanks today for
erful cooperation of
and Navy in rescue
round from the Pa-

part been advised by
H. Arnold, chief of
Air Corps of my
's rescue," Mrs. Rick-
"Of course, the
have all been under
be so little relieved
by the discovery of
lliam T. Cherry Jr.,
of the ship.
examined a thorough

Condition Good; Raft Off Samoa; 5 Others Rescued, 1 Dead

WASHINGTON, Nov. 14 (AP)—Daunt-
less Eddie Rickenbacker has been rescued,
in good condition, the Navy announced today, three weeks after his airplane radioed
that it was about out of gasoline, and then
vanished in the Pacific.

Rickenbacker, America's ace of aces in
the first World War and the country's embodied proof that you can't keep a good
man down, was picked from a raft bobbing
in the sea by a Navy Catalina flying boat

along with two of his crew. They were 60
miles north of Samoa.

Three other Army flyers who were wit
him on a survey of Pacific war zone A
Force operations have been located on a
island. The rescue of one was announce
yesterday and the seventh man of Ricken
backer's crew died in the long wait fe
rescue.

Col. Hans C. Adamson and private Joh
F. Bartek were Rickenbacker's two com
panions at the time of rescue.

Rickenbacker

Continued on Page 3

REPORT ALLIED 'CHUTISTS MOVE ON TUNIS

LONDON, Nov. 14 (AP)—The Evening Stand-
ard carried an unofficial report that the Allies are
moving parachute troops toward Tunisia for use
against Axis units which have seized airdromes there.
The source of the report was not given.

LONDON, Nov. 14 (UP)—
Great fleets of Allied planes
struck at Axis forces in Tunisia
and their invasion base in Italy
from all directions today as a
vast American and British
Army was believed crossing the
frontier from Algeria.

British press reports said the
great Allied Army, perhaps
numbering upwards of 200,000
men with armored divisions and
a great umbrella of planes, had
passed over the border at about

ported only 36 miles from the
border yesterday, an Allied
spokesman here refused to
confirm that they already were
in Tunisia.

Aiding doughty French gar-
risons at Tunis and the important naval base at Bizerte believed to have been holding out
against Axis invaders for almost
a week, British planes based on
Britain, the island fortress of
Malta and possibly Italian
Libya, and American planes
from French North Africa.

the Italian port which is the
source of their supplies and reinforcements.

As the British 8th Army, still
in unflaging pursuit of Field
Marshal Erwin Rommel's beat-
en Afrika Korps, reached Ga-
zala, in Libya, only 700 miles
east of Tunisia, there was a
chance that American and British parachute troops had been
dropped from planes ranging
ahead of the Allied Army closing in from the west.
Africa.

Britain's Eighth Army Captures Gazala

CAIRO, Nov. 14 (UP)—Brit-
ish 8th Army, pursuing the
ragged remnants of Field Marshal Erwin Rommel's once
proud Afrika Korps, seized
beyond Tobruk yesterday, a
British communique reported
today.

Following Gen Sir Bernard
L. Montgomery's exhortation
to chase the Axis "right out of
North Africa," the British land
Army drove the Germans and
Italians mercilessly while Allied
planes, ranging for about fight-
ened the Anglo-American mob

The communique said A
long-range fighters atta
the airfield at Tunis in a ti
raid Thursday night, destr
gasoline dumps, workshop
airplanes there. Axis air
then troops had been rep
in possession of the airfiel
of the first strategic obje
of the Allied Tunisian
page.

Today's communique r
Middle East command m
Bengal Air Force repeated
over attacks on Axis place
ing range from the North
can hot spot at Tunis w
terday's raid took out
planes grinding down t
main enemy escape of Tu

WAR DEPARTMENT
HEADQUARTERS OF THE ARMY AIR FORCES
WASHINGTON

October 23, 1942

Mrs. Edward V. Rickenbacker
130 East End Avenue
New York City

Dear Mrs. Rickenbacker:

The distress that I was obliged to cause you today was one of the most difficult tasks I have ever been called upon to perform.

I think you know my feeling toward your husband is one of great affection and admiration built up during the many years of our close contact and I can assure you that the news that I was compelled to pass on to you was a dreadful shock to me as well.

However, I am clinging firmly to a hope, and I want you to do the same, which I believe we are fully justified in accepting.

All planes flying such missions are completely equipped with life jackets worn by every person on board and in addition to this there are emergency rubber boats that are inflated and released when a landing is made on water.

There are many instances where men have travelled safely in these very seaworthy rubber boats for long periods of time, as they are equipped with food and water and paddles. From the facts that we can gather here, the plane had passed over its destination, which would indicate that there must have been very foggy conditions, and descended to the water somewhere not too far away from land.

They knew that they were likely to be forced down, as they had radioed in an effort to determine their exact position, and therefore there is no doubt that their preparations to abandon the plane and take to the boats would have been completed long before they actually were on the water.

You may depend upon it that no effort will be spared to discover their whereabouts and to afford a prompt rescue from what I hope is nothing more than an uncomfortable situation. I will keep you notified of every development.

Very, sincerely yours,

H. H. ARNOLD
Lieutenant General, U.S.A.
Commanding General, Army Air Forces

November 14, 1942

My dear Mrs. Rickenbacker:

I am overjoyed to learn of Captain Rickenbacker's safety, and we are all very grateful.

No one man has contributed more to air-mindedness in America than Captain Rickenbacker. His brilliant record in the last war, coupled with his civilian attainments, have stood as a glorious example for thousands of young Americans who are now proving their worth in aerial combat.

Let me offer for myself and all members of the Army Air Forces our sincere congratulations. Eddie's luck has not failed him yet, and God grant that it shall never fail him through the important work which lies ahead, and the Victory which shall eventually be ours.

Very sincerely,

H. H. ARNOLD
Lieutenant General, U. S. Army
Commanding General, Army Air Forces

Mrs. Edward V. Rickenbacker
130 East End Avenue
New York City

November 17, 1942.

My dear Mrs. Rickenbacker:

      I have received your very kind telegram on my return yesterday from an absence of a few days.

      Our success in finding your husband has made me more happy than anything that has happened for a long time, and I am sure that your devoted courage and confidence has contributed to our success in finding him. May I say also that I think our prayers helped a little too.

      I am looking forward to getting him back here safe and sound and having his help at my side again.

Faithfully yours,

Henry L. Stimson

Mrs. Edward V. Rickenbacker,
130 East End Street,
New York, New York.

CITATION TO ACCOMPANY THE AWARD OF

THE MEDAL FOR MERIT

TO

EDWARD VERNON RICKENBACKER

EDWARD VERNON RICKENBACKER, for exceptionally meritorious conduct in the performance of outstanding services to the United States from December, 1941 to December, 1944. Mr. Rickenbacker, as Special Representative of the Secretary of War and Commanding General, Army Air Forces, made numerous tours of inspection of air bases and air units in theaters of operations throughout the world, and brought to the Air Command plans and recommendations based on his observations that contributed substantially to the fund of knowledge which ultimately brought about the defeat of the enemy. He directed the full facilities of Eastern Air Lines, Inc., of which he was president, to the prosecution of the war, and made available to the Command its air knowledge and experience as well as its operational facilities. Mr. Rickenbacker's great courage and fortitude in the face of the most harrowing physical experiences, and the unflagging zeal and devotion to the cause of his country which he displayed throughout the entire period of hostilities mark him as pre-eminent in the roster of those who rose to their Nation's defense, reflecting the greatest credit on him and the Government and people of the United States.

Harry Truman

THE WHITE HOUSE

December 18, 1946.

THE UNITED STATES OF AMERICA

TO ALL WHO SHALL SEE THESE PRESENTS, GREETING:

THIS IS TO CERTIFY THAT

THE PRESIDENT OF THE UNITED STATES OF AMERICA

PURSUANT TO ACT OF CONGRESS APPROVED JULY 9. 1918.

HAS AWARDED TO

Edward V. Rickenbacker

THE DISTINGUISHED SERVICE CROSS

FOR

EXTRAORDINARY HEROISM

IN MILITARY OPERATIONS AGAINST AN ARMED ENEMY

OF THE UNITED STATES AT *Montsec, France, April 29, 1918,*

while serving as 1st Lieutenant, 94th Aero Squadron, Air Service, A.E.F.

GIVEN UNDER MY HAND AT THE CITY OF WASHINGTON

THIS *fourteenth* DAY OF *November* 1925.

Dwight F. Davis
SECRETARY OF WAR

RECORDED IN THE OFFICE OF
THE ADJUTANT GENERAL

Robert C. Davis
THE ADJUTANT GENERAL

THE UNITED STATES OF AMERICA

TO ALL WHO SHALL SEE THESE PRESENTS, GREETING:

THIS IS TO CERTIFY THAT

THE PRESIDENT OF THE UNITED STATES OF AMERICA PURSUANT TO ACT OF CONGRESS APPROVED JULY 9, 1918, HAS AWARDED IN THE NAME OF CONGRESS TO

Edward V. Rickenbacker

THE CONGRESSIONAL MEDAL OF HONOR

FOR

VALOR

ABOVE AND BEYOND THE CALL OF DUTY IN ACTION INVOLVING ACTUAL CONFLICT WITH AN ENEMY OF THE UNITED STATES,

near Billy, France; September 25, 1918, while serving as first
Lieutenant, 94th Aero Squadron, Air Service, American
Expeditionary Forces.

GIVEN UNDER MY HAND AT THE CITY OF WASHINGTON THIS *fifteenth* DAY OF *July*, 1930.

[signature]

SECRETARY OF WAR

RECORDED IN THE OFFICE OF
THE ADJUTANT GENERAL

[signature]

Major General,
THE ADJUTANT GENERAL.

THE UNITED STATES OF AMERICA

TO ALL WHO SHALL SEE THESE PRESENTS, GREETING:

THIS IS TO CERTIFY THAT

THE PRESIDENT OF THE UNITED STATES OF AMERICA
IN ACCORDANCE WITH THE ORDER ISSUED BY GENERAL
GEORGE WASHINGTON AT HEADQUARTERS, NEWBURGH,
NEW YORK ON AUGUST 7, 1782, AND PURSUANT TO ACT
OF CONGRESS, HAS AWARDED THE MEDAL

FOR MERIT

TO

EDWARD VERNON RICKENBACKER

FOR EXTRAORDINARY FIDELITY AND EXCEPTIONALLY MERITORIOUS CONDUCT

GIVEN UNDER MY HAND IN THE CITY OF WASHINGTON
THIS EIGHTEENTH DAY OF DECEMBER 1946

Harry Truman
COMMANDER-IN-CHIEF

James F. Byrnes
SECRETARY OF STATE